"This impressive volume probes several hard dialectics that have occupied Christianity from its biblical beginnings ... The authors reflect both the hard-nosed realism of seasoned lawyers and the faith-based imagination of sincere believers. The authors toe no party line, herd no sacred cows, and trade in no naïve nostalgia ... St Paul, Martin Luther, and other titans take several hits ... This is rigorous law and theology scholarship of a rare and refined sort."

John Witte, Jr., Center for the Study of Law and Religion, Emory University

Christianity, Ethics and the Law

This book examines how Christian love can inform legal thought. The work introduces love as a way to advance the emergent conversation between constructive theology and jurisprudence that will also inform conversations in philosophy and political theory.

Love is the central category for Christian ethical understanding. Yet, the growing field of law and religion, and relatedly law and theology, rarely addresses how love can shape our understanding of law. This reflects, in part, a common assumption that law and love stand in necessary tension. Love applies to the private and the personal. Law, by contrast, applies to the public and the political, realms governed by power. It is thus a mistake to envisage love as having anything but a negative relationship to law. This conclusion continues to govern Christian understandings of the meaning and vocation of law. The animating idea of this volume is that the concept of love can and should inform Christian legal thought. The project approaches this task from the perspective of both historical and constructive theology. Various contributions examine how such thinkers as Augustine, Aquinas, and Calvin utilised love in their legal thought. These essays highlight often neglected aspects of the Christian tradition. Other contributions examine Christian love in light of contemporary legal topics including civility, forgiveness, and secularism. Love, the book proposes, not only matters for law but can transform the terms on which Christians understand and engage it.

The book will be of interest to academics and researchers working in the areas of legal theory; law and religion; law and philosophy; legal history; theology and religious studies; and political theory.

Zachary R. Calo is Professor of Law at Hamad bin Khalifa University, Qatar. He is also Professor of Law (Adj.) at the University of Notre Dame Australia, Visiting Professor at The Open University (UK), Visiting Professor at Tashkent State University of Law (Uzbekistan), and Adjunct Professor at Northwestern University, Qatar, as well as Research Scholar in Law and Religion at Valparaiso University and Fellow of the Centre for the Study of Law and Religion at Emory University.

Joshua Neoh is Associate Professor of Law at the Australian National University (ANU), Australia.

A. Keith Thompson is Professor of Law at the University of Notre Dame Australia (UNDA), Australia.

Law and Religion

The practice of religion by individuals and groups, the rise of religious diversity, and the fear of religious extremism, raise profound questions for the interaction between law and religion in society. The regulatory systems involved, the religion laws of secular government (national and international) and the religious laws of faith communities, are valuable tools for our understanding of the dynamics of mutual accommodation and the analysis and resolution of issues in such areas as: religious freedom; discrimination; the autonomy of religious organisations; doctrine, worship and religious symbols; the property and finances of religion; religion, education and public institutions; and religion, marriage and children. In this series, scholars at the forefront of law and religion contribute to the debates in this area. The books in the series are analytical with a key target audience of scholars and practitioners, including lawyers, religious leaders, and others with an interest in this rapidly developing discipline.

Series Editor
Professor Norman Doe, Director of the Centre for Law and Religion, Cardiff University, UK

Series Board
Carmen Asiaín, Professor, University of Montevideo, Uruguay

Paul Babie, Professor and Associate Dean (International), Adelaide Law School, Australia

Pieter Coertzen, Chairperson, Unit for the Study of Law and Religion, University of Stellenbosch, South Africa

Alison Mawhinney, Reader, Bangor University, UK

Michael John Perry, Senior Fellow, Center for the Study of Law and Religion, Emory University, USA

Titles in this series include:

Christianity and the Law of Migration
Edited by Silas W. Allard, Kristin E. Heyer, and Raj Nadella

Christianity, Ethics and the Law
The Concept of Love in Christian Legal Thought
Edited by Zachary R. Calo, Joshua Neoh and A. Keith Thompson

Law and Christianity in Poland
The Legacy of the Great Jurists
Edited by Franciszek Longchamps de Bérier and Rafael Domingo

For more information about this series, please visit: www.routledge.com/Law-and-Religion/book-series/LAWRELIG

Christianity, Ethics and the Law

The Concept of Love in Christian Legal Thought

Edited by Zachary R. Calo, Joshua Neoh and A. Keith Thompson

LONDON AND NEW YORK

First published 2023
by Routledge
4 Park Square, Milton Park, Abingdon, Oxon OX14 4RN

and by Routledge
605 Third Avenue, New York, NY 10158

Routledge is an imprint of the Taylor & Francis Group, an informa business

© 2023 selection and editorial matter, Zachary R. Calo, Joshua Neoh and A. Keith Thompson; individual chapters, the contributors

The right of Zachary R. Calo, Joshua Neoh and A. Keith Thompson to be identified as the authors of the editorial material, and of the authors for their individual chapters, has been asserted in accordance with sections 77 and 78 of the Copyright, Designs and Patents Act 1988.

All rights reserved. No part of this book may be reprinted or reproduced or utilised in any form or by any electronic, mechanical, or other means, now known or hereafter invented, including photocopying and recording, or in any information storage or retrieval system, without permission in writing from the publishers.

Trademark notice: Product or corporate names may be trademarks or registered trademarks, and are used only for identification and explanation without intent to infringe.

British Library Cataloguing-in-Publication Data
A catalogue record for this book is available from the British Library

ISBN: 978-0-367-71005-7 (hbk)
ISBN: 978-0-367-71007-1 (pbk)
ISBN: 978-1-003-14892-0 (ebk)

DOI: 10.4324/9781003148920

Typeset in Galliard
by Deanta Global Publishing Services, Chennai, India

Contents

Foreword ix
List of contributors xii

Introduction 1
ZACHARY R. CALO, JOSHUA NEOH, AND A. KEITH THOMPSON

PART I
Law and Love in Augustine, Calvin, and Luther? 7

1 John Calvin on the Law of Love 9
   CONSTANCE YOUNGWON LEE

2 "To Heal the Wounds of Sinners": Law, Love, and Forgiveness 31
   ZACHARY R. CALO

3 Why Secularism Is No Option for a Christian Citizen: Augustine's Analysis of Love in the City 44
   RENÉE KÖHLER-RYAN

4 Why Lutheranism Is No Option for a Meaningful Jurisprudence of Love 57
   AUGUSTO ZIMMERMANN

PART II
Law, Love, and Political Theology 77

5 Law and Love in Monasticism 79
   JOSHUA NEOH

6 The Law of Love as Principles of Civility: Secular Translation or Religious Contribution? 93
ALEX DEAGON

7 The Loving Sword: The Implications of Divine Simplicity for Civil Law 112
BENJAMIN B. SAUNDERS

8 Aquinas on Love, Law, and Happiness: The Interconnection between Divine Law, Human Law, and Rational Love 130
STEFANUS HENDRIANTO SJ

PART III
The Ethics of Law and Love 147

9 From Alterity to Proximity: Emmanuel Levinas on the Natural Law of Love 149
JONATHAN CROWE

10 "Proving Contraries": Joseph Smith on Law and Love 164
DONLU THAYER

11 From Coercion to Covenant: What Kind of Higher Law Did Jesus Have in Mind? 186
A KEITH THOMPSON

12 The Forgiveness of Love in Charity: Getting Conversationally Opened Up 198
PATRICK MCKINLEY BRENNAN

Index 235

Foreword

This impressive volume probes several hard dialectics that have occupied Christianity from its biblical beginnings – law and Gospel, justice and love, rule and equity, coercion and charity, punishment and mercy, discipline and forgiveness. A dozen highly distinguished and rapidly emerging Australian and American jurists have teamed up to parse these dialectics, partly in conversation with the sages of the Western Christian tradition. Put in the dock for investigation are familiar Christian titans – St Paul and St Benedict, St Augustine and Thomas Aquinas, Martin Luther, and John Calvin – each of whom parsed these dialectics with alacrity and enduring acuity. Later chapters also introduce several more recent voices – Joseph Smith, Henry Sumner Maine, Emmanuel Levinas, Alasdair MacInytre, John Milbank, and others – who offer new insights into these dialectics, based in part on new canons, in part on fresh interpretations of older sources. The chapters range widely across the specialised fields of law, theology, ethics, history, philosophy, anthropology, political theory, religious studies, and more, cultivating and harvesting many new insights.

One central premise of this volume is the biblical insight that law is at the heart of the Gospel, justice is at the centre of love. Jesus made this clear in correcting those who regarded his message of salvation from sin and death as liberation from law and order:

> Think not that I have come to abolish the law and the prophets; I have come not to abolish them but to fulfill them. For truly, I say to you, till heaven and earth pass away, not an iota, not a dot, will pass from the law until all is accomplished.
>
> (Mt. 5:17–19)

Jesus also made clear – to a lawyer, no less – that law and love properly belong together:

> [A] lawyer, asked him a question, to test him. "Teacher, which is the great commandment in the law?" And he said to him, "You shall love the Lord your God with all your heart, and with all your soul, and with all your mind. This is the great and first commandment. And a second is like it, You shall

love your neighbor as yourself. On these two commandments depend all the law and the prophets."

(Mt. 22:35–40)

What such biblical passages teach us is that law and discipline make possible love and community. Justice and judgment enable acts of charity and forgiveness. A civil "morality of duty" sets the baseline for a spiritual "morality of aspiration." Our moral duties to neighbours and God ground our claims to civil rights and religious freedom.

A second premise of this volume is that Christians (and other people of faith) are by necessity dual citizens – occupying two paths, two cities, two kingdoms, two realms, two communities, one spiritual, one temporal. And as dual citizens, Christians come under two dispensations simultaneously – two forms of justice and morality, two orders of law and love, two powers or swords. To be sure, sometimes these spiritual and temporal communities and citizenships are closely aligned: think of medieval prince-bishoprics or Puritan New England towns. Sometimes, they are sharply separated: think of the monks and the Amish. But usually these two communities and citizenships overlap in varying ways, requiring a person of faith to constantly balance the central commandments of law and love. And even in more integrated or separated communities, people of faith must always strive to strike these balances for themselves.

A final premise of this volume is that human beings are dualistic creatures, composed of body and soul, flesh and spirit, sinner and saint. This is an ancient insight. The gripping epics of Homer and Hesiod are nothing if not chronicles of the perennial dialectic of good and evil, virtue and vice, hero and villain in the ancient Greek world. The very first chapters of the Hebrew Bible paint pictures of these same two human natures, now with God's imprint on them. The more familiar picture is that of Adam and Eve, who were created equally in the image of God, and vested with a natural right and duty to perpetuate life, to cultivate property, to dress and keep the creation. The less familiar picture is that of their first child Cain, who murdered his brother Abel and was called into judgment by God and condemned for his sin. Yet "God put a mark on Cain," Genesis 4 reads, both to protect him in his life, and to show that he remained a child of God despite the enormity of his sin. One message of this ancient Hebrew text is that we are not only the beloved children of Adam and Eve, who bear the image of God, with all the divine perquisites and privileges of Paradise. We are also the sinful siblings of Cain, who bear the mark of God, with its ominous assurance both that we shall be called into divine judgment for what we have done, and that there is forgiveness even for the gravest of sins we have committed.

Christians believe that it is only through faith and hope in God that we can ultimately be assured of divine forgiveness and eternal salvation. Christians further believe that it is only through a life of biblical meditation, prayer, worship, charity, and sacramental living that a person can hold his or her depravity in check and aspire to greater sanctity. But other traditions offer their own insights into the twofold nature of humanity, too, and their own methods of balancing the realities of human depravity and the aspirations for human sanctity. Any religious tradition that takes seriously the Jekyll and Hyde in all of us has its own understanding of the ultimate reconciliation of these two natures, and its own methods of balancing them in this life.

The authors herein offer insights into all three sets of dialectics – about law and love and their variants; about temporal and spiritual communities and their authorities; and about our sinful and saintly human natures and their reconciliation. And it is the combination of these insights that gives these chapters new three-dimensional insights into old questions. How do states and churches balance the civil and spiritual uses of the law? How do we heal the wounds of sin and crime? How do we balance punishment and forgiveness, difference and equality? How do we pursue happiness in the face of hardship? What is the role of law in the Church and attendant religious communities? What does love command of us in public life, in political discourse, in jurisprudential inquiry? How do we move ourselves and our communities from contract to covenant, from coercion to persuasion, from retribution to reconciliation?

These are the big questions of this volume. In addressing these questions, the authors reflect both the hard-nosed realism of seasoned lawyers and the faith-based imagination of sincere believers. The authors toe no party line, herd no sacred cows, and trade in no naïve nostalgia. Several perspectives come through in these pages. St Paul, Martin Luther, and other titans take several hits. And the romantic idealism of some modern Christian integrationists, chiliasts, and communitarians is (mercifully) absent. This is rigorous law and theology scholarship of a rare and refined sort.

John Witte, Jr
Director, Center for the Study of Law and
Religion
Emory University

Contributors

Patrick McKinley Brennan holds the John F. Scarpa Chair in Catholic Legal Studies and is Professor of Law at the Villanova University Charles Widger School of Law, Villanova, Pennsylvania. Brennan has published some 90 articles, essays, and book chapters as well as five books, including *Christian Legal Thought: Materials and Cases* (Foundation Press, 2017) (with William Brewbaker). Brennan clerked for the Honourable John T. Noonan Jr on the US Court of Appeals for the Ninth Circuit, and he is currently Fellow of the Dominican School of Philosophy and Theology (Berkeley).

Zachary R. Calo is Professor of Law at Hamad bin Khalifa University, Qatar. He is also Professor of Law (Adj.) at the University of Notre Dame Australia, Visiting Professor at The Open University (UK), Visiting Professor at Tashkent State University of Law (Uzbekistan), and Adjunct Professor at Northwestern University in Qatar. An attorney with McNair Chambers in Doha, he serves on international dispute resolution panels with Sport Resolutions UK and the Qatar Sports Arbitration Tribunal. He has previously taught at Valparaiso University School of Law and Notre Dame Law School (USA). He holds a JD from the University of Virginia School of Law, a BA and MA from Johns Hopkins University, a PhD in history from the University of Pennsylvania, an MA in ethics from the University of Virginia, and an LLM in dispute resolution from the Straus Institute at Pepperdine University School Law. In addition, he is Research Scholar in Law and Religion at Valparaiso University, Fellow of the Centre for the Study of Law and Religion at Emory University, and Associate Editor of the *Oxford Journal of Law and Religion*. He is the co-editor, most recently, of *Agape, Justice, and Law* (Cambridge University Press).

Jonathan Crowe is Professor of Law at Bond University, Gold Coast, Australia. He is the author or editor of 10 books and more than 100 scholarly book chapters and journal articles, primarily on legal philosophy, ethical theory, and public law. His recent books include *Natural Law and the Nature of Law* (Cambridge University Press, 2019) and the *Research Handbook on Natural Law Theory* (Edward Elgar, 2019), co-edited with Constance Youngwon Lee. He is former President of both the Australasian Society of Legal Philosophy and the Australian Dispute Resolution Research Network.

Contributors xiii

Alex Deagon is Senior Lecturer in the School of Law, Queensland University of Technology, Brisbane, Australia. His research focuses on jurisprudence, law and theology, law and religion, and religious freedom. He is the author of *From Violence to Peace: Theology, Law and Community* (Hart Publishing, Oxford, 2017) as well as numerous publications including in the *Harvard Journal of Law and Public Policy*, the *Oxford Journal of Law and Religion*, and the *Melbourne University Law Review*. He is the founding co-editor of the *Australian Journal of Law and Religion*.

Stefanus Hendrianto SJ is a Jesuit priest and legal scholar. He is a lecturer at Pontifical Gregorian University in Rome, Italy. His current research and writing have focused on the intersection of law, theology, and philosophy. In addition to his ongoing legal philosophy and theology research, his research interests include comparative constitutional law. He holds a PhD from the University of Washington School of Law in Seattle, an LLM from Utrecht University in the Netherlands, an LLB from Gadjah Mada University, Indonesia, in addition to an MDiv and a ThM degree from Boston College. His books include *Priests, Lawyers, and Scholars: Essays in Honor of Robert J. Araujo, SJ* (Franciscan University Press, 2017) and *Law and Politics of Constitutional Court: Indonesia and the Search for Judicial Heroes* (Routledge, 2018).

Renée Köhler-Ryan is Professor of Philosophy at the University of Notre Dame Australia (Sydney campus). She completed her PhD at the Catholic University of Leuven, Belgium. Her most recent book is *Companions in the Between: Augustine, Desmond and Their Communities of Love* (Pickwick, 2020). Her research interests include Political Philosophy, Philosophy of the Human Person, and the Relationship between Faith and Reason in the Catholic Intellectual Tradition.

Constance Lee is a Lecturer of Law at Central Queensland University, Queensland, Australia (Adelaide campus). She holds an LLB, LLM and PhD from the University of Queensland. Her research examines the philosophical foundations for law, examining issues like human nature and conscience to ground legal obligations in the public sphere. She has published in leading international and Australian journals, including *Oxford Journal of Law and Religion*, *Law and Critique*, the *Australian Journal of Legal Philosophy*, and the *International Journal of Law and Society*. She is co-editor of the *Research Handbook of Natural Law Theory* (Edward Elgar, 2019).

Joshua Neoh is Associate Professor of Law at the Australian National University (ANU), Canberra, Australia. He completed his LLB, LLM, and PhD at the ANU, Yale, and Cambridge, respectively. He writes in the areas of legal theory and theology. He is the author of *Law, Love and Freedom: From the Sacred to the Secular* (Cambridge University Press, 2019).

Benjamin B. Saunders is an Associate Professor at Deakin Law School, Melbourne, Australia. His research focuses on constitutional law, law and religion, and public sector governance. He is currently working on a monograph on responsible government and the Australian Constitution, and a book on civil law in the Christian perspective. He has published in journals such as *Oxford Journal of Legal Studies*, *Sydney Law Review*, and *Melbourne University Law Review*.

Donlu Thayer is Senior Fellow, formerly Publications Director, of the International Centre for Law and Religion Studies at Brigham University, Provo, Utah. She was the editor of four volumes of the Routledge Series on Law and Religion and associate editor of the *Brill Encyclopedia of Law and Religion*, and is an associate editor of the *Oxford Journal of Law and Religion*. She holds degrees (BA, MA, JD) in languages, literature, and law and was, for many years, an editor and a university writing teacher. Trained as a family and high-conflict mediator, she is a member of the Utah State Bar.

A. Keith Thompson is Professor of Law at the University of Notre Dame Australia (UNDA) (Sydney campus). His books include *Religious Confession Privilege and the Common Law* (Leiden: Brill, 2011) and *Trinity and Monotheism: A Historical and Theological Review of the Origins and Substance of the Doctrine* (Queensland: Connor Court, 2019). He formerly practised as a partner in a commercial firm in Auckland and as International Legal Counsel for The Church of Jesus Christ of Latter-Day Saints in the Pacific and through the African continent.

John Witte, Jr, J.D. (Harvard); Dr Theol. h.c. (Heidelberg), is Woodruff University Professor, McDonald Distinguished Professor, and Director of the Law and Religion Center at Emory University, Atlanta, Georgia. A leading scholar of legal history, human rights, family law, and law and religion, he has delivered 350 public lectures worldwide and published 300 articles and 45 books in 15 languages. Recent monographs include: *The Western Case for Monogamy over Polygamy* (Cambridge, 2015), *Church, State, and Family* (Cambridge 2019), *The Blessings of Liberty* (Cambridge, 2021), *Faith, Freedom, and Family* (Mohr Siebeck, 2021), and *Religion and the American Constitutional Experiment* (Oxford, 2022).

Augusto Zimmermann is Professor and Head of Law at Sheridan Institute of Higher Education in Perth, Western Australia.. He is also Adjunct Professor of Law at the University of Notre Dame Australia, (Sydney campus). From 2004 to 2006, he served as a board member of the Church and Nation Committee of Presbyterian Church of Victoria, which is charged with the responsibility of investigating moral and ethical questions on the denomination's behalf. From 2012 to 2017, he served as Law Reform Commissioner in Western Australia. He is the author/co-author/editor/co-editor of numerous academic articles and books including *Christian Foundations of the Common Law* (three volumes, Connor Court, 2018) and *Emergency Powers, COVID-19 Restrictions & Mandatory Vaccination: A Rule-of-Law Perspective* (Connor Court, 2022).

Introduction

Zachary R. Calo, Joshua Neoh, and A. Keith Thompson

The Judeo-Christian tradition is a jurisprudential tradition. The major break in the tradition, when Christianity broke away from Judaism, occurred, in large part, over a disagreement about the place of law in the tradition. What was at stake was not simply the content of law, but the concept of law. It was not simply about what law to have, but about whether to have law at all. The circumcision debate, which was all the rage in the early period of the Christian movement when it was still intertwined with Judaism, was merely a proxy for this deeper jurisprudential disagreement. Paul was a pivotal figure in this transition of tradition. Christianity proper began, not with Jesus, but with Paul.

Paul was a Pharisee, for whom law played a central role. In this Pharisaic view, which Paul would later repudiate, one's relationship with God and neighbour is mediated by law. One relates to God by obeying his laws, which include strict dietary rules and rules about circumcision. While a Pharisee, Paul experienced a conversion on the road to Damascus, and had a change of heart. He began to challenge the Pharisaic view in a series of letters. He had the zeal and fervour that is typical of a convert. His attack on the Pharisaic view became increasingly intense, which came to a head in the circumcision debate.

Jewish law required circumcision. Insofar as Christianity was a sect of Judaism, the same Jewish law would apply to Christians as well. Jews who became Christians were already circumcised, so that was not a problem. The question was whether non-Jews, also known as Gentiles, who converted to Christianity had to be circumcised. One might wonder why they were so obsessed with the male foreskin. As it turned out, all the fuss about the foreskin was not really about the foreskin after all. This debate was a proxy for the larger question about the relevance of Jewish law, and of law *tout court*, in the new Christian movement. The foreskin was a stand-in for a raging jurisprudential debate. Just as the removal of the foreskin stood for the entrance into the legal covenant between God and his people, so the refusal to remove the foreskin stood for the repudiation of law as a mode of relating to God.

Peter's vision at Joppa recounted by Luke in Acts 10 shows that Peter knew it was God's will that non-Jews should be accepted as followers of Jesus. However, it does not appear that his ministry before the Jerusalem Council, which was convened around AD 50, had required him to respond to all the consequences of

DOI: 10.4324/9781003148920-1

his visionary insight. But Paul's ministry at Antioch raised all kinds of questions and he was resolutely against imposing circumcision on Gentile converts before he attended the Jerusalem Council. Paul might have been motivated to adopt this position for both pragmatic and principled reasons. Pragmatically, he wanted to convert Gentiles, and it would be easier to convert men if you did not require them to be circumcised as part of the deal. Beyond this pragmatic consideration, it was also a matter of principle. Paul wanted to get rid of the view of law as an intermediary in the relationship between God and humanity, and replace it with love. Even if Paul was not actually an antinomian, he was potentially one, for his writings were strewn with seeds of antinomianism. The priority of love over law was part of Paul's larger vision for Christianity, which became a cornerstone of Pauline theology. In so doing, Paul introduced a dichotomy that we still live with, and continue to grapple with, today.

The Jerusalem Council was called to resolve what Jewish religious requirements should be required of Gentile converts. Circumcision was not the only issue. There were also questions about what Christian converts should eat, and how much they could interact with idolatrous worship including apparently temple prostitution. The council resolved the disagreement in the same way that many faculty disagreements today are resolved. After a detailed discussion with the contributions of Peter and James noted in Acts 15:7–11 and 13–21 and the practical difficulties of Barnabas and Paul noted in verse 12, a united decision was taken and set out in verse 29 in relation to Christian food laws and sexual morality. But the position on circumcision is more oblique. Indeed, it seems that it was not debated that much. It was a given in verse 24 that representations that the Jerusalem church leaders had commanded that all Gentile converts had to be circumcised were absolutely false. And so Paul, Barnabas, and Silas, with some unnamed others, were authorised to correct the misinformation about circumcision and to convey the new understanding of dietary norms and sexual morality to the international church such as it was then.

Uncircumcised non-Jews would come to outnumber Jews, at which point it was only a matter of time before there was a complete break between Judaism and Christianity. The Jewish authorities were not happy with what the Christians were doing. Neither were the Roman authorities. Judaism was a protected religion in the Roman Empire. The Roman authorities were fine with that concession to Judaism, as Judaism was ethnically limited. It would always be a minority religion in the empire. Christianity, insofar as it operated as a sect of Judaism, was protected, but it ceased to be protected once it broke away from Judaism. Unlike Judaism, which did not proselytise, Paul wanted to spread Christianity far and wide throughout the Roman Empire, which the Roman authorities did not like. So successful was Paul's mission that eventually the Roman Empire itself became Christian, and the rest, as they say, is history.

Starting from Paul, and because of Paul, successive Christian theologians have had to address the recurrent question about the relationship between law and love. If law were to have a place in the Christian tradition, it had to be justified in terms of love. If law cannot be justified in terms of love, then law has to go.

Introduction 3

Love is the standard by which law would be judged in Christian legal thought. Paul once wrote:

> If I speak in the tongues of men and of angels, but have not love, I am a noisy gong or a clanging cymbal, and if I have prophetic powers, and understand all mysteries and all knowledge, and if I have all faith, so as to remove mountains, but have not love, I am nothing.[1]

One could say the same of law too: if the law has no love, then the law is nothing. Love is the end of law. End can mean either telos or termination. If love is not the telos of law, then it would be the termination of law. If love is not the end of law, then that would be the end of law.

To define the place of law in Christian theology, Augustine, Calvin, and Luther all wrestled with the questions of law's relationship to love. The chapters in Part I on "Law and Love in Augustine, Calvin, and Luther?" examine and evaluate their attempts at achieving this reconciliation. Part I examines the debate about the relationship between law and love at the theological level. Part II follows these theological debates as they move into the political domain, and Part III follows them into the realm of personal ethics. The three parts of this collection weave together the theological, the political, and the personal.

In "John Calvin on the Law of Love," Constance Youngwon Lee looks at the structure of law within John Calvin's theology. John Calvin's theory of law is premised on the sovereignty of God. However, Lee argues, his theory does not translate into a theocratic form of government. Rather, for Calvin, the test of legal validity is the extent to which positive laws conform to normative standards as expressed in "the perpetual rule of love." This concept of the perpetual rule of love, which for Calvin is the final measure and destination of all law, provides the framework whereby lawmakers and citizens are made universally accountable to the transcendent laws of God.

In "'To Heal the Wounds of Sinners': Law, Love, and Forgiveness," Zachary Calo examines whether law can participate in the act of forgiveness. Calo first considers Augustine's Sermon 13 on Psalm 2:10 as an invitation to reflect on the place of love within the act of legal judgment. He next looks at the Catholic Church's statement *Memory and Reconciliation* as a way to develop an ecclesiology of forgiveness that might extend to collect acts of political reconciliation. Calo concludes by proposing that while law's capacity to enact love is provisional and limited, it can be seen within Christian thought as an act that reveals the fuller eschatological ends of creation witnessed in the Church.

Renée Köhler-Ryan also turns to Augustine to examine the relationship between love and law in the Christian tradition. In "Why Secularism is No Option for a Christian Citizen: Augustine's Analysis of Love in the City," Köhler-Ryan considers Augustine's discussion of the two orders of love that distinguish

---

1 1 Corinthians 13: 1–2.

citizenship in the City of God and in the City of Man. Citizens of the City of Man are driven by a lust for power and can love no one well, a point which has led some interpreters to propose that Augustine advocates a form of secularity in which citizens of both cities can hold a perpetual truth. Köhler-Ryan critiques the notion that Augustine promotes secularism while also proposing that Christians can witness God's love as citizens through the virtue of *latreia*.

Finally, Augusto Zimmermann's chapter "Why Lutheranism is No Option for a Meaningful Jurisprudence of Love" argues that there is little space for love within Luther's account of law. Zimmermann proposes that Luther's belief in a discontinuity between God and humans made it impossible to provide an account of the legal system by reference to the divine law, either natural or revealed. As a consequence, Lutheran jurisprudence has largely remained in the shadows of narrow legal positivism. Indeed, it is Zimmermann's position that Lutheranism not only facilitated the rise of the secular state but it also denied metaphysics in conceptualising law.

The chapters in Part I address the relationship between law and love at the theological level. In his book on *Political Theology*, Carl Schmitt famously said that "all significant concepts of the modern theory of the state are secularized theological concepts."[2] If Schmitt is right on this point, then we should expect to see the theological contestations about the relationship between law and love being replicated in political theory. The chapters in Part II on "Law, Love, and Political Theology" trace the genealogy of theological ideas as they move into the political domain and identify the structural affinity between the theological debates about law and love and the corresponding political debates.

In "Law and Love in Monasticism," Joshua Neoh traces the history of theological ideas from St Paul to St Benedict and explores the ways in which the inherited set of theological ideas shaped the history of political thought from Thomas More's *Utopia* to Alasdair MacIntyre's *After Virtue*. In tracing the history of ideas from St Paul to St Benedict, one can see two modes of community building. One might build a community on the basis of love alone, in which law plays a minimal and marginal role, as Paul dreamt of doing. In this Pauline model, one's relationship to God and to one another should be, as far as possible, unmediated by law. In contrast to this Pauline model, there is the Benedictine model, in which law moves from the margin to the centre. Law is the centrepiece of Benedictine monasticism. The Rule of Saint Benedict forges a close link between the monastic code and communal love. In this Benedictine model, law is a path to love. More's *Utopia* and MacIntyre's *After Virtue* transform Benedict's monastic ideal into a political aspiration. More's *Utopia* extrapolates the Benedictine model from a monastic community to a political community. Monastic law writ large, with suitable modifications, forms the basis of the laws and institutions of Utopia. As MacIntyre writes in *After Virtue*, "we are waiting not for a Godot, but for another – doubtless very different – St. Benedict."

---

2 Carl Schmitt, *Political Theology: Four Chapters on the Concept of Sovereignty*, trans. George Schwab (Cambridge, MA: MIT Press, 1985), 37.

In "The Law of Love as Principles of Civility," Alex Deagon suggests that the law of love supplies a theological framework for the principles of civility, which are the civic virtues that are required in a liberal democracy. Drawing on the work of John Milbank and the Parable of the Good Samaritan, Deagon argues that it is only through Christian conceptions of what it means to "love your neighbour as yourself" that the civic virtues and their transcendent foundation can properly inform public debate. The civic virtues are inherited from Christianity and find their culmination in the law of love as paradigmatically displayed through Christ, which points to their eternal nature. Any attempt to translate the law of love into a merely secular principle will fundamentally limit its effect, for the full benefit of the law of love for a legal community comes through its uniquely religious origin.

In "The Loving Sword," Benjamin Saunders challenges the notion that law and love are in contradiction. By appealing to the doctrine of divine simplicity, Saunders argues that, if God is simple, then all his attributes must be operative at all times, and God must act consistently with all his attributes whenever he acts. The doctrine of divine simplicity means that there can be no contradiction between law and love. God – the author and giver of law – must have acted lovingly when delivering the law to Moses, and when establishing the institutions of civil government. If that is so, then love, God's love, must underlie law. Saunders argues that law and love can be reconciled through a change in our understanding of love. Love can be expressed in gentle ways through compassion, forgiveness, and mercy, but it can also be expressed in ways that seem harsh and coercive. In a world of sin and violence, love can legitimately be manifested in the destruction or prevention of evil. In this fallen world, civil rulers may be called upon to carry out the loving task of executing God's wrath against wrongdoers.

In "Aquinas on Love, Law, and Happiness," Stefanus Hendrianto begins with the right to the pursuit of happiness. The right to the pursuit of happiness unites law and love. Drawing on Thomistic theology, Hendrianto argues that God is the ultimate object of happiness, and the attainment of happiness involves both sensitive and rational love. In this Thomistic model, love and happiness are connected to law. God instructs human beings through the law, which aims to foster a love of God and love of neighbour. Divine law is concerned with both the external and internal actions of human beings. Under an orientation towards the love of God and love of human beings, divine law directs human beings towards God as the source of ultimate happiness.

Part II examines how the theological debates about law and love play out in the political domain, while Part III examines how they play out in the personal domain. Just as the theological debates are replicated in the political domain, so they are further replicated in the realm of personal ethics. The chapters in Part III on "The Ethics of Law and Love" move the discussion from political theology to personal ethics.

Jonathan Crowe introduces readers to the ethical thought of Emmanuel Levinas. Levinas accepts that the ultimate end of all human life and flourishing is God or love, but he also provides an insightful account of the challenges humans face in embracing that end. While human beings are naturally inclined to self-absorption and personal enjoyment, to flourish they must approach and engage with others even though such engagement risks personal vulnerability and suffering. Ultimately, it is only through an attitude of ethical openness towards other people that we can escape the vicious cycle of self-interest and accept God's offer of unconditional love.

Donlu Thayer examines the insights of Joseph Smith Jr, American prophet-founder of The Church of Jesus Christ of Latter-day Saints, into the overarching connection of law and love, both in God's work "to bring to pass the immortality and eternal life" of humankind and in human efforts to establish a successful, ultimately holy community. Blessings from God derive from obedience to irrevocable law. God-like power and governance can be exercised only by love, guileless and unfeigned. Thayer frames her analysis with Smith's assertion that truth is "made manifest" in "proving contraries," a notion echoed both in the ideal practice of the common law adversarial system and in the Book of Mormon teaching of the necessary "opposition in all things" that underlies reality, enabling human agency, choice, and continuous progression.

Keith Thompson's chapter explores the implications of Jesus Christ's exposition of higher laws in the Sermon on the Mount, but he does that in the context of Henry James Sumner Maine's nineteenth-century hypothesis that human societies advance as they progress from relationships based on status to those based on contract. Thompson theorises that the Sermon on the Mount and Jesus' other teaching anticipate human societies differentiated by their legal orientation to coercion, contract, or covenant. And Thompson suggests that even Jesus anticipated that physical separation would ultimately be necessary in this world and in the world to come if such societies were to be able to function independently.

Patrick Brennan explores the depths of Christ's idea and practice of forgiveness after noting that Martha Minow and other contemporary thinkers believe that it can be empowering not to forgive. He uses St Thomas Aquinas' insights and gradually unfolds the reason why forgiveness empowered by grace is the better way and ultimately leads to caritas or pure love in the individuals who strive and continue to practice it. Only the practice of forgiveness can enable good to come out of evil.

What has love got to do with law? The answer that this book provides is that justice in the law is incomplete without love. The tradition of Christian legal thought has given sustained, albeit hidden, attention to the way that love might inform jurisprudence. The law itself is sterile, and judges have looked outside the law to find compelling expressions of love and justice. In that same spirit, these chapters turn to history, ethics, and theology to explore how Christian thought has aspired to find through love a transformative account of law.

Part I

Law and Love in Augustine, Calvin, and Luther?

1 John Calvin on the Law of Love

Constance Youngwon Lee[1]

Introduction

John Calvin's theory of law is premised on the sovereignty of God. However, such a theory does not translate to a theocratic form of governance as one might expect. Rather, for Calvin, the test for legal validity was the extent to which civil laws conformed to the normative standards embodied by the "perpetual rule of love."[2] Based on the Greatest Commandment in the Scripture, the rule of love prescribes that the content of civil laws be continuous with love for God and love for humanity. This framework remains continuous with Augustine's allegory of the two cities,[3] whereby the temporal realm is subsumed within a spiritual policy. Within the overarching framework of Calvin's account of providence, this chapter examines the second part of his three-pronged discussion of civil government: "[T]he laws, according to which [the magistrate] governs."[4] Calvin's ontology holds that he viewed law in terms of a teleological continuum, that he identified law with a clear moral end (*telos*). His most definitive text on this point is contained in his *Commentary on Paul's Epistle to the Romans* 10:4:[5] "indeed, every doctrine of the law, every command, every promise, always points to Christ."[6]

Calvin's detailed discussion of laws is mostly contained in Book IV, Chapter xx, 14–21 of the *Institutes*. However, references to the nature, scope, and function of law are scattered throughout his biblical commentaries, especially his *Commentary on Paul's Epistles to the Romans*.[7] The ultimate question for Calvin was: "what is the meaning of laws where God's authority is sovereign?"

---

1 I wish to acknowledge the invaluable guidance and support of the following scholars: Professors David VanDrunen, Jonathan Crowe, and Nicholas Aroney.
2 John Calvin, *Institutes of the Christian Religion*, ed. John T McNeill (Philadelphia, PA: Westminster Press, 1960): IV.x.15. Citation refers to the 1559 edition.
3 St Augustine, *The City of God* (Philadelphia: Penguin Classics, 2004). Citation refers to the revised edition.
4 John Calvin, *Institutes of the Christian Religion*, IV.xx.3.
5 John Calvin, *Commentary on Romans*, trans. Ross Mackenzie (Grand Rapids, MI: Eerdmans, 1960): 221. See also John Calvin, *Institutes of the Christian Religion*, II.vi.4 and II.vii.2.
6 John Calvin, *Commentary on Romans*, 221.
7 John Calvin, *Institutes of the Christian Religion*.

DOI: 10.4324/9781003148920-3

"Where laws are *not* the assertion of human power, how do they manifest themselves?" Calvin addresses these questions by viewing laws *not* as an embodiment of any purpose known to human beings but rather as the expression of God's perfect will. In so doing, Calvin successfully dismisses the notion of law as a human construct. However, this non-positivist approach is not synonymous with a divine command theory of law. This chapter will examine the way Calvin achieves a balanced account – one that preserves the normative weight of laws but does not eliminate the freedom of states to make and apply detailed rules to conditions which are particular to them.

To this end, this chapter begins by exploring Calvin's exposition on (1) the symbiotic relationship between laws and the magistrates. This discussion presupposes what Calvin viewed as the proper order of things – wherein the external and spiritual values transcend the temporal and civil. This hierarchal dichotomy subjects the magistrate and human-made laws to a higher moral order. Indeed, within this broader context, Calvin's emphasis on (2) the functions of laws: theological, coercive, and pedagogical, shifts his focus from the ends or goals of laws to their normative content. Upon this foundation, Calvin firmly builds his argument for (3) the proper content of laws. Here, he distinguishes between "laws" in the nominal sense (otherwise known as "law *qua* law")[8] and laws in the true sense. Calvin argues that the moral part of the divine law alone constitutes the "unchangeable rule of right living."[9] This "perpetual rule of love" captures the minimal content of law (Calvin identifies this rule with "natural law"), thereby freeing states from assuming any particular form of government (i.e. theocracy) while still subjecting them to a higher morality. By contending that the law possesses both external and internal aspects, Calvin is able to separate what the law "is" from what the law "ought to be." Paradoxically, it is by separating the two that Calvin is ultimately successful in binding them closer together – by infusing the true spirit of law into the laws themselves.

The Laws and "Their'" Magistrates

Calvin begins his chapter by reverting to a familiar metaphor, one he utilised in his previous discussion of civil government. However, this time, he uses the metaphor to liken the magistracy's relationship to laws to an individual's relationship to their sinews or soul.[10] Through this metaphor, Calvin asserts and highlights the symbiotic nature of the relationship between laws and magistrates. That is, one cannot legitimately function without the other. It is worth noting the way in which Calvin begins this section, by concluding, accordingly laws are the "stoutest sinews of the commonwealth ... the souls without which the magistracy cannot stand, as they themselves have no force apart from the magistracy."[11] He

---

8 Joseph Raz, *The Authority of Law* (Oxford: Clarendon Press, 1979): 38–39.
9 John Calvin, *Institutes of the Christian Religion*, IV.xx.16.
10 Ibid., 14.
11 Ibid.

means here that apart from the magistrate's enforcement, the laws have no real force. Mounted on this statement, Calvin goes on to claim, "the magistrate [is] a living law."[12] That is, without the support of true laws, the magistrate's proclamations lack moral force.

Calvin states, "Law is a silent magistrate."[13] McNeill observes the semblance of this statement to one advanced by Cicero: "For as the laws govern the magistrate, so the magistrate governs the people, and it can be truly said that the magistrate is the speaking law, and the law a silent magistrate."[14] However, in spite of the initial semblance, Calvin has an altogether different meaning in mind. Whereas Cicero was referring to a "speaking law," Calvin is referring to a "living law." The reference to laws that are "living" accords to laws the same status of authority (if not higher than) vested in human lawgivers. In this context, Calvin's term, "laws," engenders two distinct meanings. In the first sense, "laws" refer to those ordinances or prohibitions that simply bear "the title of laws."[15] In the second sense, Calvin uses the term to refer to those rules that also bear laws' normative character. In his view, only "laws" in this second sense are "true" laws.[16] In Book II, he identifies the "true" content of laws with the "divine mind." He then goes on to find a connection between the divine mind and the "reason inherent in nature."[17] A virtuous human is thus one whose reason is "completely developed" and is true to their "rational nature."[18] By extension, Calvin makes clear that it is by knowing "the principles of right living" that human beings are made better.[19]

The connection that Calvin establishes between human magistrates and their natural access to right standards also means that, inversely, laws are only legitimate when "the reason and mind of a wise lawgiver" conform their ordinances, "commands and prohibitions" to the divine mind.[20] Calvin is even more forthcoming in his view that both magistrate and laws bear authority when he claims, "[t]he law governs the magistrate." In Calvin's mind, the law governs the magistrate because the magistrate is only rational insofar as his laws conform to the principles of nature.[21] "The magistrate governs the people" by speaking to them the rationality of laws.[22] In other words, the magistrate is dependent on the laws, for without them his "commands and prohibitions" lack force. By "force," Calvin alludes to requisite normative content revealing a subscription to the Augustinian

12 Ibid., IV.xx.14.
13 Ibid., IV.xx.14.
14 Ibid., III.i.
15 Ibid., II.v.
16 Ibid., II.vii.
17 Ibid., II.vii.
18 Ibid., I.xvi.
19 Ibid., I.xi.
20 Ibid., II.iv.
21 This statement's semblance to the modern constitutional maxim that "nobody is above the law" is uncanny.
22 John Calvin, *Institutes of the Christian Religion*, I.vii–ix.

belief that immoral laws lack real authority (in the sense of *auctoritas* and not *potestas* or *auctoritas non veritas*).[23] The magistrate cannot speak to the rational natures of the people when "laws" so to speak – the sinews of the commonwealth – are not backed by the authority of the "divine mind." Thus, Calvin's reference to "living law" explains the association he draws, within the civil order, between the force of the magistrate and the inherently normative character of laws.

Moreover, this relationship between the magistrates and laws is inseparable but not equal. In fact, Calvin makes no attempt whatsoever to ground the authority of law in a human magistrate. This, again, highlights Calvin's commitment to the notion that civil government is, first and foremost, a "divinely appointed order." The voice of the law is its "life" force. And the life force of the law depends only on its conformity with the divine mind. This logic presents its own internal hierarchy, as follows:

 i. The silent authority of human nature ("the conscience") governs
 ii. The human authority who, in turn, forms speech
 iii. The speech then gives force to the command/prohibition only insofar as it conforms with "divine" standards
 iv. Thereby the magistrates' authority has sinew

In this way, the iterations proceeding from the mouth of a magistrate are only true laws insofar as they conform to the standards of the divine order. By this hierarchy, Calvin contends that the magistrate is not asserting power in his own name but in accordance with a "mandate from God."[24]

Calvin's doctrine of equity (*aequitas*) therefore seems a deliberate attempt to move away from any pattern of thought purporting to identify moral law with the arbitrary fiats of a despot (earthly or cosmic).[25] Calvin writes, "equity alone must be the goal and rule and limit of all laws."[26] In his political context, Calvin advises against the inclinations of fellow reformers to "degrade the authority of the law" in the process of the Reformation.[27] Compared to Luther's favoured approach of dismantling and deposing traditional regulatory systems, Calvin believed in harnessing the power of existing equitable structures in order to

---

23 Interestingly, *auctoritas* is the Latin word which is the root term for the English word for "authority." *Auctoritas* does not merely allude to political authority but refers to numinous content. It encompasses the Ancient Roman belief that the "power of command" is supported by a mysterious, even spiritual force. For more on this topic, see Saul Newman, "*Auctoritas non veritas*: On the Sovereign," in *Political Theology: A Critical Introduction* (Cambridge: Polity Press, 2018).
24 John Calvin, *Institutes of the Christian Religion*, IV.xx.6.
25 Calvin's critique of Luther's doctrine of *epieikeia* demonstrates this. For example, MacIntyre alleges that Calvin's theory of law is most consistent with the arbitrary commands of God. Alastair MacIntyre, *A Short History of Ethics* (New York: Macmillan Publishing Company, 1966) 123.
26 John Calvin, *Institutes of the Christian Religion*, II.viii.8.
27 Ibid.

reconstruct a new legal and moral order infused with God's will as manifest in natural law.

Paul Helm agrees that Calvin's views on law differ from the divine command theory of law. He argues that Calvin distinguishes between the voluntarist theory of law that holds that (1) something is "right simply because God commands it, wrong simply because God forbids it" and an ethical position that asserts (2) "knowledge of right and wrong depends upon supernatural knowledge, what God tells us in his word."[28] Whereas the first is a meta-ethical claim, the second is an epistemological one. Subscribing to the epistemological account does not necessarily commit us to the meta-ethical one. That is, it is one thing to hold that human perception of right and wrong is sourced in divine revelation, and altogether another to hold that the "divine command establish[es] what is right and wrong."[29] The first maintains that a law *ought to* conform to our knowledge of right or wrong as prescribed by divine revelation, the second that the law *is* right *because* it emanates from a divine command.

Correspondingly, Calvin never suggests special revelation is the *only* source of human knowledge of immutable norms of right and wrong. Although he consistently maintains that the fullest knowledge of the moral law is found in special revelation (and, as such, Christians must strive to adhere to this standard), Calvin still recognises that humans can generally grasp the moral good in a rudimentary and universal sense. Calvin uses a range of metaphors to describe this *continuum* between law and the gospel: special revelation is the "reality" or substance, the "whole law" that confirms and gives actuality to the "shadows." It is a "vivid portrait," while law is the "rough sketch."[30] Special revelation supplements the natural human capacity to "distinguish [between] just and unjust" through the "apprehension of conscience," which (one might recall) is itself a divine endowment.[31] Thus, Calvin employs this series of metaphors to characterise the fundamental continuum he draws between law and gospel, ultimately describing the way in which Christ "fulfils" the law.[32]

By this continuum, Calvin departs from a voluntarist approach to law. This is also the point at which Calvin's account differs subtly from Aquinas' natural law.[33] Aquinas constructs a distinct hierarchy of laws: eternal laws, divine laws, human laws, and natural laws.[34] He then goes on to divide the law of Moses into three parts: (1) moral, (2) ceremonial, and (3) judicial. By contrast, according to

---

28 Paul Helm, *John Calvin's Ideas* (Oxford: Oxford University Press, 2005): 347.
29 Ibid., 348.
30 John Calvin, *Institutes of the Christian Religion*, II.ix.4.
31 Ibid., II.ii.22. Note, Calvin's heading "political supplements." John Calvin, *Institutes of the Christian Religion*, V.xx.15.
32 I John Hesselink, *Calvin's Concept of Law* (Allison Park, PA: Pickwick Publications, 1992): 170–82.
33 R Scott Clark, "Calvin on the Lext Naturalis," *Stulos Theological Journal* 6, no. 12 (1998): 3.
34 Thomas Aquinas, *Summa Theologiae*, ed. Thomas Gilby (London: Blackfriars, 1963) I-IIae, 91,2; q91, a5; q94, a2; 95–97.

Clark, Calvin identified the Decalogue wholly with natural law. In other words, Calvin associated the moral aspect of divine law with natural law.[35] That is, "[f]or Calvin … it was a given that God had entered into a probationary, federal-covenantal relationship with Adam, and that the lex moralis … is the same law which he codified at Sinai and which Calvin called lex naturalis."[36] The implications of identifying the moral part of divine law with natural law are that the ceremonial and judicial aspects of law are mere servants to the moral law, befitting the particular circumstance of the Jews. Calvin cites Jeremiah 7:22, where God says, "I spake not unto your fathers, nor commanded them in the day that I brought them out of the land of Egypt, concerning burnt-offerings or sacrifices: but this thing commanded I them, saying 'Obey my voice.'"[37] There seems to be a difference between the spirit of the law, voice, and the form, what is spoken (reminiscent of Platonic theory of the forms), but there exists an undeniable connection between the three. For this reason, Calvin suggests that under different circumstances and in different times, these two subsidiary components of divine law may be "abrogated" by magistrates of those jurisdictions while still allowing "piety [to] remain safe and unharmed," or while "the perpetual duties and precepts of love could still remain."[38]

Thus, the clearest evidence against the allegation that Calvin's theory of law constitutes a divine command theory is found in his appeals to (natural) equity (*naturalis aequitas*) and conscience (*équité de nature – humanitas*), which together represent his natural law theory.[39] Natural law, therefore, is the moral law that the magistrate must turn to in order to discern what pious laws are. Calvin states:

> It is a fact that the law of God which we call the moral law is nothing else than a testimony of natural law and of that conscience which God has engraved upon the minds of men. Consequently, the entire scheme of this equity (*aequitatis ratio*) of which we are now speaking has been prescribed in it. Hence, this equity (*aequitas*) alone must be the goal and rule and limit of all laws.[40]

The subjects, through conscience, can also apprehend what amounts to just or unjust laws. Calvin holds natural law as the normative measure for pious or right laws. However, in advancing this claim, Calvin is careful to note that

> Surely every nation is left free to make such laws as it foresees to be profitable for itself. Yet these must be in conformity to that perpetual rule of love, so that they indeed vary in form but have the same purpose.[41]

---

35 John Calvin, *Institutes of the Christian Religion*, IV.x.15.
36 R Scott Clark, "Calvin on the Lext Naturalis," 3.
37 John Calvin, *Institutes of the Christian Religion*, IV.x.15; 788.
38 Ibid., IV.xx.15.
39 Ibid.. IV.xx.16.
40 Ibid., IV.xx.16.
41 Ibid., IV.x.15.

In this way, Calvin can be seen to be preserving the existing structure of law, choosing to recalibrate the old to create the new – a Protestant legal and moral order through natural law. In doing so, the orientation of the new order was seemingly reversed. The necessity for fixed laws and universal norms comes not from authoritarian command but from the liberty of human conscience that stems from its likeness to the image of God.[42]

Nevertheless, we must not forget that Calvin's theory of law remains subject to a continuum as part of his broader theological framework. This means that we can only make sense of his legal theory in relation to a more inclusive "moral design."[43] For this reason, David Little affixes Calvin's account of natural law with the label "derivative theory of natural law."[44] This means that in order to properly understand Calvin's theory of law, we must first consider that Calvin conceives of natural law in terms of its (divine) functions or purposes. Returning to Chapter III, Calvin states:

> "The purpose of the law, therefore, is to render man inexcusable. This would not be a bad definition: natural law is that apprehension of conscience which distinguishes sufficiently between just and unjust."[45]

In this case, the general or overall purpose of natural law is theological or spiritual (i.e. to render us inexcusable before God).[46] It is through the "secret compunctions"[47] of conscience which resides as an "inner witness and monitor"[48] that we are invited to reflect on our persistent moral shortcomings, thereby recognising our need for divine salvation. Conscience is the vehicle by which individual persons are linked to God and the moral law. It is the universal access to normative knowledge that deprives all individuals of the defence of ignorance before the moral law. However, it is also the seat of Christian liberty.[49] The liberty enjoyed by our consciences as repositories of the image of God comes hand in hand with a responsibility by the image-bearer to its Creator.

---

42 John Calvin, *Commentary on Daniel 6:22* (Grand Rapids, MI: Christian Classics Ethereal Library, 1999).
43 David Little, "Calvin and the Prospects for Christian Theory of Natural Law," in *Norm and Context in Christian Ethics*, eds. Gene Outka and Paul Ramsey (New York: Charles Scribner's Sons, 1968): 175–97.
44 Ibid.
45 John Calvin, *Institutes of the Christian Religion*, II.ii.22.
46 John Calvin, *Commentary on Acts*, trans. William Pringle (Edinburgh: Calvin Translation Society, 2005): 169–70; Benjamin B Warfield, "Calvin's Doctrine of the Knowledge of God," in *Calvin and Calvinism* (Oxford: Oxford University Press, 1931): 41–42.
47 John Calvin, *Calvin's Commentary on Genesis 4:9*, trans. John King (Grand Rapids, MI: Eerdmans, 1948).
48 John Calvin, *Institutes of the Christian Religion*, II.viii.1.
49 John Calvin, *Commentary on Galatians 5:13* (Grand Rapids, MI: Christian Classics Ethereal Library, 2009).

Interrelationship of Law and Morality

Calvin's formulations of natural law underwent steady development throughout his lifetime.[50] This development basically embodied an expansion of the scope of natural law, its functions and operations in the civil world and its purpose as the means by which God governs both earthly and heavenly kingdoms. Various references to natural law are scattered throughout the corpus of Calvin's writings – "the voice of nature," "engraven law," the "natural sense," "the sense of divine judgment," "the testimony of the heart," "the inner voice," to name a few.[51] Calvin uses these terms (not identical yet) interchangeably in discussion to describe the norms created and laid down by God for the universal governance of humankind. John Hesselink describes the order of law–morality–gospel this way: law of creation (natural law) is followed by the revealed law (the law of Moses) and finds full embodiment in the gospel, the gracious law which is the ultimate norm and guide for believers.[52]

In relation to general humanity, natural law, as objective moral norms, has been established in the world for the proper regulation of individual and social lives. These universal moral norms are described as God's commandments engraved on the conscience of individuals, summarised in the Decalogue, and fleshed out most fully in the Scripture. As we noted before, Calvin makes a particular point of observing that the *fullest* expression of natural law is found in the two tablets of the Decalogue.[53]

Moreover, Calvin's mature formulations of the spiritual and temporal dimensions reflect an expansive theory of moral law. Quoting a passage from the final edition of the *Institutes*, which, importantly, remained unaltered from the 1536 edition:

> It is a fact that the law of God which we call the moral law is nothing else than a testimony of natural law and of that conscience [*naturalis legis testimonium id est conscientiae*] which God has engraved [*a Deo insculpta*] upon the minds of men. Consequently, the entire scheme of this equity [*equitatis ratio*] ... has been prescribed in it. Hence, this equity alone must be the goal and rule and limit of all laws.[54]

In this passage, the concepts of the law of God – the moral law, natural law, conscience, and equity – are closely associated with each other. They have similar content that may lead some to mistake them as synonymous, but Calvin's thought is far subtler than conflating their meaning.

---

50 John T McNeill, "Calvin and Civil Government," *Journal of Presbyterian History* 42, no. 2 (1964): 71, 72.
51 Ibid.
52 John Calvin, *Harmony of Moses* (Edinburgh: Calvin Translation Society, 1843–59): 3:154.
53 John Calvin, *Institutes of the Christian Religion*, II.vii.1; II.viii.1; IV.xx.15.
54 Ibid., IV.iv.16.

John Calvin on the Law of Love   17

What these associated concepts do tell us is the expanded scope of Calvin's natural law account. Seen as the means by which God would govern both heavenly and earthly kingdoms, this robust natural law account brought Calvin's theology closer in line with Augustine's political theory. Augustine draws a sharp dichotomy between two kinds of righteousness – one pertaining to the spiritual realm, the other to the temporal. The first belongs to the heavenly kingdom fulfilled by Christ; the other to the secular kingdom which is characterised by fallen humanity.[55] Following in Augustine's line of thought, Calvin finds that the spiritual use of the law typically finds its place among the regenerate.[56] He deems this to be the "principal use" of the law as it demands not only outward honesty but beckons believers towards inward righteousness. In Calvin's words, the spiritual law demands "obedience of soul, mind, and will … an angelic purity which cleansed of every pollution of the flesh, savours nothing but the spirit."[57] It therefore encompasses more than external action but extends to every aspect of a person's being. In this sense, it requires a "renewed nature, which God forms anew after his own image."[58]

Moreover, the spiritual law is typified by a liberty that is sourced in justification by faith. In this sense, such a law presupposes a freedom from the shackles – the sanction or threats – that characterise civil laws.

> For the law is now acting toward us as a rigorous enforcement officer who is not satisfied unless the requirements are met. But in this perfection to which it exhorts us, the law points out the goal toward which throughout life we are to strive.[59]

By extension, the spiritual law bears an educative role. This pedagogical role involves the spiritual law instructing the regenerate who want to love God the means by which to do so. Calvin believes that this "daily instruction of the law is necessary in addition to the guidance of the Spirit, if believers are to know God's will."[60] The implication of this is to render believers subject to both laws under the broader domain of God's sovereign rule.

However, Calvin goes on to discuss the civil use of the law which he applies universally to humankind – to both degenerate and regenerate alike. The purpose of the civil law is neither to sanctify nor to condemn but to bring order to temporal society. This may involve coercion or threats. However, the mortal lawgiver's jurisdiction only extends to outward actions.[61] In Calvin's view, the reach of civil

---

55 St Augustine, *The City of God* (New York: Penguin Classics, 2004).
56 John Calvin, *Institutes of the Christian Religion*, 2.II.10.
57 Ibid., II.viii.6.
58 John Calvin, *Commentary on Romans 7:14* (Grand Rapids, MI: Christian Classics Ethereal Library, 2009).
59 John Calvin, *Institutes of the Christian Religion*, II.vii.13.
60 Ibid., II.vii.2.
61 Ibid., III.xix.16.

laws cannot extend to transform the inward person. Only when the intentions "come forth into the open" or when "actual crimes are committed" can civil laws have influence.[62] At this juncture, Calvin's anthropological reflections become most evident. His firm commitment to human depravity leads him to provide a more realistic assessment of human nature than do successive political theorists such as Rousseau's optimism on the one hand or Hobbes' pessimism on the other. Calvin presupposes that administrative or civil rules cannot disregard the natural proclivities and intuitive capacities of the citizens. In this sense, the only way to keep potential unjust habits and inclinations in check is by ensuring their alignment with the common good.[63] Calvin's account of the proper role of government flows from his natural law theory – insofar as is practicably reasonable, given the fallen nature of humanity, civil government has been commissioned to promote virtue and restrain vices in the advancement of the common good.

The Three Functions of Natural Law

Calvin's mature and expansive understanding of natural law brings him to identify law with God's "three uses of the moral law" in his governance of humanity.[64] These three functions are (1) theological, (2) coercive (or judicial), and (3) pedagogical. These duties are imposed by God on all those who inhabit the earthly kingdom regardless of their status – both upon those who hold office as well as those persons who do not. For Calvin, the basis of these duties imposed on both the ruler and the ruled is the natural law. These include the moral duties as set out in the Decalogue to respect person, property, reputation, and relationship with neighbours, premised on a foremost duty to honour God. Thus, this deontological framework for civil governance can be considered a key feature characterising Calvin's account of civil governance.

The Theological Function of Law

The first function of natural law is theological. God uses natural law to render individuals cognisant, as a means of convicting them of their depravity. This use of conscience to convict individuals compels humans to seek God's liberating grace.[65] In stating this, Calvin elaborates on his earlier writings on the dialectic between spiritual law and spiritual liberty. By holding out a model of perfective righteousness, the moral law warns, informs, convicts, and finally condemns every person of their innate depravity, making them thoroughly aware of their moral shortcomings. In this way, the theological use of natural law is to pierce the

---

62 Ibid., II.viii.6.
63 John Calvin, *Sermon on 1 Samuel 8*, trans. Douglas Kelly in Calvin Studies Colloquium, eds. Charles Raynal and John Leith (Davidson, NC: Davidson College Presbyterian Church, 1982).
64 John Calvin, *Institutes of the Christian Religion*, trans. Ford Lewis Battles (Grand Rapids, MI: Eerdmans, 1986) I.xxxiii. Citation refers to the 1536 edition.
65 John Calvin, *Institutes of the Christian Religion*, II.vii.8.

hubris of humans and drive them to despair at the inadequacy of their own efforts to attain righteousness; this despair is seen as the necessary precondition for sinners to seek God and his saving grace. Calvin uses the metaphor of a mirror to describe the theological use of natural law as a means by which persons are made aware of their need for "spiritual liberty."[66]

As discussed in Calvin's previous chapter, conscience acts as an inner monitor to "accuse," to "condemn," and to "convict."[67] In this sense, the natural law acts to puncture humans' natural proclivity for arrogance, driving them to despair at the futility of their own efforts to attain moral virtue. Only the despair borne out of true self-awareness will serve as the necessary condition for the pursuit of "spiritual liberty." This spiritual liberty is only possible through faith in God's saving grace, which, in turn, finds its foundation in a condemnation of the moral law.[68]

Coercive Function of Law

However, all this is not to say that Calvin intended that the purpose of natural law was limited to the theological. In fact, we can infer this from Calvin's passages which outline the legislative functions in addition to the significance of conscience in a judicial setting. That is, the legislative function of conscience, as the vehicle for apprehending and applying the basic norms of natural morality, remains indispensable for the preservation of civil society. Calvin defines the concept of equity as the "seed of political order" which has been "implanted in men."[69]

> Consequently, we observe that there exist in men's minds universal impressions of a certain civic fair dealing and order. Hence no man is to be found who does not understand that every sort of human organisation must be regulated by laws, and who does not comprehend the principles of those laws. Hence arises the unvarying consent of all nations and of individual mortals with regard to laws. For their seeds have, without teacher or lawgiver, been implanted in all men.[70]

In this way, the second function of natural law as God intended is to bridle humans from descent into depravity.[71] According to its legislative/judicial purpose, Calvin sees natural law as serving to restrain persons in a minimalist sense from deteriorating into complete licentiousness.

> [T]he law is like a halter to check the raging and otherwise limitlessly ranging lusts of the flesh ... Hindered by fright or shame, sinners dare neither

---

66 Ibid., II.vii.6–9.
67 Ibid., II.ii.22.
68 Ibid., II.vii.6–9.
69 Ibid., II.ii.13.
70 Ibid., II.ii.13.
71 Ibid., II.vii.10; IV.xx.3.

execute what they have conceived in their minds, nor openly breathe forth the rage of their lust.[72]

Civil righteousness is achieved through the moral law imposing upon persons constraint and force. This is primarily external and their consciences (inner beliefs) may remain "untouched" by a care for what is just and right. Nonetheless, the threat of divine punishment should compel sinners to obey the basic requirements of the law. This compliance ensures the basic maintenance of civil order in society.

Pedagogical Function of Law

The third function of natural law is pedagogical. Calvin believed that the moral law serves as an educative tool whereby believers (regenerate) may be instructed about the means and measures of sanctification. This presupposes a calling to "grow." Here, Calvin observes that this directive for spiritual development assumes that "we are not our own."[73] He goes on to observe that the faithful are not given liberty to do whatever they please unlike "[those who] were the servant[s] of their own appetites, [and] bind [themselves] to laws of their own stipulation."[74] In this way, the natural law teaches not only "civil righteousness" common to all persons but also "spiritual righteousness" for those persons already sanctified by faith in grace. In this sense, the law's purpose is not solely to curb violence and violation but ultimately to cultivate compassion and love. The law's purpose is thus twofold: not only to coercively restrain persons from doing harm through acts of murder, theft, and assault, but also to forbid immanent intentions such as hatred, covetousness, and lust. This "spiritual righteousness" is not reserved for the heavenly kingdom, but Christians are called to act on their consciences in the political dimension. Calvin charges believers with the moral duty to act "as ambassadors and stewards of treasures of salvation, of the covenant of God ... of the secrets of God."[75] It is by discharging this commission that believers not only give glory to the image of God on earth but compel degenerate individuals to realise and bemoan their own sorry states and seek God's salvation.

The Perpetual Rule of Love

Now that we have considered Calvin's expanded definition of law and its functions – the theological, legislative, and pedagogical – we turn now to consider its content. Calvin establishes his account of law, calling it "the perpetual rule of

---

72 Ibid., II.vii.10.
73 John Calvin, *Sermon on Deuteronomy*, trans. Arthur Golding (Edinburgh: Banner of Truth Trust, 1987): V:iv-vii.
74 John Calvin, *Institutes of the Christian Religion*, IV.xx.51.
75 Ibid., II.vii.12; III.iii.9; III.xvii.5–6; *Commentary on 1 Peter 1:14* (Edinburgh: Calvin Translation Society, 1855).

love."[76] By this account, all civil law ought to be judged by the moral law. He holds this rule of love as the source and aspirational end of all legal and moral obligations. So, though

> every nation is left free to make such laws as it foresees as profitable for itself, yet these must be in conformity to the perpetual rule of love, so that they indeed vary in form but have the same purpose.[77]

The perpetual rule of love encompasses natural law, the law of creation, and equity according to which "the entire natural-social order was designed."[78]

Positive and Normative Laws

Calvin begins his discussion about the content of law on a reticent note. He cautions against conversations of what constitutes "the best kind of laws" due to the presumptuousness and futility underlying such remarks.[79] He notes, "I would have preferred to pass over this matter in utter silence."[80] Regardless, Calvin still finds himself implicated to speak in the face of the "seditious" argument of some who deny that "a commonwealth is duly framed [when it conforms to the] ... political system of Moses."[81] His rejection of the denial inevitably leaves a gap in the narrative which he is then obliged to address. What laws "ought" to govern a Christian state in the absence of "the common law of nations"? Since Calvin's purpose is to ultimately exhibit political order as an aspect of God's providence, he is acutely aware of the need to understand the limits of such a discussion. He states that providence has "wisely arranged that various countries should be ruled by various kinds of government."[82] Calvin begins by pointing out the "endless" nature of such a discussion – given, firstly, the impossibility of mortal minds to penetrate the vast wisdom behind such variety and, secondly, that the limits of "the present ... place" render useless a description of such endless variety.[83] This leads Calvin to conclude, "the will of the Lord is enough."

Such caution also explains Calvin's minimalist approach to law.[84] Rather than discussing what constitutes the "best laws," Calvin instead turns his attention to

---

76 John Calvin, *Institutes of the Christian Religion*, IV.xx.15.
77 Ibid., IV.xx.15.
78 David Little, "Calvin and the Prospects for Christian Theory of Natural Law," 177; John Calvin, *Institutes of the Christian Religion*, IV.xx.16.
79 John Calvin, *Institutes of the Christian Religion*, IV.x.14.
80 Ibid., IV.x.14.
81 Ibid., IV.xx.14.
82 Ibid., IV.viii.
83 Ibid., IV.i.
84 John T McNeill suggests that to Calvin, natural law was of secondary interest but only insofar as the earthly realm was subordinate to the heavenly. Given its divine origin, it may be arguable that natural law "is not secondary but controlling" in civil affairs. Scholars dispute this however, there is less contention that Calvin believed that natural law was normatively

those laws *not* forbidden by God. His aims are not to model contemporary laws on the judicial and ceremonial laws of the Jews but to identify a standard, more general in form but robust in substance, that is *perpetual* and adaptable to a variety of different circumstances.[85] He offers a standard by which, in different circumstances, the laws of any nation could still be "abrogated while piety remained safe and unharmed."[86] According to Calvin, the moral law is the normative standard of just laws.[87] In this, Calvin is again careful to note that "every nation is left free to make such laws as it foresees to be profitable for itself."[88] The only limitation to this freedom is that every law proceeding from these nations must guarantee that "the perpetual duties and precepts of love [can] still remain."[89]

This exclusive limitation renders the rule a robust one. That is, Calvin's minimalist approach to law does not preclude an aspirational trajectory towards a higher plane of virtue. In Calvin's exposition of the Decalogue, we see him interpret a number of the Ten Commandments not only as prohibitory but also as containing positive obligations, more broadly derived from the "perpetual rule of love." For instance, on the Tenth Commandment which explicitly states, "Thou shalt not covet [thy neighbour's goods, house, wife or anything that belongs to thy neighbour]," Calvin writes:

> The purpose of this commandment is: since God wills that our whole soul be possessed with a disposition to love, we must banish from our hearts all desire contrary to love. To sum up, then: no thought should steal upon us to move our hearts to a harmful covetousness that tends to our neighbour's loss.[90]

The way the object of our affection "neighbour" is defined broadly to include "even the remotest person," evinces an aspirational aspect to the principle. William Klempa draws a penetrating conclusion on this point; he argues that Calvin seems to have followed Augustine in his interpretation of the principle, reading "love back from the end of history instead of up from a truncated nature within history."[91] In this way, for Calvin, an ideal form of love (found in Scripture) represents the aspirational end of law.

---

grounded in the divine law. See McNeill, "Natural Law in the Teaching of the Reformers," *Journal of Religion* 26 (1946): 168.
85 John Calvin, *Institutes of the Christian Religion*, IV.x.15.
86 Ibid., IV.x.15.
87 John Calvin, *Institutes of the Christian Religion*, III.xix.15. Here, Calvin's most extensive treatment of conscience is available. He describes the conscience as the inward sense of the moral law's requirements and thus, it "is a sense of divine judgement." In other words, a good conscience is "nothing but inward integrity of the heart" (III.xix.16).
88 Ibid., IV.x.15.
89 Ibid., IV.x.15.
90 Ibid., II.viii.49.
91 William Klempa, "John Calvin on Natural Law," in *John Calvin and the Church: A Prism of Reform*, ed. Timothy George (Louisville, KY: Westminster John Knox, 1990): 87: Love as it was meant to be, not as it currently is, corrupted by sin.

The Law of Love

Calvin thus establishes the perpetual rule of love as the final measure and destination of laws. The rule of love is contained under "two headings."[92] These two headings broadly govern humanity's relationship to (1) God and (2) fellow human beings. Derived from the Greatest Commandment, "[t]he first part of the law simply commands us to worship God with pure faith and piety; the other, to embrace [fellow humans] with sincere affection."[93] Thus, the moral law, or the eternal and unchangeable will of God is that he "Himself ... be worshipped by all, and that we love one another."[94] According to Calvin, this twofold requirement is the standard by which all other positive laws are to be judged. In the context of his political theory, a government which is established on the rule of love "provides that a public manifestation of religion may exist among Christians, and that humanity may be maintained among men."[95] The conceptualisation of moral law in terms of a nexus between us, an eternal God, and our neighbours on earth, allows Calvin's account to encapsulate laws governing both Christians and non-Christians alike.

That Calvin refers to a "rule" and not a "law" is significant. Here, it seems, Calvin is trying to distinguish between the spirit of the law and its form. For this reason, Calvin refrains from speaking about the end goal of love apart from its relationship to its meaning. He makes clear that the purpose of law is not its reason for being, but is the very meaning of the law itself.

> [T]he purpose of the whole law is the fulfilment of righteousness to form human life to the archetype of divine purity. For God has so depicted his character in the law that if any man carries out in deed whatever is enjoined there, he will express the image of God, as it were, in his own life.[96]

Referring to his account of the *Imago Dei*, Calvin asserts that the image of God is contained in the "gist" of the law. This "gist" is equivalent to the "aim of the law."[97] The image of God is contained in the deeds emanating from the spirit of law and not in any ends resulting from those deeds. Accordingly, the rule of love is not practised in the end of perfecting the soul, but as an expression of the law itself, "since you cannot desire a greater perfection" than that expressed in the law.[98] This is continuous with Calvin's account of human depravity – since

---

92 John Calvin, *Institutes of the Christian Religion*, II.viii.51.
93 Ibid., IV.xx.15; John Calvin, "Sermons on Deuteronomy," in *John Calvin's Sermons on the Ten Commandments*, ed. and trans. Benjamin W Farley (Grand Rapids, MI: Baker Book House, 1980): 249: "The truth and substance of the law were not [confined] to one age: they constitute something permanent which shall abide forever."
94 John Calvin, *Institutes of the Christian Religion*, IV.x.15.
95 Ibid., IV.x.3.
96 Ibid., II.viii.51.
97 Ibid., II.viii.51.
98 Ibid., II.viii.51.

our souls cannot know perfection other than that which God grants those deeds which emanate from our love.

In this way, Calvin purports to capture the true spirit of the law by defining it as a rule. Citing the Apostle Paul in 1 Timothy 1:5, Calvin writes that "the aim of the law is love from a pure conscience and a faith unfeigned."[99] Calvin thus concludes that there is no love superior to that which is practised as a rule. Calvin's focus on the spirit of the law fully expressed in the divine has led some to diminish the value Calvin accords to natural law. August Lang, for instance, erred in finding that Calvin envisaged that natural law should only play a "superficial and external" role in his account of law.[100] This interpretation fails to consider the twofold senses Calvin ascribes to his natural law. The first pertains to its ideal or fullest form as originally envisaged by God (the law as it should be). This is captured in the term "perpetual," which characterises his rule of love. The second alludes to what natural law has become as a result of sin. Natural law can only be properly understood when viewed as a sum of these two senses within a diachronic context.[101]

Calvin, rather, states that the spirit of the law is not above the law – it is set in opposition to the law but ultimately not disparate from it. In the same manner, Calvin sets the eternal sphere in clear opposition to the temporal one, the "spiritual kingdom" to the "civil jurisdiction."[102] He does so with the spirit of the law and the laws themselves. Such dualism is characteristic of the way Calvin rigorously distinguishes two aspects of a concept with the view to ultimately bind them together more perfectly.[103] The spirit is set in opposition to the law so it may infuse it more completely. It follows then that the true law comprises fear of God, spiritual worship, obedience of the commandments, sincere faith, and love.[104] But, "those who follow only *dry* and *bare rudiments* – as if the law taught them only half of God's will – do not at all understand its purpose."[105] The assumption in Calvin's statement here is that natural law is a universal starting point for humanity on the continuum towards discovering the whole truth. It is neither pre-eminent

---

99   Ibid., II.viii.51.
100 August Lang, "Die Reformation und das Naturrecht," in *Calvin and the Reformation*, ed. William Park Armstrong (Grand Rapids, MI: Baker Book House, 1980): 68–69.
101 Calvin's twofold use of the term natural law is seen in a striking way in the following passage in John Calvin, *Institutes of the Christian Religion*, II.i.11: "Therefore we declare that man is corrupted through natural vitiation [*naturali hominem vitiositate corruptum*] but a vitiation that did not flow from nature [*a natura non fluxerit*]. We deny that it has flowed from nature in order to indicate that it is an adventitious quality which comes upon man rather than a substantial property which has been implanted from the beginning [*ab initio indita fuerit*]. Sin has caused nature to be other than what it should be."
102 Ibid., IV.xx.2.
103 Ralph Hancock observes the tendency of Calvin to explode traditional conceptual dichotomies only to distinguish two concepts with the view to infusing them more tightly together. Ralph Hancock, *Calvin and the Foundations of Modern Politics* (Ithaca, N.Y.: St Augustine's Press, 1989): 25.
104 John Calvin, *Institutes of the Christian Religion*, II.viii.51.
105 Ibid., II.viii.51.

nor controlling, but neither is it secondary. Natural law is thus a fundamental aspect of Calvin's account of law which finds perfection in the divine law.

The outstanding question remains: *how* can the rule of love serve as the end and therefore the standard for all positive laws? How can a given state implement the normative standard of love in determining the content of its laws? Is there evidence of positive laws that reflect a love of God and neighbour? Calvin seems to offer little guidance on these points besides his emphasis on the diversity of civil laws and that this diversity does not ultimately detract from their potential to conform with the law of God. This emphasis and lack of elaboration goes to suggest that Calvin only envisaged that the natural law component of the rule serves minimally to determine content. Accordingly, Calvin refuses to accept any "barbarous and savage laws such as gave honour to thieves [or] permitted promiscuous intercourse"[106] as laws in the true sense but declines to go further. Similarly, he asserts that "all laws tend to the same end."[107] By the end, Calvin means more than the punishment of "murder, theft, adultery, and false witness,"[108] though these are mentioned. This causes scholars like Lang to conclude that, although the rule of love, at first, appears to set a formidably high standard for civil laws, in its implementation, it amounts to little more than punishment for acts universally recognised as abhorrent.[109]

However, a closer look at Calvin's theology reveals a deeper purpose. Although Calvin's account of law does not offer much by way of specificity regarding its purpose, it nonetheless provides a normative richness that is not overly restrictive of nations and can be applied universally. Law is identified as the revelation of God's will,[110] as the very means of maintaining the relationship of humanity to God and humans with one another. This meaning can be gleaned from the distinction and nexus he draws between (1) *inward* and (2) *outward* conformity to the rule of love. Calvin is thus able to explore another aspect of the rule of love through the relationship between a person's *inward* intention and their *outward* deeds. These entwined aspects of law are derived from the inherent dichotomy which characterises the first and second tables of the Decalogue. The dichotomy that affects spiritual and temporal, the earthly and heavenly, the divine and human, the inward and outward is made evident in passages like the following: "Our life shall but conform to God's will and the prescription of the law when it is in every respect most fruitful to our brethren."[111] The rigorous spirit of the law flows from the first table – these are requirements to pursue the pure love of God. However, the practical effect of law is manifest primarily in the second table, in our love for neighbours. The spiritual requirements to love God in purity (first table) are primary and fulfilled

---

106 Ibid., IV.x.15.
107 Ibid., V.x.16.
108 Ibid., IV.x.18.
109 August Lang, *Die Reformation und das Naturrecht* (Gütersloh: Westminster Press, 1909) 18, translated by JG Machen in "The Reformation and Natural Law," *Princeton Theological Review* 7, no. 2 (1909): 177–218.
110 John Calvin, *Institutes of the Christian Religion*, IV.iv.16.
111 Ibid., II.viii.54.

inwardly through a pure heart. However, this intention is only made visible in right conduct towards humanity (second table) which presents itself *outwardly*.[112] In this way, Calvin conceives of a law which introduces a dichotomy between the divine and natural aspects of law. Whereas the primary function of natural law is to render humanity "inexcusable" and remove any pretext for wrongdoing, the divine law is the ultimate controlling aspect. By this formulation, Calvin is capable of enfolding both Christians and non-Christians alike, in a single jurisdiction, and motivating them towards a higher plane of morality.

In this way, the perpetual rule of love serves as Calvin's final standard for civil governance. Critics justly observe that Calvin's principle of love seems circular. Like an extremely large object whose features are impossible to grasp the nearer one draws in to inspect it – for example, a planet like Mars cannot be perceived for its completely crimson surface inches from its surface – such is the nature of Calvin's rule of love. Love of humanity (outwardly manifest through action) is founded on an inward love of God (through pure inward intentions). In this sense, love of humanity without love of God is impossible and worthless. Such appearance of right conduct divorced of love of God is "hypocrisy" in God's sight.[113] The nexus between the two principles of conformity is interdependent. It follows that any attempt to source righteousness in human beings themselves would be a futile exercise – humans in their depraved nature "more often engender hate than love."[114] Only when humanity is contemplated in God and not in themselves is it possible to "embrace the whole human race without exception in a single feeling of love."[115] The proper ontological starting point for just law (begotten by active love for humanity) is therefore the contemplation of God himself. Moreover, this contemplation of God is not exhaustive in itself. The inward act of conforming one's mind to the rule of love is not a self-sufficient end but an intention that points to another act, namely, the act of loving humanity. Only by adhering to these two principles can we fulfil both the spirit and letter of the law.

Applied to politics, Calvin associates the *rule of love* with one (minimal) "purpose" – as "the limit of all laws."[116] He identifies the rule of love with "divine law," "moral law," and "that conscience which God has engraved upon the minds of men." These concepts are viewed as related and overlapping (though as aforementioned, not synonymous). Calvin's statements regarding the purpose for the rule of love thereby exhibit a conceptual continuum not present, for example, in Aquinas' legal theory. For – although Calvin establishes a clear political progression (intrinsic order) to things – God's general providence manifested in the silent authority of nature is above the authority of the magistrate who speaks the letter of the law. This spoken law only bears life insofar as the

---

112 Ibid., II.viii.52.
113 Ibid., II.viii.11.
114 Ibid., II.viii.55.
115 Ibid., II.viii.55.
116 Ibid., IV.x.16.

magistrate's utterance remains consistent with the spirit of the law (silent law). Calvin, therefore, appears to introduce a continuum to the laws themselves. This continuum between divine, moral, and natural laws allows Calvin to emphasise God's superintendence of civil government in the context of human fallibility. Perhaps best illustrated by a refusal to separate law's civil from its religious function revealed in his examination of civil laws from an ecclesiastical perspective;[117] these two realms do not occupy a disparate space for Calvin but remain part of an integral whole – within the overall realm of providence.

Once again, the clear dichotomy characterising Calvin's theory of law does not translate to a theocratic form of government premised on divine law. As we observed earlier, this conclusion can be avoided by the continuum characterising the different aspects of his account of law.[118] However, this is not to say that this apparent fluidity causes Calvin's account of law to exist independent of the idea of God. It remains firmly grounded in his theology. In his book *The Christian Polity of John Calvin*, Harro Höpfl rightly observes that Calvin denies that natural knowledge of moral law, independent of the gospel, can somehow be a sufficient adjunct for Christians.[119] For believers, natural law must always be treated as an inferior guide to the written divine law. As such, Christians must first submit to the higher law, which necessarily subjects them to the lesser. Moreover, for non-believers too, Calvin vehemently denies the possibility of a law of nature and a law of morality independent of God.[120] Unlike Scholastics, Calvin does not view natural law as the dominant force but as a minimal standard to bridle humanity from descent into utter immorality.[121] Natural law must be grounded in divine law – the dominant and controlling superstructure. However, normatively speaking, though natural law is properly sourced in divine law, it is possible for natural law to provide moral knowledge to non-believers to sustain a semblance of civility and condemn their consciences[122] while being "supplements" for Christians in political life.[123]

The Role of Conscience in Law

Calvin's understanding of conscience as comprising a moral duty therefore supports the view that civil laws ought to be grounded in natural law.[124] In keeping

---

117 Ibid., IV.x.16.
118 Mary Lane Potter observes this to be Calvin placing "the law and the gospel together in the same continuum of God's covenant of grace." See Potter, "The 'Whole Office of the Law' in the Theology of John Calvin," *Journal of Law and Religion* 3, no. 1 (1985): 117, 137.
119 Harro Höpfl, *The Christian Polity of John Calvin* (Cambridge: Cambridge University Press, 2009): 181.
120 Cf. Hugo Grotius' assertion that natural law would be valid "even if God did not exist."
121 William Klempa, "John Calvin on Natural Law," in *John Calvin and the Church: A Prism of Reform*, ed. Timothy George (Louisville, KY: Westminster John Knox, 1990): 89.
122 John Calvin, *Institutes of the Christian Religion*, II.ii.22: "If the Gentiles by nature have law righteousness engraved upon their minds, we surely cannot say they are utterly blind as to the conduct of life."
123 Ibid., IV.xx.15.
124 Henry Stob, "Natural Law Ethics," *Calvin Theological Journal* 20, no. 1 (1985): 59.

with the recurring theme of a continuum, "conscience" in Calvin's theology is what connects *natural* with the *divine will* and, as a result of sin, with *divine judgement*.[125] In turn, the established connection between nature and its proper expression (the positive law) renders normative the position that civil laws are only valid insofar as they conform with the moral requirements of natural law (the silent law). This deontological focus, situated in the broader recognition of an interconnected and interdependent relationship between God and humankind, renders civil laws the means by which "God by his providence bridles perversity of nature that it may not break forth into action; but he does not purge it within."[126] Calvin's statement on the obvious limits of common grace emphasises the shortcomings of positive laws.[127]

In this context, Calvin incisively distinguishes between "sin" and "ignorance." Sin affects an individual's inward capacity to worship God. Calvin states that without paying *spiritual* homage to God, the human instinct of self-preservation is not sufficient to enable us to reach for moral perfection.[128] Sin affects the "inward parts,"[129] and without faith in Christ's *saving grace*, we cannot be absolved of this condition. However, Calvin's elucidations on conscience reveal that individuals remain inexcusable for ignorance. Ignorance, in the civil context, pertains to our outward behaviour (or external conduct) in temporal affairs while leading our lives on earth. In other words, God's *common grace* governs the worst of human corruption, acts as the minimal check on human arbitrariness, but does nothing more. Positive laws may keep human nature suppressed, but unless they themselves appeal to a higher order, cannot expect to remain morally sound. Natural law then, given its trajectory towards a higher morality, plays a critical role in bridging the gap between positive and normative laws.

The Role of the Collective in Law

In a collective sense, Calvin sees the principle of love as realised when justice and order are preserved in society.

> "Perfect justice would undoubtedly prevail among us, if we were as faithful in learning active charity (if we may use the expression) as we are skilful in teaching passive charity."[130]

---

125 Edward Dowey, *Knowledge of God* (Grand Rapids, MI: Eerdmans, 1994): 70.
126 John Calvin, *Institutes of the Christian Religion*, II.iii.3.
127 For more comprehensive discussion of Calvin's views on "common grace," see Herman Kuiper, *Calvin and Common Grace* (Grand Rapids, MI: Smitter Book Co., 1928).
128 John Calvin, *Institutes of the Christian Religion*, II.ii.24.
129 John Calvin, *Commentary on the Book of Psalms 51*, trans. James Anderson (Grand Rapids, MI: Baker, 1979).
130 John Calvin, *Commentary on Matthew 7:12*, trans. James Anderson (Grand Rapids, MI: Baker, 1979).

Interestingly, to Calvin, the law is properly served not only in maintaining the individual rights of citizens but also in defending the authority of the civil magistrate to guard peace and equity. The requirement to obey the prince is therefore a necessary requirement of the rule of love. Citing the Apostle Paul, Calvin concludes that any individual who introduces "anarchy violates love."[131]

For Calvin, this was an important aspect of law. The rule of love necessarily involves submission to one another. We are first bound to God through our individual consciences and then to each other in our love for God. Calvin explicitly states that "no one ought to avoid subjection ... where love reigns there is a mutual servitude."[132] Our duty to God is inextricably bound to our duties to one another. This "other" includes not only family and friends but extends to the "remotest person" even rulers. Although in some instances, as a result of the Fall, rulers order acts which are contrary to morality, on the whole, Calvin finds the origins and basis of all relationships involving hierarchy – superiority and subordination – not in the Fall but in the order of nature. Such order has been preserved by God's providence, necessary not only to avoid descension into chaos but also to enable human beings to express their true humanity as first intended (*Imago Dei*). Intrinsic to this order, there is a mutual submission. It follows that the authority of rulers to subjects as found in the Scripture is not arbitrary or tyrannical. Instead, duties are owed to each other in mutual servitude. The mutuality of servitude derives from humanity's overarching duty to honour God.

Conclusion

In summary, though Calvin's theory of law is continuous with aspects of an earlier tradition of natural law, Calvin departs from this tradition in identifying natural law with moral law. By viewing the law as unitary within a continuum and not in disparate parts, Calvin extracts evidence of a universal, collective humanity. The orderly will of God is identifiable through natural law (via the conscience), finds expression in the Decalogue, and attains fullness in the gospel.

Calvin's view of natural law as a necessary but inferior aspect of law is made evident in the way he writes about the relationship between the divine law and the magistrate, made possible through conscience. Not only is the magistrate a guardian of peace and justice according to God's providence, but is also bound by mutual servitude to the individuals governed. Pursuant to the *perpetual rule of love*, individuals and governors alike are bound by mutual servitude and are accountable primarily to God.

---

131 John Calvin, *Commentary on the Epistle of Romans 13:8–10*, trans. James Anderson (Grand Rapids, MI: Baker, 1979); Arthur C Cochrane, "Natural Law in Calvin," in *Church-State Relations in Ecumenical Perspective*, ed. Elwyn A Smith (Louvain: Duquesne University Press, 1966): 187.
132 John Calvin, *Commentary on Ephesians 5:21*, trans. James Anderson (Grand Rapids, MI: Baker, 1979).

The functions or purposes – theological, legislative, and pedagogical – Calvin associates with law reinforce the dichotomy and connection between natural and divine law, spiritual and temporal realms, heavenly and earthly kingdoms. Calvin is also able to establish the different standards pertaining to believers and unbelievers, yet a universal principle that enfolds them in a unified system.

2 "To Heal the Wounds of Sinners"
Law, Love, and Forgiveness

Zachary R. Calo

Introduction

In her essay "Forgiveness, Law, and Justice," Martha Minow asks, "Should law encourage people to forgive one another – and should law be used to forgive people for wrongdoing?"[1] This question provokes an engagement with the moral ends of law and, in particular, law's relationship to love. This question also presumes that law can meaningfully relate to forgiveness. But what does it mean to speak of law forgiving? Does the concept of legal forgiveness even cohere with law's nature?

Law might potentially relate to forgiveness in a number of ways. Law can facilitate forgiveness by requiring disputes be mediated or by providing that apologies cannot be used as evidence at trial.[2] Criminal sanctions can be lessened for those who express genuine remorse. Law can adopt restorative justice practices, which incorporate aspects of reconciliation into the criminal justice system. Law can convey a form of forgiveness through a decision to not prosecute or through issuance of a pardon. Law can even express collective remorse for past injustices. In these and other ways, law might be said to encourage forgiveness.

However, to propose that law can encourage forgiveness is quite different than positing that law forgives. To imagine such a possibility is to make law an agent of forgiveness, and perhaps of love, in ways that clash with established understandings of both law and forgiveness. For one, it requires an account of forgiveness as a public act. This contrasts with the way in which forgiveness is typically framed as an act that implicates private relationships between persons. Forgiveness might have public consequences, but the act is still largely understood as a phenomenon that impacts the interior life of persons. Most instances in which law is said to encourage forgiveness involve a public authority facilitating a private action. The aim is to impact persons in their private capacities and relationships, which is different than forgiveness being directly expressed in the public life of law.

---

1 Martha Minow, "Forgiveness, Law, and Justice," *California Law Review* 103:6 (2015): 1617.
2 Minow, "Forgiveness, Law, and Justice," 1621.

In addition, the idea of legal forgiveness requires moving beyond the dominant "therapeutic" account of forgiveness.[3] The therapeutic account focuses on the emotional benefits of forgiving, especially the ways in which forgiveness allows victims to develop new attitudes that facilitate healing.[4] Forgiveness, in this sense, allows persons to "overcome" negative emotions.[5] By forgiving, Robert Enright proposes, a "path to freedom" from resentment can be found.[6] The therapeutic benefits of forgiveness operate across a range of contexts. Forgiveness might have liberating effects for both victims and perpetrators of crime. One commentator describes restorative justice as a "process of redirecting the gaze from the past to the future" so that offenders can "forgive themselves for their past actions" and "move on."[7] A similar framework has been applied to collective expressions of forgiveness or apology, which are seen to create pathways to reconciliation between persons, groups, and the state.

The therapeutic account of forgiveness contains important insights. Forgiveness can heal relationships and salve wounds. It can help people move beyond the past and open themselves to a future without resentment. Yet, therapeutic rationales are ultimately instrumental. Forgiveness is good because forgiveness works, and it works primarily at the level of subjective experience. This account of forgiveness, moreover, positions law as epiphenomenal to the act of forgiveness itself. When law encourages forgiveness, it does so by creating conditions in which the self might experience these therapeutic effects. This is one aspect of legal forgiveness but one which is limited. However, if law not only encourages forgiveness but participates directly in the redemptive process, it must transcend the private concerns of persons. Forgiveness in this respect is effected not just by law but through law. It invites the possibility that law can be an agent of grace and love.

Such an idea of legal forgiveness rests on a deeper and more complicated understanding of the ontology of forgiveness as it intersects with law. This chapter examines such an account from the perspective of Christian thought. Although significant scholarly attention has been given to various theoretical aspects of legal forgiveness, theological interventions have remained modest voices in the debate. More critically, theological interventions have not generally offered sustained attention to legal or jurisprudential considerations. This chapter considers whether law might forgive and what it could mean to envision

---

3 Mark R Amstutz, *The Healing of Nations: The Promise and Limits of Political Forgiveness* (Lanham, MD: Rowman and Littlefield, 2005): 128. See also Jesse Couenhoven, "Forgiveness and Restoration: A Theological Exploration," *The Journal of Religion* 90:2 (2010): 148–70.
4 Stephen Pope, "The Role of Forgiveness in Reconciliation and Restorative Justice: A Christian Theological Perspective," in Jennifer J Llewellyn and Daniel Philpott, eds., *Restorative Justice, Reconciliation, and Peacebuilding* (New York: Oxford University Press, 2014): 175–6.
5 Jeffrie G Murphy, "Punishment, Forgiveness, and Mercy," *Journal of Law of Religion* 35:1 (2020): 6.
6 Robert D Enright, *Forgiveness Is a Choice* (Washington, DC: APA, 2001): 3–22.
7 Joanna Shapland, "Forgiveness and Restorative Justice: Is it Necessary? Is it Helpful?" *Oxford Journal of Law and Religion* 5 (2015): 97.

law as a site of redemption. First, Augustine's Sermon 13 on Psalm 2:10 is offered as an invitation to reflect on the act of legal judgment. From within this Augustinian perspective, judgment and mercy, law and love, are neither oppositional nor irreconcilable. They are two ways that God's love finds expression in the life of the world through the operation of law. Judgment needs mercy, and mercy needs judgment, and neither is fully explicable apart from the other. Love holds them together. Second, the Catholic Church's statement on *Memory and Reconciliation* is considered in order to examine collective forms of forgiveness such as that pursued in South Africa's Truth and Reconciliation Commission. The idea that a legal process can effect forgiveness and social healing has become widely accepted and yet there remain conceptual gaps in explaining the nature of the phenomenon. This discussion explores how ecclesiology provides resources for developing a theology of collective forgiveness through law.

Christian thought has given surprisingly little attention to the relationship between law and love.[8] This situation has been fed, in part, by the individualistic account of forgiveness predominant within Christian theology. A social, political, or juridical account of forgiveness is discordant with an understanding of forgiveness framed in terms of relations between persons and between persons and God. Law is largely irrelevant to authentic forgiveness. Yet, this chapter proposes that Christian thought has resources to develop a theology of legal forgiveness. Addressing the relationship between law and love in this way not only positions Christianity to contribute to contemporary legal debate. It also offers a starting point for the development of a general Christian account of law.

Mercy in Judgment: Augustine's Sermon 13

"Be instructed, all you who judge the earth," Augustine writes in quoting Psalm 2:10, the text for his sermon. This sermon is offered as an instruction to those who wield authority to cast judgment. It is theologically rich but also decidedly practical.[9]

The sermon places the act of judgment in a tension-filled space. Judgment is necessary and good, but also dangerous. To judge rightly in love requires knowledge of the nature of judgment. It requires knowing the self and knowing God.

"If you judge the earth," Augustine writes, "you'll become heaven, and you will *proclaim the glory* of the Lord created in you." To judge the earth is to love the earth. To judge the earth is to participate in the authority and rule of God. It brings the judgment of God to bear on the affairs of the earth. The judge becomes, through the act of judgment, a point of contact between heaven and

---

8 See "Introduction," in Robert F Cochran, Jr and Zachary R Calo, eds., *Agape, Justice, and Law: How Might Christian Love Shape Law?* (Cambridge: Cambridge University Press, 2017): 1–10.
9 Augustine, "Sermon 13," in EM Atkins and RJ Dodaro, eds., *Augustine: Political Writings* (Cambridge: Cambridge University Press, 2004): 119–26.

earth. To judge the earth is to draw earthly affairs into the economy of heaven. By a similar measure, Augustine warns that "If ... you fail to judge the earth, then you will become the earth" and "belong to Adam." When not judged, the earth is turned over to itself. It is given the pretence of autonomy, even if such autonomy is illusory. To love the earth is to make it subject to the authority of God, while to not judge the earth is to cede authority to the rebellion of Adam.

Some of Augustine's most interesting remarks in his sermon address the disposition a judge should bring to the work of judgment. "To judge the earth," Augustine writes, "is to tame the body." He continues: "Those who judge the earth ought, then, to listen; they should chastise their bodies, put reins on their passions, love wisdom, overcome unruly desire. And they ought to be instructed so that they do this." Augustine is offering practical advice. This is, after all, a sermon intended to instruct judges within the Christian community. But something more is going on in the passage. Augustine is also making the point that judgment of the earth must be connected to judgment of the self. This is not only because a judge holds power over the lives of others. It is also because the judge participates in the power and authority of God. When "earth judges earth it ought to fear God who is in heaven." It is with this admonition in mind that Augustine warns that if you think "the source of your being just is yourself, then you are not serving the Lord." The power to judge is always derivative.

Before judging another "judge yourself within." This judgment of the self is not solipsistic introspection. It is an act of surrender to God that recognises the fragility of the self. Indeed, in Sermon 13 Augustine reflects on the self in ways that echo broader themes in his thought:

> [Y]ou might find yourself in him, as you have lost yourself in yourself. For in yourself, you had no power except to lose yourself; and you don't know how to find yourself unless God who made you also looks for you.

The judge, who embodies earthly power, is redefined as one who must be weak, so much so as to lose the self in God's otherness. The proud cannot be just. Thus, returning to Psalm 2:11, Augustine urges those who judge to "Serve the Lord with fear, and rejoice, not in yourself with arrogance, but in him with trembling." It is only by losing the self that one can judge others. The judge is merely "a human judging a human, a mortal judging a mortal, a sinner judging a sinner."

From this perspective, the work of judgment is a moral burden that reveals the brokenness of the self and the world. To judge is to suffer but to judge is also to love. Suffering and love are intertwined such that judgment assumes a cruciform character. The judge loves the world by suffering with the world. These themes from Sermon 13 hearken to Augustine's discussion in Book 19, Chapter 6 of the *City of God*, in which he writes that "These judgments which men pronounce on men" are "melancholy and lamentable" and yet "necessary." To judge is to interiorise moral complexities that cannot be neatly untangled. By way of illustration, in 19:6, Augustine offers the scenario in which a judge must condemn someone to torture in order to determine if the accused is guilty. What if the judge puts an innocent person to death because a wrongful confession was made under torture? Would it be better not to take a seat on the bench than to be complicit in such deeds? No, says Augustine, for "human society constrains and compels" the judge to undertake these duties, however afflicting. To judge is to endure and "recognize the misery of these necessities." In the end, all the judge can do is join the psalmist in crying to God: "From my necessities deliver Thou me."

The cruciform nature of judgment leads Augustine to consider the place of mercy within judgment. Judgment and mercy are entangled in ways that defy resolution. On the one hand, Augustine is clear that mercy does not entail the withdrawal of judgment. "Punishments should be imposed; I don't deny it; I don't forbid it." Mercy should not come "at the cost of losing discipline." On the other hand, the judge is to "foster love" for those judged. Judgment is to be carried out "in the spirit of love, in the spirit of concern, in the spirit of reform." A spirit of love should inform not only the judge's disposition but also the act of judgment. This tension between punishment and love is never overcome. The judge must simply enter into the tension, accepting it as a burden.

Augustine nevertheless offers hints as to how law might be a site for expressing Christian love. This practical counsel is most often displayed in his response to the workaday matters that come before him as pastor and bishop. In Sermon 13, for instance, Augustine makes a strong statement in opposition to the death penalty. He implores the judge to "[a]void the death penalty, so that there's someone left to repent." He explores similar themes in a remarkable set of letters (Letters 133 and 134) addressed to Marcellinius and his brother Apringius, the Christian proconsul of Africa, in which he requests mercy for two Donatists convicted of killing and mutilating Catholic priests. Augustine requests that the culprits not be "punished so harshly by law that the sufferings they will endure correspond to those they have inflicted." The "Christian judge" should "Condemn injustice without forgetting to observe humanity" in those judged. "A thirst for revenge" should be resisted so that law might "heal the wounds of sinners." By invoking the healing power of law, the Christian brings the spirit of love to the act of judgment.

Law for Augustine is primarily a way to judge and punish wrong. But his account also invites reflection on how law exists in relationship to love. To not judge, or to judge mercifully, is to make law an instrument of grace that participates in the redemptive love of God. Law stands at the intersection of judgment and mercy. Although it falls on the judge to exercise prudential wisdom in determining how to navigate the tension, Augustine's thought invites the judge into this space.

The Significance of Collective Forgiveness

Different considerations arise in connection with collective forgiveness. Collective forgiveness as a juridical and political process has been employed in a range of contexts. Governments, for instance, have apologised for past wrongs. The

36 *Zachary R. Calo*

United States apologised to Japanese-Americans for their internment during the Second World War.[10] The Canadian government apologised for the Indian Residential School System.[11] In these instances, states seek forgiveness for things done under their authority. Collective forgiveness can also involve alternative judicial mechanisms, such as the Gacaca courts in Rwanda, that promote forgiveness through legal process.[12] Most notably, collective political forgiveness has found expression in truth and reconciliation commissions, of which none has been more impactful than that of South Africa.[13] The hearings of the South Africa Truth and Reconciliation Commission are widely seen as having legitimised the practice of collective forgiveness.[14] What unites these initiatives is the idea that apology, forgiveness, and reconciliation can be part of how a political community addresses past wrongs.[15] These various processes thus aim to move beyond a narrowly legalistic account of justice to one that incorporates "a relational conception of people and the world they inhabit."[16]

The idea of collective forgiveness, particularly in the form of truth and reconciliation, marks a novel way of thinking. The juxtaposition of Nuremberg and South Africa reveals the marked shift that occurred over only a few decades, as forgiveness entered mainstream thought and brought about a fundamental shift in approaches to political justice.[17] As Daniel Philpott observes, "The most surprising, controversial, and dramatic development in the age of peacebuilding is the growth of forgiveness."[18]

---

10 The *Civil Liberties Act* of 1988 provided an apology "on behalf of the people of the United States for the evacuation, internment, and relocations of such citizens and permanent residing aliens."
11 Prime Minister Stephen Harper issued a statement in 2008 stating that, "The Government of Canada sincerely apologizes and asks the forgiveness of the Aboriginal peoples of this country for failing them so profoundly." Full text available at www.rcaanc-cirnac.gc.ca/eng/1100100015644/1571589171655.
12 Phil Clark, *The Gacaca Courts, Post-Genocide Justice and Reconciliation in Rwanda: Justice without Lawyers* (Cambridge: Cambridge University Press, 2010).
13 For a list of truth and reconciliation commissions, see Gloria Yayra Ayorkor Ayee, "Restorative Justice and Political Forgiveness: A Comparative Study of Truth and Reconciliation Commissions" (PhD dissertation, Duke University, 2016): 128–30.
14 Bonny Ibhawoh, "Do Truth and Reconciliation Commissions Heal Divided Nations," *The Conversation* (23 January 2019), https://theconversation.com/do-truth-and-reconciliation-commissions-heal-divided-nations-109925.
15 It is worth observing that the connection between forgiveness and reconciliation is a contested matter. According to some, the two must be kept separate. See Ari Kohen, "The Personal and the Political: Forgiveness and Reconciliation in Restorative Justice," *Critical Review of International Social and Political Philosophy* 12:3 (September 2009): 400–1.
16 Jennifer J Llewellyn and Daniel Philpott, "Restorative Justice and Reconciliation: Twin Frameworks for Peacebuilding," in JL Llewellyn and D Philpott, eds., *Restorative Justice, Reconciliation, and Peacebuilding* (New York: Oxford University Press, 2014): 16–17.
17 Pablo de Greiff, "The Future of the Past: Reflections on the Present State and Prospects of Transitional Justice," *International Journal of Transitional Justice* 14 (2020): 251–9.
18 Daniel Philpott, *Just and Unjust Peace: An Ethic of Political Reconciliation* (New York: Oxford University Press, 2012): 251.

Peacebuilding initiatives that utilise forgiveness are often justified on pragmatic grounds. Prosecution for crimes may not be a viable strategy if judicial structures are weak, the capacities of a legal system are exceeded, evidence is difficult to establish, and the society is deeply divided over the meaning of past crimes.[19] By this measure, political forgiveness represents a prudential accommodation to the limits of traditional legal mechanisms. Yet, highlighting the practical aspects of these initiatives does not diminish the fact that political forgiveness also represents a novel moral enterprise. Reconciliation schemes recognise the importance of addressing the past in order to secure the future. In moving beyond the strict logic of punishment, these processes seek to facilitate the reconstitution of community as an essential component of justice.

Truth and reconciliation processes have been subjected to criticism.[20] Certain critiques focus on the failure of truth and reconciliation to provide effective redress to victims; others focus on its normative shortcomings.[21] There are unique conceptual challenges with group forgiveness. Can forgiveness coherently be pursued as a collective undertaking? Can forgiveness be made on behalf of others? It is one thing for persons in their private capacity to forgive. Persons might also elect not to pursue legal remedies and thus exercise what Minow terms "a choice, held at the discretion of those harmed."[22] Collective forgiveness is of a fundamentally different nature. It involves more than the choices of persons in their individual and private capacities. It concerns persons, at times with no connection to the harms at issue, in their collective and public capacities.

Theologian Anthony Bash has argued that groups can neither forgive nor receive forgiveness.[23] He identifies a number of problems with group forgiveness. In Bash's assessment, groups lack a "moral 'self' in an organic sense." In other words, there is no "I" to express or to receive forgiveness. This moral self is essential because forgiveness requires "personal moral agency."[24] While observing that "There is a sense in which groups do carry a measure of guilt and responsibility for the actions of current and former members," the group itself cannot forgive or be forgiven as that concept is properly understood.[25]

19 Amstutz, *The Healing of Nations*, 42.
20 Philpott, *Just and Unjust Peace*, 252–4.
21 See Alice MacLachlan, "The Philosophical Controversy over Political Forgiveness," in BAM Stokkom et al., eds., *Public Forgiveness in Post-Conflict Contexts* (Cambridge: Intersentia Press, 2012): 37. MacLachlan notes that, "Where others see new hope for politics, philosophers fear an uncritical promotion of forgiveness, which risks distorting and cheapening forgiveness as a moral ideal, on the one hand, and ignoring justice, accountability and the need to end harmful relationships, on the other."
22 Minow, "Forgiveness, Law, and Justice," 1618.
23 Anthony Bash, *Forgiveness and Christian Ethics* (New York: Cambridge University Press, 2007): 14.
24 Bash, *Forgiveness and Christian Ethics*, 115. Bash's use of the term "organic" seems to address notions of legal personhood. Thus, while a corporation might have legal personhood and the capacity to take actions on behalf of the collective, this cannot be equated with moral actions taken by a biological person.
25 Ibid., 118.

Bash does not dismiss the meaningfulness of group expressions of forgiveness. Group forgiveness can still be a morally significant action but can only be applied "by *analogy*."[26] Thus, while group forgiveness is not as such logically possible, groups can nevertheless participate in certain aspects of forgiving and being forgiven. Other commentators, by contrast, defend the conceptual coherence of group forgiveness. Mark Amstutz argues that

> Although there is no such thing as a "collective will" – a concept similar to Bash's moral self – "the decisions of political communities can be viewed as possessing moral agency provided their decision-making institutions are legitimate, involve freedom of action, and are based on decision makers" moral judgments.[27]

Amstutz bypasses the ontological problem associated with locating a collective will by focusing on process and procedure.

The matter of whether there exists a collective will that can express and receive forgiveness is important for examining the nature of group forgiveness. Yet, from a theological perspective, one might question whether such considerations distract from the more central concern, which is not the existence of a moral self but rather how the moral life of a community exists across time. Communities are heritors of memory and bearers of a tradition that, regardless of whether there exists an identifiable fictive will, represent and embody the ongoingness of that group within history. In this respect, the starting point for developing a theology of collective forgiveness is the Church.

The Catholic Church's 1999 document *Memory and Reconciliation: The Church and the Faults of the Past* develops an ecclesiology of collective apology that can inform Christian approaches to political forgiveness. The task of the document is not to consider specific instances of past wrongdoing but rather "to clarify the presuppositions that ground repentance for past faults." It seeks to understand the warrant by which the Church, as a community of memory and a living reality, can seek forgiveness for things done in its name.

The concept invoked to describe this work of penance is "purification of memory." The concept is powerful in that it speaks to sins of the past that burden the present. Memory is part of "the bond" of the mystical body that holds together past and present, individual and collective. In the mystical body of the Church, "the burden of the errors and faults of those who have gone before us" are assumed and shared even by those "not personally responsible."[28] The question of whether or not there is a collective will or group self is rendered

---

26 Ibid., 117.
27 Amstutz, *The Healing of Nations*, 184.
28 See "Introduction," International Theological Commission, *Memory and Reconciliation: The Church and the Faults of the Past* (December 1999), available at www.vatican.va/roman_curia/congregations/cfaith/cti_documents/rc_con_cfaith_doc_20000307_memory-reconc-itc_en.html.

irrelevant. What matters is that the community is an ontological reality whose nature consists of more than a mere assemblage of persons. The "bond established by the Holy Spirit" forms a community that exists across time and space and which is engaged in the ongoing work of renewal, redemption, and purification.[29] When this community seeks forgiveness, it does so not merely by analogy but as an expression of the organic connection between past and present. The Church today participates, at least in a mystical sense, in the Church of history. From this perspective, communal expressions of forgiveness are not only theologically coherent but also a necessary outworking of the Church's life as a redemptive community.

There should be hesitancy in moving from collective forgiveness by the Church to collective forgiveness by the political community. Ecclesiology might nevertheless inform Christian thought about the meaning and possibilities of collective forgiveness through law. The point of contact exists because forgiveness within the life of the Church implicates the whole of creation. When the Church reconciles, it is, in the first instance, enacting a practice by which the atonement is made effective.[30] Alex Deagon similarly describes the Christian understanding of reconciliation in terms of giving shape to a "community based on true peace rather than violence."[31] Forgiveness forms the Christian community in light of the ultimate good, the final and perfect reconciliation of God and humanity. Reconciliation thus images the inner life of the Trinity and anticipates the harmony of God's peace through forms of social relation.

What occurs in the Church impacts society in ways that go beyond analogy. To be reconciled in love is an event both real and symbolic, present and expectant. Ecclesiology matters for politics. What occurs in the Church through Christ proleptically anticipates the peace that will consume all of creation. As Deagon notes, forgiveness "brought through the Incarnation and loving sacrifice of Christ" marks the way to "preserve a peaceful, loving community – the Christian community – and, by implication, the legal community."[32] Efforts to achieve peace through forgiveness in the early city thus image, however incompletely, what is already being witnessed in the Church. The state, in this sense, becomes what Oliver O'Donovan calls "a witness to the witness" of the resurrected life.[33] Reconciliation pursued through law outside the life of the Church might still be seen as participating in the reconciliation of Christ. It participates in the peace of the Kingdom of God not merely analogically but ontologically.

---

29 *Memory and Reconciliation: The Church and the Faults of the Past*, 3.3.
30 Timothy Gorringe, *God's Just Vengeance: Crime, Violence and the Rhetoric of Salvation* (Cambridge: Cambridge University Press, 2002).
31 Alex Deagon, "On the Symbiosis of Law and Truth in Christian Theology: Reconciling Universal and Particular through the Pauline Law of Love," *Griffith Law Review* 23:4 (2014): 594.
32 Ibid., 591.
33 Oliver O'Donovan, *The Ways of Judgment* (Grand Rapids, MI: Eerdmans, 2005): 88.

Towards a Theology of Legal Forgiveness

Can law forgive? It seems antithetical to the nature of law to do so. To withhold judgment is to deny law the exercise of its proper vocation. To not punish undermines law's predictability and rationality.

It might be that the concept of legal forgiveness rests on a creative tension that cannot be fully resolved but can be explored. Law cannot be reduced to love, nor love domesticated within law. Law and love are instead engaged in a complex ongoing dance. As Stephen Pope notes, it is important to establish the rule of law, but our account of justice "cannot end there."[34] Law's primary vocation is to represent and enforce the norms of justice. The law judges and punishes. And yet the work of law does not end there. Law can also enact an alternative story in which participation in love is also constitutive of justice. This is an account of law that refuses to let justice be reduced to judgment and punishment.

Forgiveness is hardly the exclusive province of religion.[35] In fact, many efforts to promote legal forgiveness have occurred within a secular framework, neither motivated by nor making reference to religious categories. Yet, what many such initiatives have lacked is an account of how the act of forgiveness can be rendered sensible in light of the nature and operation of law. There remains an ontological gap between theory and practice. One contribution of Christian legal thought is to explain the phenomenon of legal forgiveness. Christianity is not unique in being able to offer a theological account of legal forgiveness, but it might be uniquely positioned to develop a theological jurisprudence that holds together law and love.

Within the framework of Christian thought, legal forgiveness is an act that discloses, if only in limited and fragmentary ways, the fuller eschatological ends of law. Through love, law prefigures a reality that goes beyond law. It frames law as a "semi-sacramental reality where love and justice, providence and prudence, the gospel and the world, each transect and transfigure the other," according to Charles Mathewes.[36] Law becomes a space in which the possibilities and limits of the political collide. To enact forgiveness through law is to see law's judgment as a witness to the love and mercy of God.

Law's capacity to enact love is provisional and limited. Law does not itself forgive, at least not in the same way the Church understands forgiveness.[37] But law can be shaped by the presence of the Church giving witness to the forgiveness of

---

34 Stephen Pope, "The Role of Forgiveness in Reconciliation and Restorative Justice: A Christian Theological Perspective," in JL Llewellyn and D Philpott, eds., *Restorative Justice, Reconciliation, and Peacebuilding* (Oxford: Oxford University Press, 2014): 188.
35 See, for instance, Charles Griswold, *Forgiveness: A Philosophical Exploration* (Cambridge: Cambridge University Press, 2007): xvi. Griswold notes at the outset that the book's "approach to the topic is secular ... [and] will not venture into the issues surrounding forgiveness of God."
36 Charles Mathewes, "'Be Instructed, All You Who Judge the Earth': Law, Justice, and Love during the World," in Cochran and Calo, eds., *Agape, Justice, and Law*, 166.
37 O'Donovan, *The Ways of Judgment*, 87.

God. By enacting forgiveness, law moves beyond law even though it never fully escapes. Law as a semi-sacramental reality pushes towards its own negation. To say as much is not to collapse the Church into law, nor law into the Church. Both retain their spheres of authority. Yet, it does invite a recognition that these lines of division are not so segregated as to remove the possibility of porousness. While forgiveness is made possible through the life and witness of the Church, the state can in some limited respect witness a form of divine mercy.

Derrida interestingly sees the emergence of collective forgiveness as evidencing the universalisation of an "Abrahamic language." This language becomes the "universal idiom" by which a fundamentally religious concept migrates to where it is not native. However, the universalisation of forgiveness also paradoxically brings about the "erasure" of its religious dimension. In Derrida's analysis, the phenomenon of political forgiveness represents a mode of Christianisation that paradoxically renders the Church no longer necessary.[38] But maybe what is happening is less an erasure of Christianity than a concealing of it. The Church's presence in society still imbues forgiveness with a sacral quality even if its full meaning is obscured. In this sense, the fact that much talk of legal and political forgiveness unfolds in a secular key does not make it unreligious. The religious meaning already exists and the role of the Church is to provide narration.

From a Christian perspective, law can be said to forgive insofar as it participates in and witnesses God's forgiveness as enacted in the Church. Indeed, law can enact love and become an icon of God's mercy because of the Church's presence in the life of the world. Legal forgiveness acquires its semi-sacramental quality through the Church. The political is drawn up into the Church's redemptive work. This seems to be the point O'Donovan is making when he speaks of political acts being "shaped by the presence of a society in which redemption is taking effect and assuming a social form." Legal expressions of mercy and forgiveness can "witness to the Paschal judgment, but indirectly."

This witness in law must be the exception. It needs to be jarring, disruptive.[39] As Derrida writes, forgiveness "*should not be*, normal, normative, normalizing. It should remain exceptional and extraordinary."[40] Collapsing law into love would undermines law's very nature as law. If forgiveness were normalised it would upend the authority and predictability of law. However, preserving the exceptional quality of forgiveness not only protects the coherence of law in a practical sense. It also preserves the meaningfulness of forgiveness. It is the exceptional nature of legal forgiveness that makes it a radically meaningful act, for this radicality unleashes the tension between law and love that is never resolved but which nevertheless gives life.

---

38 Jacques Derrida, *On Cosmopolitanism and Forgiveness* (London: Routledge, 1997): 28.
39 Thomas Shaffer, "Forgiveness Disrupts Legal Order," *Graven Images: A Journal of Culture, Law and the Sacred* 4 (1998): 127–37.
40 Derrida, *On Cosmopolitanism and Forgiveness*, 32.

The exceptional nature of forgiveness also relativises the judgments of law. In light of the judgment of Christ, law is no longer sovereign. It exists as a provisional witness to God's judgment and God's mercy. It is the very unrealisability of perfect justice that gives meaning to its fragmented expressions within the interplay of law and love. The Church witnesses the eschatological hope of perfect justice – the reality Nigel Biggar describes as "beyond time and space" in which God will bestow full vindication.[41] The Church does so by enacting in its embodied life "a discourse that defers judgment."[42] It also does so by calling for the law to be forgiving and merciful, even while knowing such appeals will often go unheard.[43] Through the Church's witness, law anticipates the eschatological hope of a justice that remains unrealised and unrealisable.

The concept of legal forgiveness provides an interesting perspective from which to develop a more general theology of law. In his review of *Christian Perspectives on Legal Thought*, William Stuntz notes that the book might have been better if it were less conventional and more subversive.[44] Moreover, Stuntz observes that the essays in the book left the impression that Christianity can accommodate itself to most any legal theory.[45] That is, Christianity might affix itself as an adjective to a range of different jurisprudential perspectives, such that "those who like legal thought just as it is needn't worry."[46] Christianity does not disrupt the status quo. It finds a home within it.

Christian legal thought has developed in interesting ways over the two decades since *Christian Perspectives on Law* and yet many Christian perspectives remain unthreatening in the way Stuntz alleged. This is not to say that Christian legal thought should aspire to be radical and contrarian, but it should be able to surprise and upend expectations. It is in this respect that the concept of forgiveness offers a way for Christianity to critically engage regnant modes of liberal positivistic legal thought. Alex Deagon observes that liberal accounts of law "assume certainty and stability in legal doctrine."[47] This predictability signals a healthy and procedurally fair legal system yet also closes law off to the disruptive and surprising interventions of love. The peace of the liberal kingdom is ironically built on a "violence" antithetical to love. It might well be that this violence is constitutive

---

41 Nigel Biggar, "Making Peace or Doing Justice: Must We Choose?" in Biggar, ed., *Burying the Past: Making Peace and Doing Justice After Civil Conflict* (Washington, DC: Georgetown University Press, 2003): 33.
42 O'Donovan, *The Ways of Judgment*, 240.
43 On the role of Christianity in tempering justice with forgiveness, see Nicholas Wolterstorff, "Is It Possible and Sometimes Desirable for States to Forgive?" *The Journal of Religious Ethics* 41:3 (September 2013): 417–34.
44 William J. Stuntz, "Book Review: Christian Legal Theory," *Harvard Law Review* 116 (2003): 1710.
45 Ibid., 1716.
46 Ibid., 1721.
47 Alex Deagon, "On the Symbiosis of Law and Truth in Christian Theology: Reconciling Universal and Particular through the Pauline Law of Love," *Griffith Law Review* 23:4 (2014): 591.

of realising certain basic political goods, but it also means that legal liberalism cannot account for a law beyond law. It is closed in on itself and thus unable to entertain what Thomas Shaffer calls "the risk of forgiveness."[48] It cannot account for love.

If legal forgiveness rests on a logic outside of law, legal positivism can never account for the phenomenon. Perhaps then, legal forgiveness is not an achievement within secular law but a sign of its fragility and even its breakdown. In this sense, the movement for forgiveness in recent decades reveals the inability of secular law to account for the possibility of law moving beyond law. In the end, it might only be when law is embedded within a theological economy that the jurisprudence of forgiveness becomes coherent. It is where law reaches the end of law – where the logic of law is exhausted – that Christian legal thought begins. It is here that law opens the possibilities of a love beyond law. The work of Christian thought is to hold together, as much as possible, this tension between the now and the not yet, the given and the hoped for. Legal forgiveness rests on a tension that Christianity can narrate although not control. From this perspective, legal forgiveness is a radical act that disrupts norms and expectations. Yet, from another perspective, legal forgiveness is also the supreme expression of modesty. To forgive is to acknowledge that all need mercy. It is to open law to a love that might heal the world.

---

48 Thomas L Shaffer, "The Radical Reformation and the Jurisprudence of Forgiveness," in Michael W McConnell, Robert E Cochran, Jr and Angela C Carmella, eds., *Christian Perspectives on Legal Thought* (New Haven, CT: Yale University Press, 2001): 325–6.

3 Why Secularism Is No Option for a Christian Citizen

Augustine's Analysis of Love in the City

Renée Köhler-Ryan

Introduction

Liberal western democracies tend to take for granted that secular society is successful in maintaining peaceful order *because* it excludes love of God as much as possible from public discourse about intent and action. The main assumption here is that if public space is neutral about God – about his nature, his existence, and if and how he might be worshipped – then a major subjective prejudice will be removed from politics, the state will be peaceful, and its citizens will be unselfish. After all, the Rawlsian political theory that remains so influential brings with it the assumption that when citizens eschew personal beliefs and preferences for the sake of political order, a just and fair society results.[1] Augustine's understanding of the relationship between love and an ordered society turns this logic on its head. For the ancient thinker, there can be no properly ordered political society when people love themselves, rather than God first. All human action needs to put God first, and only then will the state provide well for its citizens. At the same time, Augustine realises that this is ultimately an unrealisable goal. In this fallen world, humans prove incapable of avoiding the selfishness that characterises the "earthly city." For this reason, he theorises in *City of God* that Christians must be in the world but not of it. They should abide by earthly law where possible, but defy that law when the law contradicts the dictates of Christian love. This chapter champions the importance of *latreia* (the proper worship of God through sacrament and deeds, motivated by *amor Dei*).

In so doing, the chapter argues against one of the most prevalent readings of Augustine, set forth to some extent by R.A. Markus in his monumental

---

1 Markus wrote *Saeculum* the year before Rawls' *Theory of Justice* was published. See RA Markus, *Saeculum: History and Society in the Theology of St. Augustine* (Cambridge: Cambridge University Press, 1970) and John Rawls, *A Theory of Justice* (Cambridge: Belknap Press, 1971). For an analysis of the influence that Rawls has had on political theory, see Katrina Forrester, *In the Shadow of Justice: Postwar Liberalism and the Remaking of Political Philosophy* (Princeton, NJ and Oxford: Princeton University Press, 2019). Rawls sets out his main theory in Rawls, *Theory of Justice*. The concept of overlapping consensus also discussed in this chapter is articulated most fully in Rawls, *Political Liberalism*.

DOI: 10.4324/9781003148920-5

and influential *Saeculum: History and Society in the Theology of St. Augustine*.[2] Therein, Markus argued that Augustine's view of the secular state was pluralistic – allowing for many loves and many religions. Markus argues, furthermore, that this pluralism was a civic virtue in its own right. Markus fleshes out this view in *Christianity and the Secular*, where he also admits that M.J. Hollerich is correct in the assertion that *Saeculum* comes "perilously close" to making Augustine "a precursor of modern secular liberalism," which is pre-eminently individualistic, "secular, open, pluralistic, religiously neutral – freedom plus groceries," in Hollerich's terms.[3] Markus seeks to redress his position in *Christianity and the Secular*. Nonetheless, the reading of *Saeculum* continues to exercise substantial influence on readers of Augustine's political theory.

One of the main critics of Markus' view is John Milbank, who counters in particular Markus' reading of Book XIX of Augustine's *City of God*.[4] This chapter will undertake to re-read certain passages in that book, after countering some of the more Rawlsian interpretations taken up and promoted by Markus' *Saeculum*. It should be noted that Markus wrote *Saeculum* a year before Rawls' *Theory of Justice* was published, and so his agreement with Rawls is far more explicit in *Christianity and the Secular*. This point will be discussed below. As will be seen, Augustine has a far more radical theory of political order than modern secular vision can support. Retrieving Augustine's understanding of the intrinsic links between rightly ordered love and the law will, at the same time, highlight the radical contributions that Christians can and should make to society. Christians can witness to what society can become when humans are capable of worshipping God first, even to the point of martyrdom.

These points, then, counter Markus' sense that the Augustinian citizen can readily set aside religious belief and love of God, thereby enabling peace in the earthly city. In fact, humans in such an order are fundamentally misdirected, and cannot achieve the highest good of being in a community of love with God. In matters of love, there can be no neutrality, and the entire political order is affected according to whether citizens love well or only selfishly.[5] When St Augustine's thought is understood in its fullness, it is obvious that the neutrality that the

---

2 Ibid.
3 Markus quoting Hollerich in Markus, *Christianity and the Secular* (Notre Dame, IN: University of Notre Dame Press, 2016), 50–51. See the original argument in: John Hollerich, "John Milbank, Augustine and the 'Secular,'" in *History, Apocalypse and the Secular Imagination: New Essays on Augustine's City of God*, edited by Mark Vessey, Karla Pollman and Allan D Fitzgerald (Villanova, PA: Villanova University Press, 1999), 320.
4 John Milbank, *Theology and Social Theory: Beyond Secular Reason* (Oxford: Blackwell, 1993). See especially 403–6. For an extended discussion of Milbank's position in the context of Radical Orthodoxy's greater project, see Hans Boersma, "On the Rejection of Boundaries," *Pro Ecclesia* XV, no. 4 (2006): 418–47.
5 For more on the importance of ordered love for the formation of communities in Augustine's thought, see Renée Köhler-Ryan, "Love and Friendship in the *Metaxu*: Becoming Agapeic in Community," in Renée Köhler-Ryan, *Companions in the Between: Augustine, Desmond, and Their Communities of Love* (Eugene, OR: Pickwick Publications, 2019): 101–18 and Donald

modern liberal state prioritises would nullify human love in all of its dimensions. At the same time, such neutrality would render impossible a law-based society in which substantial and meaningful relationships with other citizens are possible.

In short then, this chapter calls into question the idea that secularity in the way we usually understand it is possible, or even desirable, for Christian political thought inspired by St Augustine. At the same time, it counters the notion that the saint promoted the secular state in the first place. Examining facets of the secularism debate as it impacts on readings of Augustine's *City of God* makes clear the links between the foundations of human love – whether God or gods of our own making – and the laws that bind together human society. These findings then shed some light on the ways that Christians can be citizens and civic leaders without submitting to selfish secularity. Christians in society can witness to God's love because they make *latreia* (the service offered first to God) the most prominent human virtue. As Augustine is well aware, there will be a limit to what Christians can do in the state, but their presence is necessary if there is to be any possibility of grace and redemption for the earthly city.[6]

The Context for Debate: Two Cities and Two Loves

In *City of God*, St Augustine argues that two cities, each defined by its love, are at work throughout the entirety of human history.[7] Citizens of the City of God possess *caritas*, which orders everything that they are and do. Because they love God first, they are able to live with perfect virtue. Members of the City of Man instead love selfishly – with *cupiditas* that makes them incapable of the fullness of leading a good life. Loving themselves first, they set everything in their lives askew. Within this theologically and historically oriented framework, one can understand all of Augustine's forms of society, where a society is a form of

---

X Burt, *Friendship and Society: An Introduction to Augustine's Practical Philosophy* (Grand Rapids, MI: Eerdmans, 1999).

6 See Gregory Lee, "Using the Earthly City: Ecclesiology, Political Activity, and Religious Coercion in Augustine," *Augustinian Studies* 47 (2016): 41–63.

7 While this is the argument of the entire work, arguably the most succinct description of this can be found in *City of God*, 14.28: "Two loves, then, have made two cities. Love of self, even to the point of contempt for God, made the earthly city, and love of God, even to the point of contempt for self, made the heavenly city. Thus the former glories in itself, and the latter glories in the Lord. The former seeks its glory from men, but the latter finds its highest glory in God, the witness of our conscience. The former lifts up its head in its own glory; the latter says to its God, *My glory, and the one who lifts up my head* (Ps 3:3) In the former the lust for domination dominates both its princes and the nations that it subjugates; in the latter both leaders and followers serve one another in love, the leaders by their counsel, the followers by their obedience. The former loves its own strength, displayed in its men of power, the latter says to its God, *I love you, O Lord, my strength* (Ps 18:1)." (Augustine, *The City of God: De Civitate Dei, Books 11–22*, Vol. I/7 of *The Works of St. Augustine: A Translation for the 21st Century*, translated by William Babcock (Hyde Park, NY: New City Press, 2013), 136–7.)

community – of interrelationships between persons. As Todd Breyfogle states, *societas* in Augustine's thought denotes:

> associations or fellowship among persons, whether human or divine, including trading partnerships, friendship, marriage, household and neighborly relations (including communities of interest), political associations, the community of mankind, both demonic and angelic community, and the communion of the divine persons.[8]

Evidently, each such community is bound together by at least one form of law, which regulates its activities with respect to certain ends. That law will always be defined by the type of love that motivates it. The success of the society in reaching its ends such that they fulfil human persons will depend on how the members of that society love. One such society is that of the state – and *City of God* considers in particular the role of the Roman state, or Empire. Augustine holds that empire in deep suspicion, and cautions against thinking that any earthly state can fulfil humans' longing for God. The state will never fulfil all the needs of its citizens, and in fact Christians can only form a very uneasy alliance with the forces of domination that characterise the Roman Empire. Their longing is for something beyond, and that same pining defines them as pilgrims in this world who constantly journey towards their proper home.

Human longing, then, is properly oriented when directed towards God, and the heavenly city. In fact, throughout the entirety of *City of God* a tension is evident, whereby as Veronica Roberts Ogle argues, the Christian is to disturb the secular order, by giving witness to something more. Ogle calls the Christian witness to *amor Dei* "a vital political service" without which the earthly city would close in on itself, and becoming nothing more than an "echo chamber" with no perspective on its own culture.[9] Such witness comes with risks that Augustine claims highlight the role of *amor Dei* to be visible in the world so as to point beyond the state. The very fact that Christians are willing to die for something beyond the laws of domination of the state calls those laws into question: the *amor sui* of the earthly city is, in the end, ruled by something greater. The context for writing *City of God* brings the importance of Augustine's theory into stark relief. His stated aim when writing is to respond to Marcellinus' request for clarification on whether the Christian life was incompatible with the duties of Roman citizenship.[10] In Book I of *City of God* Augustine states:

---

8 Todd Breyfogle, "Citizenship and Signs: Rethinking Augustine on the Two Cities," in *A Companion to Greek and Roman Political Thought*, edited by Ryan K Balot (New York: Wiley-Blackwell, 2009), 531.
9 Veronica Roberts Ogle, *Politics and the Earthly City in Augustine's City of God* (Cambridge: Cambridge University Press, 2021), 177.
10 Marcellinus was "an imperial official who had been sent to Africa to end the Donatist schism, had written to Augustine in 411 or 412 and asked him to respond to the opinion of Volusian, the proconsul of Africa, who believed that the practice of Christianity was incompatible with

> I have taken up the task of defending the most glorious city of God, whether in the course of these present times when it is on pilgrimage among the ungodly, living by faith, or in the stability of its eternal home which it now awaits in patience ... but will finally attain, by virtue of its surpassing excellence, in ultimate victory and perfect peace.[11]

Augustine goes on to say that this city must be defended "against those who prefer their own gods to its founder" – that is, it must be defended against the city of Man. Understanding the nature and importance of this defence will bring Marcellinus closer to appreciating what he should do as both a Christian and a civic leader. He does not need to leave the state in order to live a Christian life, but instead can live out the law of love in his daily life. Marcellinus' question would be familiar to many contemporary Christians, and so discerning what Augustine actually has to say about this is of more than historical significance. Still, Marcellinus' biography brings with it a certain caution: the Roman official was eventually executed as a traitor – he did not survive the earthly city. Augustine is all too aware of the physical dangers in leading a Christian life, but these are no reason to submit to the laws of the City of Man (understood as the earthly city, rather than the state, *per se*). In the end, there are points of no compromise for the Christian living in a state where the love of the City of Man – *amor sui* – holds sway.

As has been foreshadowed, not every contemporary interpretation of Augustine's theory maintains such a hard reading. One of the most influential interpreters of *City of God*, R.A. Markus, claims in *Saeculum: History and Society in the Theology of Augustine*, that

> The main lines of [Augustine's] thinking about history, society, and human institutions in general (the *saeculum*) point towards a political order to which we may not unreasonably apply the anachronistic epithet "pluralist," in that it is neutral in respect of ultimate beliefs and values.[12]

In other words, Christians live in the state alongside non-Christian citizens, and their love of God need not – in effect, *does* not – affect how they act and seem. From the outside, it is difficult, if not impossible, to tell a Christian from other citizens – if the Christian is actually being a good citizen. Markus holds to this

---

the requirements of Roman citizenship." (See translator's n.3 in: Augustine, *The City of God: De Civitate Dei, Books 1–21*, Vol. I/6 of *The Works of St. Augustine: A Translation for the 21st Century*, translated by William Babcock (Hyde Park, NY: New City Press, 2012) 1–2. For correspondence between Augustine and Marcellinus, see Augustine, *Augustine: Political Writings*, edited by EM Aitkins and RJ Dodaro (Cambridge: Cambridge University Press, 2001), 28–43.

11 Augustine, ibid., 1.
12 Markus, *Saeculum*, 151.

Why Secularism Is No Option 49

"invisibility of membership in either of the two cities"[13] based on his reading of a key passage in Book XIX of *City of God*, which he interprets as Augustine's promotion of secular pluralism:

> So long as this heavenly city is a pilgrim on earth ... it calls forth citizens from all peoples and gathers together a pilgrim society of all languages. It cares nothing about any differences in the manners, laws, and institutions by which earthly peace is achieved or maintained. But it does not rescind or abolish any of these; rather, it preserves and follows them, provided only that they do not interfere with the religion which teaches that we are to worship the one supreme and true God, for, however different they may be in different nations, they all aim at one and the same thing – earthly peace. Thus, even the heavenly city makes use of earthly peace during its pilgrimage, and, so far as sound piety and religion allow, it defends and seeks an accommodation among human wills with regard to the things that pertain to humanity's mortal nature. At the same time, however, it directs this earthly peace toward the heavenly peace.[14]

Markus interprets this passage to mean that "political institutions, social practices, customs ... are all radically relativised."[15] Claiming that they are "neutral," Markus effectively argues that Augustine defines the earthly city as a secular space in a Rawlsian sense. Just why he says this and what implications it has for this discussion need to be fleshed out before this discussion continues.

Which Mode of Secularity?

In *Christianity and the Secular*, Markus both nuances the argument of *Saeculum* and at the same time responds to some of its critics. A shortcut to understanding Markus' theory can be taken by situating him within the framework of Charles Taylor's well-known work, *A Secular Age*.[16] That is, *Saeculum* can be understood in light of the three ways of discussing secularity found in Taylor's "Introduction" to that work. Notably, Markus explains his purpose in the later *Christianity and the Secular* in light of another of Taylor's discussions of the secular – a point that will be briefly articulated below.[17]

In his "Introduction" to *A Secular Age*, Charles Taylor gives three ways of discussing the meaning of secularity. The first definition refers to "public spaces [that] ... have been allegedly emptied of God, or of any reference to ultimate

---

13 James Wetzel, "A Tangle of Two Cities," *Augustinian Studies* 43, no. 1 (2012): 10.
14 This is the Babcock translation. See Markus, *Christianity and the Secular*, 40 for the translation that he uses.
15 Markus, *Christianity and the Secular*, 40.
16 Charles Taylor, *A Secular Age* (Cambridge and London: Belknap Press, 2007).
17 Charles Taylor, "Modes of Secularism," in *Secularism and its Critics*, edited by Rajeev Bhargava (Oxford: Oxford University Press, 1998), 31–53.

reality."[18] The second sense is negative. It is where "people [are] turning away from God and no longer going to Church."[19] In the third, which Taylor focuses on more fully in *A Secular Age*, the

> shift to secularity ... consists, among other things, in a move from a society where belief in God is unchallenged and indeed, unproblematic, to one in which it is understood to be one option among others, and frequently not the easiest to embrace.[20]

Exploration of the third form of secularity is one of Taylor's main concerns in *Secular Age*. Effectively, Markus' *Saeculum* combines the first mode of the secular with the third. He claims that the Roman Empire established the first sense, while he advocates for the third as the pluralistic space familiar to adherents of Rawls' neutral space of the public square. Thus, *Saeculum* argues that Augustine advocates neutrality with regard to "beliefs and values" within the secular state. This neutrality calls into question the relationship between love and the law – and asks how in fact citizens can love the law if it is not fully situated in the light of God's divinely ordered *caritas*.

Christianity and the Secular specifically addresses how Markus' theory is situated within Taylor's framework for secularism. However, Markus turns to another of Taylor's writings to make this case. Namely, in "Modes of Secularism," Taylor describes a turning point in the seventeenth century, where in order to avoid the horrors of religiously motivated sectarian warfare, two options became evident. The first was to find what beliefs all Christians, or theists, agreed upon as the basis for political consensus. The second (advocated by Hugo Grotius) was to find political norms completely outside of the scope of religious belief.[21] Markus argues that both options meld into each other within the secular state, depending on the levels and areas of consensus between citizens. That is, a state will be more or less Christian depending on the levels of Christian belief among the members of its society. Conversely, it will be more or less non-Christian according to the degree of non-Christian beliefs. In either case, consensus is considered a kind of overlap – a zone in which citizens can agree on certain points. That overlap defines the scope of where law can hold sway in the secular state.

Perhaps tellingly, Markus leaves to the side what might happen if, in our own era, a society is anti-Christian or anti-religious. Ultimately, he states that his main argument in *Christianity and the Secular* is that

> Christian tradition has a legitimate place for the autonomy of the secular, even though for many centuries this was eclipsed in its awareness, and despite

---

18 Taylor, *A Secular Age*, 2.
19 Ibid., 2.
20 Ibid., 3.
21 Markus, *Christianity and the Secular*, 7.

Why Secularism Is No Option 51

the perpetual undertow of what we have become accustomed to call "triumphalism" in Christian political and cultural attitudes.[22]

Markus claims that Augustine considers the state in this way – as a neutral, secular domain. Thus, he finds that Augustine and Rawls both fundamentally agree on this point: that neutrality is preconditioned by the "overlapping consensus" that apparently Augustine speaks about in *City of God* and upon which Rawls' *Theory of Justice* depends.[23] This link between Augustine and Rawls is significant, because it demonstrates that Markus probably does still consider Augustine as a kind of progenitor of the liberal secular state – despite the fact that he seeks to redress this point. This can be seen in the following passage, where Markus states:

> Augustine excluded religion from the scope of the consensus required by the heavenly City during its earthly pilgrimage; but he would have rejected the absolute disjunction between what John Rawls calls a "general and comprehensive" conception of justice and a "political conception" which "tries to elaborate a reasonable conception for the basic structure [or society] alone and involves, so far as possible, no wider commitment to any other doctrine." I think in terms of this vocabulary Augustine would assert a link of some sort between the two. He would see Rawls's "basic structure" as a minimum condition of social coherence, but as a minimum that societies above the level of the band of pirates would generally manage to improve on.[24]

Markus then explains that Christians will go further than this minimum condition because of their "more ultimate" goals. The "band of pirates" reference is to a discussion in Book IV of *City of God* where Augustine says that a state without justice is like a group of robbers who band together for mutual advantage, but certainly not for the common good. Christians may need to live alongside such robbers in the state, but they strive to move within the space of consensus that they can find concerning temporal goods. Markus seems to think that the Christian must bargain with robbers, but that this is really not a major issue because Christians can also move beyond that point, because they can see a greater range of political actions. What Markus does not emphasise is that Christians should also know when they have found a point of no compromise – when neutrality is by no means an option.

The above quotation, then, is significant because it explicitly claims that Augustine would agree with Rawls on the nature of the *saeculum*. The secular for both of these thinkers is the space of "overlap" between the City of God and the City of Man. In other words, Markus draws a strong analogy between the way that he claims Augustine's cities at certain points coincide and the way that

---

22 Ibid., 9.
23 Ibid., 67.
24 Ibid.

52 *Renée Köhler-Ryan*

Rawls describes a range of "overlapping consensus of reasonable comprehensive doctrines."[25] To clarify, Rawls thinks that incompatible comprehensive doctrines arise in liberal democracies, and that they need to be negotiated through agreement. In Rawls' own words, comprehensive doctrines influence how citizens think about what is good, and they inform how we make decisions about

> what is of value in life, the ideals of personal character, as well as ideals of friendship and of familial and associational relationships, and much else that is to inform our conduct, and in the limit to our life as a whole.[26]

In fact though, Augustine's understanding of love in the two cities does not make overlap possible in this Rawlsian way, because Augustine does not countenance a shared space between ordered and disordered love. The best that one can hope for is a very uneasy peace between the different kinds of lovers, where the citizens of the City of God can live in the state as pilgrims, with a vision of life that is radically incompatible with the solely earthly loves of those who surround them. In fact, the best service that a Christian can give to the earthly city is to contradict its earthly loves. Christian love does not settle down, but rises upward. This imagery will be important for understanding the role of love for Christian citizens and civic leaders elaborated below. Before proceeding to that point, the next section examines several other readings of Book XIX of *City of God*, and offers an alternative to Markus, by emphasising the importance of dissent for Christians in the political order.

Interpretations of Book XIX of *City of God* in Light of the Secularism Debate

The argument of Book XIX of *City of God* is contested within contemporary scholarship, according to how much emphasis each scholar places on the importance of love of God for human fulfilment. In this book, Augustine describes how each of the two cities has a different end, with the final heavenly end being the most important. Justice can only be defined in accordance with that final end – whereby everything human, including the social, is directed towards God. The question of the book, though, is really the question dealt with in this chapter: what is the role of the political, or earthly city, in all of this – and in particular, how are members of the City of God to orient themselves within the earthly city?

Michael J.S. Bruno and Robert Dodaro each summarise contemporary readings of the relationship between the cities.[27] In short, Peter Kaufman, for instance,

---

25 Markus, *Christianity and the Secular*, 67.
26 Rawls, *Political Liberalism*, 13.
27 Michael JS Bruno, *Political Augustinianism: Modern Interpretations of Augustine's Political Thought* (Minneapolis, MN: Fortress Press, 2014) and Robert Dodaro, "Ecclesia and Res Publica": How Augustinian are Neo-Augustinian Politics?," in *Augustine and Postmodern*

thinks that the most a Christian ruler can hope for is to "make corrupt systems less bad." John Milbank equates the City of Man with sin, and the City of God with the Church, arguing that the latter is a perfect graced society of salvation. In this context, Markus provides a midway reading, by providing for an overlap rather than an inherent and dualistic conflict between members of the cities. Robert Dodaro thinks that the Christian statesman can "harmonize temporal goods with eternal ends."[28] At the same time, the Christian statesman takes Christ as his true model for justice. As Gregory W. Lee summarises Dodaro's position:

> Contra Kaufman, the Christian statesman can and should promote institutional reform; Augustine is not hopelessly pessimistic about the possibilities of political change. And contra Markus, this reform should follow distinctly theological principles; the Christian statesman is not bound to the consensus of religiously pluralistic society.[29]

Lee's article goes on to argue that Augustine thinks that Christians should be active in the world – the earthly city – and that to be so does not mean that they must sin. In fact, there is a real role that those who love God above all else can have in influencing the law of the state.

In comparison with the above readings, the terms that James K. Lee uses for the transformative opportunities for Christians in the state are differently stimulating.[30] He argues that the eschatological reading alone – looking at the cities only as spiritual realities, with heaven or hell as end points – is as insufficient as a pluralist reading. Through a close analysis of the sermons on the Psalms that Augustine was delivering while writing *City of God*, Lee focuses on the way that Babylon and Jerusalem necessarily "mingle," and on the opportunities that this presents for Christians. By realising and even ensuring that the cities of God and Man are not kept apart, members of Babylon are presented with the opportunity to respond to grace. Babylon, Lee argues, can even "become" Jerusalem – but such an opportunity for conversion would be impossible if Christians were not constantly within the City of Man, witnessing to the life of grace through public action.

Nonetheless, one should not forget that there are as many opportunities for violence and discord as there are for conversion in the earthly city of politics. The love that characterises the City of Man all too often converges with the motivations of citizens of the earthly city. It is helpful here to tease out a difficult point

---

Thought: A New Alliance Against Modernity?, edited by Lieven Boeve, Mathijs Lamberigts and Maarten Wisse (Leuven: Peeters, 2009), 237–71.

28 Gregory Lee, "Using the Earthly City," 43.
29 Ibid.
30 James K Lee, "Babylon Becomes Jerusalem: The Transformation of the Two Cities in Augustine's *Enarrationes in Psalmos*," *Augustinian Studies* 47, no. 2 (2016): 157–80. See also MB Pranger, "Politics and Finitude: The Temporal Status of Augustine's *Civitas Permixta*," in *Political Theologies: Public Religions in a Post-Secular World*, edited by Hent De Vries and Lawrence E Sullivan (Fordham, NY: Fordham University Press, 2006), 113–21.

54 Renée Köhler-Ryan

in Augustine's language. That is, he uses one term to articulate two dimensions of the same reality. The *civitas terrena* is literally the earthly political city in which a citizen finds themselves. At the same time, this term refers to the City of Man that is characterised by a selfish love that seeks to dominate. Ogle reflects that to argue that the *civitas terrena* denotes either the sinful political domain, or that it is merely a literary device, overlooks Augustine's greater point. Augustine uses the term *civitas terrena* to refer to two dimensions because of his sacramental vision, whereby everything material (or historical) has a deeper interior meaning.[31] Thus,

> for Augustine, the earthly city *covets* the political sphere, claiming it for itself, and so gaining its name from its earthly orientation. This, however, does not mean that the earthly city invents politics, only that it co-opts the political project for its own ends.[32]

For our purposes, the question becomes whether the heavenly city can do the same. That is, can those who love God embrace the political and draw it towards heaven? The answer is complex. Citizens alone certainly cannot do this. All they can really do is be clay in the hands of God, as he transforms and then guides them as vessels of grace, so that others can see the possibilities of conversion in their lives and in society.[33]

Unlike Markus, who flattens out the political sphere, or Milbank, who equates it with sinfulness, Ogle argues that members of both cities can reach a state of consensus only with regard to temporal goods. Agreement can go no further than this when incompatible loves are at play. Referring back to *City of God* 19.17, the passage that Markus finds so crucial, she argues that: "Three elements … are noteworthy: first, that the earthly city limits the harmonious agreement, second that it limits it to a compromise, and third, that this compromise is only concerned with temporal goods."[34] Like James K. Lee, Ogle maintains that while there is a necessary distinction between the two cities, such compromises must happen. In fact though, the compromise constitutes an opportunity, because only when the cities mingle is transformation possible. Ogle argues that points of mingling – what Augustine calls *permixta* throughout the text – become opportunities for cultural renewal.[35] Ogle's nuanced and rich interpretation opens up a space for the Christian to be involved in civic life that otherwise might be deemed impossible.

Latreia: Jolting the Earthly City towards Heavenly Love

Secular readings of Book XIX of *City of God* suffer from one major oversight, which is that those who love God first above all will refuse the laws of the city

---

31 Ogle, *Politics and the Earthly City in Augustine's* City of God, 4–5.
32 Ibid., 2.
33 See Lee, "Using the Earthly City," for this argument.
34 Ogle, 154.
35 Ibid., 176–80.

where that love is incompatible. Directly before the quotation from Book 19.17 that Markus reads as Augustine's pluralistic vision, the saint articulates:

> the heavenly city knew that the one God is alone to be worshiped, and it insisted with faithful devotion that only this God is to be served with the service which in Greek is called *latreia* and which is due only to God. As a result of this difference, it has been impossible for the heavenly city to have laws of religion in common with the earthly city. Instead, it has of necessity had to dissent from the earthly city at this point and to become an annoyance to those who think differently. As a result it has had to endure their wrath, their hatred, and the assaults of their persecutions, except when it turned aback the minds of its foes, sometimes due to their fear of its sheer numbers and always due to God's aid.[36]

This point of impossibility directly challenges Markus' Rawlsian vision, because it indicates the ultimate importance of Christian worship. The point here is about laws of religion, but in fact it can be drawn out further. Namely, pagan laws of religion are inherently selfish. Unlike Christian religious love, pagan religious sensibility is driven by the desire for self-satisfaction. In this sense, it is distinctively disorienting, because it does not enable the worshipper to find his or her proper place in the world and beyond it. The main thrust of Book II of *City of God* in this respect is that worship of the pagan gods only leads to depravity, destruction, and disorder. As citizens succumb to luxury and greed, they treat others more and more selfishly – and Rome falls. Assuredly, ruling out love altogether is impossible for Augustine. Every person loves. If they cannot love well, as Christ has taught us, then the only other option is to love in a disordered way – putting themselves first. Inevitably then, spaces of communal association cannot be neutral on this point. The neutrality of the secular theorist is incompatible with Augustine's vision.

Significantly, the point of no compromise that Augustine presents is that of proper worship. In *City of God*, Augustine calls that worship of God *latreia*, which is "the worship due to divinity ... or deity."[37] Augustine is very careful to distinguish *latreia* from all other kinds of service, and selects the term because it exclusively refers to the human worship of God. This worship takes place in two ways: "in certain sacraments or in our very selves."[38] It becomes evident that Augustine thinks of *latreia* as a gift of self, through which the human person is fulfilled. Opening up an economy of love as a gift, he argues that to give ourselves to God is at the same time to become most fully human. If the state denies this possibility, then it denies the humanity of the Christian worshipper. At the same time, any law against *latreia* is a source of internal destruction, because the

---

36 Augustine, *The City of God: De Civitate Dei, Books 11–22*, 375.
37 Ibid., *Books 1–10*, 305.
38 Ibid., 307.

same-said law rules against Babylon becoming Jerusalem – the earthly city fulfilling its final purpose and promise.

Bearing this in mind, it is possible to revisit the passage Markus reads through a secular pluralist lens, to ask what Augustine means when he says that the Christian "cares nothing about any differences in the manners, laws, and institutions by which earthly peace is achieved or maintained." The answer cannot lie in the insipid acceptance of any shared customs whatsoever. Instead, Augustine's support of rich diversity in culture depends upon one factor alone. If a "manner, law, or institution" does not directly contradict the ultimate law of love of God, then it is capable of transformation from within. To translate: a law can come to transmit the deeper and higher purpose of aiming for God if it is not quintessentially harmful and if the Christian adopts it – breathing God's life into it and demonstrating its highest fulfilment. Such worship happens not only in temples, but also in daily acts that constitute a gift of self, animated by God's grace in our lives. In this respect, real works of mercy are, for Augustine, acts of properly directed love, which might also be interpreted as rebellion, within the earthly city. At the same time, they are the source of "cultural renewal" for which Ogle argues.

Notably, a work of mercy cannot be deemed such if it is devoid of love. Augustine is very firm on this point: those who think they will be saved by carrying out works that are not motivated by love are sadly mistaken.[39] Christians will only make a difference when action is motivated by love – when they would go so far as to give their lives to witness to this reality. The martyrs have the capacity to jolt citizens of the earthly city out of selfish complacency, making them aware that there could very well be much more to human life and fulfilment than their earthly loves would have it. The *saeculum* can never be neutral, because love is never neutral. It always has an object that motivates. What we love defines how we love. It breathes life into law. *Latreia* and its demands make this clear, because true service to God is only possible when we serve God with our hearts as well as our bodies. *Latreia* has, then, both visible and invisible dimensions. Each is important. This means that the *saeculum* can never be neutral, because the Christian must test any sense of neutrality so that selfishness and complacency are put under pressure. Through their love, Christians demonstrate what the law is and what it must be, if humans are to achieve the object of their longing.

---

39 Augustine, *The City of God: De Civitate Dei, Books 11–22*, 22.22 and 22.27.

4 Why Lutheranism Is No Option for a Meaningful Jurisprudence of Love

Augusto Zimmermann

First Considerations

Martin Luther (1483–1546) was born in November 1483 in Eisleben, Germany. The son of a wealthy copper miner of peasant origin, his father had planned him a promising career in law. But Luther soon abandoned his study of law after a series of traumatic personal incidents. In July 1505, he joined the Augustinian order of monks at Erfurt but spent most of his adult life serving as a theology professor at the University of Wittenberg.[1]

Gradually, Luther began to question the traditional ways of Catholicism, particularly its reliance on scholasticism. He deemed scholasticism and the study of canon law inconsistent with true biblical teaching. Instead, Luther began to focus his theology on a God who forgives sinners that turn to him in faith and repentance.[2] This insight finds its ultimate expression in the Protestant doctrine of *sola fide*, or "justification by faith." It is a doctrine that recognises salvation by God's grace alone and quite apart from salvation by works, whether sacramental or secular.[3] Unfortunately, as Dr Alex Deagon points out:

> The doctrine of *sola scriptura* also contributed to the isolation of faith from reason by rejecting the Book of Nature as an authority, effectively forcing the operating process of science to be non-theological and reject faith, embracing reason without faith. Thus, through emphasis on God's sovereignty, faith alone and Scripture alone, the Reformation further contributed to the divorce of reason and faith by continuing to allow for a space devoid of faith.[4]

It is in this context of justification by faith alone that Luther accuses St Thomas Aquinas of having elevated reason above revelation. Luther had serious doubts

---

1 Eric Metaxas, *Martin Luther: The Man Who Rediscovered God and Changed the World* (New York: Viking, 2017), 27.
2 Colin Brown, *Christianity and Western Thought – Vol 1: From the Ancient World to the Age of Enlightenment* (Downers Grove, IL: InterVarsity Press, 1990), 146.
3 Ibid., 147.
4 Alex Deagon, *From Violence to Peace: Theology, Law and Community* (Oxford: Hart Publishing, 2017), 55.

DOI: 10.4324/9781003148920-6

about the ability of human reason to investigate matters of faith.[5] He held the Christian faith to be in objective contrast to human reason. "It is perilous to wish to investigate and apprehend the naked divinity by reason without Christ the mediator," Luther argued.[6] Luther also stated: "Faith must believe against reason ... and against its understanding that grasps and admits the validity only of that which is empirical."[7] Thus, he spent most of his time attacking the Catholic notion that obeying God's law was co-instrumental with faith in our justification before God. According to Luther,

> It is a great error to attribute justification to a love that does not exist or, if it does, is not great enough to placate God; for as I have said, even the saints love in an imperfect and impure way in this present life, and nothing impure will enter the kingdom of God.[8]
>
> (Eph 5:5)

Luther's Political Theology

Luther derived much of his theology of government from one single passage in Scripture: Romans 13. This chapter reads, in part: "Let every soul be subject to the governing authorities. For there is no authority except from God, and the authorities that exist are appointed by God." Because Luther interpreted it in isolation, not only were governments assumed to be always the servants of God, but it was also assumed that there is no possible justification in Scripture for resistance against political tyranny. Indeed, Luther attempted to justify an absolute loyalty to the temporal authority by contending that "neither Joseph nor Daniel, nor many other good and godly Jews, observed Moses' laws out of their country, but those of the Gentiles among whom they lived."[9] Should this authority turn out to become a tyrannical ruler who "seizes your property on account ... and punish[es] such disobedience, we must passively submit and thank God that [we] are worthy to suffer for the sake of the divine word."[10] "Tyranny is not to be resisted but endured," Luther stated.[11]

In *Temporal Authority*, a tract that Luther wrote in 1523, Christians are said to live simultaneously in two kingdoms. The first kingdom is ruled by temporal

---

5 Justo L Gonzales, *The Story of Christianity: The Reformation to the Present Day* (New York: HarperOne, 2010), 50.
6 Martin Luther, First Disputation Against the Antinomians [1537]. Quoted from Brown, *supra* n 4, 150.
7 Payk Althaus, *The Theology of Martin Luther* (Philadelphia, PA: Fortress Press, 1966), 57.
8 Nick Batzig, "Luther, Law and Love," Reformation 21, accessed 9 November 2018, www.reformation21.org/blogs/luther-law-and-love.php.
9 Martin Luther, *Martin Luther's Tabletalk: Luther's Comments on Life, the Church and the Bible* (Fearn: Christian Heritage, 2003), 217.
10 Nick Spencer, *Freedom & Order: History, Politics and the English Bible* (London: Hodder, 2012), 65.
11 Ibid.

authorities, and the second is ruled directly by Christ, spiritually and without coercion. This type of dualism is reflected in two forms of government: the spiritual, "by which the Holy Spirit produces Christians," and the temporal, "which restrains the unchristian and wicked so that ... they are obliged to keep still and to maintain an outward peace."[12]

This distinction considers the Bible's teachings relevant only to the life of the Church and not the state.[13] Since Luther believed that the Bible brings no new laws into the world, this led to a natural rejection of the Church's separate jurisdiction.[14] Being no more than a congregation of the faithful (*congregatio fidelium*), it follows from such a premise that "the Church cannot properly be said to possess any separate jurisdiction."[15] Hence, Luther's premise committed him to support an unparalleled extension of the range of "secular powers." Indeed, if the Church is no more than a "congregation of the faithful," Quentin Skinner concludes:

> It follows that the secular authorities must have the sole right to exercise all coercive powers, including powers over the Church. This does not of course impinge on the true Church, since it consists of a purely spiritual realm, but it definitely places the visible Church under the control of the godly prince.[16]

This theological view of government activated a form of secularism that went far beyond Luther's intention.[17] Surely, one can say, the Church should always fight against injustice and political tyranny. Lutheran theology, however, inevitably weakens such a possibility by determining that law is the exclusive province of the state. Indeed, Luther believed that resistance against government is invariably a rebellion against God himself. At the outset of *On Secular Authority*, Luther goes on to argue against the idea of representative government by stating that the exercise of political power is never to be found in the consent of the governed.[18]

The Peasants' Revolt was a widespread popular revolt that resulted in the slaughter of up to 100,000 of the 300,000 peasants and farmers. When the revolt broke out in Germany in 1524, it prompted Luther to react with "shocking brutality." He called "for the most ruthless suppression of these oppressed and desperate wretches," reminding those who were oppressed that "the fact that the

---

12 Ibid., 54.
13 Jeff Myers, *Understanding the Culture: A Survey of Social Engagement* (Manitou Springs, CO: Summit Ministries, 2017), 22.
14 Quentin Skinner, *The Foundations of Modern Political Thought* – Volume 2: The Age of Reformation (Cambridge: Cambridge University Press, 1978), 12.
15 Ibid., 14.
16 Ibid., 15.
17 JR Weinberg, *A Short History of Medieval Philosophy* (Princeton, NJ: Princeton University Press, 1967), 265.
18 John R Stephenson, "The Two Governments and the Two Kingdoms in Luther's Thought," *Journal of Lutheran Ethics* (1 July 2002), www.elca.org/JLE/Articles/947.

rulers are wicked and unjust does not excuse disorder and rebellion."[19] Any faith Luther might have had in "the common man" was completely shattered. Thus, he began to communicate a message that the earthly government is of divine origin and that the political ruler has a divine mandate to expect unquestioning obedience, meaning that any resistance is unconditionally wicked.

Luther also believed that those peasants should be prepared to "suffer everything" and to "not fight against your lord and tyrant."[20] Some of the reasons provided were practical (it's easy to change a government but it is far more difficult to get one that is better), but the primary reason was essentially theological – "since the establishment of political rule lies 'in the will and hand of God,'" it follows that "those who resist their rulers resist the ordinance of God."[21] Instead of viewing those popular uprisings as an outburst against social injustices and the gross violation of God-given inalienable rights, Luther declared that even if the peasants had been treated unjustly and oppressively, as Christians they still had no right to revolt against their political rulers.[22] We can petition, but we can never have a right to resist any of their arbitrariness and tyranny.

Luther even insisted that evil rulers are ordained by God because of people's sins. It thus appears that Luther was making God the author of evil.[23] According to him, it is "blind" and "perverse" to think that sheer power is all that sustains the wicked ruler, and thus that "the tyrant rules because he is such a scoundrel." The truth, in Luther's own words, "is that he is ruling not because he is a scoundrel but because of the people's sin."[24] The reason a prince might be so dreadful, Luther continues, is because

> the world is too wicked, and does not deserve to have many wise and upright princes. If the world were composed of real Christians, that is, true believers, there would be no need for or benefits for prince, king, lord, sword or law.[25]

According to Nick Spencer, "in some ways the history of political theology is the attempt by Christians, mainly but not exclusively Protestants, to clamber out of the hole that Luther's reading of Romans 13 had dug them into."[26] Luther's interpretation of this passage was systematised in the concept of "ordinology," which assigns to the state the entire sphere of the law, leaving to the Church only

---

19 Martin Luther, "Admonition to Peace" [1525]. Quoted from Skinner, *supra* n 14, 18.
20 Martin Luther, "Whether Soldiers Can Be Saved" [1526]. Quoted from Skinner, *The Foundations of Modern Political Thought* – Volume 2, 18–19.
21 Skinner, *The Foundations of Modern Political Thought* – Volume 2, 19.
22 Justo L Gonzales, *The Story of Christianity: The Reformation to the Present Day* (New York: HarperOne, 2010), 56.
23 Skinner, *The Foundations of Modern Political Thought* – Volume 2, 19.
24 Martin Luther, "Whether Soldiers Can Be Saved" [1526]. Quoted from Skinner, *The Foundations of Modern Political Thought* – Volume 2, 19.
25 Alec Ryrie, *Protestants: The Faith that Made the Modern World* (New York: Viking, 2017), 48.
26 Spencer, *Freedom & Order*, 65.

the sphere of the Gospel.[27] As noted by Drummond, "this dualism was developed in order to suit the interests of German princes, who[se] chief aim was the preservation of power sacred and secular."[28] Eventually, the application of these ideas "sacrificed liberty to order."[29] Christian freedom is never a freedom from tyranny, but solely a "freedom of the spirit which renders the Christian patient under suffering and duress."[30]

Luther's two-kingdom analysis restricts the application of Christian love to the sphere of the individual believer. Exegetically this is highly questionable because Jesus always intended his command of love to apply to the public sphere. In Matthew 5: 39–41, for example, Jesus discusses issues that clearly pertain to the public sphere of the legal system and the authorised demands of the Roman rulers. Because the law of God is explicitly described in Scripture as "the perfect law of liberty" (Jas 1:25), the Apostle Paul counsels believers in Galatia to "stand fast therefore in the liberty wherewith Christ hath made us free" (Gal. 5:1). Sir John Fortescue (1394–1476), a chief justice of the King's Bench under King Henry VI, certainly had these biblical passages in mind when he stated:

> A law is necessarily adjudged cruel if it increases servitude and diminishes freedom, for which human nature always craves. For servitude was introduced by men for vicious purposes. But freedom was instilled into human nature by God. Hence freedom taken away from men always desires to return, as is always the case when natural freedom is denied. So he who does not favour freedom is to be deemed impious and cruel.[31]

By contrast, Luther believed that "it is in no wise proper for anyone who would be a Christian to set himself up against his government, whether it acts justly or unjustly." "There are no better works," according to Luther, "than to obey and serve all those who are set over us as superiors."[32] As a result, the Church that had grown up over the last 500 years into a major force in curbing the arbitrary power of temporal authorities was dramatically cut down and its public (and jurisdictional) authority significantly diminished. As Spencer points out:

> If there was a resulting power vacuum in this vision, it was quickly and explicitly filled by temporal power. The governing authorities now had the

---

27 Andrew Landale Drummond, *German Protestantism Since Luther* (London: The Epworth Press, 1951), 229.
28 Ibid., 214.
29 RH Murray, *The Political Consequences of the Reformation* (New York: Russell & Russell, 1960), 74.
30 Erwin R Gane, "Luther's Views of Church and State," *St Andrews University Seminary Studies* 135, no. 8 (1970): 120.
31 John Fortescue, *De Laudibus Legum Anglie* (Cambridge: Cambridge University Press, 1949), 105.
32 See George H Sabine, *A History of Political Theory* (2nd ed., New York: Henry Holt & Co., 1950), 361.

monopoly on all use of coercive power, including over the visible Church. Kings did not become sacred, at least no more sacred than anointing already made them, nor did they have the authority to pronounce on matters of doctrine, although some tried. Rather they had the monopoly on all political power, which they derived directly from God and had a duty to use it in securing religious uniformity and orthodoxy within their territories.[33]

So, it is not difficult to understand why so many German princes became Lutherans. Those princes had much to gain from embracing the Protestant faith. Nearly without exception all the most autocratic rulers of Europe – princes and kings – opted for Lutheranism. This was particularly so in the regions where the Church was the *greatest* local power. The German princes had much to gain both economically and politically.[34] By calling on the German princes to take up the work of Reformation, writes Paul Johnson,

> there was undoubtedly a monstrous danger in the line Luther adopted and consistently pursued. By the second decade of the sixteenth century the power of the State was visibly growing through all Europe: to displace clerical authority and entrust the headship of the Church, and the arbitration of the doctrine, to secular rulers was massively to enforce a process already fraught with peril to other elements of society. It meant, too, a degree of dependence on the princes which implied a blind endorsement of the social order they represented – a social order as much in need of change and reform as the clerical one.[35]

Lutheranism and the Paternal Ruler

Luther bestowed on the German princes the pompous title of "Father of the Community" (*Landesvater*).[36] The metaphor of the political ruler as a loving father eventually became "the basics of Lutheran legal and political theory for the next three centuries."[37] It undoubtedly became central to German and Scandinavian concepts of law and politics.

Luther expected the temporal authority to care for their loyal subjects as if these were their special children. In turn, the latter would have to "honour" and obey the former as if he was their loving father. Like a loving father, the temporal authority had to protect the people and prevent them from abusing themselves through gambling, drunkenness, sumptuousness, and any other conceivable vices. The temporal authority would also be in charge of educating all those

---

33 Spencer, *Freedom & Order*, 65.
34 Rodney Stark, *The Triumph of Christianity* (New York: HarperOne, 2011), 329.
35 Paul Johnson, *A History of Christianity* (New York: Touchstone Book, 1995), 283.
36 Ibid., 19.
37 John Witte, Jr, "Introduction," in *Christianity and Law: An Introduction*, eds. John Witte, Jr and Frank S Alexander (Cambridge: Cambridge University Press, 2008), 19.

Why Lutheranism Is No Option 63

under his paternal rule through public schools, public libraries, public theatres, public press, etc.[38]

Reading the writings of Luther brings to mind these comments from C.S. Lewis:

> Of all tyrannies, a tyranny sincerely exercised for the good of its victims may be the most oppressive ... Those who torment us for our own good will torment us without end for they do so with the approval of their own conscience.[39]

The Lutheran view of the role of the state is a recipe for abusive government and officious paternalism. It is therefore not surprising that the first model of "welfare state" originated in the birthplace of Lutheranism. Introduced by the Prussian Chancellor Otto von Bismarck, government-funded "social programmes" were first created in the early 1840s, first in Prussia, then in Saxony, and then finally in Germany at large.[40]

Bismarck had a notorious contempt for personal freedom and the idea of representative government.[41] As Bismarck himself once stated: "I believe I am obeying God when I serve my king."[42] He claimed to have converted to Lutheranism while visiting the house of pietistic friends. But he also thought that as a political leader he had sometimes to violate the moral principles that governed his private behaviour as a Christian. Bismarck reasoned that when acting as a servant of the state, he was not bound by the same moral dictates he would have as an individual.[43] This dichotomy goes back to Luther, who insisted that we must obey our leaders no matter how awful they might be. This double standard was taught in the German Church as a blind subjection to the temporal authority, thus emphasising that the laws of the state should always be obeyed regardless of their substantive value. Those who participated in the atrocities of the Third Reich often appealed to this Lutheran approach to laws in order to defend their immoral actions.

"Kings shall be thy nursing fathers" (Isa. 49:23). An application of this Old Testament statement that is too literal produces individuals who become far too passive, dependent, and incapable of self-government.[44] To implement social policies, the German state appealed directly to Luther's defence of paternal

---

38 Ibid.
39 CS Lewis, *God in the Dock: Essays on Theology and Ethics* (Grand Rapids, MI: William B. Eerdmans, 1948), 74.
40 Tom G Palmer, "Bismarck's Legacy," in *After the Welfare State*, ed. Tom G Palmer (Ottawa, ON: Jameson Books, 2012), 45.
41 Erwin W Lutzer, *Hitler's Cross: How the Cross was Used to Promote the Nazi Agenda* (Chicago, IL: Moody Publishers, 2016), 29.
42 Ibid.
43 Ibid., 28
44 Nancy R Pearcey, *Total Truth: Liberating Christianity from Its Cultural Captivity* (Wheaton, IL: Crossway, 2004), 61.

control over the population.⁴⁵ The primary goal of Bismarck was to forestall popular demands for political rights by giving the people a myriad of social rights that made them more dependent on the German state. This was exactly what Bismarck had in mind as he desired to prevent democratic government by giving the German people what they apparently wanted.⁴⁶

Luther pioneered the modern "welfare state" and all its social programmes: pensions, health insurance, worker safety measures, eight-hour workdays, and so on. This strategy proved disastrous little more than a generation later.⁴⁷ Not only did it give Germans a view of the state as the ultimate provider of all things, but it also saw the Church shrink from its social function in German society. Hence, in 1919, when Germany was humiliated and defeated after the First World War, general enthusiasm for paternal rule re-emerged in full force. Instead of relying on the voluntary efforts of individually responsible citizens, the Lutheran view of the "social Gospel" relied almost exclusively on government action and initiative. Hitler was thus a Bismarckian and the logical end of this distorted idea of the role of the state, ultimately paved the way for the most tyrannical of all forms of "welfare state" – namely National Socialism.⁴⁸

Lutheranism and National Socialism

To understand the role of the Lutheran leadership during the Nazi regime, one must first recognise how the Church had always been in the service of the powerful German state. Lutheran clergy traditionally saw themselves as civil servants and faithful protectors of the *status quo*. Once the Nazis came to power, they benefited from this church subservience to the German state.⁴⁹ Germans ended up suffering a great deal from the serious Lutheran error regarding the relationship between "secular" and "spiritual" orders. This error fostered attitudes of complete ecclesiastical submission to, and compliance with, the German state. The ultimate effect of this error was that it created the political environment that paved the way for National Socialism.

In April 1939, the Lutheran Church published the "Godesberg Declaration." In a nutshell, this notorious document defined National Socialism as the "natural continuation of the work of Martin Luther."⁵⁰ Erich Koch, president of the Provincial Lutheran Church, argued that National Socialism represented

---

45 Daniel Philpott, "Christianity: A Straggler on the Road to Liberty?," in *Christianity and Freedom* – Volume I: Historical Perspectives, eds. Timothy Samuel Shah and Allan D Hertzke (Cambridge: Cambridge University Press, 2016), 351.
46 Jonah Goldberg, *Liberal Fascism: The Secret History of the American Left, from Mussolini to the Politics of Change* (New York: Broadway Books, 2009), 218.
47 Ibid., 96.
48 Drummond, *German Protestantism Since Luther*, 256–7.
49 Johnson, A History of Christianity, 484.
50 Eric Metaxas, *Bonhoeffer: Pastor, Martyr, Prophet, Spy* (Nashville, TN: Thomas Nelson, 2010), 324.

the natural continuation of Luther's unfinished work of Reformation.[51] These Lutheran leaders had even the tremendous audacity to elevate Adolf Hitler to the position of a "new Moses" and the ultimate interpreter of the divine will. In April 1937, the German Church (*Reichskirche*) issued another notorious declaration that effectively substituted Hitler's authority for that of the Bible. It reads, in part:

> Hitler's word is God's law; the decrees and laws which represent it possess divine authority. The Führer being the only hundred per cent National Socialist, he alone fulfils the law. All others are to be regarded as guilty before the divine law.[52]

The Lutheran clergy justified their concordant interpretations of Scripture by directly appealing to the authority of the great German reformer. If Luther could break away from Catholic orthodoxy, so in his name even traditional Lutheran theology could also be revisited. In other words, nothing could be said to be written in stone because Luther himself had disputed the canonicity of scriptural texts. In the list of Luther's "disputed books" were Hebrews, James, Jude, and the Book of Revelation.[53] To some Nazi leaders, this theological approach was a priceless gift and saw the German Reformation completed in National Socialism. In this context, Luther became "John the Baptist" to Adolf Hitler preparing the way for the new lord and messiah of the German people. Bernhard Rust, the Nazi education minister, commented:

> "I think the time is past when one may not say the names of Hitler and Luther in the same breath. They belong together; they are of the same old stamp."[54]

It is not difficult therefore to understand why the Nazis sought to attach themselves to Luther. The teachings of Luther were regarded as the quintessence of what it meant to be a German Christian.[55] In Germany's pre-Second World War, there were more than 40 million Lutherans who viewed Luther as a national hero and, indeed, the very essence of the "German spirit" (*Volksgeist*).[56] Hence, Emanuel Hirsh, a Lutheran theologian and active member of the Nazi party,

---

51 Christopher J Probst, *Demonizing the Jews: Luther and the Protestant Church in Germany* (Bloomington, IN: Indiana University Press, 2012), 25.
52 Aurel Kolnai, *The War Against the West* (New York: Viking, 1938), 276.
53 Martin Luther, "Preface to the Revelation of St John" (1522), Bible Researcher, www.bible-researcher.com/antilegomena.html.
54 Richard Steigmann-Gall, *The Holy Reich: Nazi Conceptions of Christianity – 1919–1945* (Cambridge: Cambridge University Press, 2003), 136–7.
55 John Witte Jr, *Law and Protestantism: The Legal Teaching of the Lutheran Reformation* (Cambridge: Cambridge University Press, 2002), 297.
56 Probst, *Demonizing the Jews*, 37.

66   *Augusto Zimmermann*

argued that "the meeting with God in national existence is the only preparation for the meeting with God in the Gospel."[57] For Heinz-Dietrich Wendland, another Lutheran theologian, the Nazi ideology was "self-evident for Christian doctrine" and "an instrument of Divine Love."[58]

Needless to say, Hitler initially pretended to be a Christian. This was so in order to turn theologically ignorant Germans in favour of the Nazi regime and against the Jews.[59] Hitler particularly liked to remind the German people that Luther had called the Jews "venomous," "bitter worms," and "disgusting vermin." In one of his most notorious tracts, Luther actually recommended the burning of all Jewish synagogues, houses, and schools, as well as the confiscation of Jewish money and the coercion of every Jew into forced labour. These are his very words:

> First, to set fire to their synagogues or schools and to bury and cover with dirt whatever will not burn, so that no man will ever again see stone or cinder of them. This is to be done in honor of our Lord and Christendom ... Second I advise that their houses also be razed and destroyed ... Third, I advise that all their prayer books and Talmudic writings, in which such idolatry, lies, cursing, and blasphemy are taught, be taken from them. Fourth, I advise that their rabbis be forbidden to teach hence-forth on pain of loss of life and limb. Fifth, I advise that safe-conduct on the highways be abolished completely for the Jews ... Sixth, I advise that usury be prohibited to them, and that all cash and treasure of silver and gold be taken from them and put aside for safekeeping.[60]

Throughout the centuries these terrible words have often been quoted as proof that Christians could not be friends of the Jews. In *Mein Kampf*, a political manifesto written by Adolf Hitler in 1925, Luther is heralded as a "great reformer" and a "man of courage" who withstood the Catholic Church and, no doubt, viscerally hated the Jews.[61] By his own account, Hitler believed that eliminating the Jews was divinely mandated. Hence, he wrote in *Mein Kampf*: "I believe I am acting in accordance with the will of the Almighty Creator. By defending myself against the Jews, I am fighting for the work of the Lord."[62]

In the 1930s, many Lutherans were influenced by a theology that encouraged broad deference to the German state. They also carried the baggage of a long

---

57 Drummond, *German Protestantism Since Luther*, 164.
58 HD Wendland, Die Nation vor Gott [1934], 187, 191. Quoted from: Drummond, *German Protestantism Since Luther*, 267.
59 Metaxas, *Bonhoeffer: Pastor, Martyr, Prophet, Spy*, 94.
60 Martin Luther, *Luther's Works* – Volume 47, trans. Maring H Bertram (Philadelphia, PA: Muhlenberg, 1962), 268–72.
61 Lutzer, *Hitler's Cross*, 106.
62 Quoted from Ray Comfort, *Hitler, God & the Bible* (Washington, DC: WND Books, 2012), 116.

and disturbing history of anti-Semitism.[63] To make it more complicated, "the constant repetition of Luther's ugliest statements served the Nazis' purposes and convinced most Germans that being a German and being a Christian were a racial inheritance, and that neither was compatible with being Jewish."[64] In his notorious tract "On the Jews and their Lies," Luther describes Jews as "a base and whoring people." Oxford University historian Lyndal Roper summarises the disturbing nature of these appalling writings:

> The Jews, Luther alleges, look for biblical truth "under the sow's tail," that is, their interpretation of the Bible comes from looking in a pig's anus .... They defame Christian belief, "impelled by the Devil, to fall into this like filthy sows fall into the trough." If they see a Jew, Christians should "throw sow dung at him ... and chase him away." Luther calls for the secular authorities to burn down all the synagogues and schools, and "what won't burn should be covered over with earth, so that not a stone or piece of slag of it should be seen for all eternity." The Jews' houses should be destroyed and they should be put under one roof, like the gypsies. The Talmud and prayer books should be destroyed and Jewish teachers banned. They should be prevented from using the roads, usury banned, and the Jews forced to undertake physical labor instead. Assets from moneylending should be confiscated and used to support Jews who converted. This was a program of complete cultural eradication. And Luther meant it ....
>
> Luther's anti-Semitism then reached a crescendo of physical revulsion. He imagined Jews kissing and praying to the Devil's excrement: "the Devil has emptied ... his stomach again and again, that is a true relic, which the Jews, and those who want to be a Jew, kiss, eat, drink, and worship." In a kind of inverted baptismal exorcism, the Devil fills the mouth, nose, and ears of the Jews with filth: "He stuffs and squirts them so full, that it overflows and swims out of every place, pure Devil's filth, yes, it tastes so good to their hearts, and they guzzle it like sows." Whipping himself into a frenzy, Luther invokes Judas, the ultimate Jew: "When Judas hanged himself, so that his guts ripped, and as happens to those who are hanged, his bladder burst, then the Jews had their golden cans and silver bowls ready, to catch the Judas piss (as one calls it) with the other relics, and afterwards together they ate the shit and drank, from which they got such sharp sight that they are able to see such complex glosses in Scripture."[65]

This is the sort of behaviour that led many Lutherans to consider the Jews as great enemies of Christianity, for they emphasised law whereas the Christian faith

---

63 Michael Gerson and Peter Wehner, *City of Man: Religion and Politics in a New Era* (Chicago, IL: Moody Publishers, 2010), 13.
64 Ibid., 94.
65 Lyndal Roper, *Martin Luther: Renegade and Prophet* (New York: Random House, 2017), 392.

is primarily a matter of grace.[66] To be fair, in his last days, when the irritability of age and disease took over, Luther did not spare even those of his own faith. "Whether it was regarding the papacy or the Anabaptists or the Jews," writes Erwin Lutzer, "Luther always spoke in colourful, condemning language.[67] "Jews and papists are ungodly wretches; they are two stockings made of one piece of cloth," Luther wrote in November 1544.[68] In June 1546, John Calvin writes to Philip Melanchthon to explicitly complain that Luther's "intemperance" and "tyranny" had to be controlled "for the sake of the Reformation."[69]

Luther's treatment of the Jews made it particularly difficult for the Church in the 1930s to resist the Nazi regime. First of all, as previously stated, Luther believed that "tyranny is not to be resisted but endured."[70] This idea justified complacency and even tacit support for that oppressive regime.[71] According to Metaxas, Luther's writings ended up convincing far too many Germans that being a good Christian was not only to blindly obey the law of the state but also to be anti-Jewish. After the *Kristallnacht*, when the Nazis went on a rampage destroying Jewish businesses and synagogues, Lutheran Bishop Martin Sasse (1890–1942) wrote a tract entitled "Martin Luther on the Jews: Away with Them!" There, he specifically quotes from "On the Jews and their Lies" in order to conclude that Luther's goal had actually been accomplished by means of those appalling violations of fundamental rights.[72] Of course, when Luther wrote that pamphlet, Metaxas explains:

> he had little idea that four centuries in the future a political malevolence would rise up in his beloved Germany and that its most diabolical proponents would ferret out from the mountains of his writings those few passages of his most injudicious writings to aid their cause. That diabolical cause would end with the murder of six million Jewish noncombatants in as cold-blooded and calculated a manner as anything in the history of the world.

---

66 Justo L Gonzales, *The Story of Christianity: The Reformation to the Present Day* (New York: HarperOne, 2010), 51.
67 Lutzer, *Hitler's Cross*, 107.
68 Luther, *Martin Luther's Tabletalk*, 220.
69 R Scott Clark, "Subtle Sacramentarian or Son? John Calvin's Relationship to Luther," *The Southern Baptist Journal of Theology* 21, no. 4 (2014): 51.
70 Luther, "On Temporal Authority." Quoted from Skinner, *The Foundations of Modern Political Thought* – Volume 2, 17.
71 Metaxas, *Bonhoeffer: Pastor, Martyr, Prophet, Spy*, 281–2. To be fair, some Lutheran clergymen, those influenced not by Lutheran theology but rather Calvinistic thought, offered an important resistance against the Nazi regime. Based largely on Calvinist teachings, a few leading German theologians, including Karl Barth and Dietrich Bonhoeffer, established the Confessing Church (*Bekennende Kirche*) as an important movement within German Protestantism that arose in opposition to the official Lutheran Church and Hitler's German Christian movement.
72 Bernard N Howard, "Luther's Jewish Problem," The Gospel Coalition, accessed 19 October 2017, www.thegospelcoalition.org/article/luthers-jewish-problem/.

That the Nazis' cynical master of propaganda would find the few vile words Luther had written against Jews and broadcast them to the world, ignoring the 110 volumes of his other writings, is of course fathomlessly cynical. Even at the time, those who knew Luther's other works very well either were unaware of this pamphlet or simply ignored it, feeling that it was such a strange outlier it could hardly be understood rationally.[73]

Lutheranism, Legal Positivism, and National Socialism

Luther rejected the optimistic view of our capacity to intuitively follow the laws of God.[74] Instead, his vision of the "bondage to sin" committed him to a despairing analysis of the relationship between God and human beings. Since Luther believed that we can never hope to fathom the divine nature and will, he concluded that the commands of God are bound to be entirely inscrutable. It is at this point that Luther reveals his great debt to William of Occam by insisting that God's laws must be obeyed not because they are morally right and just, but because they are the commands of the Master of the Universe. The attack on the Thomist account of God as a rational lawgiver is one of the most distinctive characteristics of Lutheranism, where God's "immutable, eternal, and infallible will is incapable of being comprehended by men at all."[75]

According to Luther, Christ came not just to fulfil the law but "to release the faithful from its demands by His redeeming merit and love."[76] He thinks mainly in terms of the specifics rather than on the whole; and more about the individual interpretation of Scripture instead of considering this in light of Church tradition. For Luther, God does not need to justify any of his commands at the bar of reason. Indeed, God may even refuse to supply any rationale or justification beyond the fact that his commands are simply the result of his own personal injunctions.[77] The foundation for this critique of human reason rests in the belief in a divine lawmaker whose decrees are fixed in the shrouded mystery of eternity, and whose ways are higher than human reason can ever fathom.[78]

The "Formula of Concord" (1577) is the authoritative Lutheran statement of faith. There, three purposes of the law must be identified, in Article 6:

> The Law was given to men for three reasons ... that thereby outward discipline might be maintained against wild, disobedient men [and that wild and intractable men might be restrained, as though by certain bars], ... that men thereby may be led to the knowledge of their sins ... that they are regenerate

---

73 Metaxas, *Bonhoeffer: Pastor, Martyr, Prophet, Spy*, 417.
74 Skinner, *The Foundations of Modern Political Thought* – Volume 2, 4.
75 Ibid., 5.
76 Ibid., 10.
77 Stanley J Grenz, *The Moral Quest: Foundations of Christian Ethics* (London: Apollos, 1997), 154.
78 Ibid.

... they might ... have a fixed rule according to which they are to regulate and direct their whole life.

Although each of these statements is focused on the restraining aspect of the law, nothing is mentioned about these laws being necessary as a means to advance justice or have anything to do with enhancing love or freedom. There is only a formal acknowledgement of the law as regulating and directing the life of the regenerate, but in practice, the German Church historically paid very little attention to this fact as well. As a consequence, Lutheran jurisprudence has remained largely in the shadows of legal positivism. As Harold Berman points out:

> Lutheran legal philosophy rejects the definition of law proposed by Thomas Aquinas: that law is an ordinance of reason for the common good made by one having the care of the community. Such a definition, according to Lutheran thought, gives an unwarranted sanctity to both law and reason. It rests on an overoptimistic conception of human nature and consequently on an overoptimistic conception of the rule of the state as an instrument of justice. A lawfully promulgated degree of a sovereign is law, in Lutheran philosophy, even though it is arbitrary in its purpose and effect.[79]

In his letter to the Romans, the Apostle Paul stated: "God appoints governing officials as servants for human good, agents of God to bring punishment on wrongdoers (Rom. 13:1–5). Short of a universal change of heart, the law is required as a means to achieve justice by punishing evil. And since Luther was highly suspicious of any further beneficial aspect of the law, the more optimistic view of the law which is found in the letter of James was promptly rejected. In the first chapter of his letter, the Apostle James comments:

> But be doers of the word, and not hearers only, deceiving yourselves. For if anyone is a hearer of the world and not a doer, he is like a man observing his natural face in a mirror. For he observes himself, goes away, and immediately forgets what kind of man he was. But he who looks into the perfect law of liberty and continues in it, and is not a forgetful hearer but a doer of the work, this one will be blessed in what he does.[80]

At first glance this paragraph appears to contradict Romans 3:28: "Man is justified by faith apart from the deeds of the law." However, James and Paul are not contradicting each other, but completing each other. "The perfect law of liberty" identified by James can also be called "the perfect law that gives freedom." It does achieve personal freedom not by pointing to our sinful nature but by giving

---

79 Harold J Berman, *Law and Revolution II: The Impact of the Protestant Reformations on the Western Legal Tradition* (Cambridge, MA: Harvard University Press, 2003), 98.
80 James 1:22–25.

us the opportunity to seek God's mercy and forgiveness. Since Luther could not understand James' argument, he ended up calling his letter an "epistle of straw."[81] As a result, Lutheranism became "a primary source of the modern legal positivist's definition of law as the will of the state expressed in rules and enforced by coercive sanctions."[82] This theological view, noted Berman,

> broke the medieval dualism of two official hierarchies, two official legal systems, that of the Church and that of the States. In Protestant countries the Church was now conceived as invisible, a-political, a-legal, and the only sovereignty, the only law, was that of the secular State. The Reformers were skeptical of man's power to create a human law which would reflect eternal law, and explicitly denied that it is the task of the Church as such to develop human law. This Protestant skepticism made possible the development of a Christian legal positivism, which treats law as being in and of itself, as law, morally neutral solely a means of exercise of political power.[83]

Berman then explains how Luther's concept of the law

> made possible the emergence of a theory of law – legal positivism – which treats the law of the state as morally neutral, a means and not an end, a device for manifesting the policy of the sovereign and for securing obedience to it.[84]

John Austin, the eighteenth-century English legal positivist, argued that the study of God's laws is not the "province of jurisprudence."[85] Lutheranism accepts the same premise by sharply distinguishing the law of the state from the law of God, meaning that the former should never be confused with what the law *ought to be*. This kind of contribution eventually freed the state in its capacity to legislate from metaphysical considerations and ecclesiastical influences.[86] As noted by Dr Deagon:

> The very term "positivism" itself connotes the violent positing of law, a use of force to establish and preserve the law, as well as to compel obedience to it. Integral to Austin's definition of law is this notion of sanction for disobedience, namely that obedience by which the legal subject is (en)forced through inflicted evil and pain. Furthermore, this violence is integrated with the use of theological language, such as "sovereign" and "command," for

---

81 Batzig, "Luther, Law and Love."
82 Berman, *Law and Revolution II*, 76.
83 Harold J Berman, "The Influence of Christianity upon the Development of Law," *Oklahoma Law Review* 12 (1959): 94.
84 Harold J Berman, *Law and Revolution: The Formation of the Western Legal Tradition* (Cambridge, MA: Harvard University Press, 1983), 29.
85 John Austin, *The Province of Jurisprudence Determined [1832]* (London: Ashgate, 1998), 8–9.
86 Berman, "The Influence of Christianity upon the Development of Law," 94.

sovereign is an attribute traditionally ascribed to God, as it is ... God who is a willing, superior being and has the power to enforce commands through the violent threat of punishments for disobedience. Austin explicitly admits this much when he notes that God is the ultimate sovereign. Hence, not only is Austin's theory of law characterised by violence, but this violence is linked to a distorted (pagan) theology.[87]

When the Nazis came to power in 1933, most members of the German legal profession professed to be Lutherans. The vast majority of them believed that laws exist to reflect the coercive commands of the state.[88] When one looks at the German legal profession in the 1930s, it is manifestly clear that the vast majority of judges and lawyers were narrow-minded legal positivists who therefore played a decisive role in failing to stand up against the Nazi atrocities. If one considers the 84 names on the 1922 membership list of the Association of Constitutional Lawyers, legal positivists were undoubtedly the dominant group.[89] Some of these lawyers, write Seitzer and Thornhill,

> argued that the evolution of law should be viewed as following purely positive patterns, and that law should be constructed as an internally and systemically consistent unity of principles and norms, relatively closed against normative, purposive, or directly politicized external input. Legal prescriptions, in consequence, should be viewed as nothing more than inner-juridical facts, constructs formed by the law itself to facilitate its own application. On these grounds, they concluded that the validity of law depended on its status as an internally consistent set of rules, and it could not be reconstructed or interpreted on the basis of moral prescriptions.[90]

This was the view commonly shared by most German lawyers, judges, and legal academics in the 1930s.[91] Accordingly, a law can be deemed perfectly valid as long as it satisfies some formal criteria that are entirely procedural and descriptive. As noted by Hans Kelsen, the country's leading legal academic in those days, "a norm becomes law only because it has been constituted in a particular fashion, born of a definite procedure and a definite rule."[92] Kelsen also stated:

> The legal order of totalitarian states authorizes their governments to confine in concentration camps persons whose opinions, religion, or race they do

---

87 Deagon, *From Violence to Peace*, 100.
88 Fred A Brauch, *Is Higher Law Common Law?* (Littleton: Fred Rothman & Co., 1999), 474.
89 Typical of this group were Richard Thomas, Heinrich Triepel and Gerhard Anschütz.
90 Jeffrey Seitzer and Christopher Thornhill, "An Introduction to Carl Schmitt's Constitutional Theory: Issues and Context," in *Carl Schmitt: Constitutional Theory*, ed. J Seitzer, (Durham, NC: Duke University Press, 2008), 10.
91 RA Hughes, GWG Leane, and AA Clarke, *Australian Legal Institutions: Principles, Structure and Organisation* (Sydney: Lawbook Co, 2003), 32.
92 Hans Kelsen, "The Pure Theory of Law – Part 2," *Law Quarterly Review* 51 (1935): 17.

not like; to force them to perform any kind of labor, even to kill them. Such measures may be morally or violently condemned; but they cannot be considered as taking place outside the legal order of those states.[93]

Lon Fuller once explained that such a narrow legal positivism inevitably paved the way for National Socialism.[94] When the Nazis first moved against the Jews, the "good" German lawyers, those who did not agree with the Nazi regime, found themselves effectively "disarmed" by their own legal positivism.[95] This would not have been so if these lawyers had responded to the injustices of the regime with a "principled denunciation" rooted in the traditional Christian principles of natural law. However, as Professor Rice points out, the prevailing jurisprudential approach of those German lawyers who were ideologically opposed to Nazism made them "entirely defenceless against laws of arbitrary or criminal content."[96]

One such lawyer who became deeply disarmed by his own philosophy was the celebrated Gustav Radbruch (1878–1949). He believed that the secular ruler could enact any law whatsoever as long as it could be consistently enforced. A law would be valid insofar as it had been properly enacted, regardless of its substantive nature. After contending that the stability of a legal system depended on our duty to faithfully obey the law, Radbruch concluded:

> It is the professional duty of the judge to validate the law's claim to validity, to sacrifice his own sense of the right to the authoritative command of the law, to ask only what is legal and not if it is also just.[97]

Radbruch lived long enough to witness the disastrous consequences of his jurisprudential approach. After witnessing all the horrors of the Nazi regime, he gradually changed his mind and began to question whether his own positivism might have offered no jurisprudential grounds for the invalidity of Nazi legislation. Published posthumously in 1950, readers of the fourth edition of Radbruch's *Rechtsphilosophie* (*Philosophy of Law*) observed the author's embracing of a new jurisprudential approach which informed that, "where there is not even an attempt at justice, where equality, the core of justice, is deliberately betrayed in the issuance of positive law, the statute is not merely 'false law', it lacks completely the very nature of law."[98]

---

93 Ibid.
94 Lon L Fuller, "Positivism and Fidelity to Law: A Reply to Professor Hart," *Harvard Law Review* 71, no. 4 (1958): 630–72.
95 Charles Rice, "Some Reasons for a Restoration of Natural Law Jurisprudence," *Wake Forest Law Review* 24 (1989): 567.
96 Ibid.
97 Gustav Radbruch, "Legal Philosophy," in *The Legal Philosophies of Lask, Radbruch, and Dabin*, ed. Kurt Wilk (Cambridge, MA: Harvard University Press, 1950), 119.
98 Gustav Radbruch, *Rechtsphilosophie* (Stuttgart: KF Koehler Verlag, 1970), 298.

Radbruch's refreshing revisitation of his own legal philosophy came about as a natural result of the disastrous consequences of totalitarian rule under National Socialism. Of course, not every German lawyer who lived in the 1930s embraced legal positivism. However, it is clear that the majority did and this concurrence constituted a leading factor in the legitimisation of the totalitarian regime. The dominance of legal positivism, writes Gary Scott Smith, "seriously inhibited any reaction against the Nazi perversion of legal forms."[99] Positivism, at the very least, saw a considerable number of "good" German lawyers "rationalise to themselves and others their interpretation and application of laws they might, upon reflection, have considered grotesquely unjust or immoral."[100]

Final Considerations

Martin Luther did numerous things to advance the Gospel of love, including the idea that we are sinners needing God's grace, so that salvation is acquired via the mercy of God towards all those who come to him in repentance and full acknowledgement of Jesus Christ as their Lord and Saviour. However, ideas have consequences and to the sorrow of the German people there was within Lutheranism an inadequate view of God's law and its significance as a means by which believers can advance justice and demonstrate love to their neighbours. Under traditional Lutheran theology, the idea of law is perceived in a negative way, as an enemy that convicts people of sin and leads them to judgment. Believing that human selfishness and sin are pervasive in the world, advocates of this theological approach believe that a Christian cannot create a righteous society in the world through political action. At best, they can retard the spread of evil in their countries.[101]

Luther also unconsciously planted the virus of unquestioning servility in the bloodstream of the German people. He encouraged Germans to embrace a quietist form of retreat from the public life. His "Two Kingdoms" doctrine was eventually used to legitimate the all-encompassing sovereignty of the German state. Such a blind deference to temporal authority, which Lutheranism heavily promotes, results in a submissive attitude towards the government that can ultimately result in a deference to un-Christian regimes. This unquestionably contributed to the Church's shameful acquiescence to the Third Reich.[102]

There is no room in this sort of political theology for an authentic jurisprudence of love, particularly when it comes to the interpretation and application of positive laws. Luther's writings became a contributing factor to the rise of

---

99 George Breckenridge, "Legal Positivism and the Natural Law: The Controversy Between Professor Hart and Professor Fuller," *Vanderbilt Law Review* 18 (1964–1965): 950.
100 Ibid., 1826.
101 Gary Scott Smith, "Introduction," in *God and Politics: Four Views on the Reformation of Civil Government*, ed. Gary Scott Smith (Phillipsburg, PA: Presbyterian and Reformed Publishing Company, 1989), 1.
102 Robert F Goeckel, *The Lutheran Church and the East German State: Political Conflict and Change Under Ulbricht and Honecker* (Ithaca, NY: Cornell University Press, 1990), 18.

modern legal positivism and its jurisprudential view of the legal system as nothing more than the coercive commands of the state. As noted by Holborn, "submission with complete obedience was the supreme and absolute law that Luther preached, in all matters except one, namely religious conviction."[103]

Of course, nobody should be so unfair as to suggest that the great reformer would have ever envisaged the disastrous consequences of his political theology. The role of Lutheranism in the legitimisation of un-Christian regimes lies not so much in Luther's teachings concerning the amazing love and mercy of God, but instead in the practical effects of a political theology that contains a significant element of legal positivism. Combined with Luther's writings on the Jews, the role ascribed to the state in Lutheran theology undoubtedly offered an opportunity for the Nazi leadership to rationalise their evil actions as something that, in their own twisted minds, even amounted to an "endorsement" of Lutheranism and a "completion" of the German Reformation.

---

103 Hajo Holborn, *A History of Modern Germany: The Reformation* (Princeton, NJ: Princeton University Press, 1967), 190.

Part II
Law, Love, and Political Theology

5 Law and Love in Monasticism

Joshua Neoh

Introduction

Alasdair MacIntyre ends his book, *After Virtue*, with this closing line: "We are waiting not for a Godot, but for another – doubtless very different – St. Benedict."[1] This closing line is so tantalising that it has spawned a series of scholarly discussions, as well as a recent popular bestseller,[2] about what exactly we are waiting for. Its prophetic tone has added to its enigma. It is helpful to quote the paragraph in full here:

> It is always dangerous to draw too precise parallels between one historical period and another; and among the most misleading of such parallels are those which have been drawn between our own age in Europe and North America and the epoch in which the Roman empire declined into the Dark Ages. Nonetheless certain parallels there are. A crucial turning point in that earlier history occurred when men and women of good will turned aside from the task of shoring up the Roman imperium and ceased to identify the continuation of civility and moral community with the maintenance of that imperium. What they set themselves to achieve instead – often not recognizing fully what they were doing – was the construction of new forms of community within which the moral life could be sustained so that both morality and civility might survive the coming ages of barbarism and darkness. If my account of our moral condition is correct, we ought also to conclude that for some time now we too have reached that turning point. What matters at this stage is the construction of local forms of community within which civility and the intellectual and moral life can be sustained through the new dark ages which are already upon us. And if the tradition of the virtues was able to survive the horrors of the last dark ages, we are not entirely without grounds for hope. This time, however, the barbarians are not waiting beyond the frontiers; they have already been governing us for quite some time. And

---

1 Alasdair MacIntyre, *After Virtue* (London: Bloomsbury Publishing, 2013), 245.
2 Rod Dreher, *The Benedict Option: A Strategy for Christians in a Post-Christian Nation* (New York: Penguin, 2017).

DOI: 10.4324/9781003148920-8

it is our lack of consciousness of this that constitutes part of our predicament. We are waiting not for a Godot, but for another – doubtless very different – St. Benedict.[3]

St Benedict was the author of the most widely used monastic rule in the West. The Rule of Saint Benedict served as the constitution for monastic communities. The rule constituted monasticism as a form of social organisation. In the ancient world, monasticism created "new forms of community within which the moral life could be sustained so that both morality and civility might survive the coming ages of barbarism and darkness." In the present world, the appeal to St Benedict is thus an appeal to re-create such "local forms of community within which civility and the intellectual and moral life can be sustained through the new dark ages which are already upon us." Whatever it is that MacIntyre actually meant to suggest in his closing line, what he could not have meant is that everyone should be a monk, not least because in a world where everyone is a monk, and assuming monks remain celibate, the community would disappear within a generation, and there would be no community left to speak of. It would be a community to end all communities.

If MacIntyre could not have meant that everyone should be a monk, then what could he have meant? Perhaps he meant that some of the values that were central to creating the ancient monastic form of life would be needed to create the new "local forms of community" today that would enable us to preserve "morality and civility" and survive "the new dark ages which are already upon us." If so, what are the values that monasticism can recommend to us today? This chapter argues that the two candidate values that monasticism can recommend to us today are the values of law and love, particularly the way monasticism bridges those values. This chapter will mount the argument in three parts. The first part returns to the origins of monasticism to see how it brought together the values of law and love. The second part explores the ways in which those values are realised in a monastic community. The third and final part examines how those values can be transposed from a monastic community to a political community.

Origins of Monasticism[4]

Neither Christ, the first founder of Christianity, nor Paul, the second founder of Christianity, found monasticism. Monasticism was a latecomer to the scene. What Paul did was to raise a puzzle to which monasticism provided a resolution. The puzzle was the relationship between law and love. Fresh from encountering Christ on the road to Damascus, Paul's conversion led him to challenge the

---

3 MacIntyre, *After Virtue*, 244–5.
4 Parts of this section are drawn from Joshua Neoh, "Jurisprudence of Love in Paul's Letter to the Romans," *Law in Context* 34, no. 1 (January 2016): 7.

Pharisaic view of law as mediating one's relationship with God and with one another. On this Pharisaic view, law is part of Israel's juridical-theological covenant with God. The covenant with God is an "alliance between God and his people [and the] observance of the law is what cements it."[5] Righteousness requires the maintenance of status within the covenantal community through obedience to the law of God, as revealed to Israel, the people of God.[6] The law of God exists as positive law, as law that is posited by God to the Israelites. In challenging this view of law, Paul proclaims that "Christ is the end of law."[7]

For Paul, Christ is love. The new Christian community promises to be a community sustained not by law, but by love. Love is life, while law is death: "I was once alive apart from the law, but when the commandment came, sin revived and I died."[8] In place of the view of law as mediating one's relationship with God, Christ promises to restore the immediacy of the divine–human relationship. Paul claims that all the commandments of the law can be reduced to and summed up in this one single command: love.[9] As Paul says, "love is genuine."[10] Love is that "which alone effectuates the unity of thought and action in the world."[11] For Paul, love is both a verb and a noun. As a verb, it denotes a particular way of acting in the world. However, as a noun, it denotes a particular way of being in the world. Hence, it makes sense to say that God *is* love. Love as a noun precedes love as a verb: the state of being in love leads to the performance of certain acts and endows those acts with a certain quality, such that we can call them acts of love. Acts of love are not legal obligations. Speaking to the new Christian community in Rome, Paul says, "we are discharged from the law, dead to that which held us captive, so that we serve not under the old written code but in the new life of the Spirit."[12] Unlike law, love cannot be codified. That new life of the Spirit would be founded on love, not law. All you need is love.

This talk of love is all well and good, but can any community, here on earth, actually live without law? The early Christian community could not, not even after listening to Paul's soaring rhetoric about love replacing law. Those early days were heady days. Paul's uplifting letters might have been able to lift their spirits up for a while, but they needed to get on with the business of living – and living *together* – on earth. Living together requires coordination, for which law

---

5 Tracy McNulty, "The Event of the Letter: Two Approaches to the Law and Its Real," *Cardozo Law Review* 29, no. 5 (April 2008): 2209.
6 EP Sanders, *Paul and Palestinian Judaism* (Philadelphia, PA: Fortress Press, 1977), 544.
7 Romans 10:4. "End" can mean either termination or telos. In the former sense, Christ brings an end to law. In the latter sense, Christ fulfils the goal of law, but without necessarily bringing it to an end.
8 Romans 7:9.
9 Romans 13:8-10.
10 Romans 12:9.
11 Alan Badiou, *Saint Paul: The Foundation of Universalism*, trans. Ray Brassier (Stanford, CA: Stanford University Press, 2003), 91.
12 Romans 7:6.

is needed. Living together also means living with the possibility of disputes that require adjudication, again for which law is needed. Quarrelsome people need a structure of authority, which law provides, in order to live together, and there is no reason to suppose that Christians are any less quarrelsome. Not even Paul himself could live without law. Paul needed law as much as he detested it. After driving a wedge between law and love, Paul still had to "offer guidance for behavior."[13] His new Christian morals turned out to be remarkably similar to the Jewish mores that he had supposedly left behind. What Paul did, in effect, was to "reinstitute Jewish laws with Christian warrants" by "legislating rules of behaviour ad hoc."[14] He wanted to move from law to love, but he found himself repeatedly pulled back into law. If one cannot abandon law, then one has to learn to live with it, by coming to terms with it. Coming to terms with it, in the context of Christianity, means understanding law in terms of love. The question is how.

Enter monasticism.[15] After the apostolic age came the patristic age. Just as the leading light of the apostolic age was Paul, so the leading light of the patristic age was Augustine. Among the many significant contributions that Augustine made to the development of Christian theology was his endorsement of monasticism. Augustine established his first monastery in Thagaste in 388 and his second monastery in Hippo in 391, and codified a rule for monks in 397, which came to be known as the Rule of Saint Augustine. In Thagaste and later in Hippo, Augustine created an alternative society of men who rejected sex, wealth, and power in favour of chastity, poverty, and obedience. Obedience was central in creating well-regulated monasteries: the monks should obey their "superior as a father, always with the respect worthy of his position, so as not to offend God in him."[16] In his treatise on the *Work of Monks*, Augustine criticised the "hypocrites in the garb of monks, who went through the provinces, sent by no authority, never stationary, stable, or settled."[17] He contrasted the itinerant monks with the stable and stationary monks who lived under a superior and a rule. In these salutary and stationary monastic communities, the rule would be policed by the mutual surveillance of the monks themselves: "Mutually safeguard your purity ... by your mutual vigilance."[18] "Whoever happened to discover [an infraction of the rule] must report the offender," who upon conviction, "must

---

13 EP Sanders, *Paul, the Law and the Jewish People* (Philadelphia, PA: Fortress Press, 1983), 152.
14 Craig Hill, "Romans," in *The Oxford Bible Commentary*, ed. John Muddiman and John Barton (Oxford: Oxford University Press, 2007), 1087.
15 The following *very* brief history of monasticism is a summary of a longer account that I have provided in Joshua Neoh, *Law, Love and Freedom* (Cambridge: Cambridge University Press, 2019), ch. 4.
16 Augustine, "Praeceptum," trans. George Lawless, in *Augustine of Hippo and His Monastic Rule*, ed. George Lawless (Oxford: Oxford University Press, 1990), §7.1.
17 Augustine, "The Work of Monks," trans. Mary Muldowney, in *Treatises on Various Subjects*, ed. Roy Deferrari (Washington, DC: Catholic University of America Press, 2014), 384.
18 Augustine, "Praeceptum," §4.6.

submit to the salutary punishment determined by the judgement of the superior," which included corporal punishment.[19] Even if, perchance, his actions were to escape the notice of his fellow monks, he still could not escape the constant surveillance of "the One who keeps watch on high, from whom nothing can be hidden," for "God sees everything."[20] Although the rule would be enforced rigorously, the obedience had to be done out of love and not fear, for the *mores* of the monastery should be founded on the *amores* of the monks.[21] The chief goal of the rule was to enable the multitude of monks "to live harmoniously in the house and to have *one heart and one soul* seeking God."[22] To that end, "let no one work for himself alone, but all your work shall be for the common purpose."[23] Ultimate freedom was to be found in complete obedience to the common rule.

The Rule of Saint Augustine was followed by the Rule of the Four Fathers, the Second Rule of the Fathers, the Rule of Macarius, the Third Rule of the Fathers, the Oriental Rule, and the Rule of the Master, culminating in the Rule of Saint Benedict in the sixth century. As the rules developed, they became more elaborate, and the office of the abbot became more powerful. The Council of Chalcedon in 451 made clear that, although a monastery was subject to the territorial jurisdiction of the local diocesan bishop, the bishop could not exercise his episcopal powers within the monastery, and the monks, unless they were clerics, were subject to the authority of the abbot alone. When speaking of the different kinds of monks in the opening chapter, the *Rule of Saint Benedict* singles out "those who live in monasteries and serve under a rule and an abbot" as "the strongest kind of monks."[24] The *Rule of Saint Benedict* asserts its own supremacy, when it prescribes that "everybody should follow the Rule as a master in all things and nobody should rashly deviate from it," including the abbot, who "should do everything in fear of God and in observance of the Rule."[25] The rule required a total commitment to communitarianism. The monks possessed nothing individually, not even their lives. They led a well and truly common life. The vow of poverty dispossessed them of their external goods, and the vow of obedience dispossessed them of their internal will. Thenceforth, whatever they owned, they owned in common, and whatever they willed, they willed in common. They saw themselves as creating the ideal Christian community here on earth. They created a separate world within the walls of the monastery. They provided those in the City of Man with a glimpse of the City of God. In humanity's fallen condition, the monastery was "the nearest that men could get to a society in which

---

19 Ibid., §4.8-9.
20 Ibid., §4.5.
21 George Lawless, *Augustine of Hippo and His Monastic Rule*, 22.
22 Augustine, "Praeceptum," §1.2 (emphasis added).
23 Ibid., §5.2.
24 Benedict, *The Rule of Saint Benedict*, trans. Bruce Venarde (Cambridge, MA: Harvard University Press, 2011), ch. 1.
25 Benedict, ch. 3.

the bonds between its members were restored to their original [prelapsarian] integrity."[26]

When St Benedict wrote his rule in 529, after the sack of Rome in 410, it must have looked like the end of civilisation. The empire was in decay, and the future looked bleak. As the world descended into the Dark Ages, the monks made a strategic retreat from the world. The monks left the world to the barbarians and cloistered themselves behind the walls of the monastery. Within the monastery, they dedicated themselves to God and made a commitment to one another to set up a new form of moral order, as the Dark Ages descended upon Europe. The utopianism of monasticism was a form of radical protest against the existing order of the world: "Monks withdrew from the world to show how they imagined a perfectly Christian life should be," as an earthly sign of the heavenly kingdom.[27] The early monastic code writers – from St Augustine to St Benedict – were the authors of the first rules that provided "comprehensive rationalizations of behaviour and attitudes."[28] The monastery became an institutionalised utopia. These rules created a form of life, with its own form of moral order. Obedience to authority was a central feature of this new form of moral order.

It is unclear whether Paul would have approved of what the monks did. What is most striking about the transformation of ideas from Paul to the monastic ideal is in the role of law. Although Paul never crossed the Rubicon into antinomianism, he clearly saw law as a stumbling block to religious life. He was not a fan of law, to put it mildly. This lukewarm attitude to the role of law in religious life disappeared when the monk came on the scene. Law changed from being the stumbling block to being the building block of religious life. Law, with the order and regularity that it brings, is central to the religious life of the monk. This nomian change is "revolutionary," in the two senses of the word. It is revolutionary in the sense that it is a dramatic turn away from Paul's dim view of the law. But it is also revolutionary in the sense that it is a re-turn to the original Pharisaic view of the law as constitutive of one's relationship to God and neighbour, which is the view that Paul was reacting against to begin with. With monasticism, Christianity came full circle.

Monastic Community[29]

To examine more closely the monastic form of life, let's consider the word *habit*. In common parlance, habit denotes a regular way of doing things. On a larger

---

26 RA Markus, *The End of Ancient Christianity* (Cambridge: Cambridge University Press, 1990), 80.
27 Enzo Pace, "Seguy and the Monastic Utopia," in *Sociology and Monasticism: Between Innovation and Tradition*, ed. Isabelle Jonveaux, Enzo Pace and Stefania Palmisano (Leiden: Brill, 2014), 279.
28 Abbruzzese, Salvatore, "Monastic Asceticism and Everyday Life," in Jonveaux, Pace, and Palmisano, *Sociology and Monasticism*, 10.
29 Parts of this section are drawn from Neoh, *Law, Love and Freedom*, ch. 4.

scale, it can denote a way of being and acting, or even an entire way of life. In the monastic context, habit also refers to the robe that monks wear. Monks don the habit. The donning of the habit operates on two levels: it is the wearing of a physical item of clothing as well as the taking on of a particular way of life. These two levels of meaning merge through a process of allegorisation, whereby each item of clothing is made to symbolise an aspect of the monastic way of life, for example, the hood is a symbol of simplicity, the mantle is a symbol of humility, the belt is a symbol of readiness to fight for Christ, and so on.[30] Consider the other closely related word *inhabit*. Monks inhabit the monastery, thereby committing themselves to a form of communal habitation. They inhabit not only a place, but also a style of dress and a form of life.

Their form of life is created by law. Monks create their own legal structure in the monastery. Their rules are codified and read to them daily during mealtimes. They eat in silence as the lector reads them the rules. Their entire existence is regulated by the monastic code. Monastic codes contain an "imposing mass of punctilious precepts and ascetic techniques, of cloisters and horologia, of solitary temptations and choral liturgies, of fraternal exhortations and ferocious punishments."[31] They dictate, sometimes in fine detail, what to wear and what to eat, when to speak and when to keep silent, what prayers to say and what thoughts to think. In so doing, the code constructs a form of life: "A life that is linked so closely to its form that it proves to be inseparable from it."[32] The form of life is created through the mechanism of rules. Obedience to authority, entrenched in the impersonal code and embodied in the person of the abbot, is total.

Every hour of existence is regulated, such that a monk's entire existence is given up to what the Church calls the Liturgy of the Hours. The prescribed prayers throughout the day and night constitute the Divine Office, which transports the monks to a higher time than the secular time of the world. Unlike the rest of the world that lives in secular time (the *saeculum*), the monks live in sacred time, for every moment of the monk's life is sacralised by its submission to – or more accurately, its subsumption under – the monastic law. The monastic law is totalitarian, insofar as it claims to regulate, not only single acts and events, but also the entire existence of an individual.[33] The monks live their lives under the constant gaze, not only of God, but also of the other monks. Theirs is a separate and parallel community to that of the family and the state, only better, for theirs is a more perfect communion. The authority of law makes all that possible for them.

The goal of this law-based form of communal life is grand: love as union. Through this lawful form of life, the monks seek to be of "one mind and one heart," horizontally with each other and vertically with God. Augustine places

---

30 Giorgio Agamben, *The Highest Poverty: Monastic Rules and Form-of-Life*, trans. Adam Kotsko (Stanford, CA: Stanford University Press, 2013), 13–16.
31 Ibid., xi.
32 Ibid., xi.
33 Ibid., 26.

tremendous emphasis on the quality of single-mindedness in the monastery, where monks have "chosen to dwell with one accord in fellowship together under the same roof, to have 'one soul and one heart' unto God."[34] The union of love is achieved through the authority of law, for it is law that creates the common life for the monks which makes union possible. The other word for monasticism, *cenoby*, expresses this goal perfectly. *Cenoby* originates from the term *koinos bios*, which literally means the common life. The perfection that the monks seek is not individual perfection, but the formation of a perfect community. Monasticism provides us with a model of what a "total communitarian life" would look like.[35] It offers us a glimpse of another world, with a different form of social organisation.[36] The monastic community has always been anomalous amid the wider community, but "in that anomaly resided its special function": its existence as an alternative mode of social ordering "proclaims a challenge to all other forms of social existence" amidst the society of the fallen.[37]

The monastic rules constituted a total and comprehensive code of conduct for the monks. To belong to a monastery was to be part of a consecrated *order*. The monastic code not only reshaped the monk's life, but it also reshaped his sense of time. The monk's time, structured symbolically, "no longer matched with the one that regulates the universe of ordinary life."[38] In the words of Paul, the monks were "redeeming the time, because the days are evil."[39] The monastic community was to be a perfect union in perfect time. At the heart of it was the division between physical work and spiritual prayer. When the hermits first went out to the desert, they thought that they could devote themselves totally to prayer alone. They initially, and naively, "thought that they did not need to work," for "God would provide for their survival," but the early Desert Fathers soon realised that "they could not live as angels and that work was a necessity for their material or biological survival."[40] Consequently, time for prayer and time for work – *ora et labora* – were both institutionalised in the monastic rules when the first monasteries were founded. Although work responded to certain material necessities, it was also presented as a moral demand that aided the task of contemplation. Work was needed to control the desires of the flesh. The monks aimed to achieve total control of their natural impulses by living a methodical life, which involved the routinisation and rationalisation of work and prayer. The routine of work and the rhythm of prayer, as defined by the rules, constituted the regular

---

34 Augustine, *Select Letters*, trans. James Baxter (Cambridge, MA: Harvard University Press, 1930), Ep CCXI, 377.
35 Agamben, *The Highest Poverty*, 9.
36 Larry Siedentop, *Inventing the Individual: The Origins of Western Liberalism* (Cambridge, MA: Harvard University Press, 2014), 99.
37 Markus, *End of Ancient Christianity*, 81, 159.
38 Abbruzzese, "Monastic Asceticism," 7.
39 Ephesians 5:16.
40 Isabelle Jonveaux, "Redefinition of the Role of Monks in Modern Society: Economy as Monastic Opportunity," in Jonveaux, Pace, and Palmisano, *Sociology and Monasticism*, 72.

life of the monks. Monastic rules brought regulation, and hence regularity, into the lives of the monks.

The monastic life may be totalitarian, but it need not be oppressive. In fact, monasticism is a paradigmatic example of how a form of life can be totalitarian and free, as long as there is identification. Identification is doing all the work of freedom here. By setting themselves apart, spiritually and physically, from the private sphere of the family and the public sphere of the polity, the monks find their identification elsewhere. They identify with something else entirely, that is, with something entirely otherworldly. Mystics may enjoy sparks of momentary ecstasy, but for the vast majority of monks, this process of identification is "understood as a laborious, lifetime quest."[41] The distinctive vow that monks make, which other religious orders do not, is the vow of *conversatio morum*, the conversion of life, to live the rule. In monks, we find a conjoining of the joy of freedom with the vow of obedience. For them, freedom consists "in the self-imposition of rules,"[42] which is really the self-identification with the rules that are imposed by the monastic code. The self-identification is pronounced through the profession of the monastic vows at the time of admission. Freedom is to be found, not in rebellion, but in obedience: "Obedience becomes perfect when the one who commands and the one who obeys come to share one mind."[43] The freedom that the monks seek is not one of independence, but identification.

As the Church grew in power, prestige, and privilege, monasteries grew along with it from the ancient to the medieval period. "The High Middle Ages were above all a period of expansion in Christian monasticism."[44] Monasteries grew in number and size. Despite the vow of poverty, the monasteries also grew in wealth. The more wealth accumulated, the more the practice of monasticism appeared to depart from the promise of monasticism. The gap between practice and promise could only be tolerated to a certain degree before reform movements would emerge to demand that the practice fulfil its promise. Within monasticism, there were cycles of reform to return the practice to its promise. The reform of the Benedictine Order resulted in the creation of the Cistercian Order. The reform of the Cistercian Order, in turn, resulted in the creation of the Order of Cistercians of the Strict Observance. Thus, monastic orders proliferated. The cycles of reform were the inevitable consequence of the growth in wealth, which was the inevitable consequence of the work habit of the monk, which combined a strict regimentation of labour with an equally strict restriction on the consumption of the fruits of one's labour. Under such conditions, wealth would accumulate as a matter of course. Notwithstanding the actual accumulation of wealth in monasteries, the active pursuit of wealth, like that of

---

41 Siedentop, *Inventing the Individual*, 96.
42 Siedentop, 98.
43 Herbert McCabe, *God Matters* (New York: Continuum, 1987), 228–9.
44 Randall Collins, *Weberian Sociological Theory* (Cambridge: Cambridge University Press, 1986), 52.

a merchant, remained "a pudendum which was to be tolerated,"[45] but neither endorsed nor encouraged.

The actual accumulation of wealth in monasteries was thought to be an accidental accumulation. Aristotle famously said that the end of human association was "life and the good life." In monasteries, the production and accumulation of goods was necessary for life, but it did not constitute the good life for the monks. Physical labour was needed to satisfy the demands of life, but it was not the high life. The high life consisted in the High Mass, that is, liturgical worship. Physical labour was a prelude to liturgical worship. While labour and liturgy together made up the activities of the monk, labour had to be confined in order to free up time for the more important task of liturgical worship. The monks had to work, but they should not work too hard, for work had to be balanced with prayer. They had to work smart. Hence, labour was confined through the adoption of systematic and rationalised work practices. Once the requirements of labour were satisfied and life taken care of, the monks could then turn to what truly mattered. The highest form of monastic productivity was not the increase in grains, but the "increase of the *thesaurus ecclesia* [the spiritual treasure of the church] through prayer and chant."[46] Therein lay the good life.

Political Community

Is it possible for the monastic ideal to be turned into a political ideal? MacIntyre's suggestion in *After Virtue*, which is quoted at the start of this chapter, hints at that possibility, as a way to sustain us "through the new dark ages which are already upon us." As mentioned earlier, the features that are carried over from a monastic community to a political community cannot include celibacy for all. A requirement of celibacy for all would lead to the community disappearing within a generation – it would be a community to end all communities. Therefore, the transformation of a monastic community into a political community would call for the transposition of the values from a monastic community to a political community, without carrying over every single feature from the former to the latter. There is no real-world illustration of that transformation, so we have to turn to literary imagination to see what that kind of world might look like. For that, there is no better literary source than More's *Utopia*.

Utopia is isolated. The isolationism of utopianism begins with *contemptus mundi*, a contempt for the world: "Do not love the world or the things of the world."[47] A person who is contemptuous of the world would seek a retreat from it in order to create an alternative world, which is more perfect, and which is able to serve as a living critique of the world that is left behind. This sentiment

---

45 Max Weber, *The Protestant Ethic and the Spirit of Capitalism*, trans. Talcott Parsons (London: Routledge, 2001), 35.
46 Weber, *Protestant Ethic*, 106.
47 1 John 2:15-17.

underlies MacIntyre's exhortation to retreat from shoring up the contemptible world whose moral framework is crumbling, and to build instead new forms of community within which the moral life can be sustained. That, too, is the mission of monasticism, which is to leave "the world and its pomps" behind, in a flight from the world to the wilderness. The sense of *contemptus mundi* is expressed in literature, particularly in More's *Utopia*, through the literary device of estrangement, "by taking the reader to a remote and paradise-like isle, from where to criticize the society of departure."[48] Utopia is located on "an isolated island, rarely visited by foreigners and, thus, able to develop its wonderful institutions without interference."[49] "The city is surrounded by a high, thick wall with many towers and bastions,"[50] which is designed to "create a safe environment, free from the bad influence of the outer world, much like a [monastic] sanctuary, a Christian haven where perfection can at least be attempted."[51] The isolationism has to be enforced, if necessary. "If someone takes it upon himself to wander outside his territory, when he is caught without the ruler's passport, he is treated with contempt, brought back as a runaway, and severely punished."[52] The imposition of stringent constraints on travel in Utopia resembles the limitations imposed on monks, who cannot leave the monastery as they please, "since departure from the cloister is supposed to endanger the commitment to the good and holy life that the routine of communal living makes easier to follow."[53]

MacIntyre wishes for the "new forms of community" to be shining lights of civility amidst the darkness and barbarism that has descended upon the world. These new forms of community would, first, be a critique of the world, and then, be a model for the world. That wish is eminently Utopian, for that is precisely what Utopos did. Utopos, who founded Utopia, "brought its crude and rustic mob to a level of culture and humanity beyond almost all other mortals," so much so that "the neighboring peoples (who at first ridiculed the project as silly) were overwhelmed with wonder and fear."[54] Utopia is supposed to be a true *commonwealth* that is "not only the best but also the only kind worthy of the name."[55] Utopia, which is a model for the lesser mortals, is itself modelled on the monastery. For More, "the ideal commonwealth was that represented by the monastery."[56] More attributed to the Utopians many of the details of monastic

---

48 Miguel Martinez Lopez, "Utopian Happiness, Thomas More's Utopia and the Medieval Monastic Ideal," *The Grove: Studies on Medieval English Language and Literature* 8 (2001): 199.
49 Lyman Tower Sargent, "More's Utopia: An Interpretation of Its Social Theory," *History of Political Thought* 5, no. 2 (Summer 1984): 202.
50 Thomas More, *Utopia*, trans. Clarence Miller (New Haven, CT: Yale University Press, 2014), 57.
51 Lopez, "Utopian Happiness," 200.
52 More, *Utopia*, 72.
53 Lopez, "Utopian Happiness," 201.
54 More, *Utopia*, 53.
55 Ibid., 122.
56 Lopez, "Utopian Happiness," 197.

life that he had learned from his time living with the Carthusian monks at the London Charterhouse.[57] The form of life of the Utopians mirrors the "life in common," which is "practiced among the most genuine Christian communities," i.e. monastic communities.[58]

Utopians value uniformity. "Utopians incorporate the monastic proclamation of equality through the rejection of individualism and diversity."[59] They have "the same language, customs, institutions, and laws."[60] Their cities have the same layout and their clothing has the same simple monkish design, with minor variation "only to indicate sex or marital status."[61] On marital status, the Utopians consider the married life more prudent, but they consider the celibate life holier.[62] In the monastic tradition, "the wearing of the same habit, sharing the same table, the same meals, taking part in the same manual or intellectual work, having access to the same specific tradition, the use of the same furniture, the same buildings" eliminate the need for private property.[63] When those features are transposed from the monastic community to a political community in Utopia, the hope is that, where there is no private property, everyone will dedicate themselves to the public good instead of private accumulation. Where everything belongs to everyone, "no one is a pauper or a beggar there, and though no one has anything, all are rich": "For what greater wealth can there be than to be completely spared any anxiety and to live with a joyful and tranquil frame of mind."[64]

Another key feature of both monastic life and Utopian life is the strict division of time. "The day is divided into hours that must always be filled with a clear sense of purpose, avoiding idleness."[65] There is a strict schedule to work, eat, and sleep, and in "the intervals between work, meals, and sleep, they are allowed to spend however they like, provided that the time they have free from work is not wasted in debauchery and idleness but spent well in some other pursuit," particularly "intellectual activities."[66] They have meals in common, accompanied with "some reading that concerns morals."[67] With the eyes of everyone on everyone else, "nowhere is there any chance to be idle"; and with "no wine taverns, no alehouses and no brothels," there is "no excuse for laziness" and "no occasion to be corrupted, no hideouts, no hangouts."[68] Such a life is an eminently rational life.

---

57 PA Duhamel, "Mediaevalism of More's Utopia," in *Essential Articles for the Study of Thomas More*, ed. RS Sylvester and GP Marc'hadour (Hamden, CT: Archon Books, 1977), 234.
58 More, *Utopia*, 117.
59 Lopez, "Utopian Happiness," 200.
60 More, *Utopia*, 53.
61 Ibid., 60.
62 Ibid., 122.
63 Jean Seguy, "A Sociology of Imagined Societies: Monasticism and Utopia," in Jonveaux, Pace, and Palmisano, *Sociology and Monasticism*, 304.
64 More, *Utopia*, 130.
65 Lopez, "Utopian Happiness," 201.
66 More, *Utopia*, 61.
67 Ibid., 71.
68 Ibid., 73.

"In the absence of religious inspiration from heaven revealing something holier," the Utopians have to rely on their powers of reason to construct their ideal form of life.[69] What they have come up with is, to them, a rational form of life, which is, as it turns out, a mirror image of the monastic form of life. What can be inferred from this similarity, or what More wants to convey using this similarity, is that the monastic form of life is a rational form of life, with a rationalised pattern of daily activities. Rationality requires that the Utopians "do not trust the reasoning capacity of the average citizen," but instead place their trust in the basic institutions as laid out by the rational lawmaker Utopos,[70] just as how the monks place their trust, not in their individual rational capacity, but in the basic framework as laid out by the writers of the ancient monastic codes.

The basic institutions, which create the form of life in Utopia, are constituted by law. The full title of Book 2, in which More describes in exquisite detail the form of life in Utopia, is "The End of the Afternoon Discourse of Raphael Hythloday about the *Laws and Institutions* of the Little-known Island of Utopia" (emphasis added). Utopia has no lawyers, but that does not mean that it has no law. More has a dislike of lawyers, but not of the law itself. In one of those strange twists of history, despite More's disdain for lawyers, More was later canonised as the patron saint of lawyers. Like in Utopia, monastic life too is constituted by law. The Rule of Saint Benedict makes the abbot the master of the monastery, but the abbot is not above the rule of law, for the abbot himself is subject to the rule, along with all the other monks.[71] All are subject to the rule of law. The communal life, both of the monks and the Utopians, is "embedded in a network of superior–inferior relationships," in which the junior member must obey the senior member of the community, and everyone must obey the law.[72] Rules are enforced within a strict hierarchical structure of authority. Obedience to one's immediate superior and ultimately to the law is absolutely central. "Pride must be eliminated at any cost by imposing obedience."[73] Fallen human nature needs to have legal restraints to prevent it from falling even further. "The only thing which could keep people from sin was a meticulously designed set of rules and regulations, constant supervision, and harsh punishment."[74] The monastic disciplinary method, which is writ large in Utopia, prescribes major punishments even for minor infractions of the law.[75] This better-world in the monastery and on the island of Utopia is "bounded on all sides by rules and regulations."[76] It is only when human nature is kept in check by law that love can flourish.

---

69 Ibid., 91.
70 Sargent, "More's Utopia," 210.
71 Seguy, "Sociology of Imagined Societies," 313.
72 Sargent, "More's Utopia," 202.
73 Lopez, "Utopian Happiness," 202.
74 Sargent, "More's Utopia," 209.
75 Ibid., 202.
76 Ibid., 206.

Conclusion

Paul drove a wedge between law and love. For Paul, law imprisons, but love liberates.[77] Notwithstanding Paul's reservations about the law, he did not abandon law entirely. Paul never crossed the Rubicon into antinomianism. What Paul expressed was a deep scepticism about the law, a scepticism which he passed on to the nascent Christian movement. His equivocation on the role of law in religious life created a dilemma that subsequent Christian communities had to confront. The key contribution of monasticism in the history of Christianity was the restoration of the role of law in religious life. By using law as a path to love, monasticism reconciled the tension between law and love that Paul accentuated. Where Paul drove a wedge between law and love, monasticism set out to close the gap. Monasticism did not invent the idea of law as a path to love – it simply restored the idea. The idea itself can be traced back to the old Pharisaic view of the law, which Paul repudiated. The contribution of monasticism is not so much an invention as it is a restoration of an old Jewish idea, but now in a new Christian register.

In tracing the history of ideas from St Paul to St Benedict, one can see two ways of community building. One might build a community on the basis of love alone, in which law plays a minimal and marginal role, as Paul dreamt of doing. In this Pauline model, one's relationship to God and to one another should be, as far as possible, unmediated by law. The relationship should, ideally, be direct and immediate. Law, if it is unavoidable, ought to be confined and kept to a bare minimum. In contrast to this Pauline model, there is the Benedictine model, in which law moves from the margin to the centre. Law is the centrepiece of the monastic form of life. The Rule of Saint Benedict forges a close link between the monastic code and communal love. Communal love in the monastery is facilitated by collective obedience to the monastic code. In this Benedictine model, law is a path to love. As long as it leads to love, there is no problem in having a relationship, either with God or with one another, that is mediated by law.

In tracing the history of ideas from St Benedict to Thomas More, one sees how the Benedictine model can be extrapolated from a monastic community to a political community. More's extrapolation exists in the imagination, not (or not yet) in reality. Monastic law writ large, with suitable modifications, forms the basis of the laws and institutions of Utopia. Just as monastic law is a path to communal love in the monastery, so monastic law writ large is a path to communal love writ large in Utopia. In the closing line of *After Virtue*, MacIntyre appeals to St Benedict to provide us with a political ideal to create a moral haven that will serve as a beacon of hope as darkness descends upon the world. In terms of extracting, or extrapolating, political ideals from Benedict's religious vision, More's imaginative text provides an illustrative example of how that might be done and what the result might look like. More's Utopia transforms Benedict's monastic ideal into a political aspiration. Benedict, plus More, gives us the distinctly *political* idea of law as a path to love.

---

77 Joshua Neoh, "Law Imprisons, Love Liberates," *Law and Literature* 30, no. 2 (2018): 221.

6 The Law of Love as Principles of Civility

Secular Translation or Religious Contribution?

Alex Deagon

Introduction

The principles of civility are the terms of respectful civic engagement in a liberal democracy. When debating policy ideas as part of the normative structure of a political framework, citizens agree to treat each other respectfully and uphold each other's dignity and worth even while they might disagree. Citizens should, as much as possible, make themselves understandable and present good arguments for their political views, while simultaneously seeking to listen to and understand the views of others. This allows the possibility for compromise and refinement of different views in an "open marketplace" of ideas, or what political theorist Veit Bader calls "priority for democracy."[1]

This chapter proposes that the principles of civility can be best understood as part of a theological framework governed by the law of love. The "civic virtues" such as honesty, humility, and grace which comprise the principles of civility are fundamentally Christian virtues which have their meaning expressed in the maxim to "love your neighbour as yourself." The orientation and substance of the principles of civility, or what Nicholas Wolterstorff calls a "moral engagement," make most sense in a Christian framework where the law of love seeks to do justice and implement the good in a political context of profound moral evil.[2] Drawing on John Milbank and the Parable of the Good Samaritan, this chapter contends that it is through the law of love that the principles of civility find their zenith, pointing to their eternal and theological nature. An implication of this argument is that any attempt to "translate" the law of love into purely rational and secular concepts which exclude their theological origins, as Habermas proposes, will limit and dilute the effect of the principles.[3] The full benefit of the

---

1 See Veit Bader, "Religious Pluralism: Secularism or Priority for Democracy," *Political Theory* 27, (1999): 597.
2 See Nicholas Wolterstorff, *Understanding Liberal Democracy: Essays in Political Theology* (Oxford: Oxford University Press, 2012).
3 See e.g. Jürgen Habermas, "Pre-political Foundations of the Democratic Constitutional State?" in *The Dialectics of Secularization. On Reason and Religion*, eds. Jürgen Habermas and Joseph Ratzinger (San Francisco, CA: Ignatius Press, 2006).

principles of civility in a liberal democracy comes through its theological framing as part of the law of love.

The second part of the chapter outlines the principles of civility in a liberal democracy. It identifies the civic virtues of mutual understanding and respect in political discourse and the different dimensions of these virtues. It also explores the idea of moral engagement, which has two aspects. The first, which is similar to the civic virtues, is to bear in mind moral considerations in the conduct of debate, and particularly to treat others with respect. The second aspect of moral engagement broadens the concept of political debate beyond the interactions of reasons to the clash of convictions; it recognises that we live in a society which contains moral evil and so any morally engaged citizen will advocate for policies which, in their view, further justice and the common good.

The third part integrates the (secular) principles of civility with the theological framework provided by the law of love. It argues that the civic virtues and the first aspect of moral engagement are grounded in Christian virtues such as honesty, patience, generosity, grace, and forgiveness, which are purely expressed in the law of love or the maxim to "love your neighbour as yourself." It also argues that Christianity is the paradigm of (the second aspect of) moral engagement in the sense that Christianity posits the existence of profound moral evil, enables the identification of evil as such, and provides the framework for pursuing justice and the good as part of a redeemed future.

The fourth part argues that any attempt to translate the law of love into purely secular categories actually undermines moral engagement by removing the theological language of good and evil and limits the ability of religious citizens in particular to engage morally through religious categories. It also proposes that a theological context points to higher, transcendent sources which inform and strengthen the civic virtues. Therefore, the fifth part concludes, though this chapter does not advocate for a theocratic imposition of the law of love, it does contend that political discourse within the law of love framework will transcend and fulfil the principles of civility, drawing them higher and deeper and wider to most effectively further justice and the good in liberal democracies.

The Principles of Civility in a Liberal Democracy[4]

The principles of civility comprise the civic virtues and a moral engagement, and these will be considered in turn.

---

4 This part draws on my work in Alex Deagon, "Equal Voice Liberalism and Free Public Religion: Some Legal Implications," in *Religious Liberty in Australia: A New Terra Nullius?*, eds. Michael Quinlan, Iain Benson and Keith Thompson (Redland Bay: Connor Court Publishing, 2019); Alex Deagon, "Reconciling John Milbank and Religious Freedom: "Liberalism" through Love," *Journal of Law and Religion* 34, no. 2 (2019): 183.

Civic Virtues

"Priority for democracy" is a phrase coined and developed by Bader, who characterises it as a principle which accounts for the intuition that liberal democracy is not neutral, and so the phrase is "always a shorthand" for a certain approach to "liberal democracy."[5] Priority for democracy means all religious, philosophical, and scientific voices (like votes) should be considered equally when it comes to decision-making.[6] As Bader contends:

> Instead of trying to limit the content of discourse by keeping all contested comprehensive doctrines and truth-claims out, one has to develop the duties of civility, such as the duty to explain positions in publicly understandable language, the willingness to listen to others, fair-mindedness, and readiness to accept reasonable accommodations or alterations in one's own view.[7]

Rather than appealing to the state to censor religious perspectives they do not agree with, the "duties of civility" (part of the "principles of civility" more broadly expressed in this chapter) acknowledge the equal status and dignity of those with religious perspectives and recognise that they share a common identity as "democratic citizen" which allows all perspectives to be publicly displayed and considered. So, the focus is on creating a public space for free and fair discussion of contested views which are equally considered in the decision-making process. Allowing the opportunity for all views to be robustly proposed and debated in a civil manner is a primary feature of liberal democracy. One may, of course, disagree with what is expressed, but the nature of democratic discourse is that all kinds of views should be able to be proposed. It follows that a priority for a democracy model would include all religious or non-religious perspectives compatible with the democratic process, leading to a pluralistic encounter of perspectives which will combine and contribute to policymaking and allow true liberal democracy – the freedom to equally express and decide between a full array of perspectives.[8]

Bader argues that to implement priority for democracy we must focus on "civilised and decent ways of living with disagreement: liberal-democratic culture, attitudes or habits, virtues and traditions of good judgement, and good practice are crucial."[9] These "civic virtues" include "civic integrity" (principled consistency of speech and action) and "civic magnanimity" (open-mindedness and mindfulness

---

5 Bader, "Priority for Democracy," 612.
6 Ibid., 612–13. C.f. for example Jeremy Waldron, *Law and Disagreement* (Oxford: Oxford University Press, 1999).
7 Ibid., 614.
8 Alex Deagon, "Defining the Interface of Freedom and Discrimination: Exercising Religion, Democracy and Same-Sex Marriage," *International Trade and Business Law Review* 20 (2017): 252–3; c.f. Bader, "Priority for Democracy," 617.
9 Bader, "Priority for Democracy," 618.

of the equal moral status of opponents in speech and action).[10] So, the civic virtues include attitudes and actions such as honesty, humility, and patience, demonstrated through serious attempts to argue one's position in an understandable way while duly considering alternative positions, preparing to accept reasonable refinements and accommodations to one's view, and acknowledging the equal dignity and status of all citizens even when you disagree with their views. As will be discussed more below, while acknowledging that "civility" will always need to be backed by constitutional protections, Wolterstorff also advocates for a "moral engagement" between citizens as they engage in equal voice democracy, which entails substantively similar principles.[11] Billingham goes into much more depth on the civic virtues and characterises his similar "argumentative democracy" as realising "valuable relationships between citizens."[12] More specifically:

> Each citizen commits to understanding others' points of view and to engaging in public deliberation as to what decisions best promote justice and the common good. Each takes the arguments that others present seriously and seeks to grapple with those arguments and present defences of his/her own views. Citizens also recognize that the views of each person matter equally, such that decisions should be made democratically, giving each an equal vote and an equal influence over outcomes. These practices are rightly seen as embodying many important aspects of mutual respect and realizing certain goods of friendship and community.[13]

He goes on to explain how argumentative democracy is

> based upon a set of shared commitments that enable citizens to realise a valuable form of community ... Citizens should be committed to acting together based on democratic decisions, to subjecting their views to critical scrutiny, to seeking points of common cause with one another wherever they can be found and to each supporting what they believe to be the best laws – those that best serve true justice and the common good. In this way, they ... develop a sense of shared identity and social unity. In other words, they enjoy civic friendship.[14]

Consequently, Billingham also advocates these civic virtues as an essential part of his argumentative democracy framework, emphasising the communal and civic friendship which results from understanding one's place in a democracy as an equal and valued contributor who genuinely engages with the views of others to seek the common good. In fact, this "civic friendship," itself a form of love

---

10 Ibid., 618–19.
11 Wolterstorff, *Understanding Liberal Democracy*, 138–9; c.f. Hans-Martien Ten Napel, *Constitutionalism, Democracy and Religious Freedom* (London: Routledge, 2017), 92.
12 See Paul Billingham, "Does Political Community Require Public Reason? On Lister's Defence of Political Liberalism," *Politics, Philosophy and Economics* 15, no. 1 (2016): 23.
13 Ibid., 23–24. This also overlaps with Wolterstorff's "moral engagement," explained below.
14 Ibid., 25–26.

(and which is effectively advocated by Bader and Wolterstorff as well), is superior to that which is achieved under public reason liberalism because people "openly engage with other people's beliefs" rather than spurious justifications paternalistically deemed as acceptable for public consideration.[15]

John Inazu expresses this idea as a "confident pluralism" of "mutual respect and coexistence."[16] Such confident pluralism "allows genuine difference to coexist without suppressing or minimising our firmly held convictions. We can embrace pluralism precisely because we are confident in our own beliefs, and in the groups and institutions that sustain them."[17] Confident pluralism "proposes the future of our democratic experiment requires finding a way to be steadfast in our personal convictions" while also allowing fundamental disagreement; we must have a "principled commitment" to "mutual respect" sufficient for at least co-existence and even flourishing.[18] This framework includes the premises of "inclusion" (we seek for those within our boundaries to be part of the political community) and "dissent" (we allow for people to dissent from the norms established by that community).[19] Confident pluralism also includes three "civic practices": "tolerance" (people are free to pursue their own beliefs and practices even if we find them morally objectionable), "humility" (others will find our beliefs and practices morally objectionable and we can't always prove we are right and they are wrong), and "patience" (restraint, persistence, and endurance in our engagements across difference).[20]

Moral Engagement

As mentioned above, Wolterstorff also explicitly connects his "equal voice liberalism" – full, equal political voice in a democracy with constitutional limits – and civic virtues, which he calls moral engagement.[21] This involves legislators employing "moral considerations in deciding which legislation to enact"; it is a "moral engagement" with fellow legislators and citizens.[22] Importantly, it is not required that politicians regard moral considerations in their exercise of political voice, but nor are moral considerations forbidden. Wolterstorff argues that moral engagement can occur in two ways, or at two points. First, the citizen "would bring moral considerations to bear on how he engages with his fellow citizens when he exercises his own political voice and when they exercise theirs. He would in both cases treat them with respect."[23] Wolterstorff believes the "essence" of liberal

---

15 Ibid., 26.
16 John Inazu, *Confident Pluralism: Surviving and Thriving Through Deep Difference* (Chicago, IL: University of Chicago Press, 2016), 8.
17 Ibid., 7.
18 Ibid., 8.
19 Ibid., 9.
20 Ibid., 10–11.
21 C.f. Rowan Williams, *Faith in the Public Square* (London: Bloomsbury, 2012), 135.
22 Wolterstorff, *Understanding Liberal Democracy*, 138.
23 Ibid.

democracy is citizens displaying a "civility," which means respectfully listening to the arguments of others and reconsidering your own if necessary, and accepting a legitimate, democratic majority outcome where full agreement is not reached.[24]

Second, Wolterstorff also broadens the idea of moral engagement to include political advocacy on the basis of one's judgment of what justice or the common good requires.[25] Where a religiously or morally informed conscience objects to particular legislation on moral grounds, it is an exercise in moral engagement (and therefore democratically legitimate, against the public reason liberals) to use one's political voice to advocate against that legislation.[26] In deciding whether to support or oppose particular legislation and candidates for office, the citizen would consider whether the legislation "holds out some promise of correcting some significant injustice in society and of doing so without bringing about some greater injustice," or, in the case of it purporting to bring about the common good, whether it does so without "perpetrating injustice."[27] This second aspect of moral engagement can take the form of broad-based organising, movement organising, and protest organising; it occurs in a context of and is a response to "serious moral evil" which motivates people to act politically.[28] Moral engagement is therefore much broader than the substantively empty "duties of civility" which focus merely on reasons rather than the evils and passions which truly exist at the political level in "fallen societies."[29]

Thus, the category of moral engagement brings an extra dimension to political debate. It is no longer just about what is reasonable and acceptable, but about what the issues mean personally to the person offering the reasons. Some positions are preferences, and for others, citizens "care deeply" about the position for moral reasons; "we can't imagine ourselves not caring deeply about it."[30] Wolterstorff therefore rejects the public reason idea of "shared general principles" in favour of "convergence from ideologically diverse standpoints," which necessitates that those who lose "be willing to live with losing."[31]

The Law of Love as the Principles of Civility[32]

The Virtues of Christianity

Prima facie, it seems that the principles of civility are not feasible without virtues such as honesty, patience, forgiveness, and humility. These virtues have more

---

24 Ibid., 138–9; See Ten Napel, *Constitutionalism*, 92.
25 Wolterstorff, *Understanding Liberal Democracy*, 148.
26 Ibid., 150.
27 Ibid., 139.
28 Ibid., 157–8.
29 Ibid., 160–1, 164.
30 Ibid., 170.
31 Ibid., 171.
32 This part draws from Deagon, "Liberalism through Love"; Alex Deagon, "The Virtues of Public Religion," *Australasian Religious Press Association Annual Conference* (Brisbane, 2018).

significant potency in Christian theology, because they fundamentally characterise what it looks like when we implement the law of love discussed in the New Testament, to love your neighbour as yourself.

Such virtues can be discussed as part of the idea of "public religion" that originally comes from early American debates on the appropriate relationship between religion and the state.[33] A public religion is "some image and ideal of itself," a set of common, public values which reflect and consequently protect private religions.[34] The notion that a state could be neutral and lack a public religion is a philosophical fiction, and absent any shared set of values and beliefs "politicians would invariably hold out their private convictions as public ones. It was thus essential for each community to define and defend the basics of a public religion."[35] The creed of this "public religion" was "honesty, diligence, devotion, obedience, virtue, and love of God, neighbor, and self."[36]

Love of God, neighbour, and self entails the notion of "love your neighbour as yourself" – the law of love articulated by the Apostle Paul in the New Testament.[37] This fulfils the codified law since "love does no wrong to a neighbour."[38] Law can be understood as a principle or set of principles which govern individual relationships within a community. Love involves the voluntary sacrifice of oneself for another. So, the law of love, to "love your neighbour as yourself," is the voluntary giving of oneself for another as the principle which governs individual relationships within a community.[39]

This law of love, modelled on and enabled by the Incarnation and Crucifixion of Christ, consequently encourages love for one's neighbour in terms of humility and sacrifice. Importantly, this is not forced or coerced, but rather freely volunteered as an imitation of Christ in trust that the action will be reciprocated. For each member of the community participates by faith as their mind is persuaded by the revelation of love and peace in the Trinity. It is in this sense that Augustine argues that when a person is persuaded by faith, they will fulfil the law in accordance with the everlasting law (to love your neighbour as yourself) for the good and peace of the society.[40]

Fundamentally in the context of political discourse, the "law of love" approach seeks to create a harmonious space where a person can freely express, debate, and choose faith perspectives without being subject to state, community, or individual antagonism and alienation (violence). There should not be arbitrary

---

33 See John Witte, Jr, "From Establishment to Freedom of Public Religion," *Capital University Law Review* 32 (2004): 499.
34 Ibid., 504.
35 Ibid.
36 Ibid.
37 Romans 13:9.
38 Romans 13:10.
39 Alex Deagon, *From Violence to Peace: Theology, Law and Community* (Oxford: Hart Publishing, 2017), 7.
40 Augustine, *Concerning the City of God Against the Pagans* (London: Penguin, 2008), 873.

legal or political constraints on the expression of perspectives. Charity (love) or "doing good" requires something "creative" which goes beyond boundaries or precedents.[41] As Milbank exhorts, "to act charitably we must break through the existing representation of what is our duty towards our neighbour and towards God," and "break through the bounds of duty which 'technically' pre-defines its prescribed performance," just as Christ did in humbling himself to death on a cross for our forgiveness.[42] Consider, for example, Philippians 2:3–8:

> Do nothing from selfish ambition or conceit, but in humility count others more significant than yourselves. Let each of you look not only to his own interests, but also to the interests of others. Have this mind among yourselves, which is yours in Christ Jesus, who, though he was in the form of God, did not count equality with God a thing to be grasped, but emptied himself, by taking the form of a servant, being born in the likeness of men. And being found in human form, he humbled himself by becoming obedient to the point of death, even death on a cross.[43]

In this practical sense, love of neighbour entails the civic virtues which undergird the principles of civility. It means properly listening and engaging rather than judging, interpreting expressed views charitably and asking questions to clarify and learn rather than assuming or misrepresenting the views of others, and not engaging in malicious or contemptuous conduct. Love of neighbour in political discourse eschews "anger, wrath, malice, slander" and lying, and pursues "kindness, humility, meekness and patience" with honesty, forbearance, compassion, and forgiveness.[44]

The Apostle Paul groups "love" together with "faith" and "hope" as abiding virtues.[45] Faith, or trust, has "vertical" and "horizontal" aspects. The vertical aspect, between God and us, is a trust that God is just to an eminent and infinite extent that we cannot begin to fathom and a trust that his justice will eventually triumph so that a harmony of peace and order will embrace humanity.[46] The horizontal aspect, between ourselves, is a mutual dependence between each member of the community, which provides a structure for harmonious existence and the embrace of difference. As John Milbank reasons:

> It may appear that trust is weak recourse compared to the guarantees provided by law, courts, political constitutions, checks and balances, and so

---

41 John Milbank, *The Word Made Strange: Theology, Language, Culture* (Oxford: Blackwell Publishing, 1997), 134.
42 Milbank, *Word Made Strange*, 134; See Deagon, *From Violence to Peace*, 188–93.
43 See Philippians 2:3-8.
44 See Colossians 3:8-9, 12-13.
45 1 Corinthians 13:13.
46 John Milbank, "Paul Against Biopolitics," in *Paul's New Moment: Continental Philosophy and the Future of Christian Theology*, eds. John Milbank, Slavoj Žižek and Creston Davis (Grand Rapids, MI: Brazos Press, 2010), 53.

forth. However, since all these processes are administered by human beings capable of treachery, a suspension of distrust, along with the positive working of tacit bonds of association, is the only real source of reliable solidarity for a community. Hence to trust, to depend on others, is in reality the only reliable way in which the individual can extend his or her own power ... the legitimate reach of one's own capacities, and also the only reliable way to attain a collective strength.[47]

So trust or faith is a Christian virtue essential for the principles of civility. But it must be remembered that we live in a fallen world. Sometimes, people do evil rather than good, hate rather than love, and are selfish instead of sacrificial. This is part of the second aspect of Wolterstorff's moral engagement – a recognition that profound evil exists. As will be discussed below, this is actually the expression of a Christian framework (which requires a Christian resolution). Consequently, the proposal for sacrifice, trust, and humility to characterise public discourse might be viewed as problematic due to the unscrupulous. What if people selfishly take advantage of the humility and sacrifice offered? What happens if people hate and insult during a civil discussion? Paradoxically obvious yet strange, the Christian answer is located in the Crucifixion of Christ, who voluntarily allowed himself to be taken advantage of as part of his act of sacrifice.[48] People are persuaded by what attracts, namely Christ's refusal of violence which draws people to the peace of Christianity. Jesus himself said "when I am lifted up from the earth, [I] will draw all people to myself," and he "said this to show by what kind of death he was going to die."[49] There is something irresistible about the steadfast maintenance of humility, love, trust, and sacrifice even in the midst of the most horrific mistreatment. Jesus cried out "Father, forgive them! For they know not what they do"; he called upon the Father to forgive the ones who were at that moment crucifying him.[50] So while people may continue to act selfishly, the Christian virtues conversely demonstrate the radical and paradoxical nature of Christianity.

The Christian response to people taking advantage of humility, sacrifice, trust, and forgiveness is to continue offering that humility, sacrifice, trust, and forgiveness in the hope that people are peacefully persuaded to do likewise.[51] In other words, hope is just as central as trust, because it is only in the hope of redemption and perfect peace, of love reciprocated, that mutual trust and interdependence can work. Framing "moral engagement" in theological terms then, the Christian solution to the problem of evil in the world (of politics) is the exercise of the Christian virtues to pursue justice and the good. The Christian

---

47 Milbank, "Paul Against Biopolitics," 53.
48 See Alex Deagon, "A Christian Framework for Religious Diversity in Political Discourse," in *Religious Liberty in Australia: A New Terra Nullius?*, eds. Michael Quinlan, Iain Benson and Keith Thompson (Redland Bay: Connor Court Publishing, 2019).
49 John 12:32-33.
50 Luke 23:34.
51 Deagon, "Christian Framework."

perspective therefore produces a space for political discourse which is characterised by the "fruit of the Spirit": "love, joy, peace, patience, kindness, goodness, faithfulness, gentleness, self-control"; for "against such things there is no law."[52] The Christian virtues are beyond law and yet fulfil the law by their nature.[53] Manifesting this alternative framework for political discourse, governed by love beyond mere legal requirements, will persuade people there is another way to true peace and it is desirable.[54]

The principles of civility and the civic virtues, are thus, in a sense, distorted and limited forms of Christian virtues. This indicates that these "liberal virtues" can be redeemed, removed from their secular framework, and (re)placed into their proper theological framework in a way which paradoxically enhances both their Christian and liberal nature.[55] This is what makes the Christian virtues universally desirable. All religious and non-religious people can at least practise the Christian virtues according to their Christian form, even if they do not possess Christian belief.[56] Promotion of the theological virtues in Christianity does not restrict or alienate those who do not subscribe to the Christian perspective. True promotion of the theological virtues actually necessarily incorporates and redeems the virtues of secular liberalism.[57]

Milbank calls this the "democratisation of virtue," where "the most important human goods are in principle achievable by all," which "is itself also a Christian legacy."[58] Milbank argues "that the viability of democracy itself depends upon a continued constitutional commitment to 'mixed government,'" which is a blend of

> the life and implicit wisdom of the social many with the guidance of the virtuously rational few and the unifying artifice of the personal one, under the orientation of all to the transcendent Good and final vision of the Godhead.[59]

Moreover, the "Christian democratisation of virtue as charity [love] implies a transfigured version of mixed government that newly promotes the creative flourishing of all and the combined shaping of an earthly city that might remotely image the eternal."[60]

In other words, genuine democracy in a theological framework promotes the individual and communal good so that the earthly polity might echo the eternal

---

52 Galatians 5:22-23.
53 Deagon, *From Violence to Peace*, 141, 194.
54 Ibid., 194.
55 See Deagon, ibid.
56 Ibid.
57 Ibid. For a detailed account of the redemption of liberalism by focusing on a Christian dialogue with the "liberal virtues," see Bruce Ward, *Redeeming the Enlightenment: Christianity and the Liberal Virtues* (Grand Rapids, MI: Eerdmans, 2010).
58 John Milbank, *Beyond Secular Order: The Representation of Being and the Representation of the People* (Oxford: Blackwell Publishing, 2013), 264.
59 Ibid., 10.
60 Ibid., 10.

one. Such democracy is premised upon the universal practice of virtue, particularly love, which peacefully persuades the community to the good. As Milbank and Pabst clarify in a later work:

> virtue is democratic because its practice is open to all, especially the supreme virtues of love, trust, hope, mercy, kindness, forgiveness and reconciliation, which we have all in the West, whether avowedly Christians or not, inherited from the teachings of the Bible.[61]

Therefore, the better approach is not a formal, procedural duty to tolerate different views, or general secular principles which govern discussion, but a loving community of expression grounded in Christian virtue which will produce peace rather than violence.[62] This is a "politics of virtue" which eschews selfish, Machiavellian modes of discourse in favour of charity, humility, and sacrifice. We need to act with

> more receptive gratitude, more communicated generosity, and in such a way that in turn opens up the possibility of trust and further self-giving on the part of others ... Deeds must be publicly enacted and *offered*, and the highest outcome of virtuous practice is the reciprocal giving that is friendship, upon which ... the human city is founded.[63]

"Thus politics is a shared demand for a manifest mutual recognition and regard, since justice and friendship are co-original and inseparable," and the politics of virtue is then really a superfluous phrase – to act virtuously is really to truly act politically.[64] Just as love does not dispense with the law but rather fulfils it, so these redeemed civic virtues and principles of civility do not categorically reject liberalism but "recoup" its better aspects to facilitate a more loving, virtuous, and peaceful democratic community.[65]

Christianity as the Paradigm of Moral Engagement

As mentioned above, the liberal pursuit of "justice" and "the good" is predicated on the existence of serious moral evil. This acknowledgement of the morality of politics, as articulated by Wolterstorff, implies that the role of citizenship entails a moral engagement by pursuing good in a political context of evil. There is a strong correlation between Wolterstorff's idea of moral engagement bringing

---

61 John Milbank and Adrian Pabst, *The Politics of Virtue: Post-Liberalism and the Human Future* (Lanham, MD: Rowman and Littlefield, 2016), 7.
62 See John Milbank, "Against Human Rights: Liberty in the Western Tradition," *Oxford Journal of Law and Religion* 1, no. 1 (2012): 232–4.
63 Milbank and Pabst, *Politics of Virtue*, 6–7.
64 Ibid., 7.
65 C.f. John Milbank, *Theology and Social Theory: Beyond Secular Reason*, 2nd ed. (Oxford: Blackwell Publishing, 2006), xiv–xv.

a moral dimension to politics, and John Milbank's idea of a "politics of virtue" from a Christian perspective, which assumes the existence of a fallen world but does not succumb to the idea that evil is ontologically inevitable. Rather, a politics of virtue facilitates the pursuit of the good in a political community through the transcendent connection of virtue with the highest good – God Himself, who is perfect love and peace.

Christianity thus provides a more robust theoretical context for Wolterstorff's second aspect of moral engagement in the sense that the Christian framework posits a fallen world where serious moral evil exists.[66] Christianity also enables the identification of evil as such, evil as the privation of good, following Augustine's traditional account. Evil is "that which denies and takes away from Being ... [it is] the violent" or the negative.[67] The Christian ability to (temporarily and not finally) accept the existence of evil in conjunction with the ability to identify evil allows the pursuit of justice and the good as a matter of contrast, or a return to our original ontological peace – a redeemed future.[68] For Christ's Crucifixion "restores the Good" and "restores peace," enabling the "possibility of mutual reconciliation."[69] This is because in Christ is displayed the one who "endures and compensates for evil ... suffers violence without violent opposition, and yet at the same time positively opposes violence with a counter-violence to violence as such, which positively reasserts peace."[70] Aspects of this redeemed future have already been canvassed in the previous section in the form of a society governed by Christian virtues, the fruit of the Spirit, and particularly the law of love – which fulfils the law, and against which there is no law – promoting the creative flourishing of all as a reflection of and connection to the eternal.

This results in a Christian (moral) engagement in political debate which aims to bring about the good. There are many examples. After his conversion to Christianity, William Wilberforce relied on Christian ideas of intrinsic dignity and equality when arguing for the abolition of the African slave trade in the British Parliament, against the tide of his time.[71] Today in Australia, some Christian individuals and organisations have advocated for better treatment of refugees,

---

66 Deagon, *From Violence to Peace*, 3–8, 116–17. See also e.g. Stewart Goetz, "The Argument from Evil," in *The Blackwell Companion to Natural Theology*, eds. William Lane Craig and JP Moreland (Oxford: Blackwell Publishing, 2012).
67 John Milbank, "Postmodern Critical Augustinianism: A Short *Summa* in Forty-Two Responses to Unasked Questions," in *The Postmodern God: A Theological Reader*, ed. Graham Ward (Oxford: Blackwell Publishers, 1997), 269. Milbank argues that evil is the "privation of Being," following Augustine's account of evil as negative, and that evil can be committed in the most extreme sense, even inadvertently, by those who imagine they are "fulfilling the goods of order, obedience, political stability and social peace." See John Milbank, *Being Reconciled: Ontology and Pardon* (London: Routledge, 2003), 1–2, 4.
68 Deagon, *From Violence to Peace*, 3–8, 194.
69 Milbank, *Being Reconciled*, 79.
70 Ibid., 79. See also 26–43.
71 See e.g. Augusto Zimmermann, *Christian Foundations of the Common Law: Volume II United States of America* (Redland Bay: Connor Court Publishing, 2018), 185–92, especially 191–2.

fundamentally disagreeing with contemporary border protection policies on the basis of religious theories of hospitality to foreigners and "loving your neighbour as yourself" from the New Testament.[72] Even if people do not agree with the underlying theological concepts, they can rationally accept and implement the practice of loving your neighbour as yourself as pursuing good for society. If we were to divorce the neighbour principle from its Christian context, making it a secular argument rather than a religious one, the argument would lose all its force and context. We would not even know what "loving your neighbour" really means in the Christian framework without, for example, considering the Parable of the Good Samaritan in depth.[73]

Since religious groups in particular provide the associational structures (including visionary and didactic resources) for training in discourse concerning the advancement of human development and the common good, it is essential for liberal democracy that these groups be able to substantively contribute on their terms.[74] As Ten Napel argues, "it is precisely within such faith and other communities that mature visions of the good life can develop, which simultaneously contribute to the notion of the common good."[75] This Christian framing of liberal democracy consequently broadens the notion of politics beyond the immanent political process to transcendent considerations of virtue and solidarity that advance human development and public good.

Therefore, excluding a Christian framework in favour of purely secular principles presents serious challenges to holistic, inclusive public policy debate. This is especially the case in light of religious diversity and the number of varying religious and non-religious perspectives on important social issues. It would mean religious belief could not influence policy debate on issues such as same-sex marriage, abortion, euthanasia, offshore detention, poverty, and climate change – effectively disenfranchising a significant portion of citizens and limiting ways of thinking about how we can attain the common good.[76]

The Christian facilitation of a diversity of arguments will help us make the most informed decision about how the law can best implement the public good.[77] In this sense, Williams advocates a "community of communities," where the state consistently works with diverse religious groups to use their resources in the peaceful pursuit of the common good.[78] Such an approach does not eschew robust argument between competing perspectives, but the argument must be

---

72 See Alex Deagon, "Does Religion have a Place in the Marriage Debate?" *Policy Forum*, 24 October 2017, www.policyforum.net/religion-place-marriage-debate/.
73 Alex Deagon, "Liberal Secularism and Religious Freedom: Reforming Political Discourse," *Harvard Journal of Law and Public Policy* 41, no. 3 (2018): 915; c.f. Deagon, *From Violence to Peace*, 186–93.
74 Ten Napel, *Constitutionalism*, 94.
75 Ibid., 97.
76 Deagon, "Does Religion Have a Place in the Marriage Debate."
77 Deagon, "Christian Framework for Religious Diversity."
78 Williams, *Faith in the Public Square*, 3.

conducted in a way which accords with understanding, courtesy, and respect.[79] This involves the peaceful co-existence of different perspectives in the public sphere, regulated by the law of love. It entails state co-operation with diverse religious groups without precluding argument between those groups about what "the good" entails, as long as that argument is characterised by the virtues of love such as honesty, humility, kindness, and forgiveness. Williams acknowledges that the state can "move in and out of alliance with perspectives of faith, depending on the varying and unpredictable outcomes of honest social argument, and can collaborate without anxiety with communities of faith."[80] He even argues this framework requires a "strong theological grounding" because a common theme of religion is that it is less prone to violence and coercion because it does not depend on coercive power.[81] Hence, a Christian approach should in principle have the effect of creating a more harmonious public co-existence of diverse theological perspectives to augment the pursuit of justice and the good.

Furthermore, Milbank argues that since Christianity "understands all evil and violence in their negativity to be privation," "positive differences" as "instances of the Good" must "analogically concur in a fashion which exceeds mere liberal agreement to disagree."[82] In other words, as has also been considered above, Christianity goes beyond the bare, secular liberal "duty of civility" in political discourse. Instead, Christianity promotes a peaceful community of unity in diversity governed through the law of love, which entails the liberal injunction to be civil and treat fellow citizens with respect while simultaneously tethering that injunction to the eternal, entrenching and deepening the commitment to human dignity such an injunction assumes. Hence, a Christian framework satisfies the liberal democratic requirement of the principles of civility in the form of civic virtues and a moral engagement, but goes beyond the secular to the theological in order that this requirement may be more securely and consistently grounded through its connection with the eternal good. However, as alluded to already, one consequence of this approach is that the attempt to frame the principles of civility in purely rational or secular terms will necessarily jettison that security and consistency by sundering a politics of virtue from the eternal.

Secular Translation or Religious Contribution?[83]

The Limits of Translation

This chapter has so far argued that the liberal "principles of civility" are best understood, enhanced, and implemented by placing them within a theological

---

79 Ibid., 4.
80 Ibid., 33.
81 Ibid., 4.
82 Milbank, *Theology and Social Theory*, 2nd ed., xvi.
83 This part draws from Alex Deagon, "Liberal Secularism and Religious Freedom"; Alex Deagon, "The Name of God in a Constitution: Meaning, Democracy and Political Solidarity," *Oxford Journal of Law and Religion* 8, no. 3 (2019): 473–492.

framework. Schulz acknowledges that religion is an important aspect of the modern democratic society, offering "inspiration and stimuli for the philosophical-rational discourse in society."[84] However, in this sense, Schulz explains that Habermas conditions the success of religion at the level of "democratic institutions and policy makers" on "religious citizens" being able to translate

> their beliefs into rational and secular concepts. The classic example that Habermas brings up to illustrate this translation program is the biblical idea of humanity being created in the image of God. The secular translation is as follows: the human being has inviolable dignity.[85]

This sounds very much like the questionable public reason requirement of traditional political liberals like Rawls.[86] To legitimately participate in autonomous, "secular" democratic processes and adhere to the duties of civility, religious citizens must translate their religious ideas into concepts of secular or pure reason. However, requiring translation actually undermines the democratic contribution of religious citizens by removing the moral-theological language of "evil" and "good" which can inform a moral engagement from a religious perspective, and limiting their ability to appeal to eternal virtues such as the law of love.

As I have argued previously:

> Indeed, is it even fully reasonable to argue for a religious position without relying fully on the religious doctrine? Consider the claim that the legal community should be governed according to the Christian principle of the "law of love," with all the pregnant theological ideas that implies. This is obviously a religious argument based on a religious comprehensive doctrine. But it is far from incompatible with "democratic citizenship" and "the idea of legitimate law": even if people do not agree with the underlying theological concepts, they can rationally accept and implement the practice of loving your neighbour as yourself as beneficial for society. If we were to divorce the law of love from its theological context – making it a secular argument rather than a religious one – the argument would lose force and specificity. One would not even know what "loving your neighbour" [or hating them] really means without, for example, considering the Parable of the Good Samaritan contained in the New Testament [and contrasting that with the not-good action of the Levite and the Priest]. In this sense, excluding the "whole truth" of a religious comprehensive doctrine unnecessarily

---

84 Michael Schulz, "The Existential and Semantic Truth of Religion in Jurgen Habermas's Political Philosophy and the Possibility of a Philosophy of Religion," *Journal of Speculative Philosophy* 31, no. 3 (2017): 459.
85 Schulz, "Religion in Habermas," 459; c.f. Habermas, "Foundations of the State," 45.
86 See John Rawls, *Political Liberalism: Expanded Edition* (Columbia: Columbia University Press, 2005).

secularizes political discourse and undermines the pursuit of political justice by limiting conceptions of public good.[87]

In addition to restricting the mode of discourse, requiring translation undermines morally engaged democracy by restricting the kind and content of moral contributions available to religious citizens. Laborde has observed that there may be no good secular reasons for a particular proposal with moral implications, but there may be good religious reasons. An example is fundamental issues of life and death such as abortion or euthanasia which invoke the "sanctity of all human life" as an argument.[88] According to Laborde, the secular ideal of human dignity is "perhaps not robust enough" to be a purely secular justification for preserving life in this moral context.[89]

Hence, not all religious beliefs about moral issues can be easily or meaningfully framed in secular language without also importing the relevant content of that religious belief. It may well be very onerous to require the ordinary religious citizen to reframe their religious conviction on a moral issue as a secular argument. It might even be part of the moral convictions of a religious citizen that they are required to base their moral, social, and political convictions on their religion rather than a purely secular argument. A requirement for translation in this context severely restricts the ability of religious citizens to morally engage with the democratic process on their own terms, and so mandated translation actually undermines the articulation and pursuit of justice and the good.[90]

Schulz also questions the possibility of translation. If the "reason" of religion is different from secular "reason" (as seems to be assumed for translation to be conceivable) "then religious beliefs could scarcely succeed in being translated into [secular] philosophical concepts."[91] He continues:

> Religious experiences and decisions cannot be translated and transformed into universal formulas that might be applicable to all. There is a private sphere and unjustifiable (incommunicable) dimension of faith, which resists being grasped in the form of deductive concepts or conclusions. Religion is something that is deeply private, but this does not make it a merely private, socially irrelevant thing ... [Human] dignity is violated the moment someone pretends to seize, define, and possess another conceptually. Obviously, this is because we experience ourselves as a conceptually ungraspable mystery, as an ineffable – opaque – reality. In this sense, the translation of the biblical idea of humanity being created in the image of God in the secular

---

87 Deagon, "Liberal Secularism and Religious Freedom," 914.
88 Cecile Laborde, "Justificatory Secularism," in *Religion in a Liberal State*, eds. Gavin D'Costa, Malcolm Evans, Tariq Modood and Julian Rivers (Cambridge: Cambridge University Press, 2013), 180.
89 Ibid.
90 Deagon, "Liberal Secularism and Religious Freedom," 917–18.
91 Schulz, "Religion in Habermas," 462–3.

speech of the inviolable dignity of humanity takes on a central dimension of the opaque.[92]

In other words, there is a fundamental incoherence at the heart of the translation idea. Translation implies a different kind of language, but if the language is fundamentally different, then adequate translation is really impossible. Faith and religion are unique individual experiences and communal contributions on moral issues that cannot be rigidly characterised using secular categories. Any translation attempt will inevitably neglect aspects of the religious contribution. Milbank agrees, criticising the Habermasian argument that "religious claims can be 'translated' into public terms" or "norms governing fair communicative discourse" on the basis that "few religious people will accept the adequacy of such translation, since it leaves the rational aspect of specifically religious content redundant and suggests that faith makes no difference at all to the human action."[93] He even suggests that if religious people are not encouraged to articulate their own faith-based logic in the public domain it could lead to the development of "virulently fideistic and fundamentalist forms" to actually make a difference.[94] Moreover, if this kind of translation occurs, it results in a loss of transcendent ethical and moral content shared by religions and (perhaps unwittingly) non-religions alike, such as "solidarity."[95]

The Benefit of Theology

Conversely, a Christian theological framework suggests an enduring, mutually beneficial solidarity between religious and non-religious citizens, expressed through the Christian virtues and a moral engagement, as part of a desirable democratic process which entails the principles of civility. This "solidarity" takes its classical Christian meaning of deeper relationality and mutual love as a bond between citizens of a community through a co-operative order. This entails understanding mutual dependence and responsibility, culminating in communities of mercy, grace, and generosity.[96]

Reference to God, the transcendent source of virtue and the good which undergirds moral engagement, "illuminates the legal system by protecting and

---

92 Ibid., 463.
93 John Milbank, "What Lacks is Feeling: Mediating Reason and Religion Today," in *Religion in a Liberal State*, eds. Gavin D'Costa, Malcolm Evans, Tariq Modood and Julian Rivers (Cambridge: Cambridge University Press, 2013), 208–9.
94 Ibid.
95 Ibid., 209.
96 See e.g. Joel Harrison, "Dworkin's Religion and the End of Religious Liberty," in *Research Handbook on Law and Religion*, ed. Rex Ahdar (Cheltenham: Edward Elgar, 2018), 96–98 and references contained there. For a more detailed history and analysis of the classical concept of solidarity, see Meghan Clark, *The Vision of Catholic Social Thought: The Virtue of Solidarity and the Praxis of Human Rights* (Minneapolis, MN: Fortress Press, 2014).

strengthening its pillars without exploiting its internal legal structure."[97] This illumination occurs by "strengthening the commitment to respecting the universe and enhancing and embellishing the ideas of the human person, dignity, equality, moral freedom and responsibility, solidarity, subsidiarity, and human rights."[98]

For example, a moral engagement informed by Christianity strengthens the respect between and the centrality of human beings because they are in a special and unique relationship with the divine. It strengthens the dignity and equality of humans because of their creation in the image and likeness of God, and because of the human capacity to co-operate with God by assuming some responsibility for the development and care of the created order. It is a "transcendental ground" for the ontological status of the human as a pre-political bearer of rights and duties which are to be protected by law.[99]

The civic virtues reconceptualised as Christian virtues reflect this reality, ideally correlating with a real political practice of moral engagement through the law of love.[100] As Schulz observes:

> religion can, in an existential and motivational respect, elevate the operating temperature of a democratic society insofar as it motivates one to act virtuously. This function is very helpful and even crucial for a democratic society. Religions can impart worth and attitudes that support the active participation of the citizen in the democratic process.[101]

Hence, a theologically informed moral engagement is important for the liberal state because it links the immanent with the transcendent to fully take account of the human. Just as modern liberalism correctly emphasises the importance of reason and the distinction between reason and revelation, so the law of love

---

97 Rafael Domingo, *God and the Secular Legal System* (Cambridge: Cambridge University Press, 2016), 33.
98 Ibid., 34. See ibid., 34–44 for the full explanation of this claim.
99 Ibid., 35–39.
100 It should be noted that the arguments here are more conceptual and normative than empirical and descriptive. In other words, what this chapter proposes is the law of love motivates virtuous action at a conceptual and normative level. It is not making an empirical claim. Nevertheless, there is some empirical evidence that religion can motivate virtuous action. See e.g. Manuel Guillen, Ignacio Ferrero, and W Michael Hoffman, "The Neglected Ethical and Spiritual Motivations in the Workplace," *Journal of Business Ethics* 128, no. 4 (2015): 803; Vassilis Saroglou, "Religion, Spirituality and Altruism," in *Handbook of Psychology, Religion and Spirituality*, eds. KI Pargament, JJ Exline and JW Jones (Washington, D.C.: American Psychological Association, 2013, vol. 1).
101 Schulz, "Religion in Habermas," 459. This is consistent with other contemporary scholarly work arguing that religion and democracy are connected in important ways: e.g. Alex Deagon, "Liberalism through Love"; Deagon, "Equal Voice Liberalism"; Ten Napel, *Constitutionalism*; Milbank, *Beyond Secular Order*; Milbank and Pabst, *The Politics of Virtue*; Robert Woodberry, "The Missionary Roots of Liberal Democracy," *American Political Science Review* 106, no. 2 (2012): 244.

informing the principles of civility provides the background which indicates immanent (modern, liberal) political structures point towards the transcendent and are informed by eternal virtues.[102] In other words, the cultivation of higher virtues by reference to the law of love enhances the democratic process through consideration of the welfare of a citizen both as a unique and dignified individual, and as a valuable member of a community. Christianity enhances genuine democracy by promoting the individual and communal good so that the earthly polity might echo the eternal one. This is premised upon the universal practice of virtue, particularly love, which peacefully persuades the individuals in a community to do good for the benefit of individuals and the community.[103]

The Law of Love for the Love of Law

This chapter has argued that the Christian framework, expressed through the law of love, grounds and enhances the civic virtues and moral engagement which comprise the liberal principles of civility. Importantly, I am not advocating for a Christian theocracy or for a polity governed by something akin to canon law. Rather, the law of love paradoxically fulfils the principles of civility by transcending them. It produces an existence which is characterised by the "fruit of the Spirit": "love, joy, peace, patience, kindness, goodness, faithfulness, gentleness, self-control"; for "against such things there is no law."[104] The Christian virtues are able to be practised by all, regardless of belief, enabling a morally engaged pursuit of justice and the good in a fallen world by pointing to a transcendent peace.[105] That is worth seeking.

---

102 Milbank, *Beyond Secular Order*, 115–16.
103 See generally Deagon, *From Violence to Peace*.
104 Galatians 5:22-23.
105 See Deagon, *From Violence to Peace*, 194.

7 The Loving Sword

The Implications of Divine Simplicity for Civil Law

Benjamin B. Saunders

Introduction

Love and law are often thought to present something of a paradox, if not outright contradiction. Law is prescriptive, often punitive, backed by the threat of state coercion, and closely related to the idea of retributive justice, which a long tradition defines as "the rendering to each what is due."[1] Love is often considered to be precisely the opposite, requiring the forgiveness of wrongs and showing kindness and mercy not based on the merit of the recipient.[2]

Complicating matters is that respectable scriptural support can be marshalled, at least in broad terms, for both law and love. There is, of course, a great deal of law in the Old Testament. Christ famously enjoined his disciples to "render to Caesar the things that are Caesar's, and to God the things that are God's," enjoining them to obey human authorities and thus implicitly conferring at least some legitimacy on those authorities (Mt. 22:21). Civil rulers are called to bear the sword and to execute God's wrath against wrongdoers, in so doing acting as God's servants (Rom. 13:1–7).

By contrast, Christ's disciples are called to love their neighbours and turn the other cheek, exercising forgiveness where they have been wronged. Believers are told not to repay evil with evil, but to repay evil with good (Rom. 12:17–21). Christians have been forgiven, and so extend the same forgiveness to others, not being bound by a need to exact revenge (Mt. 18:21–22). In Matthew 5:38–42, Jesus seems to explicitly contrast his "kingdom ethics" with the retributive concepts of justice found in the Old Testament:

> You have heard that it was said, "An eye for an eye and a tooth for a tooth." But I say to you, Do not resist the one who is evil. But if anyone slaps you on the right cheek, turn to him the other also. And if anyone would sue you and take your tunic, let him have your cloak as well. And if anyone forces you

---

1 Emil Brunner, *Justice and Social Order*, trans Mary Hottinger (Lutterworth Press, 2002), 23.
2 Walter A Elwell, *Baker Theological Dictionary of the Bible* (Baker, 1996), 494.

DOI: 10.4324/9781003148920-10

to go one mile, go with him two miles. Give to the one who begs from you, and do not refuse the one who would borrow from you.³

Christian love, therefore, is based on forgiveness and mercy, which seems radically at odds with concepts of justice and the strict enforcement of rights which are characteristic of law. These demands made by Christ of his disciples in the Sermon on the Mount have therefore been seen as ushering in a radically new ethic, which does not sit easily with law. Dietrich Bonhoeffer argued that in the Sermon on the Mount (Mt. 5:38–42), Jesus called his disciples not to resist evil, and that "[t]his saying of Christ removes the Church from the sphere of politics and law."⁴ David VanDrunen has argued that love is a totally inappropriate category through which to view civil law. For VanDrunen, Christian love freely forgives and does not pursue retribution, whereas the purpose of law is to enforce retributive justice; as such, given the very different nature of law and love, "Christian love is not the proper category by which to organize and evaluate civil law."⁵ Nicholas Wolterstorff has argued that the New Testament rejects the *lex talionis* and the principle of retribution, which applies not just to Christians, but everybody.⁶

More radically, emphasising the differences between law and love can lead to a rejection of the legitimacy of earthly authority. Thomas Shaffer argues that once a criminal has been forgiven, there is no longer any need for civil or criminal punishment; a "jurisprudence of forgiveness" undercuts the rationale for punishment.⁷ Perhaps the clearest statement of this approach to civil authority is contained in the *Schleitheim Confession* (1527),⁸ which considers that "[t]he sword is ordained outside the perfection of Christ" and forbids Christians from serving as a magistrate:

> The government magistracy is according to the flesh, but the Christians' is according to the Spirit; their houses and dwelling remain in this world, but the Christians' are in heaven; their citizenship is in this world, but the Christians' citizenship is in heaven; the weapons of their conflict and war are carnal and against the flesh only, but the Christians' weapons are spiritual, against the fortification of the devil. The worldlings are armed with steel

---

3 Matthew 5:38–42. Scripture quotations are from the English Standard Version.
4 Dietrich Bonhoeffer, *The Cost of Discipleship*, trans RH Fuller (SCM Press, 1948), 123–4.
5 David VanDrunen, "Justice Tempered by Forbearance: Why Christian Love Is an Improper Category to Apply to Civil Law," in Robert F Cochran, and Zachary R Calo (eds), *Agape, Justice, and Law: How Might Christian Love Shape Law?* (Cambridge University Press, 2017).
6 Nicholas Wolterstorff, *Justice in Love* (Eerdmans, 2011), 120–8.
7 Thomas L Shaffer, "The Radical Reformation and the Jurisprudence of Forgiveness," in Michael W McConnell, Robert F Cochran, Jr and Angela C Carmella (eds), *Christian Perspectives on Legal Thought* (Yale University Press, 2001), 325–6.
8 Alister E McGrath, *Reformation Thought: An Introduction* (4th ed., Wiley-Blackwell, 2012), 208.

and iron, but the Christians are armed with the armor of God, with truth, righteousness, peace, faith, salvation and the Word of God.[9]

Significantly, such approaches were grounded in the character of God: Anabaptist theologian Hans Denck "appealed to the meekness of Christ and his silence before his accusers in declaring that 'force is not an attribute of God.'"[10] The debate over law and love therefore has real implications both for the legitimacy of Christian engagement in law and government, and also for the character of God.

This chapter challenges the notion that law and love are in contradiction. It reasons from the very foundation of Christian theology, namely, the character of God himself. I examine the doctrine of divine simplicity – a notoriously unsimple doctrine – and consider its implications for how we think about law and love. I do not mount a defence of the doctrine, but merely assume it to be true as a catholic doctrine of the Church and consider its implications. I argue that if God is simple, then all his attributes must be operative at all times, and God must act consistently with all his attributes whenever he acts. God must be loving, and just, and holy, and wise, and so on, at all times. But if this is so, then there can be no contradiction between law and love in God. God, the author and giver of law, must have acted lovingly when establishing law, and when establishing the institutions of civil government to enforce civil law.[11]

And if that is so, then love, God's love, must underlie law, both God's law and the human institutions established by God to administer earthly justice. The implications of the doctrine of simplicity therefore require a shift in the debate over law and love. The question becomes not *whether* law and love are reconcilable, because the character of God demands that they must be. Rather, the question is *how* law and love can be reconciled. In attempting this reconciliation, I argue that a change in our understanding of love is necessary. Love certainly can and must be expressed in ways such as compassion, forgiveness, and mercy (which I call for ease of reference "soft love"). But love can also be expressed in ways that could be considered harsh – and sometimes even violent (which I call for ease of reference "tough love").

Divine Simplicity and Its Implications

In this part, I explain the doctrine of God's simplicity. My purpose is not to make a case for the doctrine, or to defend it, but merely to explain it. That is, I assume it to be true, and in the following sections of this chapter I analyse its implications for law and love. For a defence of the doctrine the reader will have to look elsewhere.[12]

---

9 John C Wenger, "The Schleitheim Confession of Faith" (1945) 19 *Mennonite Quarterly Review* 243, 251.
10 McGrath, *Reformation Thought: An Introduction*, 208.
11 Romans 13:1.
12 See especially James E Dolezal, *God Without Parts: Divine Simplicity and the Metaphysics of God's Absoluteness* (Pickwick, 2011).

The doctrine of divine simplicity, in summary, is that God's existence and essence are identical with his attributes. The doctrine is a catholic doctrine, adhered to by Roman Catholics and Protestants alike, with a long history, being taught by the early church fathers, reaching its zenith in Aquinas, as well as being taught by later theologians. As the seventeenth-century Reformed theologian Francis Turretin said, "the orthodox have constantly taught that the essence of God is perfectly simple and free from all composition."[13] Augustine wrote:

> the knowledge of God is also His wisdom, and His wisdom is His essence or substance itself. Because in the marvelous simplicity of that nature, it is not one thing to be wise, and another thing to be, but to be wise is the same as to be.[14]

Aquinas likewise wrote:

> if the existence of a thing differs from its essence, this existence must be caused either by some exterior agent or by its essential principles. Now it is impossible for a thing's existence to be caused by its essential constituent principles, for nothing can be the sufficient cause of its own existence, if its existence is caused. Therefore that thing, whose existence differs from its essence, must have its existence caused by another. But this cannot be true of God; because we call God the first efficient cause. Therefore it is impossible that in God His existence should differ from His essence.[15]

The idea of simplicity is expressly part of the confessional standards of many churches. Article 1 of the *Belgic Confession* states that "there is only one simple and spiritual Being, which we call God."[16] Another key confessional statement is Article 1 of the *39 Articles*, which was partly adopted into the *Westminster Confession of Faith*,[17] and which provides:

> There is but one living and true God, everlasting, without body, parts, or passions; of infinite power, wisdom, and goodness; the Maker, and Preserver of all things both visible and invisible. And in unity of this Godhead there be three Persons, of one substance, power, and eternity; the Father, the Son, and the Holy Ghost.[18]

---

13 Francis Turretin, *Institutes of Elenctic Theology*, ed. James T Dennison, trans. George Musgrace Giger (Presbyterian and Reformed, 1997), vol. 1, 191.
14 Augustine, *On the Trinity*, ed. Gareth B Matthews, trans. Stephen McKenna (Cambridge University Press, 2002), 194 [book 15 ch. 13].
15 Thomas Aquinas, *The Summa Theologica of St Thomas Aquinas*, 2nd ed., trans. Fathers of the English Dominican Province (Burns, Oates & Washburne, 1920), Ia 3.4.
16 *Belgic Confession* (1561) article 1, in Arthur C Cochrane (ed.), *Reformed Confessions of the Sixteenth Century* (Westminster John Knox Press, 2003), 189.
17 *Westminster Confession of Faith* (1646) II.1 (Free Presbyterian Publications, 1985), 24–25: "There is but one only living and true God, who is infinite in being and perfection, a most pure spirit, invisible, without body, parts, or passions."
18 *The Articles of Religion Agreed upon by the Archbishops, Bishops, and the Whole Clergy of the Provinces of Canterbury and York* (London, 1562), article 1.

It is this statement that God is "without parts" that expresses the idea of simplicity. As an example of a Roman Catholic formulation of the doctrine, the *Catholic Encyclopaedia* states that "God is a simple being or substance excluding every kind of composition, physical or metaphysical," which is more fulsome and enlightening, although perhaps less elegant, than the Protestant confessional statements referred to.

Therefore, the Church has consistently held that God is a simple being, "without parts." Simplicity here does not mean lacking in complexity, rather, it is the antonym of compound: that is, simplicity holds that God "is not a compounded or composite being."[19] The underlying rationale for this idea is that God must be the sufficient explanation for himself. If God were composed of parts, then those parts must ontologically precede God. They would be more ultimate than God. But God is absolute, that is, wholly self-sufficient and the first cause of all things; he "does not possess his perfections by relation to anything or anyone other than himself."[20] Simplicity is therefore necessary to account for God's absoluteness. According to James Dolezal, the doctrine of divine simplicity teaches two propositions: "(1) God is identical with his existence and his essence and (2) that each of his attributes is ontologically identical with his existence and with every other one of his attributes."[21]

One consequence of this is that God's existence and attributes must be identical. For creatures and things a distinction can be drawn between existence and essence, which are severable from each other: there is a subject who exists to whom an essence, a variety of attributes, are added, so to speak. A person's attributes can change but the person does not thereby cease to exist. This is not the case with God. Scripture and Christian theology assign a variety of attributes to God, such as immutability, infinity, omnipotence, wisdom, justice, and so on.[22] If God is without parts, then these things are not severable from who God is. Thus, the divine attributes are not descriptions of what sort of being God is, they are not "accidents or modifications of the divine being," but are "statements of 'what' God is." Divine simplicity "asserts the essential identity of God with all of his attributes or qualities."[23] God is the sum total of everything that his attributes reveal. God's simplicity is "the end result of scribing to God all the perfections of creatures to the ultimate divine degree."[24] Theologians have drawn on scriptural texts which tell us "not only that God is truthful, righteous, living, illuminating,

---

19 Richard A Muller, *Post-Reformation Reformed Dogmatics: The Rise and Development of Reformed Orthodoxy, ca. 1520 to ca. 1725* (Baker Academic, 2003), vol. 3, 276.
20 Dolezal, *God Without Parts*, 1–2.
21 Ibid., 2.
22 See, e.g. Robert L Reymond, *A New Systematic Theology of the Christian Faith*, 2nd ed. (Thomas Nelson, 1998), 160–202; Louis Berkhof, *Systematic Theology* (Banner of Truth, 1958), 57–81; Charles Hodge, *Systematic Theology* (Charles Scribner, 1872), vol. 2, 368–441.
23 Muller, *Post-Reformation Reformed Dogmatics*, vol. 3, 43–4, 53.
24 Herman Bavinck, *Reformed Dogmatics*, ed John Bolt, trans John Vriend (Baker, 2004), vol. 2, 176.

loving, and wise, but also that he is the truth, righteousness, life, light, love, and wisdom" (Jer. 10:10; 23:6; Jn. 1:4–5, 9; 14:6; 1 Cor. 1:30; 1 Jn. 1:5; 4:8) as support for the idea of simplicity.[25]

The doctrine of simplicity serves several important theological and polemical purposes. The first is to preserve the absoluteness of God, such that there is no thing metaphysically or ontologically prior to God. God is not posterior to anything and has no cause.[26] The seventeenth-century theologian Edward Leigh noted that, "[i]f he did consist of parts, there must be something before him, to put those parts together."[27] Simplicity is therefore necessary to account for God's incommunicable attributes; as put by Dolezal, simplicity supplies the absoluteness in the attributes of aseity, unity, infinity, immutability, and eternity.[28] The doctrine of simplicity also "serves to safeguard trinitarianism from tritheistic implications."[29]

How to understand God's attributes under this doctrine is a difficult question. As noted, Christian theology assigns a variety of attributes to God, which are, to human ways of thinking, distinguishable from each other. But if God is one simple undivided essence, then this would seem to deny any basis for distinguishing between the attributes. A strong conception of simplicity denies any distinction between God's attributes, holding that all of God's attributes are really identical: all God's perfections are really identical with the others "inasmuch as each is identical with the Godhead and God cannot be really distinct from himself."[30] As the seventeenth-century Reformed theologian John Owen said, "[t]he attributes of God which alone seem to be distinct things in the essence of God, are all of them essentially the same with one another, and everyone the same with the essence of God itself."[31]

This follows from the identity of God's being and essence. If God is identical with his being, then he does not possess attributes, but rather *is* all those perfections that are ascribed to him. God's attributes are "just so many truths about the one indivisible and infinite existence and essence of God."[32] The attributes are not separate qualities of God, but describe God's simple essence. Underlying each attribute is not a distinct concept, but "the divine essence itself": God's simple unity is displayed to the human knower "under the form of creaturely

---

25 Ibid., 173; Berkhof, *Systematic Theology*, 45; Wilhelmus à Brakel, *The Christian's Reasonable Service*, ed Joel R Beeke, trans Bartel Elshout (Reformation Heritage Books, 1992 [1700]), vol. 1, 99.
26 Muller, *Post-Reformation Reformed Dogmatics*, vol. 3, 53–54.
27 Edward Leigh, *A Treatise of Divinity* (London: Printed by E. Griffin for William Lee, 1646), 27 [II.3].
28 Dolezal, *God Without Parts*, ch. 3.
29 Muller, *Post-Reformation Reformed Dogmatics*, vol. 3, 43.
30 Dolezal, *God Without Parts*, 125.
31 John Owen, *Vindiciae Evangelicae, or, The Mystery of the Gospel Vindicated, and Socinianisme Examined* (Oxford: Printed by L. Lichfield for T. Robinson, 1655), 25 (spelling and punctuation modernised).
32 Dolezal, *God Without Parts*, 136, 163.

multiplicity."[33] This, however, does not mean that God's attributes are synonyms: the sense of each attribute differs meaningfully from the others, although there is not a corresponding diversity of principles or attributes in God.[34] As put by Aquinas, "although the names applied to God signify one thing, still because they signify that thing under many and different aspects, they are not synonymous."[35] Even if it is ultimately the case that these attributes are really identical, it is meaningful to speak of the divine attributes separately, and to distinguish between them. This is because Scripture ascribes different attributes to God, such as justice, mercy, and power, and these words are not synonymous. It is entirely legitimate to speak of God consistently with the manner in which he has revealed himself to us.

Significantly for the argument of this chapter, if all God's attributes form part of one undivided essence, this means that they are all operative whenever God acts. God must act consistently with his character at all times: he is always holy and loving and powerful and just and wise, and so on. He is always consistent with all of his attributes. One implication of divine simplicity is that "we cannot rank God's attributes or make one more essential to God than another. God is love even when he judges; he is holy and righteous even in saving sinners; he is eternal even when he acts in time."[36]

One important scriptural support for this idea is in Romans 3, speaking of the righteousness of God that comes through faith in Jesus Christ for all who believe. In 3:26, Paul states that the giving of Jesus Christ as a propitiation by his blood "was to show his righteousness ... so that he might be just and the justifier of the one who has faith in Jesus." It is perhaps customary to think of the accomplishment of redemption as primarily an act of God's mercy and grace; as put by John Murray, "[t]he cross of Christ is the supreme demonstration of the love of God."[37] But in doing so, God remains "just" as well as the justifier. That is, in redeeming sinners God maintains consistency with his justice, such that the demands of his holiness and righteousness are not compromised: "in the work of Christ the dictates of holiness and the demands of justice have been fully vindicated."[38]

The doctrine of simplicity has some perhaps surprising and even uncomfortable implications. This is due to the picture that Scripture paints of God. In Scripture, as well as acting benevolently and mercifully, God reveals himself as acting in ways that seem harsh and even violent. Perhaps the most notorious example of this is the command to the Israelites to destroy the Canaanites upon dispossessing them of their land:

---

33 Ibid., 133. Muller, *Post-Reformation Reformed Dogmatics*, vol. 3, 284–98.
34 Dolezal, *God Without Parts*, 135.
35 Aquinas, *Summa Theologica*, Ia 13.4.
36 Michael Horton, *The Christian Faith: A Systematic Theology for Pilgrims on the Way* (Zondervan, 2011), 228.
37 John Murray, *Redemption: Accomplished and Applied* (Banner of Truth, 1961), 17.
38 Ibid., 18.

When the Lord your God brings you into the land that you are entering to take possession of it, and clears away many nations before you, the Hittites, the Girgashites, the Amorites, the Canaanites, the Perizzites, the Hivites, and the Jebusites, seven nations more numerous and mightier than you, and when the Lord your God gives them over to you, and you defeat them, then you must devote them to complete destruction. You shall make no covenant with them and show no mercy to them.[39]

The difficult implication of divine simplicity is that all God's attributes are always operative and can never be compromised. This means that, even when acting in ways like this, God must be acting consistently with the attribute of love. It was therefore a loving act, or at the very least not inconstant with love, for God to have ordered, and carried out, the destruction of the Canaanites.

Now this might seem an absurd thing to say. While a detailed defence of this point is beyond the scope of this chapter, a few brief points will have to suffice. Scripture records that the Canaanite peoples engaged in brutal and horrific acts such as child sacrifice. Scripture also records that these practices tended to be contagious, as other nations adopted them. For example, in the book of 2 Kings, king Ahaz "walked in the way of the kings of Israel, and even made his son pass through the fire, according to the abominations of the nations whom the LORD had driven out from before the sons of Israel."[40] Judging those nations by destroying them would have the consequence of preventing these horrific practices, thereby protecting the children who would otherwise have been subjected to them.

Implications for Law

This section considers the implications of divine simplicity for the nature of law. Christian theology has typically distinguished different categories of law, namely eternal, natural, human, and divine law.[41] This discussion has implications for all these categories of law, together with the institutions through which civil law is enforced.

Law, Love, and the Character of God

The first implication is that law and love are not opposed to each other – at least in God. Law has historically been a prominent feature of Scripture and theology. Christian theology has long held that God has created human beings subject to a natural moral order, traditionally known as the natural law, containing universally

---

39 Deuteronomy 7:1–2.
40 2 Kings 16:3.
41 See especially Thomas Aquinas, *Summa Theologica*, IaIIae 91 in RW Dyson (ed.), *Aquinas: Political Writings* (Cambridge University Press, 2004), 83–91.

applicable moral requirements knowable outside of Scripture, which is consistent with and reflects God's character.[42] The Old Testament contains many laws applicable to Israel, including the Decalogue, which many theologians have considered to be broadly equivalent to the natural law.[43] The New Testament recognises the legitimacy of the institutions of civil government instituted by God for the purpose of punishing wrong.[44]

According to the doctrine of divine simplicity, all God's attributes are operative at all times and God cannot be or act inconsistently with any of his attributes. As such, when God established these laws and the civil institutions necessary to enforce them, he must have been acting lovingly. Of course, human and divine action cannot be simplistically equated, and I consider below how this might impact the form and institutions of human law. But, in principle, this demonstrates that law and love are not in necessary contradiction to each other: God is the giver of law, and He is love, at the same time. This removes one of the principal bases of the "law vs love" conflict, and makes it difficult to argue that law and love are radically opposed to each other. In God, they are not. It is, perhaps, easier to assert that law and love are friends than to explain how this is the case. But recognising this places the burden, not on *whether* law and love are reconcilable, but *how*.

Scripture clearly draws a link between law and love. Jesus summed up the entire law in two commandments:

> "Love the Lord your God with all your heart and with all your soul and with all your mind." This is the first and greatest commandment. And the second is like it: "Love your neighbor as yourself." All the Law and the Prophets hang on these two commandments.
>
> (Mt. 22:37–40)

It is not difficult to see how this is the case. The commandments contain the content of our duties to God and to our fellow man. The first four commandments

---

42 See, e.g. Norman Doe (ed.), *Christianity and Natural Law: An Introduction* (Cambridge University Press, 2017); Stephen J Grabill, *Rediscovering the Natural Law in Reformed Theological Ethics* (Eerdmans, 2006); Aquinas, *Summa Theologica*, IaIIae 91.2.
43 See, e.g. James Durham, *The Law Unsealed, or, A Practical Exposition of the Ten Commandments* (Glasgow, 1676), 24; Edward Leigh, *A Systeme or Body of Divinity Consisting of Ten Books, Wherein the Fundamentals and Main Grounds of Religion are Opened* (London: Printed by A.M. for William Lee, 1662), 1143; William Gouge, *A Commentary on the Whole Epistle to the Hebrews* (Edinburgh: J Nichol, 1866), 123; Lancelot Andrewes, *The Morall Law Expounded, 1. Largely, 2. Learnedly, 3. Orthodoxly: That is, the Long Expected, and Much-Desired Worke of Bishop Andrewes, upon the Ten Commandments* (London: M Sparke, R Milbourne, R Cotes, and A Crooke, 1642), 83; Daniel Cawdry and Herbert Palmer, *Sabbatum Redivivum: Or, the Christian Sabbath Vindicated, in a Full Discourse Concerning the Sabbath and the Lord's Day* (London: Thomas Maxey, for Samuel Gellibrand, and Thomas Underhill, 1652), vol. 2, 56.
44 Romans 13:1–7.

express the proper manner of our love for God. If we love our fellow humans, we will honour and respect their status, life, marriage, property, and reputation, consistent with the requirements of the fifth to tenth commandments. As Paul wrote in Romans 13, we ought to love one another, because this fulfils the law of the ten commandments (Rom. 13:8–9). Underlying law, therefore, is love.

One of the primary bases for considering that there is a conflict between law and love are the commands in the New Testament for disciples of Jesus to act in ways which seem un-law like, modelling themselves on God's character,[45] which seems to contrast sharply with the more legalistic commands of the Old Testament. However, as we have seen, God's character maintains consistency with all of his attributes at all times. Any attempt to think about law from a Christian perspective must recognise that, in God, there is no contradiction between law and love.

Reflecting this, there is much greater consistency between the moral demands of the Old and New Testaments than is sometimes recognised. As has been noted, Jesus summarised the entirety of the law in two great commandments. This was not a New Testament innovation: both of these commandments were already present in the Mosaic Law (Deut. 6:5; Lev. 19:18). Even some of Jesus' more radical demands have parallels in the Mosaic Law. Jesus commanded his disciples to love their enemies and pray for those who persecute them, that they may be children of their Father in heaven (Mt. 5:43–48). In similar fashion, Exodus 23 commanded the Israelites as follows:

> If you meet your enemy's ox or his donkey going astray, you shall bring it back to him. If you see the donkey of one who hates you lying down under its burden, you shall refrain from leaving him with it; you shall rescue it with him.
>
> (Exod. 23:4–5)

The underlying principle embodied in this law – love your enemies – is very similar to Jesus' teaching. Although not precisely identical, there is much continuity between the demands of the Old and New Testaments.

The second implication is that love underlies all the institutions of civil law and government, because God has established those institutions. Romans 13 instructs "every person" to "be subject to the governing authorities." Paul says that "there is no authority except from God, and those that exist have been instituted by God. Therefore, whoever resists the authorities resists what God has appointed, and those who resist will incur judgment."[46] Thus, God has "instituted" and "appointed" the institutions of civil government, including the ruler who wields the coercive power of the sword, which ought to be exercised consistently with the requirements of the natural moral law. It might be tempting to think of this as flowing out of God's desire for justice among earthly peoples. But, according to

---

45 See, e.g. Matthew 5:43–48.
46 Romans 13:1–2.

the doctrine of divine simplicity, all of God's attributes are always operative and God acts consistently with them at all times. If God is love as well as just, then God has appointed these institutions lovingly: love underlies the appointment of these authorities for the good of the people. Indeed, Romans 13:4 describes the civil ruler as "God's servant for your good."

It is not hard to see how this can be so. As Cochran and Calo have noted, "[o]ne need only travel to one of the many countries that do not have functioning legal systems to see the harm citizens suffer," such as sex trafficking, wage slavery, rape, and police brutality.[47] The creation of law, and institutions and mechanisms for its enforcement, was an act of love to bring justice, protect the weak and innocent, promote good, and suppress evil. Love underlies all the prescriptions of the moral law, given that murder, theft, adultery, and bearing false witness cause harm to one's neighbour, and so it is loving for the civil ruler to criminalise such actions. Therefore, love is one of the foundational motivating principles for the creation of law and the institutions of government. Law, and the execution of legal judgment, are not a grudging concession to something inherently suspicious or evil, but an expression of God's character. Again, the question becomes, not *whether* law and love are reconcilable, but *how*.

What of the situation where governments are oppressive or where unjust laws are enacted? How can it be said that love underlies law and government in these circumstances? This problem is related to the problem of evil: how can a good and all-powerful God allow evil? Theologians have answered this question by arguing that God has a morally sufficient purpose or end which justifies the evil which occurs in this world.[48] For the purposes of this chapter, it may be noted that God acts consistently with his attributes, including allowing evil to occur, even if the reasons are not apparent to us.

(Re)Defining Love

As noted above, several scriptural passages form the basis for a view that there is a tension between law (and justice) and love. However, I have argued that, based on the character of God, the two seemingly opposed dispositions can, indeed must, co-exist. The same God who gave the *lex talionis*, is the same God who is love and who exhorted "kingdom ethics." As noted, the entire law can be summarised in two commandments: love God and love your neighbour.[49] The question, therefore, is not whether, but *how* law and love are reconcilable.

I argue that the perception of a contradiction arises from an inaccurate understanding of love. Love is often equated with things like tolerance, compassion, forgiveness, and mercy. For ease of reference, I will refer to this (without intending to be pejorative) "soft love." But there is another side to love. While

---

47 "Introduction," in Cochran and Calo (eds), *Agape, Justice, and Law*, 9.
48 Reymond, *A New Systematic Theology of the Christian Faith*, 377.
49 Matthew 22:35–40.

love certainly includes these things, it cannot be equated with them. Love can sometimes be expressed in ways that are stern, and potentially in ways that can seem harsh and even violent. I will refer to this (again not pejoratively) as "tough love." The doctrine of simplicity requires that God acts consistently with all his attributes at all times, and so acted lovingly (and wisely, justly, powerfully) when acting in ways that may seem harsh.

"Loving violence" is legitimate, and distinguishable from pure violence, when exercised by properly constituted authorities such as civil governments, in accordance with the scope of the authority conferred on them. Thus, a law which authorised coercive punishment for a person convicted of a crime (such as incarceration), provided that law was consistent with the natural moral law, would be an example of "loving violence."

Two examples of tough love from the New Testament are as follows.[50] In Galatians 2, Paul opposed and rebuked Peter to his face, in the presence of the whole Galatian Church, because of Peter's hypocrisy in withdrawing from the gentiles (Gal. 2:11–21). Paul explained that nothing less than the gospel was at stake, and so Paul's rebuke was necessary to safeguard the gospel (Gal. 2:15–16). Paul's actions were therefore loving for Peter himself and for the Church as a whole. A second example is Paul's injunction to the Corinthians to expel from their midst a man who had been engaging in sexual immorality which would not have been tolerated outside the Church (1 Cor. 5). While this might seem harsh, Paul explained that this was for the good of both the Church and the erring brother: "you are to deliver this man to Satan for the destruction of the flesh, so that his spirit may be saved in the day of the Lord" (1 Cor. 5:5). That is, the public rebuke may prompt the man to repent and thereby his spirit will be saved.

Thus, public rebuke and Church discipline, while unpleasant, can (and ought to be) expressions of love. Other examples of the type of love I have in mind include defending one's family against an intruder who would cause them harm, which may result in injury to the intruder. Another example is the correction of a child by a parent, which Scripture describes as an act of love.[51] Leaving aside questions of the form that discipline should take, it is coercively applied to a child for his or her good.

Thus, acting lovingly can include acting forcefully or even coercively, as with Jesus cleansing the temple. Acting lovingly can include removing a corrupting influence from, say, a Church congregation. Indeed, as Paul makes clear, Church discipline and even excommunication are for the good of the person being disciplined: it is an act of love towards them, "so that his spirit may be saved in the day of the Lord."[52] Love can mean saying things that people do not want to hear, and perhaps find deeply offensive, and so acting lovingly can irreparably breach relationships. Love can be painful. As C.S. Lewis argued, "love may cause pain to

---

50 Other examples might be cited, e.g. Matthew 21:12–17; Acts 5:1–11.
51 Proverbs 13:24.
52 1 Corinthians 5:5.

its object, but only on the supposition that that object needs alteration to become fully lovable."[53] Hebrews 12 states that "[f]or the moment all discipline seems painful rather than pleasant, but later it yields the peaceful fruit of righteousness to those who have been trained by it."[54] God disciplining his children is an act of love, which sanctifies them. Love hates evil and is consistent with righteous anger against evil that love "does not rejoice at wrongdoing, but rejoices with the truth."[55]

Love, therefore, seems to be a many-faceted thing, which will require different responses in different situations. For some types of wrongs, a person can simply forgive and move on, even if this is injurious to their interests or property, and even if it was a criminal offence. The treatment of the thief Jean Valjean by Monseigneur Bienvenu in *Les Misérables* provides a wonderful depiction of this type of self-sacrificing love.[56] Sometimes, however, tough love as well as soft love is necessary.

As noted above, Thomas Shaffer has argued for a "jurisprudence of forgiveness," which undercuts the basis for civil or criminal punishment.[57] Against this, Scripture clearly teaches that forgiveness does not mean there should be no earthly or temporal consequences for one's actions. The Book of Samuel records examples of how God forgave David for various sins, but David nevertheless suffered consequences as a result of those sins.[58] Thus, it can be loving to impose consequences.

An instructive, although distasteful, example of this is the question of how Christian communities ought to deal with a person who has abused a child. Should an abuser be forgiven and welcomed back into the Church with open arms? In many religious institutions, allegations of child sexual abuse have often been approached as a sin to be dealt with privately through the lens of forgiveness and repentance rather than as a criminal offence.[59] The Australian *Royal Commission into Institutional Responses to Child Sexual Abuse* found that a culture of ready forgiveness, coupled with naivety and "a lack of knowledge about the dynamics of perpetrators and the perpetration of sexual abuse" made certain churches vulnerable to the occurrence of abuse.[60] Perpetrators who had confessed to having committed abuse were able to abuse further children. To use the terminology of this chapter, soft love was a manifestly inadequate response, which proved

---

53 CS Lewis, *The Problem of Pain* (Harper Collins, 1940), 48.
54 Hebrews 12:11.
55 1 Corinthians 13:6.
56 Victor Hugo, *Les Misérables* (1862), ch. XII.
57 Thomas L Shaffer, "The Radical Reformation and the Jurisprudence of Forgiveness," in Michael W McConnell, Robert F Cochran, Jr, and Angela C Carmella (eds), *Christian Perspectives on Legal Thought* (Yale University Press, 2001), 325–6.
58 2 Samuel 12:15–23; 24:1–17.
59 *Royal Commission into Institutional Responses to Child Sexual Abuse* (Final Report, 2017), vol. 16, book 1.
60 Ibid., 740.

extremely *unloving* to the children who were subsequently abused as a result of the Church's failure to deal properly with perpetrators. A better approach would be for churches not only to encourage forgiveness and reconciliation, but also to ensure that abusers face consequences such as restrictions on access to children and appropriate action by the relevant governmental authorities.

Thus, the precise action to be taken in any given situation will depend on the circumstances, and may include a mix of soft and tough love. But it should be noted that the principles outlined in this chapter require a reorientation in approach. On the approach outlined by Shaffer and others, the question is essentially an either/or question: should we be loving or should we be just? Acting "justly" is an alternative to acting "lovingly." I argue that there is no contradiction between these two, and so the question is not a binary alternative. Rather, in all situations, Christians should ask how love is best demonstrated in all the circumstances, and what expression that love should take.

Those who are wronged should readily forgive. The primary import of scriptural passages such as Matthew 5:38–42 and Romans 12:14–21 is to warn Christians against maintaining a vengeful spirit. The passages are, as with so much of the New Testament, about cultivating a heart disposition, rather than a command as to specific action to be taken. They are hyperbolic, but the demands they place on us should not be muted: Jesus is calling his followers to radical, costly discipleship. But this does not mean that there are no consequences for people's wrongdoing. And they are rules directed to disciples of Jesus, not to civil rulers in their official capacity. Sometimes love requires sterner actions such as handing a person over to the authorities, or warning other people. Such actions ought, of course, not to be motivated by a desire to quench a personal thirst for vengeance, but to protect others who might be harmed by a person's conduct, as well as preventing wrongdoers from persisting in their wrongdoing.

I draw the general conclusion that, in a world of sin, violence, and evil, love can legitimately be manifested in the destruction or prevention of evil. This is, of course, a statement of principle rather than a programme for action, and it will need some qualification. First, this is not the only manner in which love can be expressed; as already noted, love can, of course, be manifested in forgiving and excusing evil. Nevertheless, one legitimate manifestation of love is in the destruction or prevention of evil. Secondly, tough love has an institutional channel, being expressed through legitimately constituted authorities such as civil governments, church leaders, and parents, and subject to standards of evidence and due process. Christians personally ought to incline towards "soft love" rather than tough love, being prepared to forgive and suffer wrong rather than insisting on their rights.

Love, Law, and the Civil State

I have argued that law and love are not opposed to each other, and I have argued that love is broader than mercy and forgiveness, and can be expressed in ways that are stern, and potentially in ways that can seem harsh and even violent, being legitimately manifested in the prevention of evil. While, of course, divine law and human law cannot be simplistically equated, this argument nevertheless has implications for human law. Although modern civil governments have not been instituted directly by God, Romans 13 states that "there is no authority except from God, and those that exist have been instituted by God" and that a civil ruler is "an avenger who carries out God's wrath on the wrongdoer," in so doing acting as "the servant of God."[61] "Ordered government is not a human device, but something of divine origin."[62] Civil rulers are the institutions appointed to carry out the loving task of preventing and punishing evil, using coercive means, by enacting and enforcing laws which are consistent with the natural moral law. If one characteristic of love is that it "does not rejoice at wrongdoing, but rejoices with the truth,"[63] then bearing the sword against the wrongdoer is a loving act.

As noted earlier, the Christian tradition has long held that there is a universally applicable moral law to which humans are subject. Further, the standard Christian view is that human law ought to conform to the natural moral law, and any human law which does not so conform is a corruption of law, and not binding as a law.[64] If, as has been argued, love underlies divine law, then human law which conforms to the natural law will similarly be based on love. Accordingly, love underlies both human law and the institutions of civil government which enforce human law.

Forgiveness and justice can operate together. The ruler should carry out his or her task of enforcing justice, but should do so consistently with the rule of personal morality established by Matthew 5:38–42. That is, any person holding a public office ought to forgive any wrongs done to him or her personally. The office requires him or her to impose punishment dispassionately and without a vengeful spirit. Further, it is important to read Romans 12:17–21 and 13:1–7 together: as David VanDrunen notes, "Paul's point in Romans 13:4 is that God commissions the civil magistrate to do the very things he prohibits his Christian readers from doing a few verses earlier."[65] By conferring the power of the sword on civil rulers, Christians are freed from the need to take personal vengeance.

The enforcement of justice is also a legitimate manifestation of love. Civil governments can show their love for the community by enforcing justice, tempered by forbearance. Taking the example of criminal law, the enforcement of criminal punishment is loving to victims of crime or oppression, by providing a means of punishing wrongdoers for their crimes. This also expresses love towards the community at large, both by providing an orderly manner for the punishment

---

61 Romans 13:1, 4.
62 Leon Morris, *The Epistle to the Romans* (Eerdmans, 1988), 458.
63 1 Corinthians 13:6.
64 E.g. Aquinas, *Summa Theologica*, IaIIae 95.2; Helen Costigane, "Natural Law in the Roman Catholic Tradition," in Doe (ed.), *Christianity and Natural Law*, 35.
65 David VanDrunen, *Politics after Christendom: Political Theology in a Fractured World* (Zondervan, 2020), 288.

of crimes, which reduces the impetus for revenge and vigilante justice, and also by punishing or incarcerating offenders, and deterring others from committing similar crimes, which together promote a safer community. It is also the case that punishment is – or can be – loving to the offender.[66] Allowing a person to commit crimes with impunity is hardly good for the person, given that God commands all people everywhere to repent and will hold all people to account.[67] A finding of criminal guilt is in effect a coercive statement of the person's wrongdoing by an impartial judicial tribunal. This can be good for the person, forcing them to reckon with their sin, and the fact that there is a higher throne before whom the person will give an account. Similar comments could be made regarding the mechanisms of civil law such as torts and remedies for breach of contract.

These things can co-exist with attributes of "soft love" such as mercy and forgiveness. Of course, a demand for justice can be the outworking of a vengeful spirit, which is to be guarded against. Where a crime has been committed, it is the victim who has been wronged, not the state. If the victim is a Christian, they are enjoined to forgive, and show mercy. But this is not inconsistent with the institutions of civil government also punishing the offender and thereby protecting the community. Further, implementing the coercive mechanisms of the state does not mean that civil rulers cannot show love when carrying out their work. The human agents of civil government should themselves act with love in so doing; indeed, placing this function in the hands of impartial prosecutors and judges (rather than aggrieved victims and family members) increases the likelihood that punishment will not be the fruit of a vengeful spirit.

The discussions of law and love in the literature perhaps contain an excessive focus on criminal justice, which, as well as being the paradigmatic instantiation of law, is also the area of law which most clearly exemplifies a tension with love. But criminal (and civil) justice is not the only thing that civil rulers do. The tentacles of the state reach into many – too many – areas of life today.[68] Governments are responsible for an enormous range of things, including emergency services, defence, essential services such as water and sewerage, infrastructure, rubbish collection, public transport, town planning, welfare, disability support, public safety, and many more. Most of these require laws for their implementation. Many could not be provided effectively otherwise than by government. In, for example, providing support to people with disabilities, the government cares for the most vulnerable; in providing sewage collection and treatment, the government cares for the good of the community. These furnish examples of where the tension between law and love is much less acute than for criminal law.

---

66 Jeffrie G Murphy notes some aspects of the American prison system that are hardly loving: Jeffrie G Murphy, "Christian Love and Criminal Punishment," in Cochran and Calo (eds), *Agape, Justice and Law*, 157, 161–2.
67 Acts 17:30; 2 Corinthians 5:10.
68 This point was well expressed in the BBC 2019 Reith Lectures, delivered by Jonathan Sumption: www.bbc.co.uk/programmes/m00057m8.

Conclusion

This chapter has argued that the tension between law and love is misconceived. The character of God demands that the two can co-exist, given that God is a simple, uncompounded being, and therefore all of his attributes are operative at all times. God can never act inconsistently with any of his attributes, including the attributes of love, mercy, and graciousness, even when acting in ways that seem harsh to us. This demands a recalibration of our understanding of love. Love certainly demands forgiveness and self-denial, but this does not exhaust the concept of love. I have argued that, in a world of violence and wrongdoing, love can legitimately be manifested in the hatred and destruction of evil, and so civil rulers ought to be acting in love when enacting and enforcing laws which do just that. Enforcing criminal and civil justice ought to demonstrate love for God, by suppressing evil, defending the defenceless from oppression, and providing an avenue to right wrongs.

Some strands of Christian teaching, especially Anabaptism, have called for a radical withdrawal from the coercive institutions of government, which they see as being fundamentally at odds with the kingdom of Christ.[69] By contrast, mainstream Christianity has taught that the office of civil ruler is legitimate and that Christians can in good conscience hold such positions.[70] The argument in this chapter helps explain how it is possible to maintain at one and the same time the command to forgive and show mercy (Mt. 5:38–42 and Rom. 12:17–21) and the coercive nature of civil rule (Rom. 13:1–7) without incoherence.

On one level, this could be seen as a semantic debate about the meaning of words. For instance, VanDrunen argues that Christian love is an improper category to apply to law, but also recognises that the enforcement of retributive justice can be an act of love.[71] He thus allows a place for "love" – but not "Christian love" – in law and its enforcement. However, the issues go deeper than a debate about the meaning of terms, having potentially serious implications for theology. Reconciling the tension between law and love is a matter which goes to the legitimacy of the institutions of government. If law and Christian love are considered to be inconsistent with each other, it is a short step from there to argue for a complete withdrawal from all earthly mechanisms of authority – a step which, as noted, many in the Christian tradition have taken. Reconciling law and love is therefore fundamental to Christian engagement in the institutions of law and government.

Further, maintaining a contradiction between law and love could potentially compromise the doctrine of God. God is the lawgiver, the author of the Mosaic code including the *lex talionis*. He is also the author of "kingdom ethics," the expectation that disciples of Jesus will act in ways that are radically self-denying

---

69 E.g. John Howard Yoder, *The Politics of Jesus* (Grand Rapids: Eerdmans, 1994), 199.
70 *Westminster Confession of Faith*, XXIII.2.
71 VanDrunen, "Justice Tempered by Forbearance," 135–6.

and sacrificially loving. If these things are in tension or even contradictory, the logical implication is that there is a tension or even contradiction in the nature of God. This chapter has argued that we need to start at the foundation, with our view of God, according to which the giving of law is consistent with the attributes of love, mercy, and forgiveness, and reason from there about the nature of law and love.

8 Aquinas on Love, Law, and Happiness

The Interconnection between Divine Law, Human Law, and Rational Love

Stefanus Hendrianto SJ

Introduction

The declarational right to pursue happiness is one of the pillars of modern constitutional order.[1] The phrase "pursuit of happiness" in the US Declaration of Independence has appeared multiple times in its country's Supreme Court cases.[2] Many constitutional drafters throughout the world have adopted the "right to pursue happiness" in the text of their nations' constitutions.[3] Nevertheless, the pressing issue is whether human law can be directed to "the happiness of a society" or a "love" that secures freedom and equality. In this chapter, I will use the thought of St Thomas Aquinas to address this question. I choose this approach because Aquinas was a philosopher who extensively addressed the interconnection of law, love, and happiness.

This chapter aims to examine the interconnection between law, love, and happiness in the Aquinas' thought. The chapter argues that according to the Thomistic view, there exists an interconnection between love and happiness, in which God is the ultimate object of happiness, and the attainment of happiness involves both sensitive and rational love. Under this model, love and happiness are connected to law in the sense that God instructs human beings through law, which aims to foster a love of God and love of neighbour. Divine law is concerned with both the external and internal actions of human beings. External actions are presupposed by both sensitive and rational love, and at the same time, love also is the first cause for every internal action. By focusing on both external and internal actions, divine law helps foster the love of God through the completion of God (internal actions) as the ultimate happiness and, at the same time, cultivates love

---

1 For an excellent analysis on the philosophical and historical meaning of the right to pursue happiness, see John C Ford, "The Natural Law and the Right to Pursue Happiness," *Notre Dame Law Review* 26, no. 3 (1951): 103–144.
2 From 1823 until 2015, the phrase "pursuit of happiness" from the Declaration of Independence appeared in 94 United States Supreme Court cases. See Carli N Conklin, "The Origins of the Pursuit of Happiness," *Washington University Jurisprudence Review* 7 (2015): 195.
3 For instance, the right to pursue happiness has existed in the constitutions of Japan (1946), France (1958–preamble), South Korea (1997), Bhutan (2008), and Brazil (2010).

DOI: 10.4324/9781003148920-11

with fellow human beings (external actions). Thus, under an orientation towards the love of God and love of human beings, divine law directs human beings towards God as the source of ultimate happiness. While human law is mostly concerned with external actions, it also indirectly brings human beings to everlasting happiness, especially through its "supernatural inclination." Through promotion of the virtues, human law has a "supernatural inclination" that directs the human mind to contemplate God philosophically on a natural level and in heaven's beatific vision on the supernatural level.

Love and Happiness

It is difficult to define Aquinas' notion of love because he has many different ways to grasp it as a concept. While there is no concise definition of love in Aquinas' thought, it is essential to disaggregate his theory of love from differing definitions. For the sake of the limits of this chapter, I will try to review Aquinas' theory on love from two perspectives: the distinction between love and appetite, and the notion of God's love in connection with Aquinas' treatise on happiness.

Love and Appetite

In his *Summa Theologiae*, Aquinas uses the word "love" when he talks about human desire and the pursuit of a good. He also sometimes used the word "love" interchangeably with "appetite." Aquinas postulated that "love is something pertaining to appetite."[4] According to Aquinas, when we notice an appetible object, we develop a desire for that object, and then "the first change wrought in the appetite by the appetible object is called love."[5] In other words, a particular object might affect our appetite, and that effect is what Aquinas calls "love."

Nevertheless, the terms "love" and "appetite" still need to be sorted out because there are subtle differences between them.[6] First, there is a natural appetite, which orients each being to seek whatever is suitable to them according to their nature. In other words, each being pursues its end in accordance with their nature as created by God. This natural inclination is always the same because it is a consequence of the mere existence of the form, e.g. gravity follows the form of all weighted bodies. Aquinas writes that "in the natural appetite, the principle of this movement is the appetitive subject's connaturalness with the thing to which it tends and may be called natural love."[7] Aquinas used the example of a heavy

---

4 Thomas Aquinas, *Summa Theologiae*, Part I-II (Laurence Shapcote trans., 2012) (hereinafter "ST I-II"), Q.26, A.1, corpus.
5 Ibid., Q.26, A.2, corpus.
6 For a more detailed analysis on Aquinas' theory on love and appetite, see Edyta M Imai, "Contemplation and the Human Animal in the Philosophy of St. Thomas Aquinas," (PhD Dissertation, Loyola University Chicago, 2011).
7 Aquinas, ST I-II., Q.26, A.1, corpus (*In appetitu autem naturali, principium huiusmodi motus est connaturalitas appetentis ad id in quod tendit, quae dici potest amor naturalis, sicut ipsa connaturalitas corporis gravis ad locum medium est per gravitatem, et potest dici amor naturalis*).

object's natural tendency to fall to the ground, in which the tendency to seek the centre of gravity may be called "natural love."[8]

Second, there are sensitive appetites, inclinations of an animal kind that require sensory perception and action on the part of an animal. While the natural appetite is an inclination following the natural form, the sensitive appetite is an inclination following sensitive apprehension. The sensitive appetite enables an animal "to desire what it apprehends and not only that to which it is inclined by natural form."[9] The sensitive appetite exists in animals because it can apprehend something as good, desire it, and seek to obtain it. According to Aquinas, there are two powers of a sensitive appetite. First is the concupiscible power through which the animal is inclined "to seek what is suitable according to the senses and to fly from what is hurtful."[10] The second power is called the irascible power, enabling an animal to resist any attacks that hinder what is suitable and inflict harm. Animal appetites are found in the soul's sensitive part, and its complacency in many concupiscible things is called "sensitive love."

While sensitive appetites exist in animals, enabling them to apprehend some good, the human apprehension of good is followed by a judgment and free choice because humans have reason and will.[11] Aquinas referred to the will as "intellectual appetite." The inclination to will the good presented by the intellect is what Aquinas called "rational love." He wrote, "in like manner the aptitude of … the will to some good, that is to say, its very complacency in good is called … intellectual or rational love."[12] Intellectual or rational love implies a choice instead of merely an attraction towards something. Aquinas explained rational love as follows:

> For love has a wider signification than the others, since every dilection or charity is love, but not vice versa. Because dilection implies, in addition to love, a choice (*electionem*) made beforehand, as the very word denotes; and therefore, dilection is not in the concupiscible power, but only in the will and only in the rational nature.[13]

Intellectual love is the will for something that the intellect understands as a good worthy of pursuing. In other words, intellectual love follows the judgment of reason and signifies the choice of good.

---

8   For an analysis on Aquinas' understanding of gravitation, see Thomas McLaughlin, "Local Motion and the Principle of Inertia: Aquinas, Newtonian Physics, and Relativity," *International Philosophical Quarterly* 44, no. 2, issue 174: 239–264 (June 2004).
9   Thomas Aquinas, *Summa Theologiae*, Part I (Laurence Shapcote trans., 2012) (hereinafter ST I), Q.80, A.1, corpus.
10 Ibid., Q.81, A.2, corpus.
11 For a more detailed analysis on judgment, will and love, see Robert Pasnau, *Thomas Aquinas on Human Nature* (Cambridge: Cambridge University Press, 2002).
12 Aquinas, ST I-II, Q.26, A.1.
13 Ibid., Q.26, A.3.

Aquinas used the term "love" to designate three kinds of appetites. The definition of "love" can be different according to natural, sensitive, or intellectual types of appetite. The word "love" in reference to natural appetites is not a passion. For instance, the stone's "love" for the ground is merely natural inclination characteristic of non-living and corporeal beings. Love in the sense of passion pertains only to sensitive appetites, which follow the sensitive apprehension of good. Love, as a passion, only belongs to the concupiscible power of the soul. In human beings, the apprehension of a good would be followed by the judgment of reason. Therefore, intellectual love is not a passion because passion precedes judgment. The intellect is supposed to consider various pieces of data presented to it by the passions and judge the situation accordingly. In sum, intellectual love presupposes sensitive love, and sensitive love presupposes natural love.

Happiness and Love of God

The previous analysis shows that Aquinas defined will as an intellectual love derived from intellectual appetite. The question is whether all human actions only belong to intellectual love. We can find an answer to this question by investigating Aquinas' theory on why human beings are drawn to love God. Aquinas argued that we are motivated to seek God and contemplate God because "the intellect needs to reach the very Essence of the First Cause."[14] Aquinas explained that our love for God is in the sense of passion, which he had defined as sensitive love. He wrote:

> [T]he words love (*amor*) signifies something more Godlike than *dilection*, was because love (*amor*) denotes a passion, especially insofar as it is in the sensitive appetite, whereas *dilection* presupposes the judgement of reason. But it is possible for man to tend to God by love, being as it were passively drawn by Him, more than he can possibly be drawn thereto by his reason, which pertains to the nature of *dilection*, as stated above. And consequently love (*amor*) is more Godlike than *dilection*.[15]

Here, Aquinas distinguishes between *dilection* and love (*amor*); and it is love of some good based on our sensitive appetite (*amor*), which caused us to pursue God as our final end.

Aquinas argued in essence that we come to know about God only through learning about other things, and so little by little, we ought to come closer to God the more we know about the natural world. He posited: "God is knowable and loveable for Himself ... but with regards to us, since our knowledge is derived through the senses, those things are knowable first, which are nearer to

---

14 Ibid., Q.3, A.8, corpus.
15 Ibid., Q.26, A.4.

our senses."[16] In sum, Aquinas' chain of argument is as follows: we love God first because He constitutes the greatest good. We are naturally drawn to love God first, although we do not know what God is and what constitutes his greatest good. Only later, we may begin acquiring enough knowledge about God and then loving him with intellectual love.

To understand Aquinas' theory on humans' love for God as passion, one must turn to his treatise on happiness[17] where he argued that we are motivated to seek "perfect happiness" because we want to know the essence of the First Cause.[18] In *Prima Pars*, Aquinas wrote that "the will tends naturally to its last end; for every man naturally wills happiness."[19] Speaking about the last end, Aquinas distinguishes between end as an object and end as enjoyment.[20] In the first sense, the object of the last end is uncreated good, namely God,[21] which, according to Aquinas, "by His infinite goodness can perfectly satisfy man's will."[22] In the second sense, a human being's last end is the "attainment or enjoyment of the last end."[23] Aquinas stated further that if we consider "man's happiness in its cause or object, then it is something uncreated, but if we consider it as to every essence of happiness, then it is something created." In short, happiness is uncreated, but the enjoyment of happiness is something created.

At this point, Aquinas' theory on happiness still needs to be sorted out because it is not clear whether happiness can be interpreted as the desire for the uncreated or created good. Aquinas argued that "it is impossible for any created good to constitute man's happiness,"[24] because happiness is the perfect good, in which God alone can satisfy a person's will for happiness. Aquinas then concluded that "God alone constitutes man's happiness."[25] Nevertheless, Aquinas also equated the word "happiness" to the enjoyment of the last end. In Aquinas' mind, whenever we speak of the attainment of the enjoyment of the last end, it is something that concerns one's soul. He argued that "since man attains happiness through his soul. Therefore, the thing itself which is desired as end, is that which constitute happiness, and makes man happy, but the attainment of this thing is called happiness."[26] Since the attainment of the last end is something created, arguably happiness is

---

16 Thomas Aquinas, *Summa Theologiae*, Part II-II (Laurence Shapcote trans., 2012) (hereinafter ST II-II), Q.27, A.4, corpus.
17 For an excellent analysis on the relationship between love and happiness in Aquinas' theory, see Daniel Shields, "Aquinas on Will, Happiness and God: The Problem of Love and Aristotle's Liber de Bona Fortuna," *American Catholic Philosophical Quarterly* 91, no. 1 (2017): 113–42.
18 Aquinas, ST I, Q.60, A.2, corpus.
19 Ibid., Q.60, A.2, corpus.
20 Aquinas, ST I-II, Q.1, A.8.
21 Aquinas, ST I, Q.3, A.1, corpus.
22 Ibid.
23 Ibid.
24 Aquinas, ST I-II, Q.2, A.8.
25 Ibid.
26 Aquinas, ST I-II, Q.2, A.7.

also related to the created good. Nevertheless, this conclusion seems contradictory with Aquinas' earlier statement, in which he strongly argued that it is God alone that constitutes human happiness. So, the pressing question is whether *God* as the object of happiness is distinct from the enjoyment of happiness in itself.

Aquinas argued that there are two things that are needed for happiness: the essence of happiness and its proper accident.[27] He argued further, "as to the very essence of happiness; it cannot consist in the act of the will."[28] Aquinas did not stop here, but he reaffirmed his argument by stating, "happiness is the attainment of the last end. But the attainment of the end does not consist in the very act of will."[29] If the essence of happiness does not consist in the act of the will, then how can one understand happiness? For Aquinas, happiness is a human operation,[30] which consists of an act of the intellect.[31] To be precise, happiness is the operation of the speculative intellect. As Aquinas stated:

> [I]f man's happiness is an operation; it must need be man's highest operation. Now man's highest operation is that of his highest power in respect of its highest object: and his highest power is the intellect, whose highest object is the Divine Good, which is the object, not of the practical but of the speculative intellect.[32]

Above all, happiness consists of contemplating God because "the intellect needs to reach the very Essence of the First Cause to reach the perfect happiness."[33] Thus, happiness is the act of speculative intellect about God, which takes place on the natural level.

In sum, Aquinas' argument on happiness is as follows: there are two elements of happiness: the object and the attainment. God is the object of happiness because only God can satisfy a human being's will. The attainment of happiness is not the act of the will, but an intellectual act directed towards God. Having traced Aquinas' argument on happiness, now we can turn back to whether human actions, i.e. loving God, only belong to the category of intellectual love.

Speaking about contemplation of God, Aquinas explained that, while God is the final cause, we can only come to know him at the end after studying his creation. Aquinas wrote:

> Since to love God (*dilectio Dei*) is something greater than to know Him ... it follows that love of God presupposes knowledge of God. And because this knowledge does not rest in creatures, but, through them, tends to something

---

27 Ibid., Q.3, A.4.
28 Ibid.
29 Ibid.
30 Ibid., Q.3, A.2, corpus.
31 Ibid., Q.3, A.4, corpus.
32 Ibid., Q.3, A.5, corpus.
33 Ibid., Q.3, A.8, corpus.

else, love (*dilectio*) begins there, and thence goes on to other things by a circular movement so to speak; for knowledge begins from creatures, tends to God, and love (*dilectio*) begins with God as the last end and passes to creatures.[34]

In explaining this love of God, Aquinas uses *dilectio*, which means he refers to rational love or intellectual love. Nevertheless, he also explained that intellectual love presupposes sensitive love. We are led to the knowledge of God through the knowledge of his creatures; by loving things created by God through our sensitive love, we are moving little by little closer to our last end, that is God.

Aquinas tells us that the journey to God's contemplation begins with an attraction to his creatures. The love of God's creatures is a passion that belongs to the sensitive appetite. If a person chooses an object for their study and then contemplates the subject, they must be directed by their sensitive appetite. It is the sensitive appetite that becomes the driving force of our actions, which eventually lead us to contemplation. The contemplation of God is love (*dilectio*) found in the intellectual appetite because it includes our rational choice. But love (*dilectio*) of God motivated by intellectual appetite must be accompanied by love as passion (*amor*), which is derived from our sensitive love. Thus, the contemplation of God always involves both intellectual appetite and sensitive appetite.

Law and Love

Aquinas' theory on love is not straightforward, but at least, we already have a few glimpses of his theory on love. Now, we can turn to the main discussion on law and love. Before we move to a detailed discussion on the connection between law and love, a few caveats are necessary to understand the notion of law in Aquinas' mind. In *Summa Theologiae*, Aquinas explained that there are four types of law: an eternal law (*lex aeterna*), a natural law (*lex naturalis*), a human law (*lex humana*), and a divine law (*lex divina*).[35]

In this chapter, I will limit the discussion to divine law's role in human law.[36] This chapter's point of departure is Aquinas' argument on the distinction between divine and human laws, in which he explains:

> Again, it must be observed that the end of human law is different from the end of Divine Law. For the end of human law is the temporal tranquility

---

34 Aquinas, ST II-II, Q.27, A.4, ad 2.
35 Aquinas, ST I-II, Q.91.
36 This chapter is taking an unorthodox approach to investigating the link between divine law and human law. Most of the scholarship on Aquinas' Treatise on Law usually focuses on the nexus between the divine law and natural law. For instance, see Jean Porter, *Ministers of the Law: A Natural Law Theory of Legal Authority* (Grand Rapids, MI: Wiliam B Eerdmans Pub. Co., 2010); Fulvio Di Blasi, *God and the Natural Law: A Rereading of Thomas Aquinas* (South Bend, IN: St Augustine's Press, 2006).

of the state, which ends law effects by directing external actions, as regards those evils which might disturb the peaceful condition of the state. On the other hand, the end of the Divine Law is to bring a man to that end which is everlasting happiness; which end is hindered by any sin, not only external but also of internal action.[37]

The passage suggests that the purposes of human and divine law are different. Several pressing questions arise from Aquinas' proposition on the distinction between divine law and human law: whether divine law is meant only to direct humans to their supernatural end; whether human law has anything to do with the supernatural end; and, finally, whether there is a point of contact between divine law and human law.

External and Internal Actions

Before one can answer these questions, it is necessary to review Aquinas' theory of action, as it helps us understand the distinction between the purpose of divine law and human law. In Aquinas' philosophy of action, he distinguished *actus interioris* (internal act) and *actus exterioris* (external act).[38] Aquinas postulated that the end is the proper object of the internal act, while the object of the external action is the action that it brought to bear.[39] In other words, an external action derives from the object on which it bears, and the internal act derives from its end.

Both internal and external acts are voluntary actions, which are commanded by the human will. Aquinas argued that

> exterior action is the object of the will, inasmuch as it proposed to the will by the reason, as good apprehended and ordained by the reason and thus it is prior to the good in the act of the will.[40]

Based on this proposition, one can presume that all external actions are an object of love; it is presupposed by a good apprehension of sensitive love and ordained by rational love. Moreover, Aquinas posits that "when one power is the mover of the other, then their acts are, in a way one,"[41] which means that sensitive love

---

37 Aquinas, ST I-II, Q.98, A.1, corpus.
38 For a more detailed analysis of Aquinas' theory of external and interior actions, see Duarte Sousa-Lara, "Aquinas on Interior and Exterior Acts: Clarifying a Key Aspect of His Action Theory," *Josephinum Journal of Theology* 15, no. 2 (2008): 277–316; see also Dana L Dillon, "As Soul to Body: The Interior Act of the Will in Thomas Aquinas and the Importance of First-Person Perspective in Accounts of Moral Action" (PhD Dissertation, Duke University, 2008).
39 Aquinas, ST I-II, Q.18, Art 7, corpus.
40 Ibid., Q.20, A.1, ad 1.
41 Ibid., 17, A.4, ad 1.

and rational love propose to the will some good that eventually manifests into an external action altogether.

Concerning internal actions, Aquinas argues that "the will moves the intellect and all the powers of the soul."[42] Nevertheless, "there is no other passion of the soul that presuppose love of some kind,"[43] because in every passion of the soul, there is love that moves towards something or rests in something. Aquinas argues, "every movement towards something or rest in something, arises from some kinship of aptness to thing; and in this does love consist."[44] While every desire of the soul will not be caused by love, some particular love may cause some desire. Aquinas used an example of a man who loves pleasure, but every pleasure is "caused by another love; for none takes pleasure save in that which is loved in some way."[45] The bottom line is that Aquinas believed that love causes all the inner dynamics of human beings, as he wrote, "desire, sadness and pleasure and … all other passions of the souls result from love." Finally, Aquinas postulated that "love is the root and cause of every emotion." Therefore, love is the first cause of every internal action.

In sum, both internal and external actions are related to love. Based on Aquinas' explanation of the relationship between human action and love, I now examine in more detail the purpose of divine law and human law regarding human action and love.

What Is the Purpose of Divine Law?

In his Treatise on Law, Thomas argued that it was necessary to have divine law for directing human conduct for four different reasons.[46] First, since humans are directed to a supernatural end that goes beyond natural law and human law, humans must then be directed by another law given by God. Second, because of the uncertainty of human judgment, different people can form different judgments; therefore, so that humans may know without any doubt what they ought to do and what they ought to avoid, God gave divine law. Third, since human law could not sufficiently direct internal acts, yet the perfection of virtue requires that humans have both the right internal and external acts, it was necessary for this purpose that a divine law should supervene (*superveniret*). Finally, since human law cannot punish or forbid all evil acts, it was necessary to have a divine law so that no evil deed might remain unforbidden and unpunished.

When we read Aquinas' argument on divine law, we must keep in mind that the term divine law (*lex divina*) involves a possible textual ambiguity engendered by Aquinas' practice of using a general term to refer to a particular part of divine

---

42 Aquinas, ST I, Q.82, A.4.
43 Aquinas, ST I-II, Q.27, A.4, corpus.
44 Ibid.
45 Ibid., Q.27, A.4, ad 1.
46 Ibid., Q.91, A.4.

Table 8.1 How the Old Law Shows Forth the Precepts of the Natural Law

The Four Purposes of Divine Law	The Specific Part of Divine Law Directed to Each Purpose
1. Directs humans to their supernatural end	New Law (and perhaps moral precepts of the Old Law)
2. Corrects uncertain judgments	Moral precepts of the Old Law (and perhaps ceremonial and judicial precepts)
3. Deals with the interior movements of the soul	New Law alone
4. Forbids all evil deeds	Both Old Law and New Law together

Source: This table was adapted from Randall Smith, "How the Old Law Shows Forth the Precepts of the Natural Law: A Commentary on Certain Questions Concerning the Law in the Summa of Theology of Thomas Aquinas" (PhD Dissertation, University of Notre Dame, 1998), 48.

law. Divine law includes both the Old Law (*lex vetus*) and the New Law (*lex nova*). Furthermore, Aquinas explained that there are three kinds of precepts in the Old Law: the moral precepts (*scilicet moralia*), the ceremonial precepts (*caeremonialia*), and the judicial precepts (*iudicialia*).[47] When Aquinas explained the purpose of divine law, he might have been referring to either divine law in general or to one of the particular kinds of divine law.

If we try to match divine law's four different purposes to the particular part of divine law, we generate Table 8.1.

One of the purposes of divine law is to direct humans towards their supernatural end. In the *Summa Contra Gentiles*, Aquinas said, "the end for the human creature is to cling to God, since in this does happiness consists."[48] The best way for a human to cling to God, according to Aquinas, is through an act of love.[49] Nevertheless, the role of divine law is not merely to direct humans to the love of God; it also aims to help humans know "how to live in relation to other men according to the order of reason."[50]

How could humans live with others according to the order of reason? Aquinas answered the question by providing an answer within the context of the precepts of justice. He said, "it was necessary that through Divine law, precepts of justice be given so that each man would give his neighbor his due."[51] Furthermore, Aquinas stressed that the precepts of justice must accompany the virtue of charity. He said:

> Now, man is moved in two ways to observe this justice that is prescribed by the Divine Law: first, from within; second, from without. From within, when

---

47 Ibid., Q.99, A.4.
48 Thomas Aquinas, *Summa Contra Gentiles* (Laurence Shapcote trans.) (hereinafter "SCG") Book III, Chapter 115.3.
49 Ibid., Book III, Chapter 116.1.
50 Ibid., Book III, Chapter 128.1.
51 Ibid., Book III, Chapter 128.6.

> man is willing to observe the precepts of the divine law. This is the result of man's love of God and his neighbor: for anyone who loves another gives him his due willingly and with pleasure and gives even more with liberality. Hence the entire fulfillment of the law depends on love, according to the word of the Apostle: *Love is the fulfilling of the law* (Rom 13.10). Again, our Lord says that *on these two commandments,* that is, on the love of God and of neighbor.[52]
> (Mt. 22.40)

The bottom line is that divine law prescribes justice's precepts, which enable humans to love their neighbour.

Why is there a need for an order in the relation between a person to other persons? Why doesn't divine law just direct each person individually to the knowledge of God? Aquinas argues that all persons are united in having God as their ultimate end to know and to love God. Therefore, there must be "a union in affection among those for whom there is one common end."[53] By sharing a common end, all persons are bound only to love God and love other persons. Aquinas argued further that whoever loves a person must also love those loved by that person. If one loves God, then one must love other people who are loved by God.[54] Furthermore, Aquinas argued that the love of God and neighbour is mutually interdependent because the help of others would foster one's love for God. He said:

> Again, the end of Divine law is that a man may adhere to God. Now, in this, one man is assisted by another both in his knowledge and in his affections, because one man helps another to know the truth, and one urges another to good, and withdraws him from evil.[55]

In short, Aquinas posited that there is a mutual relationship between the love of God and the love of neighbour.

Based on Aquinas' analysis of divine law, we can conclude that divine law directs humans to two ends primarily: the love of God and the love of neighbour. A human's natural end is to love and to know God; this fundamental love of God must then be extended to all those loved by God. In summary, a person is bound to love all those who share a common end, mainly because humans can help each other reach their common goal to love God.

What is the Purpose of Human Law?

After exploring Aquinas' treatment of divine law, this chapter now addresses the purpose of human law. Aquinas envisioned the role of human law in the context

---

52 Ibid., Book III, Chapter 128.8.
53 Ibid., Book III, Chapter 117.2.
54 Ibid.
55 Ibid., Book III, Chapter 128.2.

Aquinas on Love, Law, and Happiness 141

of moral education; that of checking the bad people's inclination to vice or at least their facility for acting on those inclinations.[56] Here, Aquinas provided a negative narrative of human law as a pedagogical exercise for bad people.[57]

Aquinas began his argument by stating that "human beings have a natural aptitude for virtue, but the perfection of virtue must be acquired by man by means of some kind of training."[58] In Aquinas' view, human beings are not readily self-sufficient regarding this training, since the perfection of virtue consists chiefly of human beings' restraint from excessive pleasures, towards which they are most prone.

Aquinas explained:

> [f]rom becoming accustomed to avoid evil and fulfill what is good, through fear of punishment, one is sometimes led on to do so likewise, with delight and of one's own accord. Accordingly, law, even by punishing, leads men on to being good.[59]

This passage suggests that Aquinas constrained human law only for moral pedagogy, which means human law contributes more directly to the achievement of political peace than directing humans to the supernatural end.

If Aquinas envisioned the role of human law as moral education for bad people, the next question is whether good people are subject to the law. Aquinas argued that "the virtuous and righteous are not subject to the Law, but only the wicked."[60] Aquinas asserted further that "to those young people who are inclined to acts of virtue, by their good natural disposition, or by custom, or rather by the gift of God, paternal training suffices, which is by admonitions."[61] In short, Aquinas believed that there is no real need for human law to provide training for a mature virtuous person. The good person needs laws only to compel the bad to leave them alone, and for those inclined to do good, parental training is sufficient.

Aquinas' position seems clear that virtuous and righteous people are not subject to the law. Nevertheless, in a different part of *Summa Theologiae*, Aquinas expressed a different opinion. He stated:

> [E]very law was imposed on two kinds of men. Because it is imposed on some men who are hard-hearted and proud, whom the law restrains and

---

56 Aquinas, ST I-II, Q.95–97.
57 Mary Keys originally developed the distinction between Aquinas' negative and positive narrative on the law in Mary Keys, *Aquinas, Aristotle, and the Promise of the Common Good* (Cambridge: Cambridge University Press, 2006). For an excellent treatment of Aquinas' theory of how law can curb moral vice, see Robert P George, *Making Men Moral: Civil Liberties and Public Morality* (Oxford: Clarendon Press, 1993).
58 Aquinas, ST I-II, Q.95, A.1.
59 Ibid., Q.92, A.2, ad. 4.
60 Ibid., Q.96, A.5.
61 Ibid., Q.95, A.1.

tames: and it is also imposed on good men who, through being instructed by the laws, are helped to fulfill what they desire to do.[62]

Apparently, Aquinas suggested that every law was imposed on both good and bad people.

Aquinas' proposition on the role of law in directing good people raises a question of whether his thoughts on the subject matter were merely muddled or contradictory. It is important to note that Aquinas discussed the imposition of law upon good people in the section on divine law. Thus, to understand the purpose of law in directing the good person, we must explore Aquinas' analysis of divine law. Aquinas explained:

> [E]very law is given to people. Now people contains two kinds of men: some, prone to evil, who have to be coerced by the precepts of the law, as stated above (I-II 95, 1); some, inclined to good, either from nature or from custom, or rather from grace; and the like have to be taught and improved by means of the precepts of the law. Accordingly, with regard to both kinds of the law. Accordingly, with regard to both kinds of men it was expedient that the Old Law should contain many ceremonial precepts.[63]

Aquinas suggested that the good lawgiver must formulate and promulgate the law to both good and bad persons. This suggestion also applied to human lawmakers, who are supposed to enact a law for both good and bad persons.

Aquinas further argued, "with regard to good men, the Law was given to them as a help; which was most needed by the people, at the time when the natural law began to be obscured on account of the exuberance of sin."[64] Aquinas saw the necessity for divine law to aid the good person because "the natural law can be blotted out from the human heart, either by evil persuasions ... or by vicious custom and corrupt habits."[65] The bottom line is that moral evil and corrupt habits can infect those with fundamentally good hearts.

While Aquinas argued that human law's objective is to direct bad people, there is also another positive aspect of human law that could help good people towards a state of flourishing and perfection. Human law and divine law share a mutual interest to direct both good and bad people. While divine law is directing good and bad people towards a union with God, human law is directing good and bad people towards a perfect community.

Love: The Point of Contact between Divine Law and Human Law

Having explained divine law and human law's objective, I now propose a thought experiment suggesting that there is contact between divine law and human law. I

---

62 Ibid., Q.98, A.6.
63 Ibid., Q.101, A.3.
64 Ibid., Q.98, A.6.
65 Ibid., Q.98, A.6.

argue that the contact between divine law and human law lies in their relationship to love.

As explained earlier, divine law brings people to love God as their supernatural end and leads people to love their neighbour. Moreover, divine law even directly commands people to love their neighbour. Human law, however, does not command the love of persons because legislators are only concerned over external acts of human beings,[66] instead of internal acts. Nevertheless, human law commands acts of virtue, and it tends to produce habits of virtue. Although human law will not command acts of love, it could secure friendship between virtuous people. In the friendship between virtuous persons, Aquinas said, "those who are alike in virtue wish one another good inasmuch as they are virtuous. But they are good in themselves, for virtue is a kind of perfection making man good and his work good."[67] Considering that human law could secure friendship between virtuous persons, it somehow could lead humans to mutual love. In other words, although human law does not command acts of love, it could indirectly bring humans to love one another.

Human law could also indirectly lead people to love God through its "supernatural inclination," in which it can help people avoid sin. Aquinas argued that "sin diminishes the natural inclination to virtue."[68] Furthermore, Aquinas stated that "wherefore as sin is opposed to virtue, from the very fact that a man sins, there results in a diminution of that good of nature, which is the inclination to virtue."[69] If human law is an effective training for the perfection of virtue, presumably human law will also help humans to combat sin, which tends to diminish humans' inclination to virtue.

To understand the "supernatural inclination" of human law, one must revisit Aquinas' treatment of the state of "original justice" before original sin. Aquinas said, "original justice was a gift of grace, conferred by God on all human nature in our first parent. This gift the first man lost by his first sin."[70] Aquinas explained further that

> the original justice was forfeited through the sin of our first parent; so that all the powers of the soul are left, as it were, destitute of their proper order, whereby they are naturally directed to virtue; which destitution is called a wounding of nature.[71]

Aquinas continued to argue that the soul's destitute powers after the original sin could be the subject of virtue. Aquinas said, "the reason, where prudence

---

66 Ibid., Q.100, A.9.
67 Thomas Aquinas, *Sententia libri Ethicorum* (Commentary on the Ethics of Aristotle), Book VIII Lecture 3, 1575.
68 Aquinas, ST I-II, Q.85, A.1.
69 Ibid., Q.85, A.1.
70 Ibid., Q.81, A.3.
71 Ibid., Q.85, A.3.

resides, the will, where justice is, the irascible, the subject of fortitude, and the concupiscible, the subject of temperance."[72] Considering that the human inclination to virtue is diminished on account of original sin, then human law could contribute to healing the wounded soul through the promotion of virtues. In the state of "original justice," there was no need for law and specifically human law promulgated by the political government. After the fall, however, the government needed to promulgate a human law, which could help people heal their wounded nature due to their first parent's sin. In sum, while human law directs man towards the temporal aims, it also has a "supernatural inclination" that may direct the human mind to love God by healing its wounded nature.

Conclusion

This chapter begins with an analysis of the meaning of love. Aquinas used the term "love" to designate three types of appetites: natural, sensitive, or intellectual. Consequently, the definition of "love" can be different according to appetites: natural love in reference to natural appetite; sensitive love that pertains to sensitive appetite; and intellectual love or rational love that derives from intellectual appetite. Based on this classification, Aquinas distinguishes love (*amor*) as a sensitive love and the dilection (*dilectio*) in the sense of rational love.

Aquinas explained further the distinction between these two types of love in his analysis of human love for God. Aquinas posited that we are naturally drawn to God first through our sensitive love, and later at some point, we begin acquiring knowledge about God through our rational love. Aquinas' theory of love for God as both sensitive and rational love fall into place in his Treatise on Happiness. Aquinas posited two elements of happiness: first, God is the object of happiness as it is only God who can satisfy a human's will for happiness. Second is the attainment of happiness, which is an act of speculative intellect directed to God. Thus, the attainment of happiness consists of the contemplation of God on the natural level. Nevertheless, while the contemplation of God is love (*dilectio*) in the sense of rational love, it must be accompanied by love (*amor*) as passion because human beings must be directed by their sensitive love about God first before it leads us to contemplation about God. In sum, the contemplation of God as perfect happiness always involves both rational and sensitive loves.

This chapter then explores the interconnection between law and love by first looking into Aquinas' theory on human action. In Aquinas' philosophy of action, he distinguishes *actus interioris* (internal act) and *actus exterioris* (external act). Aquinas explained that both internal and external actions are voluntary actions, commanded by human will. The will is the efficient cause of all external actions presupposed by both sensitive love and rational love. With regard to internal actions, Aquinas postulated that love is the root of all emotions and the inner

---

72 Ibid.

dynamics of human beings, such as desire, sadness, pleasure, and all other passion of the souls. Thus, love is the first cause of every internal action.

In his Treatise on Law, Aquinas explained the different types of law, which relate to the external actions and internal actions. This chapter primarily focuses on Aquinas' treatment of the difference between divine law and human law. The former is ordered towards everlasting happiness by directing both external and internal actions. Nevertheless, the latter only directs external actions with the focus on the temporal tranquility of the state.

One of the purposes of divine law is to direct human beings towards God as the perfect happiness. Here, Aquinas is speaking about contemplating God philosophically on the natural level and in heaven's beatific vision on the supernatural level. Divine law also deals with the soul's interior movement, which means that it directs internal actions of human beings. Nevertheless, divine law also directs the external actions by directing human beings to love their neighbour. The bottom line is that Aquinas argued that the love of God and love of neighbour are mutually interdependent because to love fellow human beings would foster one's love for God.

While divine law directs people to God as the ultimate happiness, human law's focus is more on the external actions; that is directing both good and bad people in a perfect community. Nevertheless, there is a point of contact between divine law and human law, with love as their point of contact. Human law commands an act of virtue, which could help to secure friendship between virtuous people. Through friendship among virtuous people, human law can lead people to love one another. Moreover, human law also can indirectly lead people to love God through its "supernatural inclination." The notion of supernatural inclination must be understood in the context of original sin. The original sin diminished human inclination to virtues. Therefore, after the fall, there is a need to promulgate a human law, which could help people to heal their wounded nature due to original sin. Human law also has a "supernatural inclination" that directs the human mind to the beatific vision by promoting virtues. In sum, while human law primarily concerns external acts, it also indirectly leads human beings to love God and love their neighbour.

This chapter aims to address whether human law, such as a constitution, can be directed to the "happiness of a society" or foster "love" among citizens. The answer is no insofar as we define happiness and love in the context of wealth, honour, glory, power, bodily good, and pleasure. Aquinas argued that human beings would not find ultimate happiness in created goods, for only God can satisfy the human desire for happiness. Aquinas posited that the object of happiness is God, and the attainment of happiness is an act of rational love preceded by sensitive love. Such happiness can be obtained with the help of both divine law and human law, in which the former directs human beings to love God and their neighbour and the latter indirectly also leading human beings to love God and their neighbour through the perfection of virtues. In sum, there is an interconnection between law, love, and happiness, in which both divine law and human law help foster sensitive and rational love in human beings so that they can reach God as the perfect happiness.

Part III
The Ethics of Law and Love

9 From Alterity to Proximity

Emmanuel Levinas on the Natural Law of Love

Jonathan Crowe

Introduction

Emmanuel Levinas' account of ethics emphasises the face-to-face relation with the other. Levinas' rich and nuanced phenomenology of this relation traces a dynamic movement – akin to a dance – where the self is continually compelled to both separate herself from and approach the other. Levinas' emphasis in his first major work, *Totality and Infinity*,[1] falls on the radical alterity of the other. It is the utter strangeness of the other that compels me to leave the comfort of my own enjoyment and recognise her ethical demands. His second major work, *Otherwise than Being*,[2] shifts the focus to the subject's need to approach the other. This desire for the other places the subject in a relation of proximity, where the suffering and vulnerability of the other is laid bare. Ultimately, for Levinas, the proximity of the other necessitates substitution, the unconditional love of one who is ultimately responsible.

This chapter argues that Levinas' two major works yield a coherent and compelling account of the diachronic movement of ethical life. Levinas shows, first, how the subject is naturally inclined to self-absorption and enjoyment; second, how this egoistic outlook is inherently unstable; and, third, how the subject's initial focus on enjoyment creates the separation necessary to assume responsibility for the other. I contend that Levinas' theory traces what might properly be described as the *natural law of love*. This conception of natural law captures and resolves the central tension of human ethics: I am responsible before God, but because I am not God, I must fail in my responsibilities. Love, as the ultimate good, imposes infinitely demanding duties on us while also offering forgiveness for our inevitable failures. Ethics becomes the "spiritual optics" that connects earthly and heavenly love (TI, 78).

---

1 Emmanuel Levinas, *Totality and Infinity: An Essay on Exteriority*, trans. Alphonso Lingis (Pittsburgh: Duquesne University Press, 1969) (hereinafter TI).
2 Emmanuel Levinas, *Otherwise than Being or Beyond Essence*, trans. Alphonso Lingis (Pittsburgh: Duquesne University Press, 1998) (hereinafter OB).

From Alterity …

Who is the other? Not a thing, but not another self either. The other, for Levinas, is ungraspable: she eludes our attempts to instrumentalise her or reduce her to concepts or language. That is not to say that these forms of reduction cannot be attempted. Indeed, we are continually drawn to attempt them. These attempts, however, are ultimately doomed to failure and therefore inherently unstable. One may describe an object and situate it for one's use; where the self is concerned, one may form priorities and projects, even introspect to pin down one's deeper values and motivations. The other, however, resists these modes of enquiry. Any attempt to pin down the other runs up against the irresistible fact of her subjectivity, which signals numerous shifting possibilities in terms of her plans and responses.

The other's subjectivity is not fixed in place and time, but strikingly open. The other is other in a deeper sense than mere objects in the world that are, in a less radical way, other than me. "The other metaphysically desired," as Levinas puts it, "is not 'other' like the bread I eat, the land in which I dwell, the landscape I contemplate" (TI, 33). These things are not me, but can nonetheless be reduced to their use for me, employed as means to satisfy my lack. "Their *alterity* is thereby reabsorbed into my own identity as a thinker or a possessor" (TI, 33). However, it is not possible to straightforwardly possess the other in this way. The other engages the subject's attention at a primordial level while also threatening her sense of control. It is, in this sense, a profoundly unsettling experience. My need and desire to approach the other "tends towards *something else entirely*, toward the *absolutely other*" (TI, 33). The ineffability of the other opens infinity and "overflows the thought that thinks it" (TI, 25).

The unsettling nature of the encounter with the other arises from the way in which it challenges the subject's sense of comfort and control over the world. Humans, for Levinas, naturally seek comfort and security. Our natural mode of being takes the form of what he calls "a *sojourn* [*séjour*] in the world" (TI, 37). "The *way* of the I against the 'other' of the world," he claims, "consists in *sojourning*, in *identifying oneself* by existing here *at home with oneself* [*chez soi*]" (TI, 37). The sojourner is comfortable in the world; she explores it freely and positions it for her use and enjoyment.

> "The 'at home' [*le 'chez soi'*]," Levinas says, "is not a container but a site where I *can*, where, dependent on a reality that is other, I am, despite this dependence or thanks to it, free … Everything is here, everything belongs to me."
>
> (TI, 37)

The sojourner is at home, as if in her armchair, with everything conveniently within reach. She can enjoy the world without interruption. Happiness, as the sojourner experiences it, "suffices to itself"; it "consists in satisfying its needs and not suppressing them" (TI, 118). Enjoyment accordingly involves "a withdrawal into oneself, an involution"; "[i]t is precisely as a 'coiling', as a movement toward oneself, that enjoyment comes into play" (TI, 118). The sojourner is like a cat, curled up in a ball, enjoying her place in the sun. She enjoys the world, basks and bathes in it. "Through the home," as Levinas puts it, "our relation with space as distance and extension is substituted for the simple 'bathing in the element'" (TI, 132). This relation of basking or bathing in the world is adequate from the sojourner's point of view. The person at home is a pure consumer. "In enjoyment," Levinas remarks, "I am absolutely for myself ... without ears, like a hungry stomach" (TI, 134).

The question of what is on the other side of my four walls does not occur to me while I remain at home with myself. I can immerse myself in the elemental world as an unconstrained consumer, situating nature as well as material objects as something that exists for my enjoyment. "One does not know, one lives sensible qualities: the green of these leaves, the red of this sunset" (TI, 135). I am content, but this contentment cannot last forever. The sojourner, at home with herself, is always conscious on some level that her happy existence is insecure. There is, after all, a world beyond those four walls. The subject is therefore aware, even in the comfort of the home, of "an insecurity which throws back in question" the cosiness of her enjoyment (TI, 137). This insecurity puts into motion an oscillation where the subject continually finds her enjoyment interrupted and then seeks to regain it.

The subject is vulnerable partly because she must venture outside the four walls of the home to obtain the things she needs to live. The fact that the dwelling space has an exterior disturbs the subject, but she can make this exterior world bearable by seeking refuge in the dwelling. The body reflexively appropriates the exterior as an aspect of its enjoyment by "recollecting [to itself] [*se recueillant*]" (TI, 137). This process of recollection is "produced concretely as *habitation in a dwelling*" (TI, 150). The subject, in other words, instinctively retreats from the exterior world that poses a threat to her enjoyment. Comfort and fear are two sides of the same coin. "The primordial relation of [humans] with the material world," Levinas says, "is not negativity, but enjoyment and agreeableness [*agrément*] of life. It is uniquely with reference to this agreeableness – unsurpassable within interiority, for it constitutes it – that the world can appear hostile, to be negated and to be conquered" (TI, 150).

The necessity of engaging with the exterior world paves the way for the subject's encounter with the other. Nature cannot be entirely possessed; the subject cannot appropriate the whole of the exterior world for her enjoyment. There is therefore always an exterior; the whole world cannot be home. This exteriority manifests itself as insecurity; "[t]o be affected by a [plane] [*face*] of being while its whole depth remains undetermined and comes upon me from nowhere is to be bent toward the insecurity of the morrow" (TI, 142). The subject staves off this uncertainty by recollecting to itself, but the uncertainty reappears in the guise of the future. I may be safe and secure today, but there is always tomorrow. Enjoyment always presages "an 'other' inasmuch as a future is announced ... and menaces it with insecurity" (TI, 137). Pure enjoyment is therefore inherently unstable; it is "without security" (TI, 142). "In the concern for the morrow," Levinas remarks, "there dawns the primordial phenomenon of the essentially uncertain future of sensibility" (TI, 150).

The subject is therefore not only obliged to venture into the world, but is also drawn to retreat from it. She scuttles back and forth from her dwelling to the dangerous exterior, before retreating to the safety of her enjoyment. The insecurity of the subject in the world leads to recollection and taking refuge in the dwelling. The subject therefore engages with the world in a conditional way; he "abides in the world as having come to it from a private domain, from being at home with himself, to which at each moment he can retire" (TI, 152). He is of the world, but not fully in it. The dwelling that Levinas describes here is both empirical and metaphorical; "[b]ecause the I exists recollected it takes refuge empirically in the home. Only from this recollection does the building take on the signification of being a dwelling" (TI, 154). The dwelling is where the subject takes stock, tending to her needs. "Recollection," for Levinas, "designates a suspension of the immediate reactions the world solicits in view of a greater attention to oneself, one's possibilities, and the situation" (TI, 154).

The subject in the dwelling looks to her own needs, as she must to survive. She engages in self-care, prioritising her enjoyment. "With the dwelling," Levinas says, "the separated being breaks with natural existence, steeped in a medium where its enjoyment, without security, on edge, was being inverted into care" (TI, 156). The dwelling is necessary for our survival in the world; it is profoundly human. However, the dwelling is tenuous; one cannot remain there forever. The subject must venture out to get what she needs. The dwelling therefore structures the world as interior and exterior, making labour and the economy possible. The subject in her interiority grasps at the exterior world and brings it back into the dwelling for her enjoyment. "The hand," Levinas remarks, "is the organ of grasping and taking, the first and blind grasping in the teeming mass: it [reverts] [*rapporte*] to me, to my egoist ends, things drawn from the element" (TI, 159). The hand reaches into the world, grasps something, and deposits it in the dwelling, "conferring on it the status of a possession" (TI, 159).

The subject's insecurity, provoked by her consciousness of the uncertain future, leads her to acquire more things than she can immediately enjoy. The hand "gathers the fruit but holds it far from the lips, keeps it, puts it in reserve, possesses it in a home" (TI, 161). At the same time, however, "[t]he hand that acquires is burdened by what it takes" (TI, 161). The same possessions that were supposed to stave off an uncertain future beget further uncertainty, because now the subject must defend what she has from those who would demand it. The subject in her dwelling, with her possessions, cannot avoid being aware that there are other people out there, with their own needs and desires. The subject is not so much bothered by the fact that the other may seize her possessions by force; that could be overcome with fortifications. However, the subject is profoundly bothered by the awareness that the other *needs* her possessions; the other has a claim that competes with her own. The other "paralyses possession, which he contests by his epiphany in the face. He can contest my possession only because he approaches me not from the outside but from above" (TI, 171).

The appearance of the other is the beginning of ethics. The other interrogates the subject's egoistic enjoyment; "[t]he strangeness of the Other, his irreducibility to the I, to my thoughts and my possessions, is precisely accomplished as a calling into question of my spontaneity, as ethics" (TI, 43). The subject's encounter with the other is made possible – and, indeed, necessitated – by the subject's separation from the exterior world. "Without separation," as Levinas puts it, "there would not have been truth; there would have been only being" (TI, 60). Truth, however, does not undo separation; it does not bring about the union of self and other. Rather, it signals a different and more profound separation; one that must be continually negotiated. "The quest for truth," for Levinas, "unfolds in the apparition of forms. The distinctive characteristic of forms is precisely their epiphany at a distance" (TI, 60). The subject cannot simply evade the other; indeed, she desires the other profoundly. The other, once encountered, cannot be forgotten; she fascinates the subject, obsesses her. This other who claims the subject's possessions haunts her dreams and nightmares. The other demands to be known, even as she radically resists knowing.

The fascination produced by the other arises from the way in which she both holds and exceeds the subject's attention. The other is "that which is approachable by a thought that at each instant *thinks more than it thinks*" (TI, 62). The other is excessive, immoderate, incommensurable. This excessiveness [*démesure*] is found in the face [*visage*] (TI, 62). The face, as Levinas describes it, is not merely a visual phenomenon. Vision tends to commensurate; it processes the perceptual material, rendering it accessible to the subject's understanding. "Vision," as Levinas puts it, "moves into grasp. [It] opens upon a perspective, upon a horizon, and describes a traversable distance" (TI, 191). The excessiveness of the face does not relate to its form, but rather its ethical significance. "Total alterity, in which a being does not refer to enjoyment and presents itself out of itself, does not shine forth in the *form* by which things are given to us, for beneath form things conceal themselves" (TI, 192).

The encounter with the face is defined by this significance that exceeds mere form and appearance. The distinctiveness of the face lies precisely in "its refusal to be contained … [I]t cannot be comprehended, that is, encompassed" (TI, 194). The subject's inclination is to process the visual appearance of the face in the same way as other phenomena. However, in so doing, she is aware that "the invoked is not what I comprehend: *he is not under a category*" (TI, 69). The face is not merely a face, as a chair is a chair. It is, rather, the face *of the other*. And the other, who appears in the face, is "absolutely foreign to me – refractory to every typology, to every genus, to every characterology, to every classification" (TI, 73). The strangeness of the other lies in her status as another locus of consciousness; she is a person with her own plans, needs, and desires that potentially conflict with my own. "To manifest oneself as a face is to impose oneself above and beyond the manifested and purely phenomenal form … in one's nudity, that is, in one's destitution and hunger" (TI, 200).

The eyes of the other look at me and demand things that are mine. They call into question my carefully cultivated home, my practices of self-care, my light and joyous way of being in the natural world. "The gaze that supplicates and demands," for Levinas, "is precisely the epiphany of the face as a face. ... To recognise the Other is to recognise a hunger. To recognise the Other is to give" (TI, 75). The other cannot be grasped and appropriated in the same way as the material world; I cannot simply install the other in my dwelling for my use. The other is inconvenient, because any attempt to envelop or dominate her is rendered vulnerable and unstable by the "absolute upsurge" of her subjectivity and freedom (TI, 89). I fear the other, because at any time she may overflow my positioning of her, expressing needs and desires that are irreducible to my own. "The face resists possession, resists my powers. In its epiphany, in expression, the sensible, still graspable, turns into total resistance to the grasp" (TI, 197). At the same time, however, the other invites me to form a relation with her; once aware of the other, I can no longer simply live alone. I must engage the other on her own terms. "[T]he face speaks to me and thereby invites me to a relation incommensurate with a power exercised, be it enjoyment or knowledge" (TI, 198).

The other demands my attention, but simultaneously threatens my comfortable existence. I am compelled to engage her, but also to keep my distance. The result is a kind of engaged separation that creates the possibility, although not the inevitability, of ethical relations. "Separation," for Levinas, "is the very constitution of thought and interiority, that is, a relationship within independence" (TI, 104). The other can be encountered, but not understood; she can be engaged, but not known. Encountering the other is, in this sense, like encountering God – and the prospect of relating authentically with an other who eludes understanding is like a gift from the divine. "An infinity that does not close in upon itself in a circle but withdraws from the ontological extension so as to leave a place for the separated being exists divinely" (TI, 104). The separation between self and other "inaugurates a society" (TI, 104); it signals a move from the dwelling, where the subject's focus is on pure enjoyment, to the community, which is open to all. At the same time, it signals a shift in the subject's priorities from enjoyment to responsibility.

It is only by embracing this call to responsibility that the subject can escape the perpetual insecurity that pervades the dwelling. "[T]he other absolutely other – the Other – does not limit the freedom of the same; calling it to responsibility, it founds and justifies it" (TI, 197). Responsibility is, however, not another form of security. It consists, rather, in embracing vulnerability. This authentic relationship with the other can be achieved only by becoming radically open to her demands.

> The facing position, opposition par excellence, can be only as a moral summons. This movement proceeds from the other. The idea of infinity, the infinitely more contained in the less, is concretely produced in the form of a relation with the face.
>
> (TI, 196)

Any residual resistance to responsibility – that is, any attempt to carve out an impermeable dwelling in the midst of society – replicates the problem of insecurity previously described. Remaining open to the other, on the other hand, involves embracing uncertainty and ambiguity, because the other is inscrutable; her demands are both constantly shifting and beyond our understanding.

To Proximity ...

The alterity of the other unnerves the subject, because it reveals the other as a source of needs, desires, and ethical demands. The other is nonetheless unavoidable. This is partly for the practical reason that it is impossible to go through life without encountering some trace of the face. However, it is also because the subject is inherently drawn to the other. This desire for the other is unquenchable; it is not satisfied by a specific encounter or person. "The metaphysical desire [for the other] does not rest on any prior kinship. It is a desire that can not be satisfied ... it desires beyond everything that can simply complete it" (TI, 34). Humanity, for Levinas, has an inbuilt sociality and generosity of spirit that cannot be completely suppressed, even though it is in tension with the desire for security and recollection described previously. The subject at home with herself is, as we have seen, always insecure, because she is aware of the ethical demands the other makes on her. However, the subject's cosy existence in the dwelling is also unsustainable for another reason – namely, that the subject deeply desires to be in a relational mode of being.

A person at home in her dwelling does not find this desire for the other diminished by separation; rather, it grows under such conditions. The desire for the other is

> a generosity nourished by the Desired, and thus a relationship that is not a disappearance of distance, not a bringing together or ... a relationship whose positivity comes from remoteness, from separation, for it nourishes itself, one might say, with its hunger.
>
> (TI, 34)

The desire that Levinas describes here is "desire for the absolutely other" (TI, 34). It is "[a] desire without satisfaction which, precisely, *understands* [*entend*] the remoteness, the alterity, and the exteriority of the other" (TI, 34). It is not that I need the other, but that I desire to be near her on a primordial level. A need, Levinas notes, can potentially be satiated and overcome; "in need I can sink my teeth into the real and satisfy myself in assimilating the other" (TI, 117). A desire, by contrast, potentially overflows any action one might take to meet it; "there is no sinking one's teeth into being, no satiety, but an uncharted future before me" (TI, 117).

The defencelessness of the other, as shown in the face, obsesses the subject; it is impossible to simply look away, as much as it might be convenient to do so. It is for this reason that the subject may sometimes be tempted even to kill the other as the only possible way of evading her ethical demands (TI, 198). Levinas expresses the subject's desire for the other in the term *proximity*. Proximity, in this sense, is not physical closeness, but rather a kind of ethical gravity that draws the subject to the other precisely because of her radical strangeness. "Infinity," as Levinas puts it,

> presents itself as a face in the ethical resistance that paralyses my powers and from the depths of the defenceless eyes rises firm and absolute in its nudity and destitution. The comprehension of this destitution and this hunger establishes the very proximity of the other.
>
> (TI, 200)

We saw previously that the subject's attempts to remain at home with herself are inherently unstable; the only way out of this insecurity is to render oneself open to the demands of the other. Proximity yields the same result, but for different (albeit complementary) reasons.

The desire to approach the other cannot be eradicated by keeping one's distance; indeed, distance only exacerbates the hunger. Proximity cannot be abolished or fully satiated, but neither can it be suppressed or denied without creating a schism within the self. A flourishing life requires acknowledging proximity; this, in turn, necessitates an attitude of ethical openness. The subject, for Levinas, is inherently vulnerable to the other; any attempt to deny or eradicate this vulnerability is doomed to backfire, because it renders the subject's egoistic security ever more precarious in the face of the other's demands. The answer to this dilemma lies in embracing vulnerability through what Levinas terms *substitution*. "This breakup of identity," Levinas remarks, "this changing of being into signification, that is, into substitution, is the subject's subjectivity, or its subjection to everything, its susceptibility, its vulnerability, that is, its sensibility" (OB, 14). The subject who embraces her vulnerability to the other finds her way of being in the world transformed. "In sincerity, in frankness, in the veracity of this saying, in the uncoveredness of suffering, being is altered" (OB, 15).

Philosophical ethics, for Levinas, has normalised the notion that we owe responsibilities to other people. At the same time, however, it risks obscuring the radical nature of those duties. "Perhaps because of current moral maxims in which the word *neighbour* occurs," Levinas observes, "we have ceased to be surprised by all that is involved in proximity and approach" (OB, 5). We must regain our sense of surprise to appreciate the depth of our entanglement with the other. Alterity and proximity are, in this respect, mutually supporting, because the strangeness of the other unsettles our complacent ethical discourses, rendering us open to the level of intimacy demanded by proximity. "Alterity," in this sense, "figures as what is near in a proximity that counts as sociality, which 'excites' by its pure and simple proximity" (OB, 16). The other, in her radical difference, eludes my understanding. I cannot adequately conceptualise her being. This sense of the other's alterity sparks the realisation that "[t]he other to whom

From Alterity to Proximity 157

the petition of the question is addressed does not belong to the intelligible sphere to be explored." Rather, she "stands in proximity" (OB, 25).

Proximity is not a static relation, where the parties involved are "at peace and in agreement," but rather takes the form of a "restlessness of the same disturbed by the other" (OB, 25). My vulnerability before the other renders me permanently open to her, whether I like it or not. Proximity signifies "the proximity of the other and in a certain modality of my responsibility for the other, this response preceding any question, this saying before the said" (OB, 26). The mode of being this relation necessitates is performed "on the basis of the one-for-the-other, of substitution of the same for the other" (OB, 26). Proximity, authentically realised, is substitution. Substitution, in turn, reconstitutes the subject as an inherently relational being, thereby relieving her from the burden of her egoistic insecurities. It is in substitution, paradoxically, that the subject finds her authentic self. "Proximity is quite distinct from every other relationship, and has to be conceived as a responsibility for the other; it might be called humanity, or subjectivity, or self" (OB, 46).

Proximity, in this sense, produces a similar result to alterity in preventing the other from being understood purely in terms of the self. The self, authentically understood, does not exist in any self-contained way that would enable me to encapsulate the other as being inherently similar or different to me. The other is not like or unlike me; she is "precisely *other*" (OB, 87). The other is the one who is already there and whom I am drawn to approach. And in this approach "I am first a servant of the neighbour, already late and guilty for being late" (OB, 87). There is, as such, an inversion in proximity of the problematic that Levinas poses early in *Totality and Infinity*. We saw previously how the other interrupts the subject's cosy existence at home with herself [*chez soi*]. However, this interruption does not take the form of a visitor formally announced to the subject sitting in her armchair. Rather, the other is like a ghost in the house of the self; she is *already there*. The subject cannot hide from the other, not only because the dwelling is permeable, but also because *she* is permeable; the other is always already among her, constituting her as a relational being.

Proximity, for this reason, also recasts the nature of time. Synchronic time is unstable in the face of the other; it becomes a succession of uncertain moments, continually pregnant with threats that unsettle the subject's retreat to herself. However, the subject in substitution can experience time not as a series of threats, but rather as pure diachrony, an extended sensible undergoing:

> The subjectivity of a subject is vulnerability, exposure to affection, sensibility, a passivity more passive still than any passivity, an irrecuperable time, an unassemblable diachrony of patience, an exposedness always to be exposed the more, an exposure to expressing, and thus to saying, thus to giving.
> (OB, 50)

The subject, thus constituted, is stripped bare in her relation to the other; however, this existential nudity, far from robbing the subject of her identity, reveals her as a unique and irreplaceable ethical agent. Proximity is "a denuding of the unqualifiable *one*, the pure *someone*, unique and chosen; that is, it is an exposedness to the other where no slipping away is possible" (OB, 50). My identity is produced precisely by my answerability for the other. "The most passive, unassumable, passivity, the subjectivity or the very subjection of the subject, is due to my being obsessed with responsibility for the oppressed who is other than myself" (OB, 55).

The other, for her part, is revealed in this relation in her complete ethical dependence on the subject. This dependency, far from rendering the other familiar to me, underscores her alterity. The other, in being "reduced to having recourse to me," is unveiled in her "homelessness or strangeness" (OB, 91). She is a wanderer, uprooted from institutions and context, whereas I in my home am acutely aware of what I have to offer. The other in her recourse is "incumbent on me"; this relation of need "presses the neighbour up against me" (OB, 91). The temptation of the subject is to respond to this recourse through reversion to oneself, coiling up like a cat in the homely comforts of the *chez soi*. However, as we have seen, there is no home that is not rendered permeable by the haunting presence of the other:

> To revert to oneself is not to establish oneself at home … It is to be like a stranger, hunted down even in one's own home, contested in one's own identity and one's very poverty, which, like a skin still enclosing the self, would set it up in an inwardness, already settled on itself, already a substance.
> (OB, 92)

The recourse of the other is also recursive. The other does not appear once and then leaves me alone. She recurs to me again and again. Recourse, then, may be followed by reversion, but recourse recurs, instantiating a cycle of insecurity that renders the home nobody's refuge. The refuge of reversion is illusory; it is based on a rejection of that which cannot be refused. The alternative is that relation of "proximity or fraternity" in which I offer the other things that are mine (OB, 92). This openness to the other might at first appear to the subject as a compromise, "a troubled tranquility in a subject that wants to be absolute and alone" (OB, 92). There is, however, no absoluteness or aloneness; there is only relationality. And, in this context, the "restlessness and emptying and diachrony" of substitution is revealed as the only true refuge, albeit one unlike the world of static boundaries imagined from the subject's armchair (OB, 92). It is the refuge one finds in a flowing river, when one stops fighting against the current and instead allows the water to support one's body, to flow over, around and past it, even occasionally to pull it under.

Substitution is not a fusion of self and other where the parties lose their respective identities. It is, rather, "a substitution in separation, that is, responsibility" (OB, 54). I do not cease, even in my radical openness to the other, to be shocked by her incomprehensible strangeness. The depth of my love for the other in proximity gives me pain, because she obsesses me at the same time as she resists my grasp. "The exposure to the other is disinterestedness, proximity, obsession by the neighbour, an obsession despite oneself, that is, a pain" (OB, 55). I am compelled to love that person whom I can never understand. This love is intensely embodied; one is "for the other, despite oneself, starting with oneself, the pain of labour in the patience of ageing, in the duty to give to the other even the bread out of one's own mouth and the coat from one's shoulders" (OB, 55). I feel the other's pain as my own, rendering pure isolation and egoistic enjoyment both impossible and intolerable. "[A]s a passivity in the paining of the pain felt, sensibility is a vulnerability, for pain comes to interrupt an enjoyment in its very isolation, and thus tears me from myself" (OB, 55).

Love for the other entails suffering, but at the same time the idea of a life without suffering is both empty and a mirage. It is empty, because it tears me away from the part of myself that desires openness, vulnerability, and authentic relations with other people. It is a mirage, because I cannot hide from love. The other haunts me, even when I am at home with myself. "Pain penetrates into the very heart of the for-oneself that beats in enjoyment, in the life that is complacent in itself, that lives of its life" (OB, 56). My awareness of the other and her demands occurs prior to cognition and rationalisation. It belongs, unlike reflective knowledge and understanding, to "the pure passivity of the sensible" (OB, 61). Proximity, then, is "the signification of the sensible"; it "does not belong to the movement of cognition" (OB, 63). My responsibilities for the other are apprehended to me through intuition, which is "the sensible conceptualised" (OB, 63). I perceive, rather than deduce, my ethical duties; my understanding of what these duties involve is produced over time by repeated ethical encounters, rather than being derived through the exercise of reason. "Sensation already functions as sensible intuition; it is the unity of the sensing and the sensed in the divergency, and recoveries, of temporality, where the past is rememberable" (OB, 63).

Sensible experience is both the location of self-centred enjoyment and also, at the same time, the source of my awareness of the other. The sojourner at home with herself is seduced by "the ease of enjoyment, more immediate than drinking, the sinking into the depths of the element, into its incomparable freshness, a plenitude and a fulfilment" (OB, 64). This sensible enjoyment, as we have seen, leads the subject to put up boundaries, to hoard material possessions. There is, however, an emptiness at the core of this satisfied existence, due to the continual presence of the other, who represents another dimension of sensibility. "[T]here is," as a result of the other's appearance, "a coring out [*dénucléation*], of the imperfect happiness which is the murmur of sensibility. There is a non-coinciding of the ego with itself, restlessness, insomnia, beyond what is found again in the present" (OB, 64). The encounter with the other "has the form of sensibility or vulnerability, pure passivity or susceptibility" (OB, 67). It is "passive to the point of becoming an inspiration" (OB, 67). It rouses me to relationality; the culmination of this movement is substitution.

The hand that grasps material goods becomes, in this movement, the "hand that gives even the bread taken from its own mouth" (OB, 67). The egoistic self undergoes "a peculiar dephasing, a loosening up or unclamping of identity:

the same prevented from coinciding with itself, at odds, torn up from its rest, between sleep and insomnia, panting, shivering" (OB, 68). The subject takes on a new identity, which is not an abandonment of the self, but rather a spirit of vulnerability and self-sacrifice. "This identity is brought out by responsibility and is at the service of the other" (OB, 69). Levinas is not arguing that this movement is inevitable; if it were, the problems of ethical responsibility would not arise. Rather, the subject cannot help but be aware of the sources of this movement and, at least implicitly, of its teleological destination. The subject may then choose whether to embrace this movement or, as is more common and tempting, to resist it. The experience of proximity therefore frequently leads to a retreat into egoism and separation.

However, proximity is not only a phenomenon, it is also a normative demand. My metaphysical desire for the other is simultaneously an awareness of her ethical subjectivity and my concomitant accountability for her needs. "Contact is not an openness upon being, but an exposure of being. In this caress proximity signifies as proximity, and not as an experience of proximity" (OB, 80). "It is vulnerability, susceptibility, denuding, circumscribed and concerned by the other, irreducible to the appearing of the other" (OB, 80–81). This vulnerability founded in proximity bridges, but cannot erase, the metaphysical distance between self and other. Proximity is "a certain measure of the interval narrowing between two points or two sectors of space, toward a limit of contiguity and even coincidence ... Its absolute and proper meaning presupposes 'humanity'" (OB, 81). It signals a responsibility for the other prior to rationalisation; it demands justice. Proximity, then, is "the human signification of justice before all difference" (OB, 81). It motivates our explorations of what justice demands, while simultaneously holding them to account.

And Beyond ...

The hallmark of natural law thinking is its emphasis on the good.[3] Contemporary natural law theory often elucidates a plurality of basic human goods.[4] This is accurate on one level: human life is characterised by a range of modes of flourishing.[5] However, the danger of this approach is that it may elide a deeper truth: ultimately, there is only one good that unites all flourishing, one end at which human life aims.[6] That ultimate end is God or love. It is precisely this end that, for Levinas, is sought and revealed in the face of the other. "Responsibility for

---

3 Jonathan Crowe and Constance Youngwon Lee, "The Natural Law Outlook," in *Research Handbook on Natural Law Theory*, ed. Jonathan Crowe and Constance Youngwon Lee (Cheltenham: Edward Elgar, 2019), 2, 10.
4 The *locus classicus* is John Finnis, *Natural Law and Natural Rights*, 2nd ed. (Oxford: Oxford University Press, 2011), ch. 3–4.
5 See generally Jonathan Crowe, *Natural Law and the Nature of Law* (Cambridge: Cambridge University Press, 2019), ch. 2.
6 Crowe, *Natural Law and the Nature of Law*, 56–57.

the other ... is human fraternity itself, and it is prior to freedom" (OB, 116). More than this, however, it is "an unrepresentable trace, the way of the infinite" (OB, 116). The ethical demands of the other, through their simultaneous alterity and irrepressibility, appeal to "the irreplaceable singularity that lies in me" (OB, 153). They render me uniquely responsible and, in so doing, make me aware of the possibility of a better future, even just a little better than the present, which it is within my hands to deliver. And beyond that there is another possible future and another, each a small improvement on the present.

"It is through the condition of being hostage," Levinas says, "that there can be in the world pity, compassion, pardon and proximity – even the little there is, even the simple 'After you, sir'" (OB, 117). The pursuit of the good, on this view, lies in an attitude of responsibility and openness to the future to come. This good is not merely good *for me*; nor is it merely good *for the other*, although it is my attitude of openness to the other that constitutes it. The good is, rather, permanently beyond the world; it is *otherwise than being*. "Goodness is ... the sole attribute which does not introduce multiplicity into the One that a subject is, for it is distinct from the One" (OB, 118). It is "an abandon of all having, of all *one's own* and all *for oneself*, to the point of substitution" (OB, 118). It does not consist in reaching some state of repose where the needs of one – or indeed of all – are satisfied. "[S]ignification, the one-for-the-other, is never an *enough*, and the movement of signification does not return" (OB, 138). Rather, "[g]oodness in the subject is anarchy itself" (OB, 138). It is an attitude of "never enough," a peaceful restlessness, a "passivity of unconditionality" (OB, 139).

Kantian ethics famously holds that *ought implies can*. Immanuel Kant himself claims "if the moral law commands that we ought to be better human beings now, it inescapably follows that we must be capable of being better human beings."[7] However, Levinasian ethics has the opposite result; on this view, *ought implies can't*. The first part of Kant's dictum holds true for Levinas: "the moral law commands that we ought to be better human beings now." However, the recursivity of the ethical demand falsifies the second part of Kant's statement. No matter how much we may strive to live up to our ethical responsibilities – and thereby participate in the unity of the good – there is always more to be done. The good is infinite, so our responsibilities are infinitely demanding. There is, indeed, a sense in which the more responsible we become, the closer we move to accepting the weight of our duties as humans, the more distant we become from discharging them entirely. The more we become acquainted with the infinite, the more we realise its infinity. As Levinas puts it:

> No theme, no present, has a capacity for the Infinite. The subject in which the other is in the same, inasmuch as the same is for the other, bears witness

---

7 Immanuel Kant, "Religion Within the Boundaries of Mere Reason," in *Religion and Rational Theology*, trans. and ed. Allen W. Wood and George di Giovanni (Cambridge: Cambridge University Press, 1996), 94.

to it. The difference of proximity is absorbed in the measure that proximity becomes closer, and by this very absorbtion is brought out gloriously, and accuses me always more.

(OB, 146)

The other goes before me anywhere; however far I move towards her, she has always passed on, moving always into the light. "In approaching the other," Levinas says, "I am always late for the meeting" (OB, 150). The infinite is not, after all, a fixed horizon that I can ever reach. I pass inexorably through the space of human time, but infinity does not pass through time; it only passes itself. It goes on interminably, continually surpassing its own appearance. Infinity "cannot be assembled into a present, and refuses being recollected" (OB, 151). It finds its only "positive form in proximity, responsibility and substitution" (OB, 151). This picture of the good gives rise to a deep and painful tension at the heart of human existence: *I am responsible before God, but because I am not God, I must fail in my responsibilities.* This tension, I claim, is integral to both Levinasian and biblical ethics (although I cannot argue that fully here). It can be found, for example, in Job's powerful lament, "I shall be condemned; why then do I labour in vain?"[8] The resolution of the tension, on the other hand, appears in New Testament ethics, which teaches in essence that (1) you must strive to be perfect in your love[9]; (2) you will inevitably fail in this aim[10]; (3) you will be forgiven for failing[11]; and (4) the only unforgivable failure is to cease to pursue love.[12]

The other holds me hostage, imposing demands that are infinitely demanding. This makes me insecure and vulnerable, not just to the other, but to God, who sees all my failures. However, I can be freed from this insecurity by rendering myself vulnerable through love. The other reveals to me the one from whom I cannot hide, the one who overflows being, who is *beyond essence*. "[God's] very epiphany," Levinas says, "consists in soliciting us by his destitution in the face of the Stranger, the widow and the orphan" (TI, 78). Love, the ultimate good, contains both love of the other and love of God. Earthly love is unidirectional; I must offer the other what is mine, without expecting or demanding anything in return. Heavenly love, however, flows both ways – and, ultimately, God's love for me, expressed through forgiveness for my inevitable failures, outstrips anything I can humanly offer.[13] The presence of God signals the simultaneous conceivability and practical unattainability of perfect love. Direct comprehension of God is impossible, but direct experience of God can be attained by rendering myself

---

8 Job 9:29 (ESV).
9 Matthew 5:48.
10 Romans 3:23.
11 Matthew 12:31–32; Mark 2:28–29.
12 Ibid.
13 For a discussion of divine forgiveness in the Talmud, see Emmanuel Levinas, "Toward the Other," in *Nine Talmudic Readings*, trans. Annette Aronowicz (Bloomington: Indiana University Press, 1990), 12–29.

open and vulnerable before the face of the other. "Ethics is the spiritual optics" that connects the earthly and heavenly realms (TI, 78).

"It is necessary to have the idea of infinity," Levinas claims, "in order to know one's own imperfection" (TI, 84). Perfection "is not an idea but desire" (TI, 84); it manifests itself through "[t]he work of justice" (TI, 78). Justice is the attitude of striving for a better world by participating in the good of love. Love, for Levinas, is not an end state but a movement. It necessarily "goes beyond the beloved" (TI, 255). "[T]hrough the face [of the other] filters the obscure light coming from beyond the face, from what *is not yet*, from a future never future enough, more remote than the possible" (TI, 255). Justice is fundamentally inexpressible; it eludes human imagination and understanding. Nonetheless, we must try. Philosophy, then, becomes the attempt to put into words and themes our inexpressible responsibilities towards the other. It is "the measure brought to the infinity of the being-for-the-other of proximity" (OB, 161). It is a leap of faith where one seeks to express the inexpressible, to conceptualise what is beyond comprehension, as part of our never-ending and ultimately unattainable quest for perfection in our loving relations. "Philosophy," as Levinas puts it, "is the wisdom of love at the service of love" (OB, 162). It is an attempt to orient oneself towards the divine by meeting the other on her own ground.

10 "Proving Contraries"
Joseph Smith on Law and Love

Donlu Thayer

Proving Contraries: Joseph Smith on Law and Love

> Happiness is the object and design of our existence; and will be the end thereof, if we pursue the path that leads to it; and this path is virtue, uprightness, faithfulness, holiness, and keeping all the commandments of God. In obedience there is joy and peace ... and as God has designed our happiness ..., He never has – He never will ... give a commandment to His people that is not calculated in its nature to promote that happiness which He has designed.[1]
>
> – Joseph Smith

Truth

> Truth is knowledge of things as they are, and as they were, and as they are to come ... The glory of God is intelligence, or, in other words, light and truth.[2]

In early June 1844, Joseph Smith Jr of Nauvoo, Illinois, wrote to Pennsylvania historian and bookseller Israel Daniel Rupp acknowledging receipt of Rupp's book, *He Pasa Ekklesia: An Original History of the Religious Denominations at Present Existing in the United States*. As founder and prophet-leader of The Church of Jesus Christ of Latter-day Saints,[3] Joseph was among the 43 "theological professors, ministers, and lay members" who had been invited to contribute.[4]

---

1 *History, 1838–1856*, volume D-1 [1 August 1842–1 July 1843], Addenda 27 August 1842, 1387, JSP.
2 Doctrine and Covenants [hereinafter D&C] 93:24, 36.
3 Since 1838, this has been the official name of the organisation founded by Joseph Smith in 1830 as the Church of Christ, commonly and at first slanderously known as the "Mormon" church, after the Book of Mormon. Members of the Church are properly called Latter-day Saints. Some people known as "Mormons" are not affiliated with the Church, whose headquarters is in Salt Lake City, Utah.
4 This book, edited by Rupp and originally published in 1884 in Philadelphia by JY Humphreys and in Harrisburg by Clyde and Williams, is available from Kessinger Publishing as part of its Legacy Reprint Series.

DOI: 10.4324/9781003148920-14

Thanking the sender "for so valuable a treasure," Joseph praised the "design, the propriety, the wisdom of letting every sect tell its own story." For although "all is not gold that shines, any more than every religious creed is sanctioned with the so eternally sure word of prophecy, satisfying all doubt with 'Thus saith the Lord'; yet, 'by proving contraries', truth is made manifest."[5]

Joseph[6] left no account of what he meant by the proving contraries aphorism or where he learned it.

> Was "proving contraries" or "proving contrarieties" a familiar phrase, a cliché? Or was it a term of art? It ... sounds like a term of art in logic or rhetoric or both, and thus a term that Joseph Smith could have learned in the "juvenile debating club" he sometimes attended as an adolescent in Palmyra, to discuss "some portentous questions of moral or political ethics."[7] Or [it] might have been a term used in the later School of the Elders or School of the Prophets.[8]

Did Joseph know of William Blake's assertion in his 1794 *The Marriage of Heaven and Hell*: "Without contraries is no progression .... Attraction and repulsion, reason and energy, love and hate, are necessary to human existence"?[9] Surely, this passage has resonance with an important Book of Mormon doctrine: there, "must needs be an opposition in all things." Otherwise "righteousness could not be brought to pass, neither wickedness, neither holiness nor misery, neither good nor bad" (2 Nephi 2:11). Without such opposition, "things" would not exist; human agency could not be exercised, and the choices that enable human advancement could not be made. Without such "opposition," the purposes of God would be thwarted.

Joseph Smith learned that these purposes, the very "work and glory" of God, are "to bring to pass the immortality and eternal life" of humankind (PGP-Moses 3:19), spirit children of God born into mortality, to be "proved" to see if "they will do all things whatsoever the Lord their God shall command them" (PGP-Abraham 3:24–25). All this in preparation for post-mortal realms of glory, where losses are restored, and the opportunity for eternal advancement continues.

---

5 "Letter to Israel Daniel Rupp, 5 June 1844," punctuation as in the original. In the apparently original letter, written in the hand of William W Phelps, one of Joseph's scribes, "contraries" is written as "contrarreties." Subsequent copies show "contrareties" and eventually "contraries." See *History of Joseph Smith, the Prophet*, Introduction and Notes by BH Roberts, 6 (1842–1843), ch. 20, 428.
6 A common practice of Latter-day Saints is to refer to early Church leaders by their first names only.
7 Richard Lyman Bushman, *Joseph Smith: Rough Stone Rolling* (Knopf, 2005) 37–38.
8 Bruce Jorgensen, "Proving Subcontraries: In Memoriam G. Eugene England, 1933–2001," (Winter 2019) 52(4) *Dialogue: A Journal of Mormon Thought* 113–14.
9 William Blake, *The Marriage of Heaven and Hell* (1794), Project Gutenberg reproduction of publication by John Luce & Company (Boston, 1906) 7.

In this scenario, even damnation must be freely chosen, in full knowledge of, and prideful rejection of, God's benevolent plan for human happiness.

Important to note before we proceed is a caution from Joseph Smith's biographer Richard Bushman:

> [Joseph's] teachings came primarily through his revelations, which, like other forms of scripture, are epigrammatic and oracular. He never presented his ideas systematically in clear, logical order; they came in flashes and bursts. Nor did he engage in formal debate. His most powerful thoughts were assertions delivered as if from heaven. Assembling a coherent picture out of many bits and pieces leaves room for misinterpretation and forced logic. Even his loyal followers disagree about the implications of his teaching.[10]

Unlike his scribes and many others of his associates, including his parents, his older siblings, and his well-educated wife, Joseph Smith had almost no formal schooling. But he

> made intellectual pursuit a quest of holiness, founding the School of the Prophets, establishing a fledgling university, and devoting himself to the study of ancient languages and lore even as he claimed to bypass the learned systems of men with his powers of seership and translation.[11]

From his earliest childhood, in a home where Scripture was frequently read aloud, Joseph's mind "was thoroughly steeped in biblical words and rhythms." In expressing his revelations, and in the works he translated "by the gift and power of God," he was "telling a sacred story, and this demanded a sacred language, which for him meant the English of the King James Bible."[12] It is essentially Joseph's version of King James English that we encounter in the scripture he produced.[13]

Joseph Smith was, of course, not the only religious leader to experience visions or establish a church during the Protestant religious revival in early nineteenth-century United States. Characteristic of such movements was a rejection of notions of human depravity and limited human agency found in colonial Christianity in favour of optimistic, motivating concepts of free will, the "restoration" of biblical truths, and evangelical, reformist zeal.[14]

---

10 Richard Lyman Bushman, *Joseph Smith: Rough Stone Rolling* (Knopf, 2005) xxi.
11 Terryl L Givens, *People of Paradox: A History of Mormon Culture* (Oxford University Press, 2007), xiv–xv.
12 Philip L Barlow, *Mormons and the Bible: The Place of the Latter-Day Saints in American Religion* Updated Edition 2013 (Oxford University Press, 1991 and 2013) 13.
13 A surprising discovery of linguist Royal Skousen's Critical Text Project, begun in 1988, is "the frequent occurrence of vocabulary from Early Modern English" in Joseph Smith's translation, with usage and meanings already obsolete before the time of the King James Bible, though preserved in the OED. See Royal Skousen, "Editor's Preface," in Skousen, ed., *The Book of Mormon: Earliest Text* (Yale University Press, 2009) xxvii.
14 See, for example, Grant Wacker, *Religion in Nineteenth Century America* (Oxford University Press, 2000). Also Ryan S Gardner, "A History of the Concepts of Zion and New

But in opening the canon of scripture, Joseph did something truly outrageous. He first produced the 270,000-word Book of Mormon. Additional revelations would be compiled into two additional books of scripture (the Doctrine and Covenants and the Pearl of Great Price) and a revision of some parts of the Bible, meant to "restore plain and precious things" and correct scribal errors and "mistranslations."

The letter to Daniel Rupp does not have such "thus saith the Lord" status in the Joseph Smith corpus.[15] However, its poignant context (written three weeks before Joseph's death), and its significant resonance with doctrines at the core of Joseph's understanding of the nature of the cosmos and of God's purposes, combine to lend the letter a sort of "last words" heft. And the "proving contraries" aphorism is a useful framework for considering what Joseph Smith taught about those most useful of "contraries" – law and love.

Characterising law and love as contraries does not, of course, suggest they are rivals, or moral or ethical opposites, one good, the other evil. "Contraries" are differences held in useful tension, even useful proximity. On a fundamental physical level, the material world depends upon the stable "oppositions" of the subatomic realm. The process of proving contraries is thus not a battle, not a contest with mere victory as its end. "Proving" is trying, testing, learning by reason and by experience. Proving contraries happens best in a "safe space," a rhetorical or physical space allowed by good faith (love) operating within a structure (law). A "space of co-operation,"[16] where justice and mercy are in balance in the service of truth.

Human senses develop and discernment increases as we learn to distinguish what *is*, from what is not. For Joseph Smith, mortality is designed to provide opportunity for God's children to learn to discern God's presence, to hear God's voice through the mortal cacophony. As we shall presently see, young Joseph found his way to God only as, conflicted and distressed, he found God's loving invitation in the Gospel of James.

Human brains are "hardwired" for stories,[17] and the importance of narrative in human cognitive and moral development perhaps goes without saying. But how

---

Jerusalem in America from Early Colonialism to 1835 with a Comparison to the Teachings of the Prophet Joseph Smith," *BYU Scholars Archive* (Brigham Young University, 2000).

15 By this is meant the "Standard Works" of The Church of Jesus Christ of Latter-day Saints – the Bible (KJV, and others used for study), the Book of Mormon (BoM), the Doctrine and Covenants (D&C), and the Pearl of Great Price (PGP). In addition, all known "papers" of Joseph Smith have been collected, some published in print volumes, and all exquisitely indexed and searchable in the online version of *The Joseph Smith Papers* (JSP), available at www.josephsmithpapers.org/.

16 See Paul Babie and Vania-Ivan Savić, "Introduction: Law's Love," in *Law, Religion and Love: Seeking Ecumenical Justice for the Other* (Routledge, 2018) 9.

17 See discussion in Darryl L Tippens, "'Love Calls Us to the Things of this World': The Pauline Tradition and 'The Law of Christ,'" in Robert F Cochran, Jr and Zachary R Calo, eds, *Agape, Justice, and Law: How Might Christian Love Shape Law?* (Cambridge University Press, 2017) 45–48. See also, for example, Carl Alviani, "The Science Behind Storytelling:

do we know which stories are "true"? If something "rings true" to us, how can we be sure we are right? God will "give unto the faithful line upon line, precept upon precept," Joseph learned, and "will try you, and prove you" (D&C 98:12).

In this same revelation, received in Kirtland, Ohio, in 1833, Joseph learned:

> [T]hat law of the land which is constitutional, supporting that principle of freedom in maintaining rights and privileges, belongs to all mankind, and is justifiable before me ... I, the Lord God make you free, therefore ye are free indeed; and the law also maketh you free. Nevertheless, when the wicked rule, the people mourn.
>
> (D&C 98:5, 8–9)

An underlying premise of the adversarial system of the common law is that "a just result is more likely to be reached if the parties are allowed to tell their own stories and frame their own arguments."[18]

> The practical impact of fair procedures is to give those involved the opportunity to express their often differing viewpoints on a problem. If the process is allowed to work properly and does not become unduly polarized, solutions are often found that are better than anything those involved would have thought of in advance on their own.[19]

In a rhetorical space made "safe" by the rules of law, truth may be established. In practice, of course, what happens in the courtroom is often less a process of parties telling their own stories until the truth can be discerned than it is an exercise of lawyers using forensic skills in a battle for victory. (Prompting many to seek instead, when possible, a well-conducted mediation.)

They were lawyers, after all, who came to Jesus with questions not seeking answers, not to know him – who is the way, the truth, the life, who is Love itself – but to conquer, thwart, impede. To the probably less than forthright question "Who is my neighbour?," Love answered with a story – the Parable of a Good Samaritan, a member of a despised minority – which manifested the true answer to the question to all who would hear it.

The notion of proving contraries has an echo in an invitation issued by the prophet Isaiah: "Come now, and let us reason together, saith the LORD: though your sins be as scarlet, they shall be as white as snow; though they be red like crimson, they shall be as wool" (Isa. 1:18 KJV).

Our Brains are Hardwired for Narrative" (Protagonist Studio and Jag Bhalla) and "It is in our Nature to Need Stories," *Scientific American*, 8 May 2013.

18 W Cole Durham, Jr, Foreword to Theodor Viehweg, *Topics and Law: A Contribution to Basic Research in Law, Translated with a Foreword by W. Cole Durham, Jr.* (5th ed., Peter Lang, 1993) xxv.

19 Ibid.

Explaining to his sometimes fractious followers how they must organise according to the laws of God, Joseph conveyed a similar invitation:

> And now come, saith the Lord, by the Spirit, unto the elders of his church, and let us reason together, that ye may understand; Let us reason even as a man reasons one with another face to face ... [E]ven so will I, the Lord, reason with you that you may understand. Wherefore, I the Lord ask you this question – unto what were ye ordained? To preach my gospel by the Spirit, even the Comforter which was sent forth to teach the truth.
>
> Wherefore, he that preacheth and he that receiveth, understand one another, and both are edified and rejoice together. And that which does not edify is not of God, and is darkness. That which is of God is light; and he that receives light, and continues in God, receives more light; and that light grows brighter and brighter until the perfect day.
>
> (D&C 50:9–14, 22–24)

A year before writing to Daniel Rupp, Joseph Smith taught:

> There is a law, irrevocably decreed in heaven before the foundations of this world, upon which all blessings are predicated; And when we obtain any blessing from God, it is by obedience to that law upon which it is predicated.
>
> (D&C 130:20–21)

God's working for the good of humankind is made possible by law. In an orderly universe, love flows through the operation of law. Law provides the proving ground. Love brings us home.

In more than one sense, it was in a continual process of the "proving" of "contraries," in (most often) productively enduring the necessary "opposition in all things," that Joseph Smith lived out his controversial, strife-filled, nineteenth-century life on the American frontier. An opportunity to tell his story, to be heard in a safe space in which "contraries" could be tested until truth could "manifest." This, for Joseph, would have been treasure indeed.

Revelation

> Could you gaze into heaven five minutes, you would know more than you would by reading all that ever was written on the subject.[20]
>
> – Joseph Smith

---

20 *History*, 1838–1856, volume E-1 [1 July 1843–30 April 1844] 1750, *Joseph Smith Papers* [hereinafter JSP].

170 *Donlu Thayer*

Joseph began his entry for Rupp's *He Pasa Ekklesia* with a bold assertion.

> The Church of Jesus Christ of Latter Day Saints was founded upon divine revelation, as the true church of God has ever been, according to the scriptures (Amos, iii. 7, and Acts i. 2). And through the will and blessings of God, I have been an instrument in his hands, thus far, to move forward the cause of Zion. Therefore ... I shall commence with my life.[21]

Joseph had spent his earliest years in relative security in Vermont, the fifth of his parents' 11 (9 surviving) children. When Joseph was six years old, typhoid fever swept the region, and all the Smith children were stricken. All survived, but Joseph would suffer continual returns of infection, which eventually invaded the bone of his left leg. Despite surgery that saved his life and his leg, he was left physically weak during his adolescence, and with a lifelong limp.

In 1816, the Northern Hemisphere's "Year without a Summer" caused by the eruption of Mount Tambora in Indonesia, "battered the Smith household economy" in Vermont.[22] After crop and business failures, the family took the decision to make the difficult journey over the mountains to New York, in hopes of better opportunities near the newly opened Erie Canal.

Their new life, however, was a

> never-ending struggle to convert dense forest into fields, to plant and harvest wheat, to tap maple trees and manufacture sugar, to make baskets, barrels, and brooms for supplementary income, and to build homes and utility structures on land not previously inhabited.[23]

And the harmony of the Smith's family life was interrupted by religious differences that flowed from the Second Great Awakening in their so-called "burned-over district" (a term coined to express the extreme religious fervour of the times[24] in western and central New York).

While Joseph felt some attraction to the Methodists and his mother, sister, and two brothers joined the Presbyterians, his visionary father remained aloof from formal gatherings, and Joseph often remained home with him. As he told the story for Daniel Rupp, Joseph "began to reflect upon the importance of being prepared for a future state." But, in his words:

---

21 Joseph Smith in Rupp, 405.
22 See Bushman, *Rough Stone Rolling*, 16.
23 Richard Lloyd Anderson, "Joseph Smith's Home Environment," *Ensign*, July 1971.
24 See, for example, Whitney Cross, *The Burned-Over District: The Social and Intellectual History of Enthusiastic Religion in Western New York, 1800–1850* (Harper & Row, 1950). For the notion that the fervour characterising this area was typical rather that exceptional, see Linda K Pritchard, "The Burned-Over District Reconsidered: A Portent of Evolving Religious Pluralism in the United States," (Summer 1984) 8(3) *Social Science History* 243–65.

> So great was the confusion and strife ... that it was impossible for a person young as I was, and so unacquainted with men and things, to come to any certain conclusion who was right and who was wrong ... In the midst of this war of words and tumult of opinions, I often said to myself: What is to be done? Who of all these parties are right; or, are they all wrong together? If any one of them be right, which is it, and how shall I know it?
>
> (JSH 1:8, 10)

> While I was laboring under the extreme difficulties caused by the contests of these parties of religionists, I was one day reading the Epistle of James, first chapter and fifth verse, which reads: *If any of you lack wisdom, let him ask of God, that giveth to all men liberally, and upbraideth not; and it shall be given him.*
>
> (JSH 1:11)

This passage "seemed to enter with great force into every feeling" of Joseph's heart and he went into the woods near his home to pray. He reports that as he struggled against dark powers that threatened to overcome him, calling upon God to rescue him from darkness and despair, he was delivered from "the enemy that held [him] bound." And then,

> I saw two Personages, whose brightness and glory defy all description, standing above me in the air. One of them spake unto me, calling me by name and said, pointing to the other – This is My Beloved Son. Hear Him!
>
> (JSH 1:17)

Joseph was told that his sins were forgiven, that he should join none of the striving sects, for "they draw near me with the lips, but their hearts are far from me, they teach for doctrines the commandments of men, having a form of godliness, but they deny the power thereof" (JSH 1:19).

Three years later, in September 1823, despite severe "persecution ... because [he] continued to affirm that [he] had seen a vision," another earnest prayer brought about the first of several visits from a heavenly messenger, Moroni, who would tutor Joseph, and prepare him to receive a record, compiled by Moroni's father, the ancient prophet Mormon, and engraved on gold plates, "giving an account of the former inhabitants of this continent ... [and also] the fulness of the everlasting Gospel ... as delivered by the Savior to the ancient inhabitants" (JSH 1:34).

Among many things Joseph would learn from Moroni was the importance of "The Spirit of Elijah," a manifestation of God's love for his children on the earth in human families, and the basis of eternally efficacious "sealing" ordinances, for the living, and vicariously for "kindred dead," a process of "turning the hearts of the fathers to the children and the children to the fathers," lest the earth be "utterly wasted" at the coming of the Lord (see Mal. 4:6 and JSH 1:39).

After three attempts to receive the record from Moroni, rejected each time because he was yet unprepared, Joseph at last took possession of it in 1827, when he brought with him to the meeting place Emma Hale, his wife of nine months. The rumours that Joseph Smith had a "gold treasure" made finding a safe place to live and work challenging. Such challenges would follow Joseph and Emma to the end.

Joseph translated essentially the entire Book of Mormon as it now exists, dictating to scribes between April and June 1829, a period of between 60 and 120 days, when he was 23 years old.[25]

Finding a publisher was another challenge, but with the logistical and financial assistance of friends, Joseph was able to publish the Book of Mormon in March 1830. Less than a month later, the Church of Christ was organised with six official members, and the work of sharing the news began. In short order – because of often violent persecution, exacerbated by internal strife – the Church would move from New York to Ohio and Missouri, to Illinois, and finally, after Joseph's death, to the part of Mexico that would become the State of Utah.

Law

> [T]his is the whole meaning of the law ... that great and last sacrifice ... the Son of God ... infinite and eternal. And thus he shall bring salvation to all those who shall believe on his name ... to bring about ... mercy, which overpowers justice ... And thus mercy can satisfy the demands of justice.
>
> (Alma 34:14, 16)

Necessary Opposition: A Fortunate Fall, Pride, and Redemption

The Book of Mormon "contains a record of a fallen people" (D&C 20:9), whose history is played out in repeated "pride cycles," as righteousness brings the blessings of God, leading to prosperity, then pride, leading to contention, failure, pain, wickedness, warfare, destruction. But the Book of Mormon also contains "the fulness of the gospel of Jesus Christ," and the stories recount how sorrow leads to humility and repentance, and to the healing made possible by the love of God, manifest in the atonement of his Son. Contraries are perpetually proven, and the solution, the truth, is always the same.

Nearing the end of his life, the first Book of Mormon prophet, Lehi, speaking to his fifth son, Jacob, acknowledges the "afflictions and much sorrow" that Jacob has suffered because of the "rudeness" of his older brothers, Laman and Lemuel. Nevertheless, Jacob knows "the greatness of God," who shall consecrate his afflictions for his gain (2 Nephi 2:1–2). Jacob's "soul shall be blessed" as he lives safely with his righteous old brother Nephi, his days being spent in the service of his God (2 Nephi 1–4).

Lehi continues with insight into the connection between law and justice, love and mercy, grace and truth.

---

25 See John W Welch, "Timing the Translation of the Book of Mormon: 'Days [and Hours] Never to Be Forgotten,'" (2018) 57(4) *BYU Studies Quarterly* 12.

"*Proving Contraries*" 173

> And men are instructed sufficiently that they know good from evil. And the law is given unto men. And by the law no flesh is justified; or, by the law men are cut off ... Wherefore, redemption cometh in and through the Holy Messiah; for he is full of grace and truth ... Behold, he offereth himself a sacrifice for sin, to answer the ends of the law, unto all those who have a broken heart and a contrite spirit; and unto none else can the ends of the law be answered.
>
> (2 Nephi 2:1–7)

"Opposition" is "necessary" and underlies this process:

> [God has] created all things, both the heavens and the earth, and all things that in them are, both things to act and things to be acted upon. And to bring about his eternal purposes in the end of man, after he had created our first parents, and the beasts of the field and the fowls of the air, and in fine, all things which are created, it must needs be that there was an opposition; even the forbidden fruit in opposition to the tree of life; the one being sweet and the other bitter. Wherefore, the Lord God gave unto man that he should act for himself. Wherefore, man could not act for himself save it should be that he was enticed by the one or the other.
>
> (2 Nephi 2:14–16)

In an "extract from the translation of the Bible as revealed to Joseph Smith the Prophet, June 1830–February 1831"[26] is a vision of Moses, who is shown God's plan for redeeming humankind from the inevitable conditions of mortality. To fulfil the plan, a redeemer is required, one who can conquer both physical death and spiritual death (hell, estrangement from God). Two among the hosts of heaven volunteer: Jehovah, God's "Beloved and Chosen from the beginning" (Moses 4:1), and Lucifer, "the Son of the Morning" (see Isa. 14:12), "an angel of God who was in authority in the presence of God" (D&C 76:25).

Jehovah makes his offer: "Father, thy will be done, and the glory be thine forever" (Moses 4:2). Lucifer counters: "Send me, I will be thy son, and I will redeem all mankind, that one soul shall not be lost, and surely I will do it; wherefore give me thine honor" (Moses 4:1).

God answers: "I will send the first."

> Wherefore, because that Satan rebelled against me, and sought to destroy the agency of man, which I, the Lord God, had given him, and also, that I should give unto him mine own power; by the power of mine Only Begotten, I caused that he should be cast down; And he became Satan, yea, even the devil, the father of all lies, to deceive and to blind men, and to lead them captive at his will, even as many as would not hearken unto my voice.
>
> (Moses 4:2–4)

26 Heading to PGP-Moses.

This first, foundational opposition, this confrontation of contraries, establishes the mortal proving ground. Ultimately, Jehovah, in his earthly role as Jesus Christ, will conquer Satan, the enticer, who in prideful rebellion continues to seek to thwart God's plan. Satan's first target in the mortal realm: Eve, the Mother of all Living (Moses 4:26).

The fall of humankind is a fortunate event, Joseph Smith learned, necessary to God's purposes for the advancement of humankind. "Adam fell that man may be," said Lehi," and men are that they might have joy" (2 Nephi 2:45). The "fall" of humankind into mortality was a choice between contraries, a "transgression," not a sin. And Mother Eve's role is hero, not villain.

After the expulsion from Eden, Eve declares:

> Were it not for our transgression we never should have had seed, and never should have known good and evil, and the joy of our redemption, and the eternal life which God giveth unto all the obedient. And Adam and Eve blessed the name of God, and they made all things known unto their sons and their daughters.
>
> (Moses 9–12)

Furthering the Cause of Zion: Learning the Law in Ohio and Missouri

> We consider that God has created man with a mind capable of instruction, and a faculty which may be enlarged in proportion to the heed and diligence given to the light communicated from heaven to the intellect; and that the nearer man approaches perfection, the clearer are his views, and the greater his enjoyments, till he has overcome the evils of his life and lost every desire for sin; and like the ancients, arrives at that point of faith where he is wrapped in the power and glory of his Maker, and is caught up to dwell with Him.[27]
>
> – Joseph Smith

Self-mastery achieved by repentance and the ministrations of Christ and the Holy Spirit were Book of Mormon themes that Joseph Smith carried into his ministry. The object was to purify men and women on earth so that they became holy – worthy to be "caught up" to dwell with God. The Church was established to enable such people to establish Zion, the dwelling place of the pure in heart.

Joseph Smith was once asked by an Illinois legislator "how it was that he was able to govern so many people, and to preserve such perfect order." Joseph replied, "I teach them correct principles, and they govern themselves."[28]

---

27 Letter to the Church, circa February 1834, 135, JSP.
28 John Taylor, article in (1851) *Latter-Day Saints' Millennial Star* (13) 339, JSP.

How are "correct principles" identified? By attending to trusted voices (prophets) and sources (scripture).

The Book of Mormon prophet Alma, who had known both the pain of rebellion and the joy of repentance in his own youth, gave relevant counsel to an already righteous son:

> See that ye are not lifted up unto pride; yea, see that ye do not boast in your own wisdom, nor of your much strength. Use boldness, but not overbearance; and also see that ye bridle all your passions, that ye may be filled with love.
>
> (Alma 38:11–12)

The benevolent Book of Mormon King Benjamin worked alongside his people to ease their burdens, teaching that the "natural man" is God's enemy, unless he "yields to the enticings of the Holy Spirit" and becomes submissive to God, "meek, humble, patient, full of love" (Mosiah 3:19).

Everyone who is motivated by love and who is willing to search, can learn eternal truth: "If thou shalt ask, thou shalt receive revelation upon revelation, knowledge upon knowledge, that thou mayest know the mysteries and peaceable things – that which bringeth joy, that which bringeth life eternal" (D&C 42:61).

Joseph thus expected Church members to study things out in their minds, to consider the contraries and receive revelation confirming that what was taught by the prophets and scriptures was correct and should be applied in their lives. People attuned to inspiration from God could also recognise truth by how it affected their spiritual senses. In his final public address, delivered at a conference of 20,000 people, outdoors on a rainy, windy day in April 1844, Joseph is reported to have said that good doctrine "*tastes good* ... I can taste the spirit *and principles* of eternal life, *and so can you.*"[29]

The necessary companionship of law and love is nowhere seen more clearly than in Joseph Smith's attempt to learn and convey correct principles in what he accepted as his divine mandate to "establish Zion." God told Joseph that in Zion,

> You shall be a free people, and ... shall have no laws but my laws when I come, for I am your lawgiver, ... [T]each one another according to the office wherewith I have appointed you; And let every man esteem his brother as himself, and practice virtue and holiness before me.
>
> (D&C 38:22–24)

For Joseph, the result of proving contraries is unity. If the "provers" are motivated by pure love, they will listen with honest hearts, and they can find and settle upon

---

[29] See Stan Larsen, "The King Follett Discourse: A Newly Amalgamated Text," (1978) 18(4) *BYU Studies Quarterly* 204. This discourse was preserved in manuscript form by four of Joseph's scribes. Italics indicate passages occurring only in the manuscript prepared by Wilford Woodruff.

common ground. The Lord commanded the Saints to "be one; and if ye are not one ye are not mine" (D&C 38:27).

An essential characteristic of such "oneness" is the absence of contention. The Book of Mormon contains an account of an appearance of the Risen Lord to his "other sheep" (see Jn 10:16) in the Americas. Among Christ's teachings to the people was a warning that there should be "no disputations" among them, for "the spirit of contention is not of me, but is of the devil, who is the father of contention," who stirs up the hearts of people to contend with one another in anger (3 Nephi 11:2–29). Obedience to this command brought peace to the Nephite civilisation for 200 years.

When the Church was organised in 1830 in Fayette, New York, this Book of Mormon teaching about avoiding contention would have been fresh on Joseph's mind. At this moment, Joseph received instruction that "all things shall be done by common consent in the church, by much prayer and faith, for all things you shall receive by faith" (D&C 26:2). A later revelation called simply "The Law" (D&C 42) contained instructions for the establishment of Zion: The Saints were to live together, without idleness. A "member in good standing in the Church" must "feed the hungry ... clothe the naked, ... provide for the widow ... dry up the tear of the orphan ... comfort the afflicted, whether in this church, or in any other, or in no church at all, wherever he finds them."[30]

In this place, in nineteenth-century America, Church members were to model themselves after the people of Enoch. In the days of this ancient prophet, Joseph learned, "The Lord called his people Zion, because they were of one heart and one mind, and dwelt in righteousness; and there was no poor among them" (Moses 7:17–18).

Given small space in the Old Testament, Enoch, the father of Methuselah and grandfather of Noah, was restored to prominence by Joseph Smith. In most translations of the Hebrew Bible, Genesis tells us only that "Enoch walked with God: and he was not; for God took him." The epistle to Hebrews 11:5 adds more detail: "By faith Enoch was translated that he should not see death; and was not found, because God had translated him: for before his translation he had this testimony, that he pleased God." Joseph Smith revealed where Enoch went, and what Enoch saw.

For Joseph Smith, "translation" was not necessarily and not only a word-for-word rendering of a text into another language. "Translation was also concerned with the transformation of human beings and the worlds they were capable of inhabiting. These twin senses of translation run together in early Latter-day Saint thought."[31]

Joseph learned that all of the inhabitants of the City of Enoch, Zion, were "translated," "taken up into heaven," where they remain "in the bosom of the

---

30 *Times and Seasons*, Nauvoo, 15 March 1842, JSP.
31 See Samuel Morris Brown, *Joseph Smith's Translations: The Words and Worlds of Early Mormonism* (Oxford University Press, 2020) 4.

Father, and of the Son of Man." In a conversation with God, Enoch was given a view of "all the inhabitants of the earth," and the contrary power of Satan upon its face. In that process, Enoch learned something remarkable about the Creator of humankind.

> And it came to pass that the God of heaven looked upon the residue of the people, and he wept; and Enoch bore record of it, saying: How is it that the heavens weep, and shed forth their tears as the rain upon the mountains? And Enoch said unto the Lord: How is it that thou canst weep, seeing thou art holy, and from all eternity to all eternity?
>
> (Moses 7:23–24)

> The Lord said unto Enoch: Behold these thy brethren; they are the workmanship of mine own hands, and I gave unto them their knowledge, in the day I created them; and in the Garden of Eden, gave I unto man his agency; And unto thy brethren have I said, and also given commandment, that they should love one another, and that they should choose me, their Father; but behold, they are without affection, and they hate their own blood ... wherefore should not the heavens weep, seeing that these shall suffer?
>
> (Moses 7:28–29, 32–33, 37)

Seeing the destruction in the days of his great-grandson, Noah, Enoch also "wept and refused to be comforted." But God promised Enoch that through the redeeming work of his Only Begotten, a new Zion would be built on earth.

> And the Lord said unto Enoch: Then shalt thou and all thy city meet them there, and we will receive them into our bosom, and they shall see us; and we will fall upon their necks, and they shall fall upon our necks, and we will kiss each other; And there shall be mine abode, and it shall be Zion, which shall come forth out of all the creations which I have made; and for the space of a thousand years the earth shall rest.
>
> (Moses 7:63–64)

For Joseph Smith, the contraries that all must suffer, in a world where human beings exercise their freedom of choice, are part of the process of becoming as God is. While the pain that flows from suffering never ends, it is not punishment. It is one of the contraries that identifies and exalts the happiness that flows from voluntary obedience to the laws of God.

Joseph Smith's life was courageous, often discouraging, and mercifully short. He never claimed perfection. He was, he said, like a rough stone rolling down a hill, desiring the learning and wisdom of heaven, "polished" as he encountered adversity – weakness, error, opposition.[32] And persecution, always persecution.

---

32 *History*, 1838–1856, volume D-1 [1 August 1842–1 July 1843] 1556, JSP.

Latter-day Saint attempts to "establish Zion" in Missouri, supported by a "stake of Zion" 800 miles away in Ohio, ultimately failed.

Joseph's account in Rupp's compendium explains some of the refining persecution of this period:

> [Our neighbors] commenced at first to ridicule, then to persecute, and finally an organized mob assembled and burned our houses, tarred and feathered and whipped many of our brethren, and finally drove them from their habitations; these, houseless and homeless, contrary to law, justice, and humanity, had to wander on the bleak prairies till the children left the tracks of their blood on the prairie. This took place in the month of November, and they had no other covering but the canopy of heaven, in that inclement season of the year. This proceeding was winked at by the government; and although we had warrantee deeds for our land, and had violated no law, we could obtain no redress. There were many sick who were thus inhumanly driven from their houses, and had to endure all this abuse, and to seek homes where they could be found. The result was, that a great many of them being deprived of the comforts of life, and the necessary attendance, died; many children were left orphans; wives, widows; and husbands, widowers. Our farms were taken possession of by the mob, many thousands of cattle, sheep, horses, and hogs were taken, and our household goods, store goods, and printing press and types were broken, taken, or otherwise destroyed.[33]

In response to Joseph's anguish, he was given the revelation recorded as Section 101 of the Doctrine and Covenants:

> I say unto you, concerning your brethren who have been afflicted, and persecuted, and cast out from the land of their inheritance – I, the Lord, have suffered the affliction to come upon them ... in consequence of their transgressions; Yet I will own them, and they shall be mine in that day when I shall come to make up my jewels. [They must be] chastened and tried ... For all those who will not endure chastening ... cannot be sanctified.
>
> (D&C 101:1–5)

> Therefore, let your hearts be comforted concerning Zion; for all flesh is in mine hands; be still and know that I am God. Zion shall not be moved out of her place, notwithstanding her children are scattered.
>
> (16–17)

Scattered indeed. The Saints moved to other sparsely settled areas in Missouri, but persecution continued. In early 1837, a schism in the Church in Kirtland over a failed economic plan, led to the relocation of Church headquarters to Far West, Missouri, and the arrival of hundreds more Saints from Kirtland and elsewhere. The

---

33 Joseph Smith in Rupp, 407.

resulting "Mormon War" of 1838 would lead to the governor issuing the infamous "extermination order," requiring all Latter-day Saints to leave Missouri or be killed.

On 1 November 1838, Joseph, his brother Hyrum, and other Church leaders surrendered to authorities in an agreement to stop the violence. The prisoners escaped execution by firing squad when General Alexander William Doniphan refused to obey the order. They would instead be held in jail in Missouri, on charges including treason against the state, while their people made another harrowing winter exodus – to Quincy, Illinois, where they found relief.

The eight-year attempt to "establish Zion" in Missouri had come to its close.

Crucible

> Verily, thus saith the Lord unto you whom I love, and whom I love I also chasten that their sins may be forgiven, for with the chastisement I prepare a way for their deliverance in all things out of temptation, and I have loved you.
>
> (D&C 95:1)

Joseph Smith was no stranger to the processes of human law. At the time of his death age 38, he had been involved in approximately 220 legal disputes in five US states, as plaintiff, defendant, witness, or judge.[34] He was charged in some 50 criminal cases and was convicted in none.[35] He became expert in the law of habeas corpus, and had known the help and friendship of some of the best legal minds in Illinois.[36] He was twice imprisoned on charges of treason after he surrendered himself to protect his followers. On neither occasion was he heard on those charges. The first time he escaped during a change-of-venue excursion, permitted, it has been asserted, to avoid the embarrassment of an acquittal.[37] The second time he was murdered before the hearing could take place.

The Prison-Temple at Liberty, Missouri

Joseph, Hyrum, and four companions spent the winter of 1838–1839 imprisoned in Liberty, Missouri. In this crucible of adversity, in miserable conditions,

---

34 See Joseph I Bentley, "Road to Martyrdom: Joseph Smith's Last Legal Cases," (2015) 55(2) *BYU Studies Quarterly* 9 fn 8.
35 Ibid., 9.
36 See Elder Dallin H Oaks of the Quorum of the Twelve Apostles, "Behind the Extraditions: Joseph Smith, the Man and the Prophet," *Newsroom*, 23 September 2013.
37 See, for example, discussion in A Keith Thompson, "The Habeas Corpus Protection of Joseph Smith from Missouri Arrest Requisitions" (2018) 29 *Interpreter: A Journal of Mormon Scripture* 293–4, citing Jeffrey N Walker, "Habeas Corpus in Early Nineteenth-Century Mormonism, Joseph Smith's Legal Bulwark for Personal Freedom," (2013) 52(1) *BYU Studies Quarterly* 34–37. An account in "Extract, from the Private Journal of Joseph Smith Jr. July 1839," JSP, says merely that the prisoners escaped when their guard became intoxicated.

180   *Donlu Thayer*

and in anguish over the suffering of his people, Joseph would receive the most significant of his revelations on the interplay of law and love – including a manifesto of righteous leadership – delivered as letters to his people. In the process, Liberty Jail became what a later church historian would call a "prison-temple."[38]

> A cry of pain and a plea for redress, for himself and for his people, begins: "O God, where art thou? ... Remember thy suffering saints, O our God." Joseph reports God's response:

> My son, peace be unto thy soul; thine adversity and thine afflictions shall be but a small moment. And then, if thou endure it well, God shall exalt thee on high ... Thy friends do stand by thee, and they shall hail thee again with warm hearts and friendly hands. Thou are not yet as Job.
>
> (D&C 121:1, 6–10)

Even if Joseph should "be cast into the pit, or into the hands of murderers, and the sentence of death passed upon" him, even if the "very jaws of hell should gape open the mouth wide" after him, God promised that all these things would give him experience, and would be for his good (D&C 122:7).

> The Son of Man hath descended below them all. Art thou greater than he? Therefore, hold on thy way ... Thy days are known, and thy years shall not be numbered less; therefore, fear not what man can do, for God shall be with you forever and ever.
>
> (D&C 122:8–9)

Joseph reported these words of loving rebuke and comfort in an "epistle to the Church" dated 20 March 1839 (see headings to D&C 121, 122, 123). This document also delivers Joseph's revealed understanding of the righteous exercise of authority of one person over another.

"We have learned by sad experience that it is the nature and disposition of almost all men, as soon as they get a little authority, as they suppose, they immediately begin to exercise unrighteous dominion" (D&C 121:39). People may be "called" to authority, but not "chosen" for the work. Why?

> Because their hearts are set so much upon the things of this world, and aspire to the honors of men, that they do not learn this one lesson – That the rights of the priesthood are inseparably connected with the powers of heaven, and that the powers of heaven cannot be controlled nor handled only upon the principles of righteousness.
>
> (35–36)

> [W]hen we undertake to cover our sins, or to gratify our pride, our vain ambition, or to exercise control or dominion or compulsion upon the souls

---

38 BH Roberts, *A Comprehensive History of the Church of Jesus Christ of Latter-Day Saints, Century One* (The Church of Jesus Christ of Latter-day Saints, 1930) 521.

of the children of men, in any degree of unrighteousness, behold, the heavens withdraw themselves; the Spirit of the Lord is grieved; and when it is withdrawn, Amen to the priesthood or the authority of that man.

(37)

No power or influence can or ought to be maintained by virtue of the priesthood, only by persuasion, by long-suffering, by gentleness, and meekness, and by love unfeigned; By kindness, and pure knowledge, which shall greatly enlarge the soul without hypocrisy, and without guile.

(41–42)

Reproving betimes with sharpness [promptly, with clarity], when moved upon by the Holy Ghost; and then showing forth afterwards an increase of love toward him whom thou hast reproved, lest he esteem thee to be his enemy; That he may know that thy faithfulness is stronger than the cords of death.

(43–44)

Let thy bowels also be full of charity towards all men, and to the household of faith, and let virtue garnish thy thoughts unceasingly; then shall thy confidence wax strong in the presence of God; and the doctrine of the priesthood shall distil upon thy soul as the dew from heaven. The Holy Ghost shall be thy constant companion, and thy scepter an unchanging scepter of righteousness and truth; and thy dominion shall be an everlasting dominion, and without compulsory means it shall flow unto thee forever and ever.

(45–46)

The Saints, Joseph wrote,[39] had "an imperative duty ... to all the rising generation, and to all the pure heart" (D&C 123:9) to continue to teach truth and to counter error:

[W]e should waste and wear out our lives in bringing to light all the hidden things of darkness, wherein we know them; and they are truly manifest from heaven – These should then be attended to with great earnestness. Let no man count them as small things; for there is much which lieth in futurity, pertaining to the saints, which depends upon these things. You know, brethren, that a very large ship is benefited very much by a very small helm in the time of a storm, by being kept workways with the wind and the waves. Therefore, dearly beloved brethren, let us cheerfully do all things that lie in our power; and then may we stand still, with the utmost assurance, to see the salvation of God, and for his arm to be revealed.

(D&C 123:13–17)

---

39 Note: "Joseph wrote" usually means "Joseph dictated to a scribe."

In April 1839, after most of the Saints had left Missouri, Joseph and his friends escaped from custody. They made their way, a 200-mile journey, to Illinois, where the Saints, battling cholera, malaria, and typhoid, would build again, in Commerce, a failed community in a mosquito-infested swamp on a bend in the Mississippi River. As the city rose, Joseph renamed it "Nauvoo," from a Hebrew word meaning "beautiful" (Isa. 52:7).

A "Necessary Murder": Joseph Smith Dies at Carthage Jail

Writing in his journal in 1842, Joseph insisted:

> If it has been demonstrated that I have been willing to die for a Mormon, I am bold to declare before heaven that I am just as ready to die for a Presbyterian, a Baptist or any other denomination. It is a love of liberty which inspires my soul. Civil and religious liberty were diffused into my soul by my grandfathers.[40]

From Liberty Jail, Joseph had written of his belief that the US Constitution is "a glorious standard ... founded in the Wisdom of God ... a 'heavenly banner.'"[41] Joseph concluded his entry for Daniel Rupp's book with a list of 13 statements of belief that he had previously prepared for publication by John Wentworth, proprietor of the *Chicago Democrat*.[42] Two of these statements concern the laws of the land:

> We claim the privilege of worshiping Almighty God according to the dictates of our own conscience, and allow all men the same privilege, let them worship how, where, or what they may. We believe in being subject to kings, presidents, rulers, and magistrates, in obeying, honoring, and sustaining the law.
> (PGP-Articles of Faith 11, 12)

Enemies of the Church in New York and Ohio, in Missouri, and finally in Illinois, were sceptical of such sentiments. Oaks and Hill have noted the "bitter opposition from Illinois citizens" who charged that Mormons

> followed their prophet implicitly and had little respect for man-made law. In advancing their opposition to the increasing political power of the Mormons, the anti-Mormons appealed to two versions of the higher law – the right of self-preservation and popular sovereignty.[43]

---

40 *Journal*, December 1842–June 1844; Book 2, 10 March 1843–14 July 1843, 301, JSP.
41 Letter to Edward Partridge and the Church, circa 22 March 1839, in the hand of Alexander McRae, JSP.
42 *History of the Church*, 4, 535–41, JSP. The Wentworth Letter was originally published in Nauvoo in the *Times and Seasons*, 1 March 1842.
43 See Dallin H Oaks and Marvin S Hill, *Carthage Conspiracy: The Trial of the Accused Assassins of Joseph Smith* (University of Illinois Press, 1979) xiii.

To many, such "higher-law" response seemed essential, given what they saw as the increasing power of an arrogant and dangerous Joseph Smith.

There can be no doubt that people in the places where the Saints attempted to settle considered them a threat, though not always for reasons common in popular imagination. A leader of the mob that tarred and feathered Joseph and his associate Sidney Rigdon in Ohio in 1832 said their actions were not motivated by religious differences. The people of Hiram, Ohio, "were liberal about religion and had not been averse to Mormon teaching." The problem, he said, was a fear of a Mormon "plot" to take away their property,[44] perhaps a mistaken interpretation of Church members' attempts to "hold all things in common."

One student of pre-1850 antipathy towards the Mormons has asserted that

> the distrust and hate which came to dominate the citizens of Illinois in relation to the inhabitants of Nauvoo can be traced to the Mormons' attitudes and actions in local and national politics, more than to talk of polygamy or their economic and religious views.[45]

The anti-slavery beliefs among Saints in southern Missouri played a considerable role in their expulsion from that state, no matter how strongly they professed their belief in obeying the law. And local fears of "too much political clout, too quickly"[46] contributed to the growth of anti-Mormon sentiment in Hancock County, Illinois, where by 1844, the Mormons were in the majority, and deciding elections.

As Joseph Smith wrote to Daniel Rupp, tensions were building to impasse between the "old settlers" of Hancock County and the people of Nauvoo, which in only four years had become a thriving city with "more than 15,000 inhabitants,"[47] rivalling Chicago as the largest city in the state. Joseph's followers and new converts were steadily gathering, not only from the United States but also from Canada, the British Isles, and elsewhere abroad. While there were "no correct data by which the exact number of members of [the Church] can be known," wrote Joseph for Daniel Rupp, "150,000 ... might [still] be short of the truth."[48]

In 1840, Nauvoo had been granted state-like powers by the Illinois general assembly, in a city charter that included provision for a university and for an independent militia. Four years later, Joseph was not only prophet-president of the Church, mayor of Nauvoo, and lieutenant general of the Nauvoo Legion, but he was also a recently declared candidate for president of the United States,

---

44 See, for example, Donna Hill, *Joseph Smith: The First Mormon* (Doubleday, 1977) 146.
45 George R Gayler, "The Mormons and Politics in Illinois: 1839–1844," (1956) 49(1) *Journal of the Illinois State Historical Society* 48.
46 Armand Mauss, quoted by James Janega, "160 Years Later, Illinois Ready to Offer Mormons an Apology," *Chicago Tribune*, 7 April 2004.
47 Joseph Smith in Rupp, 409.
48 Ibid.

with a platform including provisions for freeing the slaves, for strengthening "the federal government's ability to ensure justice and redress for all the citizens, and to ensure that the Constitution was applied equally in the states."[49]

It was Joseph's calling up of the Nauvoo Legion and declaring martial law – rights granted in the Nauvoo Charter – to prevent a threatened imminent hostile invasion of Nauvoo,[50] that led to the June 1844 charges of treason. Joseph and Hyrum surrendered to authorities in Carthage, the county seat 15 miles from Nauvoo. Both were shot four times by a mob that stormed the keeper's upstairs quarters, where the brothers were resting with friends, in the Carthage Jail.

These were troubled times on the United States frontier. In Abraham Lincoln's first public address in January 1838, he lamented "the increasing disregard of the law – the growing disposition to substitute the wild and furious passions in lieu of the sober judgment of courts, and the worse than savage mobs for the executive ministers of justice."[51]

The killing of Joseph and Hyrum Smith was characterised by its perpetrators as a summary execution, encouraged and committed by "a respectable set of men,"[52] who might have "regretted the necessity of murder but did not doubt that the Smiths deserved it."[53] A year after this "necessity," those accused of committing it were acquitted by a jury of their peers.

Love

> Fear not, little flock; do good; let earth and hell combine against you, for if ye are built upon my rock, they cannot prevail ... Look unto me in every thought; doubt not, fear not ... Be faithful, keep my commandments, and ye shall inherit the kingdom of heaven.
>
> (D&C 6:34, 36–37)

Since the moment of his first vision at age 14, Joseph Smith had devoted his life to understanding the will and ways of God. When he wrote to Daniel Rupp 24 years later about finding truth in the proving of contraries, he knew whereof he spoke.

Joseph had worked in his last years to transmit revelations about sacred covenants, endowments of godly power, and family sealing ordinances, which should take place in a temple, the House of the Lord. The Nauvoo Temple was only half completed when Joseph died, and the Saints worked for two more years to

---

49 Oaks, "Behind the Extraditions."
50 Oaks and Hill, *Carthage Conspiracy*, xiii.
51 Abraham Lincoln, Address before the Young Men's Lyceum of Springfield, Illinois (27 January 1838), *Collected Works of Abraham Lincoln* (Rutgers University, 1953) 1:108–15. Cited in Oaks, above n 35.
52 "The Mormon Settlement in Illinois": Address delivered by OF Berry, before the Illinois State Historical Society Springfield, Illinois, 24 January 1906, 97.
53 "George Rockwell to Thomas H Rockwell," 2 August 1844, Kansas Historical Society.

complete the building and perform ordinances that would strengthen them for the road ahead, even as opposition and persecution began again. They began leaving in February 1846, crossing the Mississippi River into Indian Territory.

The temple was finished and dedicated by 1 May, and most of the Nauvoo Saints were gone by September, when another mob of 800 men with two cannons invaded the city. In 1848 – when those who had survived perilous thousand-mile journeys "across the plains" had begun establishing communities in the Valley of the Great Salt Lake – the Nauvoo Temple was destroyed by fire.

The Book of Mormon ends with the words of Moroni, the last Nephite, in hiding because his enemies would kill anyone who would not deny Jesus Christ. While awaiting his fate, Moroni added to the record some sermons of his father, Mormon. In translating one of these sermons, Joseph Smith reproduced most of I Corinthians 13 as it is rendered in the King James Bible, including the translation of agapē as "charity," with the addition of Mormon's explanation that charity, "the pure love of Christ," is a gift from God, bestowed upon "all who are true followers" of Jesus Christ, if they will pray to the Father "with full energy of heart" to be filled with this love, so "that when he shall appear we shall be like him" (Moroni 7:47–48).

Moroni's own last words convey Joseph Smith's ultimate understanding of law and love:

> I would exhort you that ye would come unto Christ, and lay hold upon every good gift ... come unto Christ, and be perfected in him, and deny yourselves of all ungodliness; and if ye shall deny yourselves of all ungodliness, and love God with all your might, mind and strength, then is his grace sufficient for you, that by his grace ye may be perfect in Christ.
>
> (Moroni 10:32)

Proving contraries is a process requiring patience. Joseph learned that truth may manifest in a flash, but sure understanding and lasting strength will develop over time, which must be "endured well." In words of the psalmist much beloved by the followers of Joseph Smith:

> Rest in the Lord, and wait patiently for him: fret not thyself because of him who prospereth in his way, because of the man who bringeth wicked devices to pass. Cease from anger, and forsake wrath: fret not thyself in any wise to do evil. For evildoers shall be cut off: but those that wait upon the Lord, they shall inherit the earth.
>
> (Ps. 37:7–9 KJV)

11 From Coercion to Covenant

What Kind of Higher Law Did Jesus Have in Mind?

A Keith Thompson

Introduction

Henry James Sumner Maine's thesis was that human societies progress when human individuals can transcend the shackles of status within kinship groups and redefine themselves in contractual associations with anyone they choose. His thesis captured intellectual attention when it first appeared in 1861.[1] In the age of Darwin, he had nutshelled social anthropology in a sentence. The book went through 12 editions, and a final version was published with notes by Frederick Pollock after Maine's death in 1906.

In the spirit of Maine's insight about human society, I consider whether human progress in law from coercion to co-operation and covenant could be the product of educated choice and whether it could be achieved before heaven. I accept that my suggestion runs against Maine's tide since I anticipate a retreat from progressive individualism back towards social community, but I believe I am justified since the enlightened contractual societies Maine envisaged were not hedonistically selfish in orientation. I approach this task in four parts.

In the first part, I sketch Maine's theory and briefly discuss the question of whether progressive societies must prioritise individual accomplishment over community interest if they are to succeed economically and socially. In the second part, I extract my idea that more enlightened legal systems are possible by comparing Jesus' higher view of the Mosaic Law expressed in the Sermon on the Mount with the contemporary interpretations he encountered and which he intended his higher view to succeed. I also briefly contrast Christ's vision with the general nature of law in practice in twenty-first-century Western society. In the third part, I outline the nature of the different law that might operate within systems described as coercive, co-operative, and covenantal. And in the fourth part, I discuss the separation that would have to exist before co-operative and

---

[1] Henry Sumner Maine, *Ancient Law: Its Connection with the Early History of Society, and Its Relation to Modern Ideas* (John Murray, 1861). Maine was Regius Professor of Civil Law at Cambridge from 1847 to 1854, but wrote the book as one of the Readers of the Inns of Court before his appointment to the Chair of Historical and Comparative Jurisprudence at Corpus Christi College, Oxford in 1869.

DOI: 10.4324/9781003148920-15

covenantal systems could operate in contemporary twenty-first-century society. I conclude with the aspirational thought that the very fact that we can conceive of higher-order legal systems suggests that they are possible, but I reflect that the achievement of such society seems unlikely absent Christ's personal leadership this side of heaven.

Maine's Theory: From Status to Contract

Maine's discussion begins with the suggestion that the social origins of law had not been subjected to scientific analysis before his own time and that Greek and Roman analysis involved little more than educated guesses.[2] Locke had merely copied their social contract idea[3] and while Montesquieu in France had shown some originality, his ambiguous expression was flawed because his sociological conclusions were premised on the plastic nature of the human race when, in fact, human nature is constant.[4] Bentham was not as easily disposed of. While it was difficult to say that his utilitarian theory was false, it was "unfruitful."[5]

Instead, comparative jurisprudence established the "Patriarchal Theory" or the idea of primogeniture as the common foundation of all primitive societies.[6] Those societies were not "a collection of individuals ... [but rather] an aggregation of families."[7] These aggregated families were, in effect, corporations with perpetual succession and collective responsibility for wrongs.[8] Aliens could be adopted in and even recruited, but these recruits acceded to the established aggregate family norms at the time of their adoption and the original families became aristocracies.[9] This analysis explained all ancient societies before modern Europe but the "family dependency" had been gradually broken down and replaced with "individual obligation."[10] And "the tie between man and man which replace[d] by degrees those forms of reciprocity in rights and duties which have their origin in the Family ... [wa]s Contract."[11] The "free agreement of individuals" signalled a new social order where even slavery has been "superseded by the contractual relation of servant to his master."[12] Human society had progressed from a relation based on family status to one based on contract.[13]

That is the essence of Maine's insight. He embellished his theory with examples from the law of testamentary succession and real property, but the "wheels

2 Ibid., 93–94.
3 Ibid., 94.
4 Ibid., 95–96.
5 Ibid., 97.
6 Ibid., 101–3.
7 Ibid., 104.
8 Ibid., 104–5.
9 Ibid., 106–9.
10 Ibid., 110–40.
11 Ibid., 140.
12 Ibid.
13 Ibid., 141.

and bolts" of modern society were only differentiated from those more ancient by an individualism seated in the idea of contract.[14] Maine's view of contract enabled understanding of individual moral duty separate from the extended family.[15] European feudal societies manifested the early stages of this transition when the lord of the manor, who "had many of the characteristics of a patriarchal chieftain," bound himself to new recruits by contract.[16]

Maine also added two generalisations about human societies which are useful in the discussion that follows. He observed that young nations were always characterised by "a period of ungoverned violence"[17] and that it takes time for ideas of sin, wrong (tort), and crime to separate in developing human societies.[18] That is because the idea of a crime against the state or a remote sovereign is a vicarious substitution for a wrong against a known family member in a primitive society.

The primary question I have about Maine's theory is whether the individualism he sees as part of societal progress is essential? That is, does individualism have to trump communitarianism if human societies are to progress towards unforced co-operation? I hope not because my sense is that some form of communitarianism is required to displace the selfishness which is so easily a product of individualism if human society is to progress further still. But in advocating care for others as bedrock in the best human societies, I am not suggesting that individual talent and entrepreneurship have to be suppressed if we are all to live together in peace and plenty. But I do think selfishness has to go.

Are More Enlightened Legal Systems Possible?

In writing this part, I draw on Christian New Testament Scripture. I try to do that in an ecumenical way without relying on the interpretative approach of any particular tradition, but I recognise that true objectivity is impossible because of autobiography.

In his letters to various European Christian communities in the first century AD, the Apostle Paul referred to the Mosaic Law as a "schoolmaster to bring us to Christ."[19] The gospel was a higher law which relied on spirit-guided compli-

---

14 Ibid., 258–60.
15 Ibid., 280–3.
16 Ibid., 304.
17 Ibid., 307.
18 Ibid., 307–24.
19 Galatians 3:24 (King James Version) (all biblical references in this chapter are from the King James Version). Note that while Paul used this specific phrase only once in the letters we have from him in our current New Testament, his letters to the Romans and Hebrews in particular include the same idea. Consider Romans 3:20–31 and particularly his reference to the "law of faith" in verse 27. Similarly, in Romans 7, he testifies that the law of Moses is fulfilled in Christ as he admonished those saints to live according to the spirit of the law (verse 7 and Romans 8:2) which Christ had outlined. In 2 Corinthians 3, he said that the gospel of Christ surpasses the law of Moses, and in Hebrews 9 he said that the ordinances of the law of Moses prefigured Christ's ministry and gospel.

ance rather than scrupulous letter-bound obedience. Indeed, he used the spirit/letter dichotomy so often that his references to "the letter" became shorthand for the law of Moses and "the spirit" became shorthand for the gospel law of Christ.[20] Paul's famous theme is not obvious in the other New Testament epistle writers, but the comparison between different understandings of the meaning of the law of Moses is clear in Christ's Sermon on the Mount. While he did not analyse the law of Moses commandment by commandment, the samples he used to teach the quest for character perfection are clear. First, there was a change from an emphasis on the restrictions of the Ten Commandments themselves to the celebration of nine affirmative character traits in the Beatitudes. The message was not that his disciples were no longer obligated to worship God the Father on the Sabbath day nor to kill, steal, bear false witness, nor covet.[21] These requirements remain, but Jesus wanted his disciples to pay affirmative attention to "the weightier matters of the law" and to strive to become like God rather than be side-tracked by minutiae including the tithing of herbs growing by themselves in one's kitchen garden.[22] Christ said that he did not come to take away the requirements of the law of Moses but to ensure that the greater purpose of that law was not missed.[23] Indeed, he made the Father's expectations of disciples very clear when he summarised traditional attitudes towards simple law obedience with the virtues God really intended his children to strive for (Table 11.1).

It is not just the *actus reus* of the crime of murder that the ancient law was proscribing. The law was always intended to fence the top of the cliff and intercept the *mens rea* of that crime before it crystallised in the mind of a would-be disciple. But since our thoughts are not known to any other mortal, control over the formation of sinful intent was required of each mortal as an act of conscious will and self-denial in the quest for character completeness.

Lust was similarly a sin of mind that could be controlled with mental practice, and thought control was expected of every disciple on the path to perfection.[24] Nor was it ever intended that Moses' divorce procedure should be universally available. Divorce was only ever legitimate in cases of infidelity. All other marriage difficulties were to be worked out. Expletives were unworthy of anyone on the path of discipleship. In Christ's ideal society, all human oral communication would be controlled so that it neither made light of sacred things nor contributed to the formation of anger in others. Christ's disciples were to strive for holiness in thought, word, and deed.

Then he provided counsel about how his would-be disciples should behave when they were provoked. Contemporary Roman law allowed serving soldiers to compel civilians to carry their load for a mile. Christ's disciples were not to merely

---

20 Consider for example, Romans 2:27; 2:29; 7:6; 8. Similar use of the contrast is also clear in 2 Corinthians 3 and in Galatians 3 and 5.
21 Exodus 20:1–17.
22 Matthew 23:23; Luke 11:42.
23 Matthew 5:17.
24 Matthew 5:48.

Table 11.1 Christ's Understanding of the Law of Moses

The Law of Moses	The Law of the Gospel
Ye have heard that it was said by them of old time, Thou shalt not kill; and whosoever shall kill shall be in danger of the judgment:[a]	But I say unto you, That whosoever is angry with his brother without a cause shall be in danger of the judgment: and whosoever shall say to his brother, Raca, shall be in danger of the council; but whosoever shall say Thou fool, shall be in danger of hell fire.[b]
Ye have heard that it was said by them of old time, Thou shalt not commit adultery:[c]	But I say unto you, That whosoever looketh on a woman to lust after her hath committed adultery already with her in his heart.[d]
It hath been said, whosoever shall put away his wife, let him give her a writing of divorcement:[e]	But I say unto you, That whosoever shall put away his wife, saving for the cause of fornication, causeth her to commit adultery: and whosoever marrieth her who is divorced committeth adultery.[f]
Again, ye have heard that it hath been said by them of old time, Thou shalt not forswear thyself, but shalt perform unto the Lord thine oaths:[g]	But I say unto you, Swear not at all; neither by heaven; for it is God's throne: Nor by the earth; for it is his footstool: neither by Jerusalem; for it is the city of the Great King. Neither shalt thou swear by thy head, because thou canst not make one hair white or black. But let your communication be, Yea, yea; Nay, nay; for whatsoever is more than these cometh of evil.[h]
Ye have heard that it hath been said, An eye for an eye, and a tooth for a tooth:[i]	But I say unto you, That ye resist not evil: but whosoever shall smite thee on thy right cheek, turn to him the other also. And if any man will sue thee at law, and take away thy coat, let him have thy cloak also. And whosoever shall compel thee to go a mile, go with him twain. Give to him that asketh thee, and from him that would borrow of thee turn not thou away.[j]
Ye have heard that it hath been said, Thou shalt love thy neighbour, and hate thine enemy.[k]	But I say unto you, Love your enemies, bless them that curse you, do good to them that hate you, and pray for them which despitefully use you, and persecute you.[l]

[a] Matthew 5:21.
[b] Matthew 5:22.
[c] Matthew 5:27.
[d] Ibid.
[e] Matthew 5:31.
[f] Matthew 5:32.
[g] Matthew 5:33.
[h] Matthew 5:34–37.
[i] Matthew 5:38.
[j] Matthew 5:39–42.
[k] Matthew 5:43.
[l] Matthew 5:44.

suppress their anger if their services were requisitioned. Rather, they were to prove that they understood the requirements of God's law by treating the Roman law as imposing only a minimum requirement. God expected Christ's disciples to be an example of their faith to all who knew them.[25] They were expected to exceed the requirements of the temporal law with a cheerful countenance so that no one would perceive any discontent.[26]

However, this counsel was not the *summum bonum* of Jesus' expectation of his disciples when they suffered provocation. He dramatised that expectation with the example of face slapping which may have been the response allowed or even expected by the rabbis when one witnessed blasphemy first hand.[27] In these circumstances, Jesus' disciples were not to respond in kind as the principle of reciprocity embedded (and misunderstood) in the law of Moses suggested.[28] Rather, they were to turn the other cheek in a sincere effort to de-escalate the conflict and to suck the life out of the provocation. Contention of any kind was to be completely expunged from the vocabulary and lives of Jesus' disciples. Any other response was evil.[29] Jesus expected all of his disciples to be as guileless as Nathanael[30] and he demonstrated his expectations with frequent instructive rebukes.[31]

Modern political campaigns regularly feature calls for legislators to craft laws with punishments that fit the crime. And while we can accept that the idea of restitution is more enlightened than revenge when we discuss tort law, the need

---

25 Compare with Paul's admonition that Timothy should be an example of the believers: I Timothy 4:12.
26 Compare also Christ's requirement that his disciples not disfigure of paint their faces when fasting so their good works were manifest which diluted one's reward in heaven: Matthew 6:16.
27 John W Welch, *Legal Cases in the Book of Mormon* (Brigham Young University Press, 2008): 263–5, referring to Gwilym H Jones, *New Century Bible Commentary* (Eedrmans, 1984) [2:368]; Carl Friedrich Keil, *Biblical Commentary on the Prophecies of Ezekiel*, trans James Martin (T and T Clark, 1857) [1:312]; George A Butterick et al. (eds), *The Interpreter's Bible* (Abingdon Press, 1956) [5:969]; William L Holladay, *A Commentary on the Book of the Prophet Jeremiah* (Fortress, 1986) 542.
28 That is, the law of Moses has often been caricatured as a law which justified vengeful retribution (*lex talionis*). However, when even the "eye for eye," and "tooth for tooth" phrases are considered in their Levitical context, they express a restitution principle which included fourfold reimbursement in many cases: see, e.g. Exodus 2; Leviticus 24; Deuteronomy 19; see especially Leviticus 6:2–5; 2 Samuel 12:6; Luke 19:8. Christ co-opted the "eye for eye" concept for other uses. These included his observation that his disciples were better off half blind in heaven that fully sighted in hell (Mk 9:47); more qualified to criticise the motes in others' eyes if they first removed the beams from their own – a carpentry analogy he was of course more than qualified to make (Lk. 6:41); and more like their Father in Heaven when their eyes were single to his glory (Lk. 11:34). In doing so, he not only emphasised the restitution principle over the retribution idea; he taught his disciples that self-denial in the quest for character perfection was to be preferred even over earthly ideas of restitution.
29 Matthew 5:37.
30 John 1:47.
31 Consider Christ's rebukes to Peter (Mt. 16:23; Mk 8:33; Lk. 4:8; Jn 18:10) and to James and John (Lk. 9:52–56).

to punish rather than forgive is never very far from the surface whenever there is public debate about immigration law and refugees, even though the Mosaic Law required its adherents to be kind to strangers.[32] Despite the Judeo-Christian foundations of Western civilisation, human beings remain reluctant to explore unfamiliar paths to social justice however it is conceived.[33]

In my brief analysis of Christ's views of law in the Sermon on the Mount above, I have noted a contrast between a view of law premised in obedience and a view of law premised in what is variously called, "care for other," charity, or love. However, both of these views of law pre-suppose a lower anarchic view of law. At the most basic level, law must be imposed to bring order to chaos. My suggestion is not that these three views of law correspond with Maine's idea that human societies progress when they make space for individual human autonomy, but that both insights suggest that higher orders of human society are possible when we reason about them.

Maine perceived that economic development was not possible until societal rules allowed for and enabled individual accomplishment and profit. Rules privileging the status of the oldest male had to give way to contract before the Industrial Revolution was possible. I am suggesting that social justice will not be achieved until we recognise and differentiate between legal systems premised in coercion, contract, and covenant. And I suggest too, that these divisions correspond not only with Christ's analysis of the nature of law in his Sermon on the Mount, but with Paul's expectations of differences in the life to come when he briefly discussed the nature of the resurrection in his first epistle to the Corinthians,[34] possibly after reflection on Christ's Parable of the Talents.

More specifically, in Matthew's version of Christ's parables of the ten virgins, the talents, and the sheep and goats,[35] he confirms that the kingdom of heaven

---

32 See, e.g. Exodus 22:30, Leviticus 19:34; Deuteronomy 10:18, 10:19; 24:14, 24:17, 27:19. Note that the authors of the Reform Judaism website observe that the commandment to care for one's stranger is mentioned more times than *any* other commandment in the Torah; more than the command to love God (*v'ahavta*): see Reuven Firestone, "The Commandment to Love and Help the Stranger," *Reform Judaism* (web page, 24 September 2016) https://reformjudaism.org/learning/torah-study/torah-commentary/commandment-love-and-help-stranger. According to the Talmud, Rabbi Eliezer the Great noted that "the Torah warns 36 times, and some say 46 times, not to oppress the stranger": Babylonian Talmud, *Bava M'tzia* 59b.
33 In their 1990 text titled *What is Justice? Classic and Contemporary Readings*, Robert C. Solomon and Mark C. Murphy explore the many different meanings of the word "justice." These include the idea of justice as vengeance, retribution or desert, through the religious idea that "justice" is a synonym for "righteousness" or "right conduct," through to the property rights inspired thought that justice means "overall public good," otherwise known as "social justice": see Robert C Solomon and Mark C Murphy, *What is Justice? Classic and Contemporary Readings* (Oxford University Press, 1990).
34 I Corinthians 15:37–44.
35 Matthew 25. Note that in Matthew's gospel narrative, these three parables immediately follow and respond to questions from the disciples about the time and nature of the final judgment in Matthew 24.

will feature divisions[36] and he alludes to the nature of some of those divisions. In Matthew 24, the divisions have to do with human character and the difference between real intent and hypocrisy.[37] In Matthew 25, they have to do with the difference between wisdom and foolishness which is manifest as preparedness in the Parable of the Ten Virgins[38]; as diligence resulting in spiritual profitability in the Parable of the Ten Talents[39]; and as charity or the pure love of Christ in the Parable of the Sheep and Goats.[40] There is also recognition in the Parable of the Talents that God's servants/children differ in ability,[41] although they appear to be rewarded proportionately in the same place as in Luke's exposition of the Parable of the Pounds.[42] Paul's summary presents as an undeveloped reflection on the nature of the resurrection, but the lack of development may be on purpose.[43] He says:

> And that which thou sowest, thou sowest not that body that shall be, but bare grain, it may chance of wheat, or of some other grain: But God giveth it a body, as it hath pleased him, and to every seed his own body. All flesh is not the same flesh; but there is one kind of flesh of men, another flesh of beasts, another of fishes, and another of birds. There are also celestial bodies, and bodies terrestrial: but the glory of the celestial is one, and the glory of the terrestrial is another. There is one glory of the sun, and another glory of the moon, and another glory of the stars: for one star differeth from another star in glory. So also is the resurrection of the dead. It is sown in corruption; it is raised in incorruption: It is sown in dishonour; it is raised in glory: it is sown in weakness; it is raised in power: It is sown a natural body; it is raised a spiritual body. There is a natural body and a spiritual body.[44]

It is not clear how many divisions Paul sees in the resurrection since there may be as many differences in glory as there are stars. Nor is it clear how they shall

---

36 Matthew 25:1, 25:14, 25:31–33. This teaching about divisions in the life to come also responds to the end teaching in Matthew 24:51 where he taught that there would be a division between those who kept his commandments and those who did not. The same division is evident in Luke's record of the Parable of the Rich Man and Lazarus: see Luke 16:19–31.
37 Matthew 24:51. In verses 24 and 31, he describes those who "hear" (hearken to his commandments) as the "elect." These are those who are always "faithful and wise": Matthew 24:45–47. Those who do not heed the Lord's teachings, despite his grace, are "evil servants" who will be "cut asunder": Matthew 24:48–49; 24:51.
38 Matthew 25:1–13.
39 Matthew 25:14–30.
40 Matthew 25:31–46.
41 Matthew 25:15.
42 Luke 19:12–27.
43 The three synoptists all record Christ's explanation that he spoke in parables on purpose to hide his meaning from those who were not spiritually prepared to receive it. See Matthew 13:10–17; Mark 4:9–12; and Luke 8:9–10. Indeed, the Parable of the Sower which formed part of the context of this explanation in each case may be regarded as teaching about spiritual preparedness to receive and implement the word of God in our lives.
44 I Corinthians 15:37–44.

be divided since the different flesh of men, beasts, fish, and birds cohabit on this planet and interface without communication. But it is clear that divisions will continue and the parables of Christ appear to make it plain that the divisions among humans hereafter will have a lot to do with their attitude towards others.

Are More Enlighted Systems Possible Now?

Christ encouraged genuine soul deep care for others. That was the human character trait that would be of most value in the world to come. If some humans have to be coerced to respect even the most fundamental rights of others, those inclined to co-operate without coercion may not be able to achieve a fully co-operative society if they are obliged to live in the same place or space as those who cannot treat them honourably, or as Maine would have it, in accordance with the terms of a contract. But Jeremiah appears to have foreseen an even higher order of human society inhabited by those who have unselfish care for others written in the flesh of their hearts and who are willing to live bound only by mutual covenants of love.[45] Because those who have to be coerced to obey law would not naturally respect the persons or interests of those willing to be governed only by love, it is likely that those willing to live by covenant alone would not be able to achieve their societal vision in the same space as those willing to live only to a lesser standard.

Jesus taught that those who must be forced by law (social customs [common law] or detailed legal codes [civil law]) to respect the autonomy and dignity of others because they are not law obedient by choice or nature, will lead eternal lives separate from those who have charity in the marrow of their bones. That appears to be because those who must be coerced to respect others have identified themselves during their lives on earth as inherently anti-social beings. Because it is not as encouraging to dwell on the negative, I discuss Christ's encouragement of human virtue as laid out in the Sermon on the Mount, especially since he emphasised that all human beings can become charitable enough to live with him in the life to come through repentance.[46]

When he summarised the parables which Matthew has recorded in his 25th chapter, Jesus said that the charitable will have a place at his Father's right hand in the life to come:

> Then shall the King say to them on his right hand, Come ye blessed of my Father, inherit the kingdom prepared for you from the foundation of the world: For I was an hungred, and ye gave me meat: I was thirsty, and ye gave me drink: I was a stranger, and ye took me in: Naked, and ye clothed me: I was sick, and ye visited me: I was in prison, and ye came unto me. Then shall the righteous answer him, saying, Lord, when saw we thee an hungred, and fed thee? Or thirsty, and gave thee drink? When saw we thee a stranger, and

---

45 Jeremiah 31:31–34.
46 For example, Matthew 4:17, 9:13, 11:20–21; Mark 2:17; Luke 5:32, 13:3,5, 15:7, 17:3–4, 24:47.

took thee in? or naked, and clothed thee? Or when saw we thee sick, or in prison, and came unto thee? And the King shall answer and say unto them, Verily I say unto you, Inasmuch as ye have done it unto one of the least of these my brethren, ye have done it unto me.[47]

The reason the charitable will have a place at the Father's right hand in the life to come appears to be because they can be trusted with authority and care for others.

Can contemporary societies and legal systems be changed so that they encourage the behaviours which he encouraged throughout his mortal ministry? Must we wait for his leadership before implementing the underlying principles? How would mortal laws be different if they were established to accord with his teachings?

Christianity as a whole is the story of human effort to answer these questions and to re-engineer society in holy ways to enable Christ's vision of ideal human relationships. My purpose is not to suggest that our efforts to date have been futile or are destined to remain so without his personal leadership. However, I do suggest that we are more likely to understand the utopian city of God, and prepare for its advent under his leadership, if we reflect on the nature of its likely laws in advance. I therefore suggest that we can identify three levels of law from our experience in human society and from the teachings of Jesus.

When human law relies on coercion to secure order, a reluctant peace is possible though it is tentative. To achieve peace when a significant number of members of the society are unwilling to co-operate (coercees) requires that we articulate legal rules in detailed codes and build criminal courts and prisons to secure the safety of those willing to obey the law without coercion (co-operators).

The insight that most members of human societies that rely on coercion for peace are inclined to obey the law by choice if not by nature (co-operators), suggests that if we were able to physically separate them from those who must be coerced to obey, we would only need courts to resolve civil disputes and there would be no prisons. Absent separation of coercees and co-operators in any human society, prisons are required to protect co-operators.

If citizens were so empathetic that they have no mind to harm one another and could resolve accidental harm by clear and guileless communication (covenantors), a higher level of society seems possible. In that society, like-minded citizens could maintain their peace by observing mutual covenants and courts would not be necessary at all. But once again, it seems that such society would only be possible if the citizens were physically separated from those incapable of living up to their standards.

Outlines for Future Human Societies?

The philosophical challenge for the citizens of co-operating and covenant societies is how to justly insulate their societies from those outside (coercees) who

---

47 Matthew 25:37–40.

would steal their material product or invade them for the sake of dominion. The perceived need for insulation infers enduring selfishness in those citizens and the perceived need for protection infers that defensive military technology would be necessary for protection. It also seems that the development of defensive technology would be anathema to covenantors, but technological separation alone might be sufficient to protect both co-operators and covenantors since it is unlikely that the coercees would ever co-operate sufficiently to bridge a significant technological gap.

Would co-operators and covenantors need to be physically separated from each other to ensure peace in a combined society? Could covenantors "turn the other cheek" when co-operators wanted to take them to court, and how would covenantors respond to court findings against them in the unlikely event they were found to have broken co-operator-level law?

The answers to these questions are difficult to resolve in a vacuum. However, it seems likely that covenantors would not be able to live to a full covenant law standard in a society they shared with co-operators since they would necessarily be subject to some co-operator-level law. This insight suggests that human societies are entropic in nature. That is, the legal standards to which they conform are those dictated by their least law-obedient member. If this insight is correct, then physical separation will be necessary if human beings are to establish and maintain co-operative and covenant-level societies.

Is such physical separation selfish and is it inconsistent with the altruism here identified as a necessary characteristic of those who would inhabit a covenant society? More specifically, is such separation intrinsically selfish? The answer here seems to be that non-imperial and possibly unseen charitable help is not necessarily inconsistent with altruism, though it is possible that co-operators and coercees might resent it if they saw and recognised it.

For the time being, it is, of course, unnecessary to resolve all the details of how the higher-level societies here suggested would operate. Evolved solutions would appear as these societies developed. The point of this philosophical exercise is to identify the general differences in laws that might differentiate human society if we were able to create them and to suggest that these differences and the need for physical separation in the life to come may be inferred from the teachings of Christ. I believe that the most significant suggestion that flows from this reflection is that higher-level legal systems would not need to use coercion to ensure compliance with their law.

Conclusion

I believe that human beings can realise anything they can conceive and believe. I think the technology conceived in the Jetsons cartoon series demonstrates that, but it is also conceptually clear in the teachings of Christ about prayer.[48] But I

---

48 Matthew 7:7–11; 18:19; 21:21–22; Luke 11:1–13; John 14:12–14.

am also aware of my lack of faith since I have suggested in this chapter that it is unlikely that we can realise non-coercive societies without Christ's physical presence and leadership. However, I do think reflection on the differences in law that may be involved is profitable for Christians and even non-Christian philosophers.

Many of the things I have written here are practically controversial. My idea that non-coercive society is likely impossible without physical separation annoys me because it runs contrary to my beliefs about how we should treat strangers in this current world. I want Australia to open its doors more fully to refugees including "co-operative" economic refugees. In part, that is because I would like to translate my vision of the gospel of Christ into contemporary society. I want Australia's collective laws to reflect my vision of his gospel and I am uncomfortable when the laws my country passes do not fully conform to my vision of that gospel.

Such dissonance always leads to reflection and more questions. Should I aspire to use the law to coerce others to my vision of what the world should be, especially if lesser laws respect my physical autonomy? When is it consistent with the gospel of Christ to coerce others at all? Only when they would break my leg or pick my pocket as Jefferson might say? What of the unborn child? Or should I be patient, do the best I can for others in the current world, and accept that the creation of a better world must wait for Christ? Or is that laziness rather than patience? If it is lazy, how might I best co-operate with like-minded others to realise a social version of Christ's gospel here and now? Would I most efficiently strive for that politically in an interfaith setting or within the confines of a single congregation since Christ did his temporal work in a small place named Galilee? I do not know the answers to all these questions, but I continue to reflect upon them.

So, I end my conclusion where I began it. I believe that human beings can realise anything they can conceive and believe. I therefore challenge my listeners and readers to argue with me, to show me why my ideas are myopic and morally wrong, and thus why we can do better now even before Christ comes.

12 The Forgiveness of Love in Charity
Getting Conversationally Opened Up

Patrick McKinley Brennan

Making the Most of the Natural

The crisis of normativity from within which we make our daily bread and choose how, or even whether, to love one another has spared no ideal.[1] Even forgiveness, not as *obviously* tantalising a target as true religion, marriage, or fatherhood, is being cancelled by redefinition. Christ commanded his followers to love their enemies (Lk. 6:37) and forgive one another 70 times 7 times (Mt. 18:22), and he nowhere suggested that anyone was absolutely incapable of doing what he asked. Perhaps rankled by the possibility that God does not command the impossible, many theorists have not been content merely to ignore Christ's summons to self-transcending love in unconditional forgiveness. They have instead reduced forgiveness to therapeutic terms worthy of valentines. Forgiveness needs to be rescued, above all from expressive individualism.[2]

Descended from Rousseau's reaction against the bourgeois life of possessive individualism of the sort launched by Hobbes and domesticated by Locke, expressive individualism is the diffusion of semi-romantic ideals according to which "persons are conceived as atomized individual wills whose highest flourishing consists in interrogating the interior depths of the self in order to express and freely follow the original truths discovered therein toward one's self-invented destiny."[3] A sophisticated, seductive, and potentially sobering example of what forgiveness looks like on expressive individualist terms is provided in the prodigious work of Martha Minow. It is characteristic of Minow's account, which will provide a starting point for conversation here, that while she concludes that "ours

---

1 On the nature of the current crisis, Jeremy D Wilkins, *Before Truth: Longergan, Aquinas, and the Problem of Wisdom* (Washington, DC: Catholic University Press, 2018), 37–95, and DC Schindler, *Freedom from Reality: The Diabolical Character of Modern Liberty* (Notre Dame, IN: Notre University Press, 2017) are especially helpful.
2 "You rescue something *from* something." GA Cohen, *Rescuing Justice and Equality* 1 (Cambridge, MA: Harvard University Press, 2008), 1.
3 O Carter Sneed, *What It Means to Be Human: The Case for the Body in Public Bioethics* (Cambridge, MA: Harvard University Press, 2020), 5.

is an unforgiving age, an age of resentment,"[4] she nonetheless contends that "to forgive is not an obligation."[5]

Reading Minow and like-minded theorists of forgiveness, one can easily form the impression that we are predestined to create and inhabit an unforgiving world, and sometimes even that such an unfriendly world is preferable *on principle*. Expressive individualism is just one especially successful truncated horizon that comes out of a long line of rationalising that counsels us, sometimes on the basis of a "theological secularism," to set our collective sights very low.[6] In some but not all of its forms, the *tendency* of this reductive way of thinking and living is to call for "respect for *any* decisions a person happens to make, or for *any* moral contents or 'life-style' to which people happen to commit themselves."[7] This might even take the form of a life in which *ressentiment* itself becomes a source of moral valuation such that "genuine acts of forgiving someone" are blocked.[8]

There exists another line of reflection, however, and what it sets out to do is "to make the most of the natural in light of the supernatural."[9] Refusing "reductionism – not only of the supernatural to the natural, but also of the natural to sin,"[10] this tradition of thought, above all in the work of St Thomas Aquinas, strives to allow the natural to achieve its full and proper stature, by showing how the natural is corrected, transformed, and perfected by the supernatural. On Thomas' account, as I will develop it here in conversation above all with Bernard Lonergan SJ and Frederick G. Lawrence, the Holy Spirit works in humans by endowing us individually by grace with the form of *caritas*, charity, by which we are transformed such that we take spontaneous joy in the good and, if we choose, overcome evil with good by forgiving our enemies.

While the reductionist tells us, through one justificatory narrative or another, to brace ourselves for the decay of the natural into enmity, envy, and resentment, among many other failures to love, the Christian committed to making the most of the natural through the supernatural invites us into a conversation

---

4 Martha Minow, *When Should Law Forgive?* (New York: Norton, 2019), 1.
5 Martha Minow, "Forgiveness, Law and Justice," *California Law Review* 103 (2015): 1615–45, 1618.
6 The work of Nomi Stolzenberg, such as "The Profanity of Law," in *Law and the Sacred*, ed. Austin Sarat et al. (Stanford, CA: Stanford University Press, 2006), 29–90, develops this position with great sophistication, crediting Amos Funkenstein, *Theology and the Scientific Imagination: From the Middle Ages to the Seventeenth Century* (Princeton, NJ: Princeton University Press, 1986), for the narrative of theological justification of what she terms "accommodation." Along similar lines, on liberal political theory, especially Rawls', as one attempted but unstable resolution of the Pelagian questions through "secularization," see Eric Nelson, *The Theology of Liberalism: Political Philosophy and the Justice of God* (Cambridge, MA: Harvard University Press, 2019).
7 Frederick G Lawrence, *The Fragility of Consciousness: Faith, Reason, and the Human Good* (Toronto, ON: University of Toronto Press, 2017), 360. My debt to Lawrence's appropriation and development of Lonergan is considerable.
8 Manfred S Frings, *Max Scheler* (Marquette, WI: Marquette University Press, 1996), 55.
9 Lawrence, *Fragility*, 374.
10 Ibid.

about human possibilities for the good. When conducted with the probity called for by the unrestricted desire for the true and the good that is constitutive of us *as* human, this conversation *in the good*, already the beginning of the moral life, can bring us into friendship not only with God but also with our enemies.[11] If the reductionist should object at the outset that this is a bridge too far, the Christian who in faith and with the theological virtue of hope accepts Thomas' supernatural solution will counter, in words such as those of Thomas Gilby OP, that "[g]race broods over the whole course of history, and consequently should not be excluded from Christian social philosophy, however severely the rational evidences are attended to."[12] The Catholic theology of grace *in its political vein* will counter the rational evidences with the assurance that good can overcome evil through forgiveness and thereby build up a socio-political order rooted in the good, animated by friendship, and leading us back to God.

Conversing with Martha Minow

"People as human exist conversationally in relation to everything that is,"[13] and so any exploration of "forgiveness" in search of correct understandings, as opposed to mere solipsistic assertion, must start from somewhere within the relevant conversation as it comes down to us. Martha Minow's influential work provides a worthy starting point for conversation because of its clarity and its capacity to represent an important strand of what I have called reductionism. In a departure from theorists who cluster around the idea that forgiveness involves overcoming resentment for moral reasons,[14] Minow carefully defines forgiveness as "a conscious, deliberate decision to forgo rightful grounds for grievance against those who have committed a wrong or harm," and to this definition she adds, for good measure, that "to forgive is not an obligation; it is a choice held at the discretion of those harmed."[15] I take these statements together as synthetic and programmatic and, therefore, worthy of a sequence of questions aimed at illuminating how far Minow has succeeded in understanding forgiveness.

A first question concerns whether Minow believes that humans sometimes have *good reason* to grant forgiveness (as she understands it). Minow never, to

---

11 For an introduction to the notion of the "unrestricted desire for the real and the good" to which I will return repeatedly, though without ever undertaking a comprehensive account, see Patrick H Byrne, *The Ethics of Discernment: Lonergan's Foundations for Ethics* (Toronto, ON: University of Toronto Press, 2016), 58–60, 210–27.
12 Thomas Gilby, *Between Community and Society: A Philosophy and Theology of the State* (London: Longmans, 1953), 191.
13 Lawrence, *Fragility*, 173.
14 Theorists who hold that letting go of angry feelings, in some cases for "moral reasons," is constitutive of or an essential part of forgiveness are collected in Margaret Urban Walker, *Moral Repair: Reconstructing Moral Relations after Wrongdoing* (Cambridge: Cambridge University Press, 2006), 154 n.3.
15 Minow, "Forgiveness," 1618.

my knowledge, specifies any such reasons. Although she does mention some possible benefits associated with what is commonly called forgiveness, "including not only psychological release but also a chance for moral betterment,"[16] Minow does not understand even "a chance for moral betterment" as exactly providing reasons, let alone good and *sufficient* reasons, for granting forgiveness (as she understands it).[17] Likewise, although Minow allows that "[t]hrough forgiveness, we can renounce resentment, and avoid the self-destructive effects of holding on to pain, grudges, and victimhood,"[18] she refuses to say that anyone *should* forgive anyone else.

This leads to a related question concerning Minow's rather authoritative assertion that forgiveness is "not an obligation." Is Minow's judgment that forgiveness is "not an obligation" tantamount to the claim, which she does not, to my knowledge, make explicit, that people can *never* have good and sufficient reasons to forgive? No, it is not, and her ambivalence about *whether to forgive* will turn out to be chronic, despite occasional rhetorical flourishes in one direction or another. Although Minow does lament, in oddly dissociated language, that "the supply of forgiveness [is] deficient"[19] in our time, she half-counsels against forgiveness as she understands it. On her account, the deliberate decision to forgo rightful grounds for grievance is "not an obligation" but instead a "choice" to be made in "discretion," and there are, she further contends, sometimes other – perhaps better? – choices for people to make: "The choice *not* to forgive can be empowering."[20]

"Empowering" is perforce a word of power, if only in the sense of a grab, but what does it mean as used by Minow? The clarity of Minow's definition of forgiveness is followed in this context by ominous obscurity in terms of the meaning of the gerundive "empowering," although in a much earlier book she defined the substantive noun "empowerment" as "restoring a sense of power and control."[21] Still conversing with Minow's text in a hermeneutic of charity, we can at this point pose two more questions. First, are there good and sufficient reasons to choose that which is said to be "empowering?" Minow does not provide them; perhaps taking it as self-evident, she instead changes the topic by once again noting the difficulty of forgiving and by underscoring the importance of expressing "a fair expectation of accountability and fairness."[22] One way reductionism works in the domain of forgiveness is by attaching preconditions some of which are

---

16 Minow, *When Should Law Forgive?*, 5.
17 The most that Minow is willing to say, it seems, is that "[p]erhaps forgiveness should be reserved, as a concept and a practice, to instances where there are good reasons to forgive." Martha Minow, *Between Forgiveness and Vengeance: Facing History after Genocide and Mass Murder* (Boston, MA: Beacon, 1998), 17.
18 Minow, *Between*, 14.
19 Minow, *When Should Law Forgive?*, 1.
20 Minow, "Forgiveness," 1619 (emphasis added).
21 Minow, *Between*, 65.
22 Minow, "Forgiveness," 1619.

beyond the would-be forgiver's capacity to satisfy. Contrition and repentance are common examples.

Second, can there be good and sufficient reasons *not* to forgive? Almost but not quite, according to Minow, and here at last is where Minow utterly gives away her game: "It is not bad to not forgive. Some acts are simply unforgiveable."[23] Minow is an accomplished stylist of the English language, and so in its signal awkwardness her double-negative combined with a split infinitive amounts to a quiet but clear concession that her account of forgiveness has run aground. Minow, it seems, can give her readers no *good and sufficient reasons* for refusing to forgive, only the conversation-stopping *ipsa dixit* that "[s]ome acts are simply unforgiveable" and the intimation that "a sense of power and control" is choice-worthy. One is reminded of Arthur Leff's "Sez who?"[24]

A clear giveaway that this is an expressive-individualist account of forgiveness is how the overwhelming focus on a "conscious, deliberate decision," "held in discretion," breezes right past any reckoning with the claim, as by philosopher Jeffrie Murphy, that "forgiveness is the sort of thing one does for a reason, and where there are reasons there is a distinction between good ones and bad ones."[25] Kathryn Abrams reads Minow as understanding forgiveness itself as one of "a vital set of emotions,"[26] and so it would be on some such fluid basis, then, that Minow has divided the world's population into two categories. First, there are those who are the hapless victims of "unforgiveable acts," whatever the contents of that authoritarian category. These are Minow's victims, too, it merits saying, precisely because she has denied them the opportunity to forgive, thereby confirming this as a reductionist position. Second, there are those who, not the victims of acts deemed by Minow "unforgiveable," are negatively free to forgive (or not) but who are, nonetheless, without benefit of any good and possibly sufficient reasons for choosing between forgiving their enemies and "empowering" themselves.

In sum, apart from cases of "unforgiveable acts," Minow has given every man a "choice" to forgive but not so much as one good reason, let alone good and sufficient reasons, to make that choice. Possessed of "rightful grievance" and "discretion," what is Minow's heroine to do?[27] The answer, I suppose, is "whatever she wants" or "whatever feels good," so long, as I further suppose, as it does

---

23 To which Minow adds in a footnote: "I assert this here as, at minimum, a psychological truth. As for normative analysis, the subject is debated." Minow, "Forgiveness," 1619. For my counterargument to the asserted "psychological" "minimum," see seventh section *infra*.
24 Arthur Leff, "Unspeakable Ethics, Unnatural Law," *Duke Law Journal* 28 (1979): 1229–49, 1249.
25 Jeffrie G Murphy, "Forgiveness and Resentment," in *Forgiveness and Mercy*, ed. Jeffrie G Murphy and Jean Hampton (Cambridge: Cambridge University Press, 1988), 14–34, 15.
26 Kathryn Abrams, "Seeking Emotional Ends with Legal Means," *California Law* Review 103 (2015): 1657–78, 1671. "Forgiveness marks a change in how the offended feels about the person who committed the injury." Minow, *Between*, 15.
27 In a related context, Minow postulates a moral equivalence between forgiveness and revenge: "If the legal framework inevitably affects emotions, pushing toward forgiveness may be no

not "harm" anyone else, an interpretive point to which I will return in the third section.

Like the atoms of Hobbes and Locke, the loci of free and equal autonomy of Rousseau and Rawls, and the self-sovereigns of J.S. Mill and Elizabeth Cady Stanton, Minow's individual with a "rightful grievance" and a "decision" to make is going it alone, or so she would have us believe: a person with little more than a satchel of "discretion" traveling, perhaps in search of "a sense of power and control," a lonely road across a field of acts some of which have been peremptorily declared by Minow "unforgiveable." The atomised or atomising quality of Minow's programme comes crashing in as she inveighs that "[i]ndividual human beings are just that, individual beings, both before and after anyone is victimized and then labeled as a victim."[28] One doubts that Minow is here making the unnecessary point that persons are biologically individuated before and after any act that introduces the possibility of forgiveness. It seems more likely that she is advancing a normative thesis, akin in some respects to Stanton's in "The Solitude of the Self," about how biological individuals ought rightly to understand one another *apart from their situatedness* and the relations by which, I had thought, they (we) were constituted as the persons they (we) are.

Minow's is a world in which "the human being [is] artificially," and most deliberately, "removed from the political, economic, and social relationships in which it is embedded."[29] The reason Minow's individual is faced with what she is told is an unreasoned choice between forgiving and "empowering" is that she has been denatured to a world in which, we are told without our usually noticing, "social relationships are something people choose (or once upon a time chose) to enter into, out of a calculation of their own advantage."[30] But this account of relatedness, the one at work in Minow's preserve, will not withstand even a first round of questioning because, in an example we can hardly escape, I and we belong to our languages far more than they belong to me or us. The reason Minow's heroine is in so much trouble, even if she cannot bring herself to own it, is that "[t]he purely autonomous ego was mortally wounded when it was found that if language was not its instrument, then the subject was not in control."[31]

People *as* human, it bears repeating, exist conversationally in relation not only to everything that is but also to every good they could possibly choose. In order for us to begin to *understand* forgiveness, we necessarily had to join a conversation and become participants in something larger than ourselves by which *as* human we are related to all that is and that can yet come into being. All the key

---

worse than pushing toward revenge, adversariness, or bitterness." Minow, "Forgiveness," 1627.
28 Minow, *Between*, 20.
29 Lawrence, *Fragility*, 298.
30 Nicholas Boyle, *2014: How to Survive the Next World Crisis* (New York: Continuum, 2010), 119–20.
31 David Tracy, *Plurality and Ambiguity: Hermeneutics, Religion, Hope* (Chicago, IL: University of Chicago Press, 1987), 82.

terms in Minow's analysis – "empowering," "discretion," "victim," "victimised," and "unforgiveable" – embody understandings and judgments that are just as socially constructed as the lone individual to whom they try in vain to do justice, and individuality is no exception:

> [I]ndividuality is a social category, in the sense that it is a category of collective human life: What it means for us to be individuals is determined by the society that gives us names and a language in which to say "I" (and in many cases the various due gradations of "you," "we" and "they"), by the economy in which we gradually construct ourselves through our productive work for each other, and by the state that safeguards our physical integrity, prohibits our being sold as chattels, protects our lives and limbs and maintains the institutions within which we can have duties and expectations and freedoms.[32]

The fact that the terms are socially constructed by no means entails that they are false, but it does establish the need to understand them and judge them for their truth, falsehood, or probability. The person who believes she has, and may indeed have, "rightful grounds for grievance" owes the possibility of that earnest judgment, which we try to respect and so ask her to account for, along with the notion of her sacrosanct "discretion," to an inherited but dynamic language, an imperfect but functioning economy, and a reasonably effective state (political order) from within which she can deliberate about whether on particular occasions to exercise something called "discretion," not a concept she invented or will bury, nor a capacity she generated all by herself.[33]

Injustice at the Cruxes of Interpretation Leading to Judgment

"How often," Minow writes, "I feel a desire for revenge even over minor matters! Forgiving family members and neighbors who harm us is a daily challenge."[34] Minow makes this confession of daily "harm" in the context of a law review article on forgiveness, and so it will not be amiss to ask how she understands "harm" here. Her choice of the word "harm," central as it is to our legal culture increasingly formed around the Millean harm principle, invites us to inquire whether many instances of what constitutes Minow's "daily challenge" are not instead just so many "offences" as understood by Mill.[35] Even so, is it possible that Minow is

---

32 Boyle, *2014*, 119.
33 On the demands of "conversational justice" and making ourselves and our choices intelligible to others, I am following in some respects Alasdair MacIntyre, *Dependent Rational Animals: Why Human Beings Need the Virtues* (Chicago, IL: Open Court, 1999), 11–13, 147–58.
34 Minow, "Forgiveness," 1619.
35 John Stuart Mill, *On Liberty*, chapter V. Joel Feinberg's four-volume work on *The Moral Limits of the Criminal Law* (Oxford: Oxford University Press, 1987–1990) provides an

suggesting that every offence is a potentially proper object of forgiveness? Or are only the contents of some still-to-be-designated subset of offences within forgiveness' domain? Not everything is forgivable, and the question to which I now turn is how we go about deciding the proper domain of forgiveness.

In colloquial English and under the sway of certain defective philosophy, we may sometimes say that we perceive injustice, but there are no percepts of injustice. Brute experience is never a possible starting point for our responses *as* human. Rather than say that we experience injustice, it would be closer to adequate to say that we interpret and in turn judge our experience to be unjust. Nothing in this life comes authoritatively pre-stamped as "forgiveness eligible." Minow's authoritarian category of "unforgiveable" acts notwithstanding, a threshold question, always, for someone deliberating about whether to forgive is whether *this* – whatever "this" turns out to be – falls within forgiveness' proper domain, and any judgment about whether *this* falls within forgiveness' proper domain must be reached through a series of questions and answers all depending, decisively, on interpretive *acts* of understanding. This is because we do not know the way angels know.

"Angels need only intuit to know. And each does so alone, not in a community of inquiry, for each exhausts its own species. But we humans," David Tracy continues, "must reason discursively, inquire communally, converse and argue with ourselves and one another."[36] Not capable of knowing by intuition or just "taking a good look" with the mind of eye, we must engage in conversation, where "conversation in its primary form" is understood as "an exploration of possibilities in the search for truth."[37] These possibilities are what we commonly call *interpretations*, and they are not epiphenomenal to human knowing but partially constitutive of it. With respect to every person, thing, or possibility that is the potential object of human knowing, the data must first be *interpreted*, and

> [t]o give an interpretation is to make a claim. To make a claim is to be willing to defend the claim if challenged by others or by the further process of questioning itself. When there are no further relevant questions either from the text or from myself or from the interaction that is questioning, then I find relative adequacy. I then present my interpretation to the community of inquiry to see if they have relevant further questions. They often will.[38]

Relative adequacy is not everything, but it is enough for now, and whether more is needed will emerge from relevant further questions.

---

excellent starting point for the interpretive issues presented in an attempt to implement the harm principle, the category of offence ("harmless wrongdoing"), and so forth, and Bernard E Harcourt, "The Collapse of the Harm Principle," *Journal of Criminal Law and Criminology* 90 (1999): 109–94, considers the interpretive strains on the harm principle when it is asked to do too much.

36 Tracy, *Plurality*, 27.
37 Ibid., 20.
38 Ibid., 25.

Texts, smiles, and even situations must be interpreted for possible understandings in the search for truth. No brute experience self-certifies that anyone was injured, robbed, disrespected, abandoned, smothered, defiled, victimised, cheated, betrayed, denied, harmed, or the like. Interpretation and the consequent need for the judgment, of the truth or probability of the preceding interpretation, are built into any starting point from which to deliberate about possible responses to experience. "The skills used in every act of interpretation are analogous to those used in moments of phronesis or practical wisdom that teach us how to act in a concrete situation."[39]

While it may ordinarily be far easier to judge what is a "harm" than it is to judge what is an injustice, this is not because any experience at all comes pre-understood and authoritatively categorised, but instead because, in part, in the conversation in which we are participating, the relevant criteria of interpretation allow us to judge that as to some particulars, under some circumstances, we have the answers to all relevant questions. "On any particular, we can know when we have no further relevant questions. It is possible, therefore, to know when we know enough."[40] This is no exception, however, to the *de facto* rule that a reasoned decision about whether forgiveness is possible and also appropriate must be preceded by *relatively adequate* resolution of what I will refer to as relevant *cruxes of interpretation* in the concrete situation.[41]

I have emphasised that there is no honest way to avoid the burden of reaching (relatively adequate) interpretation but also that we do not start from scratch. Within the relevant conversation about forgiveness' proper domain, some reliable markers are available to us. The first is the requirement of a human act, or what Thomas understood as an *actus humanus*. Earthquakes and other less dramatic "acts of God" are not within forgiveness' domain. Roger Scruton makes the same point when he observes that

> Dogs don't forgive because dogs don't resent. Forgiveness is unique to rational beings, and is a gift of metaphysical freedom. Only the accountable being, able to take responsibility for his own actions and mental states, can forgive or be forgiven.[42]

We do not resent rocks when they fall and hurt us, nor lightning bolts when they strike us, because as accountable beings we do not abuse our metaphysical freedom by trying to hold non-accountable beings accountable and eligible for forgiveness. What about an epileptic when he seizes and strikes us? It might be relevant to the adequate resolution of this crux of interpretation whether he was

---

39 Ibid., 22.
40 Ibid., 61.
41 I borrow the notion of "cruxes of interpretation" from Jaroslav Pelikan, *Interpreting the Bible and the Constitution* (New Haven, CT: Yale University Press, 2004), 38–75.
42 Roger Scruton, "*What is Forgiveness?*"; Review of Charles Griswold, *Forgiveness: A Philosophical Exploration*, *Times Literary Supplement*, TIMESONLINE (12 December 2007).

"negligent," not a self-defining term, in failing to take his anti-seizure medicine, and this leads to a second marker: culpability.[43]

We are familiar from the criminal law with the ideas that culpability can be greater or lesser with respect to the same, free act, and that greater culpability justifies (and perhaps, for Kantians, requires) proportionately greater retribution. Proportionate retributive punishment meted out by the lawful authority may be not only just, but even, in Simone Weil's observation, "a *need* of the soul"[44] who has received and experienced forgiveness, or yet hopes for it.[45] The interpretive question about the proper domain of forgiveness, however, must confront the fact that, whatever the judgments and punishments of the criminal law, we can never know, and for that reason alone (though there are others) we may never judge, another person's heart. As Remi Brague writes:

> I alone can accuse myself of sin. I can observe that some else commits a misdeed. But I do not have the right to accuse anyone else of sin. This in fact would itself be a sin. Of myself alone can I say that I am fully responsible for what I did.[46]

How, we may then ask, is interpersonal forgiveness ever even possible? Timothy Jackson writes that "[e]ven if not all candidates for forgiveness flow from positive malice, there must be some kind of turpitude for forgiveness to be well-founded."[47] Perhaps, but Josef Pieper echoes Thomas when he endorses the consensus view that

> [i]n the realm of justice good and evil are judged purely on the basis of the deed itself, regardless of the inner disposition of the doer; the point is not how the deed accords with the doer, but rather how it affects "the other person."[48]

It is how the deed affects the potential forgiver, in the objective order, when he becomes aware of it, that brings its doer within the proper domain of forgiveness.[49]

---

43 On how culpability is often subsumed within the concept of a "wrong" in discussions of forgiveness, see Lucy Allais, "Wiping the Slate Clean," *Philosophy & Public Affairs* 36 (2008): 33–68, 33 n.1.
44 Quoted in Timothy Jackson, *The Priority of Love* (Princeton, NJ: Princeton University Press, 2003), 39.
45 On the need for "satisfaction" on Thomas' account, see Eleonore Stump, *Atonement* (Oxford: Oxford University Press, 2018), 102–104.
46 Remi Brague, *On the God of the Christians (and on One or Two Others)* (South Bend, IN: St. Augustine's Press, 2013), 148.
47 Jackson, *The Priority*, 140.
48 Josef Pieper, *The Four Cardinal Virtues* (South Bend, IN: Notre Dame University Press, 1966, 2007), 60–61. See also St Thomas Aquinas, *Summa Theologiae* II.II 58.10. Most quotations from the *Summa Theologiae* will be taken from the English Dominican translation.
49 "Forgiveness can occur only in the objective context of the agent having been wronged and in the conceptual and epistemic context of the agent recognizing that she has been

The next, and central question, is whether the deed itself was unjust, and here we encounter a third crux of interpretation: the domain of justice.

To begin to understand the terms of justice we must join a conversation stretching from Plato through Rawls (and his critics). For his part in the conversation, Thomas understands justice to be a virtue, and further defines it as "the perpetual and constant will to give each one his right."[50] Just action, in turn, in the idiom familiar since Cicero, is giving each person his or her due, *suum cuique*.[51] Justice is the virtue that orders persons in their relations with one another and, according to Thomas, it "denotes a kind of equality."[52] Martin Rhonheimer explains that, on Thomas' account,

> [t]he concept of justice, which extends to the right of the other, only arises from the recognition of the other as a fellow human being, as "equal to me." This act of recognition is, as it were, the fundamental act of justice; and so injustice is always a form of inequality.[53]

It is to Christianity, not to Greek philosophy or even Stoic philosophy, that we owe what clarity we have on the recognition of human equality as the first act of justice.[54]

The just act, as Thomas and the tradition understand it, does not honour the basic commitment to equality by giving each person the same thing, but instead determines commutative, distributive, and social justice according to norms of both arithmetic and geometric equality. The demands of equality can therefore be satisfied in ways that look quite different among themselves. This is just one aspect of the crux of interpretation of what justice requires. Rather than elaborate it here, I will simply note that what one person may (in good faith) judge to be a failure of justice may turn out to amount only to an annoyance or inconvenience responsibly caused by what most people would regard as, precisely, a *just* person doing under the circumstances exactly what justice allows or requires of him or her.

Is such a person eligible to be forgiven? Perhaps even in need of being forgiven? Person A's perhaps eccentric, idiosyncratic, or precious sensibilities that he has been mistreated do not state injustices *per se* by Person B whose actions causally contributed to them. We are not *owed* all sunshine and unicorns and

---

wronged." Nicholas Woltertorff, *Justice: Rights and Wrongs* (Princeton, NJ: Princeton University Press, 2008), 106.
50 II.II 58.1. I have benefited from Jean Porter, *Justice as a Virtue: A Thomistic Perspective* (Grand Rapids, MI: Eerdmans, 2016), 115–46.
51 II.II 58.11.
52 II-II 57.1.
53 Martin Rhonheimer, "Sins Against Justice (IIa IIae qq. 59–78)," 287–303, 290, in Stephen J Pope, ed., *The Ethics of Aquinas* (Washington, DC: Georgetown University Press, 2002).
54 John E Coons and Patrick M Brennan, *By Nature Equal: The Anatomy of a Western Insight* (Princeton, NJ: Princeton University Press, 1999) and Larry Siedentop, *Inventing the Individual: The Origins of Western Liberalism* (Cambridge, MA: Harvard University Press, 2014), 62, 67–78, 83, 88, 96, 116, 118–19, 354–55.

compliments. Our culture of hyper-sensitivity makes it important to insist that hurt feelings do not *entail* antecedent injustice. In fact, "there is something morally offensive about undue sensitivity to injury, even although forgiveness follows from consciousness of injury."[55]

Taking a step back, the question of whether forgiveness is possible, because something within forgiveness' domain has happened to the person in question, emerges from within "the conversation that we are," a phrase I borrow from the German Romantic poet Friedrich Holderlein.[56] We get angry, hurt, even resentful, and emotions such as these, over which we have what Aquinas called "political" or diplomatic,[57] but not despotic, control, can be important pointers towards right choices concerning the good. But if forgiveness is to be an act taken for good and sufficient reasons, not just a chosen shift in emotions, our individual capacity *correctly to understand* particular situations and possible instances of injustice must be won from within the interpretive stories we tell ourselves in the conversation that we are. A righteously angry person on the verge of judging, perhaps correctly, that someone has done her a grave injustice is not exempt from our general "need," as Frederick Lawrence calls it:

> to be conversationally opened up and made sensitive to the depth of our involvement in the sinfulness of the situation brought about by the stories that have grown out of the waves of modernity in our culture; our need to absorb in detail how much we have constituted ourselves individually and collectively in these stories to the detriment of others, even Jesus.[58]

Among the familiar stories we tell about ourselves is the one according to which "[i]ndividual human beings are just that, individual beings, both before and after anyone is victimized and then labeled as a victim." Allowing myself to be *conversationally opened up*, however, I may well discover that "my behavior is never simply 'my own,'"[59] that everything I do or fail to do in some way affects somebody else, and that my emotions or desires as such do not provide good and sufficient reason for choice and action.

Allowing ourselves to be conversationally opened up, we may discover that we owe others far more than the self-soothing stories we tell ourselves

---

55 RS Downie, "Forgiveness," *Philosophical Quarterly* 15 (1965): 128, 134.
56 Lawrence, *Fragility*, 64, 163, 172, 192, 240, 382.
57 Sherwin, *On Love*, 50. "When Aquinas discusses *how* we can restrain our emotional impulses, he gives much the same kind of explanation we might hear today from a cognitive therapist. He does not believe that we can restrain our emotional impulses directly. We can, however, take an indirect approach." Bonnie Kent and Ashley Dressel, "Weakness and Willful Wrongdoing in Aquinas' De Malo," in *Aquinas's Disputed Questions on Evil*, ed. MV Dougherty (Cambridge: Cambridge University Press, 2016), 34–55, 40.
58 Lawrence, *Fragility*, 346.
59 Paul J Waddell, *Happiness and the Christian Moral Life*, 3rd ed. (New York: Rowman and Littlefield, 2016), 50.

indicate, even that they do not in fact owe us what we thought they owed us. Ominously, the domain in which we need to be forgiven, not just to forgive (the preferred perspective of Minow's tergiversating heroine), may be a whole universe broader than we have been habituated to imagine by the expressive-individualist languages that have, in Fred Lawrence's judgment, "invaded us."[60] The perhaps *unintended* quality of the consequences of my behaviour does not render my behaviour simply "my own." Not even emotions of rage, anger, and resentment, nor desires to avenge, retaliate, or punish render pointless the questions: "How will acting on this emotion or desire affect others? And do I, then, have good and sufficient reasons to do it?" The point is that every decision about "whether to forgive" invites the potential forgiver to hold herself accountable.[61] Especially in grave cases, we should not hesitate to say that what is called for on the part of the potential forgiver is her own further *conversion*, a category alien to expressive individualism: not casting stones without first taking inventory of one's own involvements in the distortions of evil and injustice, not "seeing" injustice in the other where there exists either less than we first thought or none at all, and, what is not yet forgiveness, having *mercy* and pitying the offender's defect precisely because one can look on his distress as in a way *one's own*.[62]

Inasmuch as we *as* human are conversational beings, both our problems, such as injustice, and their potential solutions, such as forgiveness, arise conversationally. In emphasising the interpretive burdens on the would-be forgiver, even his or her own need to undergo conversion of a sort in order to judge correctly, I must not be misinterpreted as denying absolute truth. "[T]o acknowledge ... that all human judgments regarding this-worldly realities are as conditioned as the things known thereby ... by no means entails the rejection of the human ability to attain absolute truth."[63] Some acts are truly evil, and some cultures, languages, horizons are better than others at allowing us to judge them to be such, and the possibility of forgiveness, like everything else that distinguishes *as* human, arises from within the context of possible true judgments and possible false judgments as measured by the demands of the constitutively human unrestricted desire to understand the real and the good. The interpretive task will be easier for those with good habits, and we call such people *virtuous*, but there is no honest way to circumvent the cruxes of interpretation. Those who have disinterestedly given themselves over to the search for the truth, by following the demands of the unrestricted desire to understand the real and the good, will be better friends, for reasons to which I am coming.

---

60 Lawrence, *Fragility*, 343.
61 "Human beings are, so to speak, narrative creatures, full of mixed motives, so they need to remember the likelihood of hidden narcissism, through a sensitive reading of both self and others." Martha Nussbaum, *Anger and Forgiveness: Resentment, Generosity, Justice* (Oxford: Oxford University Press, 2016), 88.
62 II-II 30.2.
63 Lawrence, *Fragility*, 105.

Bringing Good Out of Evil

Nancy Rosenblum writes that "[e]very injustice arouses anger, or should."[64] Especially in light of what I have called the cruxes of interpretation and the burdens on the interpreter, it is worth asking whether Rosenblum is right about the "should." If the question is when we have *good* reason to be angry, Thomas answers that we have good reason to be angry at, even to hate, what is evil: "the anger which is directed against sin is good."[65] This anger is good, according to Thomas, because it is an exercise of reason whose aim or object is *justice*. Unlike anger that is mere base passion with an evil object (e.g. envy), righteous anger, conversationally informed and limited by reason, merges into the legitimate judgment of wrongdoing: "when a man is angry with reason, his anger is no longer from passion: wherefore he is said to judge, not to be angry."[66] It is for this reason that Thomas even concludes that "[i]f one is angry in accordance with right reason, one's anger is deserving of praise."[67] Notably, when anger is called for according to reason, the anaesthetic effects of the platitudes of popularised stoicism would deform the moral life by deadening proportionate resistance and objection to injustice: "[L]ack of the passion of anger is also a vice, even as the lack of movement in the will directed to punishment by the judgment of reason."[68]

What Thomas invites us to affirm, precisely, is that whether the reasons for the anger are *good* reasons turns on the nature of the *objects* of the anger. The reason that the anger at the injustice *per se* is good is that the injustice represents an evil, and the reason that it is good to be (proportionately) angry at evil, on Thomas' account, is that the evil is a *privation*. Evil is a privation of being, and what is evil about evil, so to speak, is that it is a privation of what is good, for, on Thomas' account, being and goodness are convertible, which is to say that *what is, is good*. "[T]rue and false are in the mind, but good and evil are in things. The good is in things; it is something existing."[69]

Now, to talk this way – about being as good and evil as a privation and a privation as evil – is not to speak from Mount Olympus or Mount Tabor. It is to take a position, to offer an interpretation as a possibility in search of truth, from within an historically extended conversation. Over against positions (such as Zoroastrianism and Manichaeism) that give evil its own substance, Thomas' position, here in the words of Christian Smith, is that

---

64 Nancy Rosenblum, "Introduction," in *Breaking the Cycles of Hatred: Memory, Law, and Repair*, ed. Martha A Minow (Princeton, NJ: Princeton University Press, 2002), 1.
65 "Anger at sin is good." Thomas Aquinas, *On Evil*, trans. Richard Regan (Oxford: Oxford University Press, 2003), 375.
66 II-II 158.8.
67 II-II 158.1.
68 II-II, 158,1, 8.
69 Bernard Lonergan, *Topics in Education*, ed. Robert M Doran and Frederick E Crowe, Collected Works of Bernard Lonergan 10 (Toronto, ON: University of Toronto Press, 1993), 29.

badness and evil do not possess their own positive, distinct, independent ontological being in rivalry to the good. Ontologically, evil has only a "shadow" existence that is parasitical on the good. Ultimately, only good is independently real, and all of reality is ultimately good in being.[70]

Smith himself adopts and defends this last view, the *privatio boni* understanding of evil, following Thomas in the judgment according to which, in Smith's words, "[a]ll it takes for evil to spring in existence ... is the absence of what is good."[71]

Does this account risk trivialising evil? Anticipating such a concern, Smith considers several examples to show how it does not. They include violent vigilante revenge and the physical battery of wives by husbands. He also considers the evil of rape:

> Rape is inexpressibly wicked and morally reprehensible in the extreme – but in a deeply twisted and depraved way it is evil exactly in virtue of the privation of the goods of consent, mutuality, and loving communion in sex properly engaged, or a hideously misdirected attempt to achieve the true goods of sexual intimacy and the exercise of the power of personal agency.[72]

In rape as in the other two examples Smith considers,

> explaining these as *privatio boni* does in no way trivialize their evils. We speak here about matters of life and death, of violations and ruptures of unspeakably grievous wrong and destruction. So real and rightful is the true good in life,

Smith continues, "that its privation or misdirection proves to be of shattering consequence. Rather than seeing the absence of good as negligible, then, this account compels us to recognize it as catastrophic."[73]

Smith's pointed reference to the "catastrophic" was anticipated by Thomas' judgment that here we have reached the domain of *sin*. Sin, or what Lonergan refers to as "basic sin," is his/her free choice of a *privatio boni*. This happens, on Lonergan's account, when a person freely fails to choose an intelligible and intelligent course of action or fails to reject an unintelligible and unintelligent course of action.[74] Here it is worth belabouring, against possible misunderstanding, that basic sin is "simply irrational"; "basic sin is not an event; it is not something that positively occurs; on the contrary, it consists in a failure of occurrence, in

---

70 Christian Smith, *To Flourish or Destruct? A Personalist Theory of Human Goods, Motivations, Failure, and Evil* (Chicago, IL: University of Chicago Press, 2015), 234.
71 Smith, *To Flourish or Destruct?*, 235.
72 Ibid.
73 Ibid.
74 Bernard JF Lonergan, *Insight: A Study of Human Understanding* (New York: Philosophical Library, 1970), 666.

the absence in the will of a reasonable response to an obligatory motive."[75] As Lawrence explains,

> Whatever exists must do so for a sufficient reason that provides the grounds for our judging it to exist. The lack of intelligibility and reasonableness of an immoral act (or a basic sin) results in an objective falsehood or the objective surd. Only in this improper sense do we speak of evil (which according to Augustine and Aquinas, is always a privation of being) as existing.[76]

The failure to act on good reasons, or the failure to avoid acting in the known absence of known good reasons, would constitute basic sin, from Montaigne's "ordinary vices," "the common ills that we inflict upon one another every day,"[77] such as dishonesty, disloyalty, and treachery, to grave evils such as rape and sexual trafficking of children. No matter its magnitude, basic sin represents a failure to act on good and sufficient reasons, a preference for a course of action for which good and sufficient reasons cannot be provided.

Basic sin is not ethereal, nor is it at all unusual, and here, inasmuch as we are trying to understand the context of possible forgiveness, it may be beneficial to be conversationally opened up by Lonergan:

> Men are sinners. If progress is not to be ever distorted and destroyed by the inattention, oversights, irrationality, irresponsibility of decline, men have to be reminded of their sinfulness. They have to acknowledge their real guilt and amend their ways.[78]

The difficulty of amendment reflects the fact that *moral evils*, as Lonergan calls them, follow on and compound the effects of our basic sins. The person guilty of basic sin becomes, as a consequence of that sin, less effectively able to follow intelligent courses of action and avoid morally reprehensible courses of action. This moral evil, the lack of effective freedom for the real and the good, is itself a reduction in being and the good, of course, and, unless and until reversed, will lead to more.

The lack of effective freedom for the good is not just individual; it is also systemic, as when the setup that makes particular goods possible or likely is broken or even missing. This kind of evil is a privation of what Lonergan refers to, in a most useful phrase, as the *good of order*.[79] The good of order is the set of facilitating conditions that allow people to operate by co-operating, and people who cannot co-operate, because of the lack of effective freedom to do so, will suffer their own particular temptations to irrational and unreasonable alternative

---

75 Lonergan, *Insight*, 667.
76 Lawrence, *Fragility*, 144 n. 169; Lonergan, *Insight*, 666–9.
77 Judith Shklar, *Ordinary Vices* (Cambridge, MA: Harvard University Press, 1984), 1.
78 Bernard Lonergan, *Method in Theology* (Minneapolis, MN: Seabury Press, 1979), 117.
79 Lonergan, *Topics*, 34–36.

courses of action, a point of great importance to which I will return in the eighth section.

Whether with respect to particular goods or the goods of order that supply particular goods on a regular basis, we humans are conditioned beings whose conditions happen, providentially, to be satisfied, at least for now. Evil is not some nominal defect but, instead, a shortcoming or failure in real-world processes to which, if we choose, under the right circumstances, we can make positive, transformative contributions that would be called *good* precisely as contributions to increasing the good (being) in the world in which, as we know at a common-sense level already, good things and bad emerge as more or less *probable* based in part on the decisions people make. At this point, the phrase "emergent probability," a complex notion of great heuristic value introduced by Lonergan, can be helpful.[80] The planetary system can be explained in terms of emergent probability and of the survival of the relevant schemes of recurrence. So, too, can the ecosystems of the planet earth or, for that matter, the organs of the human body. But he or she, as Lonergan observed, "does not have to wait for his environment to make him."[81] He or she can freely contribute to the emergence of his or her own probability. Conversely, she can block it.

"Emergent probability is the great equalizer."[82] Every human on the planet is equally an emergent probability. It may help here to recall that "in this present life it is true of us that we do not merely have, but are our bodies."[83] The single-shot-to-the-head suicide immediately reduces the probability to nil, but suicide comes in degrees and does not always dress in black. Everyone contributes to his own emergent probability, or to his slow suicide, every day of the year. There is a growing literature on the skyrocketing phenomenon of "deaths of despair." None of us exists by necessity, and we ineluctably face the choice, as Christian Smith puts it, "to flourish or destruct." We either choose things that are good for ourselves and our emergent probability, or we do not, or, more often, it is a mixed bag of choices. The good does not exist apart from evil, good choices can bring good out of evil, and every person has to decide for herself the extent to which – if "extent" is not too cold a category – how much and how well she will choose what is good for her emergent probability. She will do so conversationally, asking herself what the right course of action is, whether to take it, or instead, and for no good reason, to give perverse pride of place to privation.

---

80 In addition to Lonergan's own many texts on the topic, I have especially benefited from Kenneth R Melchin, *History, Ethics, and Emergent Probability: Ethics, Society, and History in the Work of Bernard Lonergan*, 2nd ed. (The Lonergan Website, 1999) and Mark T Miller, *The Quest for God & the Good Life: Lonergan's Theological Anthropology* (Washington, DC: Catholic University Press, 2013), 10–25.
81 Lonergan, *Insight*, 210.
82 Tad Dunne, *Lonergan and Spirituality* (Chicago, IL: Loyola University Press, 1985), 62; Coons and Brennan, *By Nature Equal*, 139–40.
83 MacIntyre, *Dependent Rational Animals*, 6.

"St Augustine made perhaps one of the most profound remarks in all his writings, and for that matter in the whole of theology, when," Lonergan writes, "he said that God could have created a world without any evil whatever, but thought it better to permit evil and draw good out of evil."[84] What God wants for us is to draw good out of evil:

> We must not forget what God wants, the world God foreknew from all eternity in all its details and freely chose according to his wisdom and infinite goodness, is precisely the world in which we live, with all its details and all its aspects. This is what gives meaning to a phrase that might at times be considered trite: resignation to the will God. God does not will any sin, either directly or indirectly. He wills only indirectly any privation or punishment. What he wills directly is the good, and only the good. Yet the good that God wills and freely chooses with infinite wisdom and infinite goodness is this world. It is a good, then, that is not apart from evil. It is a good that comes out of evil, that triumphs over evil.[85]

The good that comes out of evil does not come out of it automatically, according to some blueprint. Lonergan writes that "that coming out of evils is another dynamic aspect of the good in this world,"[86] and each human contribution to that possible stage-by-stage increase in being and goodness can be the more adequate the more adequately we are conversationally opened up to *how* God's will, that we overcome evil with good (Rom. 12:21), is to be done. Often, the next stage will be to forgive one another as we have already been forgiven (Col. 3:13).[87]

The Forgiveness That Is Love

Any human who judges that she has suffered injustice, and so experiences emotions such as anger and resentment that we associate with being attacked and undervalued, faces several possible choices vis-à-vis her offender. The usual questions include the one about whether "to forgive" the offender, and while it is true that "[w]hatever else we may say about forgiveness, it is 'other directed,'"[88] any rush to judge what the offended has good reason to do to or for *the offender* risks eliding the starting point of the answer to that very question: the offended person herself.

For the reasons discussed above, the offended person has good reason to be angry and object to, and perhaps even to hate, the evil of the injustice she has been

---

84 Lonergan, *Topics*, 39.
85 Ibid., 30.
86 Ibid.
87 Miroslav Wolf, *Exclusion and Embrace: A Theological Exploration of Identity, Otherness, and Reconciliation* (Nashville, TN: Abingdon, 1996), 124–5.
88 J Harvey, "Forgiving as an Obligation of the Moral Life," *International Journal of Moral and Social Studies* 8 (1993): 211, 213.

done. She has no good reason, however, to hate herself, and this is so *because she exists*. What exists, is good. Especially, but not only, when treated in a way she judges to be unjust, she has good reason to say to herself: "It is *good* that you exist!" In a situation in which I judge that I have been offended, my possible judgment about myself that my existing is good will travel in tandem with my other judgment that what strikes at my being is bad or evil. In fact, it is because my very being is *good* that I can judge that the offence, that which I judge to threaten my being or to reduce the probability of my continuing, is evil. Forgiveness presupposes, and in no way denies or minimises, evil, specifically, the privation of my own being. Properly understood, forgiveness does not excuse, justify, pardon, condone, or minimise evil.[89] Instead, as Josef Pieper writes, "[w]e forgive something only if we regard it as distinctly bad, not if we ignore its negative aspect."[90]

Before, then, I direct any judgment or statement to the "other" who has caused or threatened the privation of my own being, I have good reason to say to myself, in the face of offence and the offender: "It is good that you exist!" Having *said* that, what then am I to *do*? Thomas' answer is that I am, *first*, to love myself and then, second, to love my neighbour, who happens in this case to be, or so I believe, my enemy. Love is indeed the answer, then, starting with self-love, in the specific sense still to be developed here. Thomas' theological account of love is complex, but for present purposes several points of broad outline will suffice to provide an account of forgiveness as the extension of proper love of self from the offended person to her offender.

The first point is that simply in virtue of creation we, like the angels, have a *natural love* for ourselves, by which Thomas means an impulse or desire for own fulfilment or perfection; Thomas' usual term for this love is *amor*. "Such needlove," as Pieper unapologetically terms it, "whose goal is its own fulfillment, is also the nucleus and the beginning in all our loving. It is simply the elemental dynamics of our being itself, set in motion by the act that created us."[91] The Creator created us to love ourselves, and others, unto himself.

Second, the love that is *amor* is just the beginning of the love of which humans *as* human are capable, according to Thomas, because there is also a form of love proper to us *as* human, *dilectio*. This kind of love takes two forms, *amor concupiscentiae* and *amor amicitiae*, "the love proper to desire" and "the love proper to friendship," respectively.[92] We are accustomed to the idea that love is to be the form of the Christian moral life, but it can be surprising to discover that *friendship*, an idea Thomas adapted from Aristotle, is the model of not only human-to-human love but, in a different way, for the relationship between him or her and God.

---

89 On avoiding some of these possible miscommunications, see Trudy Govier, *Forgiveness and Revenge* (London: Routledge, 2002), 54–61.
90 Josef Pieper, *Faith, Hope, Love* (San Francisco, CA: Ignatius Press, 1986), 189.
91 Pieper, *Faith*, 222.
92 Michael S Sherwin, *On Love and Virtue: Theological* Essays (Steubenville, OH: Emmaus, 2018), 99.

The Forgiveness of Love in Charity 217

Third, the love proper to friendship is defined by Thomas as follows: "to love is to will good to someone,"[93] where the good is understood as *that which perfects something as its end*. As Michael Sherwin OP explains Thomas' account, the love proper to friendship

> is the act of willing good to the beloved. This willing, however, must be oriented toward the good we will for our friend, and thus entails as an integral component an *amor concupiscentiae* for the good we will for him. This, in Aquinas's view, is the essence of the love of friendship. When we love a person, we are always affirming some good for that person. These are not two separate loves.[94]

The love of friendship necessarily *includes* the willing of particular goods for the friend, but

> most fundamentally, the good we will for the beloved is simply the good of existence. "The first thing that one wills for a friend is that he be and live" [ST II 25.7]. Only subsequently do we then will particular goods for our beloved and direct our actions accordingly.[95]

In the love of friendship proper to humans, then, the lover wills good to the friend and, as an integral component of that willing, wills *particular* goods, as Sherwin explains:

> [H]uman love always has two components, one of which is subordinated to the other. Love of concupiscence [that is, the love proper to desire] is contained within the dynamism of our love of friendship for ourselves and for someone else.[96]

With his reference to "love of friendship for ourselves," Sherwin returns us to our starting point in the *priority* of the proper love of self[97]: it is good that you exist and, therefore, right to will the good to yourself.

---

93 I-II 26.4.
94 Sherwin, *On Love*, 99.
95 Ibid.
96 Ibid.
97 "For Thomas, the primacy of self-love over love of neighbor on this level is not a statement of normative ethics ... In a specific way, the human will also stands under the fundamental law of all creaturely being according to which *being*-one (*unitas est potior unione*). The natural assertion of one's own good precedes the free love that is supposed to reach the neighbor, just as it already includes the self of the one loving." Eberhard Schockenhoff, "The Theological Virtue of Charity (IIa IIae, qq. 23–46)," in *The Ethics of Aquinas*, ed. Stephen J. Pope (Washington, DC: Georgetown University Press, 2002), 244–58, 253. On the question of proper love of self according to Thomas, see Anthony T Flood, *The Root of Friendship: Self-Love and Self-Governance in Aquinas* (Washington, DC: Catholic University Press, 2014);

About the priority of love of self, Thomas is crystal clear: "the love we have for ourselves is the type of love that is proper to friendship (ST I-II 28.1 ad 2)."[98] The love proper to friendship that we owe first ourselves, and with it the love proper to desire that we owe ourselves, provide the model: "friendship is the image and self-love is the original; we love our friends as we love ourselves."[99] Pieper anticipates the standard objection to this thesis, and his way of handling it is worth following:

> Granted, it sounds at first rather odd, and almost like a deliberate provocation, that self-love should serve as a paradigm from which we may read off what love in general is. But suppose we once more apply our "test" formula: It's good that you exist. To whom do we refer that expression, instantly and with sincerity, if not to ourselves? We do so even if at the moment we have been critically examining ourselves and do not find ourselves especially lovable.[100]

The love of self by which we will our own good is the free choice to act for the happiness for which we were in the depths of our soul created. It is to co-operate with the Creator in achieving that for which we were created. It would be hubris in the extreme to decline on the ground of "altruism" to do what the Creator created us to do with and for our very selves.

When we judge correctly that it is good that we exist and that we have therefore good and sufficient reasons to will goods to ourselves, we do so, nonetheless, from within a world of mixed messages. On the one hand, it is good that I exist, but, on the other, I can, and sometimes must, accuse myself of sin. On the one hand, it is good that I exist, but, on the other, my offender has seen fit, or so it seems, not to love me. And so, as Pieper observed, we sometimes "do not find ourselves especially lovable." Herbert McCabe OP calls attention to the *fear* that is "very deep in us ... that our existence as a subject is precarious, and contingent, and perhaps an illusion."[101] In the context of offence especially, the situation of felt degradation, and perhaps partial annihilation, may hinder and therefore make more exigent the judgment "It is good that you exist!"

On this judgment depends the possibility of moving oneself out of the mire, past the paralysis of the "grievance" held in the "discretion" on which Minow's heroine rested, and onward to the task of treating oneself *as* good. Unless we

---

Anthony T Flood, *The Metaphysical Foundations of Love: Aquinas on Participation, Unity, and Union* (Washington, DC: Catholic University Press, 2018); Thomas Osborne, *Love of Self and Love of God in Thirteenth-Century Ethics* (South Bend, IN: Notre Dame University Press, 2005), DM Gallager, "Thomas Aquinas on Self-Love as the Basis for Love of Others," *Acta Philosophica* 8 (1999): 23–44.

98 Sherwin, *On Love*, 99 n. 144.
99 Pieper, *Faith*, 236.
100 Ibid., 235–6.
101 Herbert McCabe, *God, Christ, and Us* (New York: Continuum, 2005), 120.

start with ourselves, we can be of no good to others: "as a man is to himself, so also he is to his friend."[102] Whatever our own sins and whatever the true (rather than apparent) sins that others have committed against us, it is good that we exist and, as Thomas goes on to remind us, we have good and sufficient reasons to will goods to ourselves:

> The love that a man has for others arises in man from the love that he has for himself, for a man stands in relation to a friend as he does to himself. But a person loves himself inasmuch as he wishes the good for himself, just as he loves another person by wishing him good. So, by the fact that one is interested in his own good he is led to develop an interest in another person's good.[103]

At the moment when a person judges that she has been offended, it may yet be a stretch – the proverbial bridge too far – for her to reach out to her offender "to forgive." If, however, she starts where Aquinas tells her to start, where Pieper emphasises that she is by creation and nature inclined to start, her first act – in a sequence leading to the possibility of forgiveness, though she need not yet recognise it as such – is to love herself with the love proper to friendship. It is neither unseemly nor "selfish" to do what we were created to do.

If the first component of forgiveness consists of the acts of proper self-love, then, the second component *follows on* the judgment that the existence and goodness of his offender are just as real as his own. This would be the judgment that he and his offender are *each other's equals* as fellow seekers of the good.[104] This judgment of equality, as we saw in the third section, is the *fundamental act of justice*, and it reflects a refusal, which will elude the romantic, to identify someone definitively with his or her predicates.[105] Inasmuch as my offender and I are fundamentally one another's equals, despite the secondary inequalities that include our unjust and even wicked choices, the same reasons I have for saying to myself that it is good that I exist *apply equally to my offender*.[106] As Pieper observes, "the New Testament … establishes self-love as the measure for all love among human beings: Thou shalt love thy neighbor as thyself!"[107]

If my "offender" were Scruton's dog, a gorilla, or a Martian, the reasons I have for loving myself *qua* he or she would not apply to my "offender." I therefore

---

102 "Finality, Love, Marriage," *Collection*, Collected Works of Bernard Lonergan 4, ed. Frederick E Crowe and Robert M Doran (Toronto, ON: University of Toronto Press, 1993) 17–52, 35.
103 Thomas Aquinas, *Summa Contra Gentiles*, III.153.
104 II.II 26.4.
105 Robert Spaemann, *Persons: The Difference Between 'Someone' and 'Something'*, trans. Oliver O'Donovan (Oxford: Oxford University Press, 2017), 232.
106 On human equality as the unity of mankind in nature and grace, see "Human Equality," Jacques Maritain, *Redeeming the Time*, trans. Harry Binsee (London: Bless, 1946), 1–28, 18.
107 Pieper, *Faith*, 238.

could not attempt to befriend it in the sense of loving it with *amor amicitiae* and so willing for it, in *amor concupiscentiae*, goods of the sort I will for myself. It is the unity in human form, a certain human equality, that provides the basis of the judgment and the reason for action, as Thomas explains:

> [F]rom the fact that two things are alike, having as it were one form, they are in a certain manner one in that form, as two men are one in the species of humanity and two white persons in whiteness. And therefore the affection of the one inclines the one toward the other as toward what is one with himself: he wills the good for him as he does for himself.[108]

This particular judgment of equality, when it is reached, provides the good and sufficient reasons for willing the good of the other person as I will it, or have good and sufficient reasons to will it, for myself. Love for others "proceeds from the similarity to the love we bear ourselves."[109]

What I propose as an understanding of forgiveness, then, is one human's *extension* of the love proper to friendship that she owes herself to the person she believes has offended her. The judgment of human equality on which the extension pivots can be hard or seemingly impossible to reach in good times because, even then, we are familiar with just how evil humans are capable of being. That judgment is presumably the harder to reach in the context of felt offence to one's own person. But it is the truth of that judgment, that we are one another's equals as fellow seekers of the good, that shapes forgiveness as the answer to this question: What should a person do vis-à-vis her offender in response to the offence? She should love her enemy *as* another self. Or, in other words, forgiveness, understood as the *extension* of proper love of self to one's offender, is the form love takes in the context of offence, and it has no conditions precedent that must be satisfied. The offender is equally another lovable self irrespective of whether he ever performs an act of contrition or even offers an apology: there are no preconditions to another person's being lovable, just as there are no preconditions to my own self's being lovable. Forgiveness is indeed other-directed, but it starts with the offended person's own judgment that "It is good that I exist!", proceeds on that basis to love of self, judges the fundamental equality between the offended and the offender, and *extends* the love he rightly has for himself to his offender, despite whatever he judges to be wrong with his offender. *How* he is to do this is the question to which I now turn, and the answer is principally *charity*.

From Love to Charity

Unless blocked, the question properly arises for individuals in all kinds of situations whether they have what it takes to contribute to the emergence of specific

---

108 I-II 27.3.
109 Pieper, *Faith*, 236.

probabilities. Some people can, but others cannot, contribute to sustaining Latin as a spoken language, to the building of shelters for people who have lost homes in a particular recent hurricane, or to the reform of a particular political order to raise it closer to the level that charity demands. The question of *who can do what* also arises for a person about himself, and the question is categorically at its most acute, we can suppose, when forgiveness is what love calls for. He is my equal, but *can* I love him?

Cyril O'Regan captures this acuteness when he asks whether forgiveness is a term "*of* the impossible, or even *for* the impossible" and goes on to suggest that, as we disambiguate the term, forgiveness, and specify the "this" to which it refers, we recognise that "[f]orgiveness in any of its forms has contexts and even more importantly conditions," but "the truly important question is whether forgiveness has *sufficient* conditions."[110] If but only if forgiveness is not impossible, we must ask whether – and if so when and how – its sufficient conditions are satisfied. As Lonergan noted, the ability to bring good out of evil is itself a good and is, therefore, contingent, but is it a good whose conditions happen to be satisfied?

The reductionist has his doubts or denials. The Christian, however, when she asks herself, "Can I forgive him for this?", knows in faith that her natural desires and experiences of moral impotence, as in *ressentiment*, are never the whole picture. Our struggles to meet the responsibilities of natural love of self, not to mention of one's enemy, need not be, if they ever were, without benefit of the supernatural solution. "Common English usage commonly associates the supernatural with the spooky,"[111] but what Thomas has in mind by the supernatural concerns how he or she enters into the divine life and, in a real way, participates in it. As Thomas develops the supernatural solution, it is understood as our being the recipients of the self-communication of the triune God that always already offers to correct and transform us so that we can live on the level of love and friendship with one another, even with those who persecute us, and with God.

The way Thomas goes about making the best of natural in light of the supernatural gives effect to his judgment that "the universe really and not just metaphorically has a conversational structure."[112] This is so, according to Thomas, because the triune God, in whom the three divine persons are conversationally related to one another, such that we can speak of God "as conversational," self-communicates to humans through the *inner word*, the Holy Spirit, and the outer Word, Christ, so as to allow human consciousness to respond through mind and heart in conversation and choice. *Acting* in history as intended from the foundation of the universe, God as conversation offers conversationally to open us up

---

110 Cyril O'Regan, "Forgiveness and the Forms of the Impossible," *Proceedings of the American Catholic Philosophical Association* 82 (2008): 67, 68.
111 "Mission and Spirit," Bernard Lonergan, *A Third Collection*, Collected Works of Bernard Lonergan 16, ed. Robert M Doran and John D Dadosky (Toronto, ON: University of Toronto Press, 2017), 21–33, 25.
112 Lawrence, *Fragility*, 275.

and bring us into the life of that friendship in charity of which we would be, left to our own devices, incapable:

> "Thomas knows on the basis of revelation ... that the God of our Lord Jesus Christ 'wills all men to be saved' (1 Tim. 2:4); that that God is faithful, by whom you were called into the fellowship [*koinonia*] of his God, Jesus Christ our Lord" (1 Cor. 1:9). In Aquinas's overarching vision, God out of unbounded love for this Triune nature, and in a movement in response to this original event of love, draws all creatures in accord with their own dignity back to himself as end. In creation, election, and incarnation the Triune God enters into intimate companionship and communication with human beings: *societas, convivere, conversation*.[113]

The sufficient conditions of our being able to live on the level of love, including in the form of forgiveness, are established not incidentally, peripherally, or contingently, but as a working out of the "original event of love" of the triune God in the Word and in the Holy Spirit.

The shorthand way of describing this is, first, that God works on us through grace to effect charity that, with our free co-operation, brings us into the divine friendship into which we can in turn invite others through our willing their good, too. It is, second, that God instructs us through the outer Word. I will briefly elaborate both ways.

The Development of Charity

"Charity is love, yet love is not always charity."[114] By charity, Thomas understands an infused virtue whereby a person is ordered towards friendship with God and friendship with other persons in relation to God. Beyond our natural means and in us only through infusion by the Holy Spirit, charity is the form that inclines us individually to acts of love *by rendering them delightful*.[115] By the grace of charity, we come to enjoy "a certain pleasing affective affinity for the good."[116] Paul Waddell explains the way in which

> charity is an implication of grace, an activity, a way of life derived from a genuine understanding of who we are. In grace we are not merely human, we are sharers in God's life, men and women who already participate in the friendship that is God; thus, to act in charity is to live in harmony with ourselves, to act according to, not in opposition to, who we truly are.[117]

---

113 Ibid., 365.
114 I-II 62.2 ad 3.
115 Lawrence, *Fragility*, 366.
116 Sherwin, *On Love*, 52.
117 Paul J Waddell. *Friendship and the Moral Life* (Notre Dame, IN: Notre Dame University Press, 1989), 126.

Within our world of emergent probability, "[g]race is not a scheme of recurrence that more or less probably emerges from natural processes"; "grace is absolutely beyond what nature could achieve on its own."[118]

When Thomas presents charity as a certain friendship with God and friendship with other people, including oneself, in relation to God, he understands that it must pass through stages, which we anticipated, in part, in the discussion of *dilectio* in the fifth section. The first phase is one of *desire*. In the love proper to desire, now under the grace of charity, we begin by desiring another, and this is not a bad or unhealthy thing, as Lawrence explains, giving ample scope to Thomas' mereology, because it is

> how we all manifest the desire of parts to be integrated in the whole; or, in our desire for self-preservation, it is how we want to have our needs secured in community (i.e., the legitimate aspect of liberal democracy's passage from the state of nature to civil society).[119]

When we judge that we have been offended, our concupiscent desire to be integrated into the whole has been frustrated, even our "self-preservation" upset, and the first stage of love of others in response to offence will be to act on that desire to be restored to the rightful place vis-à-vis one's offender and the overall community.

The next stage in the development of charity towards friendship is *benevolence*, "that well-wishing by which we love another for his or her own sake ... For Aquinas," Lawrence, notes,

> *benevolentia* lays no claim on another, and manifests no greed to possess the other. It is the affective counterpart to disinterested inquiry into the truth for its own sake, and so is a kind of desire that is unaffected by concupiscence.[120]

It is at this point that the true sense of the political, the self-transcending pursuit of the common good of the community, can emerge, to the possibility of which I will return in the eighth section. Immediately in the context of response to offence, however, the grace of charity leads the offended person to benevolence (well-wishing) and even sometimes beneficence, where our opportunities for the former, including through prayer for our enemies (Mt. 5:4), will often exceed our opportunities for the latter.[121] If God has given prayer "all power over good," as Tertullian says God has, then our benevolent prayer for our enemies

---

118 Mark T Miller, *The Quest for God and the Good Life* (Washington, DC: Catholic University Press, 2013), 144.
119 Lawrence, *Fragility*, 366–7.
120 Ibid., 367.
121 Michael Sherwin, *By Knowledge and By Love: Charity and Knowledge in the Moral Theology of St. Thomas Aquinas* (Washington, DC: Catholic University Press, 2005), 67, 147–52.

in forgiveness can indeed change them, but it is certain that forgiveness changes the one giving it.

The third stage in the affective development of the self in the love of charity is *friendship* itself, in which, from the proper starting point in love of self, "[a] higher love comes circling back ... The movement, which has turned first on the lover and then gone out to another, now returns," Gilby explains,

> but from the other, and this return, *redamatio*, both diminishes the effort and increases the nobility of the activity ... This circling of love between two persons, which includes desire and benevolence and adds a stability and ease denied to both, supposes a union between them, a *communication*.[122]

Forgiveness consists of a reciprocal love, a loving-back (*redamatio*) based on a union of equals in the pursuit of the good.

Remarkably, Thomas does not hold that in charity we are to love all equally. *Unlike* theorists (such as Gene Outka) who understand charity as a form of "equal regard," Thomas affirms that charity requires different treatment for different people. What Thomas refers to as the "order of charity" follows our natural loves:

> The primary object of charity is, of course, God. The second object of charity is the self, for the self directly partakes of the divine good, but a neighbor is loved for his or her fellowship in pursuit of that good ... Not only is the self to be loved above the neighbor,

as we saw in the fifth section, "but some neighbors are to be loved more than others,"[123] a notion Thomas works out in terms of "nearness." According to Thomas, we are required to love some neighbours more than others because of our nearness to them in blood, marriage, family, "and friendship amid the roles and practices that shape the moral life."[124] We can think here of "the disciple whom Jesus loved" (Jn 13:23).

In the context of possible forgiveness, some offenders come from afar but others from close at hand, and their comparative nearness will, in turn, determine the charity that is owed in response to offence. "At some point in any real friendship, benevolence and beneficence must be expressed through forgiveness."[125]

---

122 Gilby, *Between*, 192.
123 Michael Moreland, "Justice, Love, and Duties of Care in Tort Law," in *Agape, Justice, and Love: How Might Christian Love Shape Law?* ed. Robert Cochran and Zachary Calo (Cambridge: Cambridge University Press, 2017), 188–208, 202. "Thomas denies that charity as neighbor love requires each of us to love all our neighbors equally (2a2ae 26.6)." Jean Porter, "*De Ordine Caritatis*: Charity, Friendship, and Justice in Thomas Aquinas's *Summa Theologiae*," *The Thomist* 53 (1989): 197–213, 199.
124 Moreland, "Justice," 205.
125 Paul J Waddell, *Happiness and the Christian Moral Life*, 3rd ed. (Lanham, MD: Rowman & Littlefield, 2016), 70.

Forgiveness in response to offence by a spouse will ordinarily have a return to friendship as its end, as will the forgiveness a person gives to anyone with whom he or she delights to spend time in conversation in the good. Even when offence is caused by strangers, however, or enemies who in no way reciprocate our love, we have good and sufficient reason to extend the love of charity as benevolence, in which Thomas claims there should be no inequality,[126] or perhaps even beneficence of some sort, but certainly through prayer. On Thomas' account, even those who hate us are "not ... contrary to us, as men capable of happiness: and it is as such that we are bound to love them."[127]

In the standard literature on forgiveness, there is much handwringing over whether forgiveness *entails* something called "reconciliation." On the foregoing account, forgiveness includes the willing of another person's good and, as possible or appropriate, the doing of some good for him or her. Precisely what beneficence is called for will reflect the nature of the relationship before the offence made forgiveness possible. In what Gaelle Fiasse calls "integral forgiveness,"[128] friends are brought back into harmonious relations as the final term of forgiveness, but in some circumstances benevolence and prayer may be as far as the forgiver can rightly go, either permanently or at least for the time being. How precisely the parts are to be fitted together, or back together, to make, or to remake, the whole is worked out one stage at a time.

In sum, "[b]y the gift of charity God acts in us, and by our natural capacities we act in relation to our neighbor and the world,"[129] and all of this life together is best understood as at least approaching a conversation in the good that joins friends:

> It is appropriate to speak of the society of friendship as a conversation in the good because it reminds us that the focus of friendship is not primarily the friends, but the good which joins them. To be friends they must be turned to the good they love, and they must understand their friendship to be a conversing in this good, an ever deepening participation in the good. This conversation in the good of the friendship makes possible the conversion to the good the friendship intends.[130]

A conversation in the good that would be impossible without grace is rendered possible by the virtue of charity, the form of all of the virtues, and how such a life looks in practice is what Christ gave us in his human love for us *as* human, to which I now turn.

126 II-II 26.6 ad 1.
127 II.II 25.8.
128 Gaelle Fiasse, "Forgiveness and the Refusal of Justice," *Proceedings of the American Catholic Philosophical Association* 82 (2008): 125–34, 131–3.
129 Lawrence, *Fragility*, 369.
130 Waddell, *Friendship*, 136.

From the Inner Word to the Outer Word

The preceding discussion of the power and effects of the charity of God diffused in our hearts by the Holy Spirit is the familiar stuff of Christian theological discussion of how the divine love works on us humans, and its bearing on forgiveness as an act of love is clear. Less familiar but of special importance for the present discussion, of charity as friendship in the context of offence, is *the love of Christ as human* for us as human or, as Lonergan wrote, "the love of Christ as man for men."[131]

As we look to what precisely the divine self-communication communicates in Christ's human love for us as human, Lonergan invites us to attend to the facts concerning how "a single divine identity or Person became at once the subject of a divine consciousness and the subject of a human consciousness."[132] On the one hand, Christ enjoyed immediate and ineffable divine knowledge: he knew God face to face. But this beatific knowledge, however, according to Lonergan, did not give Christ knowledge of what it means to be unconditionally in love with God, as we are called to be, "in human, this-worldly terms. He had to discover that during his earthly life."[133] It was Christ's work as human through his human consciousness, by way of the mediated (as opposed to immediate), conversational knowledge of which humans are capable, to show us how to live lives of unconditional love:

> Jesus knows God face to face along with everything that ever actually occurs in the created world order in the past, present, or future by the light of glory, but before actually living his human life he does not know it, nor can he express it, in human terms. To convey God's meanings and values to us in terms that are humanly understandable, Jesus had to move dialectically from not knowing how to communicate what he already apprehended by his beatific knowledge to gradually finding out how to express and communicate it to us.[134]

The love of Christ as man for us as human, then is, as Lonergan elaborates it,

> the love of the Sacred Heart of Jesus, the love of a human will, motivated by a human mind, operating through human senses, resonating through human emotions and feelings and sentiments, implemented by a human body with its structure of bones and muscles, flesh, its mobile features, its terrible capacities for pleasure and pain, for joy and sorrow, for rapture and agony.[135]

---

131 "The Mystical Body of Christ," Bernard Lonergan, *Shorter* Papers, ed. Robert Croken et al. 20 Collected Works of Bernard Lonergan (Toronto, ON: University Toronto Press, 2007), 106–11, 107.
132 Lawrence, *Fragility*, 396.
133 Ibid., 398.
134 Ibid., 399.
135 Lonergan, "Mystical Body," 107–8.

Christ the man had a message to communicate. He communicated it to his followers by calling them "friends" rather than servants (Jn 15:15), and so mystified them. He affirmed that message before the Sanhedrin and earned himself death on a cross. He did not shout it from the rooftops and render himself a fool.[136] He communicated it by everything he ever did or said as he conversed through his human consciousness with the world as he found it, experienced it, understood it, judged it, and deliberated about how, precisely, to contribute to its salvation. One day at a time, in eliciting his own free acts of knowing and willing, Christ had to will the means of communicating to us God's unconditional, unbounded, forgiving, saving love. So it was, as Lawrence explains, that

> because Jesus was sent to share the divine friendship in a sinful world, he had to overcome enmity due to human transgressions; and because he had to show what it means to live human life simply for love, he had to learn how to overcome evil with good.[137]

The Word showed those he died to redeem how to overcome evil with good, and so he forgave his enemies and prayed his Father to forgive even his crucifiers "for they know not what they do" (Lk. 23:34).

God Does Not Command the Impossible

If *we* are to overcome evil with good, we must, like Christ, learn how to do so in the conversational ways by which humans come to know, and Christ's own words and deeds offer to serve as our conversation partners as we struggle to do so. Those who believe in Christ and his words and deeds also believe, moreover, in that work of the Holy Spirit by which they are graced and made capable of charity (Rom. 5:5) leading to friendship and the giving of forgiveness. "[C]harity, and all the virtues born from charity, are nothing more than grace expressed in activity, for they accomplish day-by-day the transformation of our self unto God which grace enables and always intends. This is why," Waddell continues, "Thomas says grace is a gift but charity is a virtue, the power or skill to make good on the promise of grace, to sustain and deepen the love that is our life."[138]

Those who have received the gift of charity often still carry psychological and cognitional baggage, at least at the start, and it is in this vein that Michael Sherwin inquires about the situation of a beginner in the Christian life, an adult person who has recently repented of a life of serious sin, converted, and been baptised. Such a person will believe in faith that he or she has the power (grace) to do what love demands, but he may not *feel* capable of living here and now on the level of love. Sherwin's analysis and answer are worth meditating on.

---

136 Ibid., 108.
137 Lawrence, *Fragility*, 401.
138 Waddell, *Friendship*, 127.

Depending on how the convert has lived before his conversion and the coming of sanctifying grace into his life, "virtues such as chastity, sobriety, or even justice may feel unnatural to him. In other words, he may still experience the morality of the Gospel as an external imposition on him,"[139] not, instead, as the liberation through grace of the person he was created to be. "If, therefore," Sherwin continues,

> he is going to act according to what grace enables him to do, he must live from a twofold trust: he must trust that Gospel morality is good for him and he must trust that God gives him the grace (power) here and now to live according to this morality.[140]

This trust is necessary because "on the level of psychological experience, neither feature of Gospel morality may *feel* true."[141] The recently former habitual sinner may believe that he is free to live at the level of love, here and now, but he may nonetheless *feel* the pull of bondage rather than the promised freedom, the pleasure of virtue, and the delight in the good. The residual effects of sin war at the psychological level against the moral potency for the charity promised by grace.

Seasoned moral theologian that he is, Sherwin addresses this situation in part on the basis of those who have struggled with addiction and affirmed the availability of a solution. Here, I will reproduce Sherwin's discussion in precisely the way it converses with the testament of Bill Wilson, one of the founders of Alcoholics Anonymous, and of Wilson about his friend:

One of the cofounders of *Alcoholics Anonymous* describes how trust in God played the decisive role in overcoming his addiction. There was first an encounter with a friend who had made the discovery before him.

> My friend sat before me, and he made the point-blank declaration that God had done for him what he could not do for himself. His human will had failed. Doctors had pronounced him incurable. Society was about to lock him up. Like myself, he had admitted complete defeat. Then he had, in effect, been raised from the dead, suddenly taken from the scrap heap to a level of life better than the best he had ever known!

This encounter and other preparatory events eventually led the future co-founder to the following experience:

> At the hospital ... I humbly offered myself to God, as I then understood him, to do with me as he would. I placed myself unreservedly under his care and discretion. I admitted for the first time that of myself I was nothing;

---

139 Sherwin, *On Love*, 180.
140 Ibid.
141 Ibid.

The Forgiveness of Love in Charity 229

that without him I was lost. I ruthlessly faced my sins and became willing to have my new-found friend take them away, root and branch. I have not had a drink since.

Although aspects of Alcoholics Anonymous' approach remain controversial, Bill Wilson articulates in these passages the almost universal experience among former addicts that their road to recovery began with a personal encounter with a loving God and a twofold act of loving trust that this encounter elicited. My thesis is that the best way to understand the dynamics of this healing conversion is by appealing to Aquinas' theology of the relationship between the residual effects of acquired vice, the infused cardinal virtues, and the theological virtues. In the beginning, the former addict still feels drawn to his addiction but has the ability from the infused moral virtues to act against it. To do so successfully, however, he must trust that God gives him the power to do so and that so doing is truly for his good.[142]

My own conversations with a number of former addicts in long-term recovery have confirmed what Wilson reports and what Sherwin describes as the almost universal experience among former addicts.[143]

Can anyone, then, claim absolute impossibility? Are there humans whose situations are such that they can truly judge that the sufficient conditions of living on the level of love and granting forgiveness cannot be fulfilled? Is anyone absolutely exempt from the Great Commandment?

I answer that it is straightforward Catholic doctrine that it is God's antecedent will that all people be saved (1 Tim. 2:4). As I have considered it here, the divine self-communication expresses "God's astonishing desire for the flourishing of each and every person and thing in creation in all their specificity and particularity."[144] It follows from this that God must give everyone sufficient grace. This universality does not deny, indeed it depends upon, the unicity of Christ as the mediator of salvation. It does not deny, indeed it depends upon, God's working uniquely through the seven sacraments of the Catholic Church but also and extensively through other means known to God alone. Through all these means, which after all are invisible in their causality and efficacy, God does for all persons (1 Tim. 2:4) what they could not do for themselves, which is to order them to divine friendship and equip them to love one another, and sometimes the form that love must take will be to forgive one's offender, even when it seems impossible to do so. Once we affirm the truth of the promise of the grace that makes the "impossible" possible, we need not worry about precisely where the natural "ends" and the supernatural takes over, as Pieper explains: "If you row your boat in the same direction as the wind is driving it – how are you to distinguish between the motion that is caused by your own efforts and what is caused by the wind?"[145]

---

142 Ibid., 181–2.
143 Waddell develops similar themes. Waddell, *Happiness*, 176–9.
144 Lawrence, *Fragility*, 271.
145 Pieper, *Faith*, 242.

God does not command the impossible, nor does he cancel our freedom.[146] To forgive one's offender is to overcome evil with good, and to do this is the noble activity of persons freely participating in a human conversation caught up by grace in the divine conversation.[147] But it would be a choice.[148]

Love and Forgiveness in the Political Order

When understood as the mere forgoing of rightful grounds of grievance, forgiveness is guilty as charged by S.J. Perelman: "To err is human, to forgive, supine."[149] When understood instead as the love of friendship in response to offence, forgiveness, as Lord Herbert appreciated,

> is the most necessary and proper work of every man; for, though, when I do not a just thing, or a charitable, or a wise, another man may do it for me, yet no man can forgive my enemy but myself.[150]

From this understanding of forgiveness it follows that no civil power, no matter how it is constituted, can forgive my enemy for me.

The short answer to the question posed by Martha Minow in the title of her book *When Should Law Forgive?*, then, is that the question assumes a capacity not in evidence. A more elaborate response to the reductionist project would begin by observing that to philosophise as Minow does about the bureaucratic state's "forgiving debt," and even "forgiving youth,"[151] is to divert attention from the indispensable work of charity. As even Minow acknowledges, "[p]erhaps a society infused with Christianity," as opposed (in Minow's terms) to the "more secular, diverse community" in which we live, "would especially support a notion of forgiveness that celebrates the virtue of charity with a rich sense of common humanity, common evil, and original sin."[152] In fact, a society conversationally opened up by the Christ event would attend, on the one hand, to the political implications of the real work of forgiveness when a person loves his enemy as another self, but also, on the other, to a true Christian state's capacity to forgive,

---

146 "*Deus impossibilia non iubet*" is straightforward Catholic doctrine, much maligned by reductionists of all kinds. John Mahoney, *The Making of Moral Theology: A Study of the Roman Catholic Tradition* (Oxford: Clarendon Press, 1987), 48–57. Moral perplexity can only be *secundum quid*, not absolute.
147 "[C]harity cannot be excessive, for it regards not the means but the end. Hence the great commandment is to love God with all one's heart and all one's soul, with all one's mind and all one's strength. And the second is like the first, to love one's neighbor as oneself, to love one another as Christ has loved us, toward the fulfillment of Christ's prayer at the Last Supper ...." Lonergan, "Mystical," 111.
148 I agree with Minow that "no one can be made to forgive." Minow, *Between*, 155 n.65.
149 Quoted in Nussbaum, *Anger*, 10.
150 Quoted in Harvey, "Forgiving," 221.
151 Minow, *When Should Law Forgive*, 35–112.
152 Minow, *Between*, 155 n.65.

The Forgiveness of Love in Charity 231

in a way the Catholic analogical imagination will grasp, those who offend against the temporal common good. The true import of the forgiveness of love for the political order is radical, and it works from the bottom up and from the top down, about which a few things can be said in conclusion.

From the bottom up, humans conversant in the love of friendship will not be content when from time to time A forgives B and C forgives D. Grasping the practical implications of the fact that human operating is, to a notable extent, human co-operating, they will strive to structure the political order through that *benevolentia* described above. This occurs when the person

> breaks out of the circle of himself ..., acts no longer as a child on the pain-pleasure principle, ... and [h]is group becomes political, the object of detached judgments, which engages his service according to the dues of objective justice, even to the point of self-sacrifice.[153]

The result will be ongoing collaborative contributions to reform of the entrenched but dynamic goods of order that are laws and legal institutions aimed at true human goods as publicly specified.[154]

Refusing to release the legal order "from the exhausting demands of goodness,"[155] individuals will choose, even against the bureaucratic undertow of the day, ordering institutions that proceed as much as possible on the basis of what the ancients understood as the *conversatio civilis*, of which person-to-person forgiveness will be a regular incident. While "[p]erfect friendship may be rare, and so may the perfect balance of contrasting forms, but nothing less should be the exemplar whenever human beings dwell together."[156] Even from within the bureaucratic state and its hobbling forms, humans will seize opportunities to act with self-transcending vigour for the common good. Anyone who doubts that disinterested benevolence and sometimes even beneficence are often at work even in our bureaucratic state would do well to read the works of the late Judge John T. Noonan, Jr,[157] and of Joseph Vining, above all his magnum opus *From Newton's Sleep*, where he marshals the evidence that, even now, "[f]or law, mind is caring mind. Mind that does not care is no mind to seek, no mind to take into oneself, no mind to obey: it has no authority."[158]

---

153 Gilby, *Between*, 192.
154 The good as understood on the account pursued here is emphatically not a matter of private invention. Alasdair MacIntyre, "The Privatization of the Good," *Review of Politics* 52 (1990): 344–77.
155 Eric Gregory, *Politics & the Order of Love: An Augustinian Ethic of Democratic Citizenship* (Chicago, IL: University of Chicago Press, 2008), 25.
156 Gilby, *Between*, 65.
157 "Love is a movement of the rational will seeking the good. That movement manifests two human desires, always mixed: the desire to meet the needs of one's own insufficiency and the desire to share one's goodness. The two 'great commandments' of Christ inculcate love." John T Noonan, Jr, "Posner's Problematics," *Harvard Law Review* 111 (1998): 1768–75, 1775. Noonan cites Thomas, I-II 27.3, for the definition of love.
158 Joseph Vining, *From Newton's Sleep* (Princeton, NJ: Princeton University Press, 1995), 32.

What our contemporary politico-legal order altogether lacks, however, is an even barely adequate reckoning with charity and forgiveness as they come *from the top down*. The priority of charity as the friendship of God, showered on his friends and his foes alike, through the forgiveness of our sins, is packed with political possibility, as Lonergan elaborates:

> But when [redemption] comes, it comes as the charity that dissolves the hostility and divisions of past injustice and present hatred; it comes as the hope that withstands psychological, economic, political, social, cultural determinisms; it comes with the faith that can liberate reason from the rationalizations that blinded it.[159]

The Christian operating under the power of charity and animated by theological hope will not tire of calling down the grace of God on the political order, begging forgiveness and pledging service. The faithful Christian, however, is not a lone ranger but a member of the mystical body of Christ, and the Church has a God-given role to play in breathing the life of grace and forgiveness *into* the body politic. The liturgical polity of Christendom, oriented in justice around the divine love and its originating forgiveness, is not at present a possibility, but it nonetheless provides the model that alone gives effect to the political order's due role in directing persons to their last end subject to the authority, jurisdiction (Mt. 18:18), and sacred ministry of that good of order, of supernatural foundation, that is the Catholic Church.[160]

Strange as it may sound to say, "the church, too, is a good of order. It gets people to heaven – not just one, but a flow of people into heaven,"[161] and it does so in part by raising up, transforming, and correcting through grace in charity the legal order that the reductionist would abandon to its own devices. The Church will have a structural role to play in a political order wherein the shared hope is for the supernatural to make the most of the natural, mediating the friendship of God and graciously making the world a more friendly place. Even where the Church is denied its rightful place, however, and fear rather than love thereby becomes the ordering principle to keep chaos at bay, the Christian in love with God and his neighbour will resist reductionism wherever it rears its ugly head.

---

159 Bernard Lonergan, "Mission and Spirit," Bernard Lonergan, *A Third Collection*, ed. Frederick E. Crowe SJ (New York: Paulist Press, 1985), 23–34, 31–32; Lawrence, *Fragility*, 381.
160 On the need for the Church as mediator of grace in the political order, see Christopher A Ferrara, "Luther's Disembodied Grace and the Graceless Body Politic," in *Luther and His Progeny*, ed. John C Rao (Kettering, OH: Angelico Press, 2017), 115–42. On the right relationship between the Church and the civil power, see Thomas Crean and Alan Fimister, *Integralism: A Manual of Political Philosophy* (Havertown, PA: Casemate, 2020); Patrick McKinley Brennan, "An Essay on Christian Constitutionalism: Building in the Divine Style, for the Common Good," *Rutgers Journal of Law and Religion* 16 (2015): 478–540.
161 Lonergan, *Topics in Education*, 34.

Contributing choice by choice to what he judges and hopes will be the emergent probability of a more friendly and forgiving political order, he will overcome evil with good in charity:

> The good Christian does not oscillate between two different worlds, now occupying himself with spiritual exercises and now, grudgingly, attending to the business of mere earthly living. But one world exists, and that is God's, and everything can be for his love. So it started; so it may end.[162]

---

162 Gilby, *Between*, 193.

Index

actus exterioris 137, 144
actus humanus 206
actus interioris 137, 144
actus reus 189
Adam 14, 34, 174
After Virtue (2013), Alasdair MacIntyre 4, 79–80, 92
agrément 151
Alcoholics Anonymous 228–9
alterity 149–63
altruism 110, 196, 218
amor 133, 136, 144, 216
amor amicitiae 216, 220
amor concupiscentiae 216–17, 220
amor Dei 44, 47
Amstutz, Mark 38
antinomianism 2, 58, 84, 92
anti-Semitism 67
appetite 131–3, 136, 144
Aquinas, St Thomas 5, 6, 13, 26, 57, 69, 70, 115, 118–20, 126, 130–46, 198, 199, 207–9, 211, 213, 217–19, 222–4, 229
Aristotle 88, 141
Augustine, St 3, 4, 7, 9, 17, 22, 33–5, 44–56, 82–6, 99, 115, 213
Austin, John 71–2

Bader, Veit 93, 95, 97
band of pirates 51
Bash, Anthony 37–8
Belgic Confession (1561) 115
believers 16–17, 20, 27, 30, 60, 61, 74, 112, 191
Benedict, St 4, 79–80, 83–4, 91–2
Benedictine order 4, 87, 92
benevolentia 223, 231
Bentham, Jeremy 187
Berman, Harold 70–1
Bienvenu, Monseigneur 124

Biggar, Nigel 42
Billingham, Paul 96
Bismarck, Otto von 63–4
Blake, William 165
Bonhoeffer, Dietrich 68, 113
Book of Mormon 6, 164–7, 172, 174–6, 185; Alma 175; Benjamin, King 175; Jacob 172; Laman 172; Lehi 172, 174; Lemuel 172; Mormon 171, 185; Moroni 171, 185; Nephi 172
Brague, Remi 207
Brennan, Patrick McKinley 6, 198–233
Breyfogle, Todd 47
Bruno, Michael JS 52
Bushman, Richard 166

caeremonialia 139
Caesar 112
Calo, Zachary R 1–6, 31–43, 122
Calvin, John 3, 7, 9–30, 68
care for other 62, 188, 192, 194–5
caritas 6, 46, 50, 199
Catholic Church 3, 33, 35, 38, 58, 65–6, 114–16, 200, 214, 229, 231, 232
Catholic Encyclopaedia (1907–1914) 116
cenoby 86
charity 28, 100, 102–3, 132, 139, 181, 185, 192–6, 198–233
chastity 82, 228
chez soi 150, 157–8
Chicago Democrat 182
Christ, Jesus 5–6, 9, 13, 17, 39, 42, 53, 55, 58, 59, 61, 69, 74, 80–1, 85, 99–101, 104, 112–14, 118, 128, 172, 174, 185, 187–9, 191, 193–4, 196–8, 221–2, 225–7, 229–31
Christianity 1–2, 5, 33, 40–3, 45, 47, 49–50, 52, 67, 80, 82, 84, 92, 94, 98–106, 110–11, 128, 166, 195, 208, 230

Index

Christianity and the Secular (2016), RA Markus 45, 49–50
Christian Perspectives on Legal Thought (2001), Michael W McConnell, Robert E Cochran Jr and Angela C Carmella 42
The Christian Polity of John Calvin (2009), Harro Höpfl 27
Christian/s 1–6, 13, 15, 20–1, 23, 26–7, 32–5, 38–40, 42–56, 58–61, 63, 65–9, 71, 73–5, 81–4, 87, 89–90, 92–4, 99–107, 109–14, 116–17, 119, 121, 124–8, 188, 192, 197, 199, 200, 216, 221, 226–7, 230, 232–3
Christian virtues 93–4, 98–102, 104, 109–11
Church of Jesus Christ of Latter-day Saints 6, 164, 167, 170
Cicero 11, 208
circumcision debate 1–2
Cistercian order 87
City of God 4, 34, 44–9, 51–6, 83, 195
City of God (Penguin Classics, 2004), St Augustine 45–56
City of Man 4, 44–9, 51–6, 83, 102
civic virtues 5, 93–7, 100, 102–3, 106, 110–11
civility 5, 27, 79–80, 89, 93–111
civitas terrena 54
Cochran, Robert F Jr 122
coercion 5–6, 10–11, 17–20, 59, 62, 66, 71–2, 75, 99, 106, 112, 121, 123, 126–8, 142, 186–97
communitarianism 83, 86, 186, 188
comprehensive doctrine/s 52, 95, 107
congregatio fidelium 59
conscience 12–16, 18–19, 22, 24, 26–9, 46, 63, 98, 128, 182
contemptus mundi 88–9
contention 21, 172, 176, 191
contract 6, 127, 186–8, 192, 194
conversatio civilis 231
conversatio morum 87
conversion 1–2, 53–4, 80, 87, 104, 183, 210, 225, 228–9
convivere 222
co-operation 106, 186, 188, 195, 222
correct principles 174–5
Council of Chalcedon (451) 83
covenant 1, 6, 20, 27, 81, 119, 186–97
Crowe, Jonathan 5, 9, 149–63
cupiditas 46

Darwin, Charles 186
David, King of Israel 124
Deagon, Alex 5, 39, 42, 57, 71, 93–111
Decalogue 14, 16, 18, 22, 25, 29, 120
démesure 153
democracy 5, 93–8, 102–3, 105, 108, 110–11
democratisation of virtue 102
Denck, Hans 114
dénucléation 159
Derrida, Jacques 41
dialectics 18, 93, 226
dilectio 136, 144, 223
dilectio Dei 135
dilection 132–3, 144
discretion 37, 200–204, 218, 228
divine simplicity 112–29
divisions 192–4, 232
divorce 57, 105, 107, 189
Doctrine and Covenants 167, 178
Dodaro, Robert 52, 53
Dolezal, James 116–17
Doniphan, Alexander William 179
Drummond, Andrew Landale 61, 64, 66
Drunen, David van 9, 113, 126, 128

earthly city *see* City of Man
emergent probability 214, 223, 233
empowerment 6, 201–4
enjoyment 6, 134–5, 149–54, 159
Enoch 176–7
Enright, Robert 32
entend 155
entropy 196
equality 73, 90, 100, 104, 110, 130, 208, 219–20
equity 12, 14, 16, 19, 21, 29
Eve 174
evil 5–6, 60, 70–1, 74–5, 86, 93–4, 98, 101, 103–4, 106–7, 112–13, 122, 124–6, 128, 138–42, 167, 173–4, 185, 190–1, 193, 199–200, 207, 209–16, 220–1, 227, 230, 233
expressive individualism 198–9, 210
extermination order 179

face 151
face slapping 191
family 29, 85, 87, 123, 127, 170, 184, 187–8, 204, 224
Fiasse, Gaelle 225
forgiveness 3, 5–6, 31–43, 71, 94, 98, 100–101, 103, 106, 112–14, 122, 124–9, 149, 162, 198–233;

collective forgiveness 33, 35–9, 41; integral 225; legal forgiveness 31–3, 40–3; political forgiveness 36, 38, 41; therapeutic benefits 32, 198
Formula of Concord (1577) 69–70
fortunate fall 172–4
friendship 29, 47, 52, 63, 66, 96, 103, 120, 143, 145, 172, 179–80, 182, 184, 200, 210, 216–27, 229–32
From Newton's Sleep, Joseph Vining 231
fruit of the spirit 102, 104, 111
Fuller, Lon L 73–4

Gilby, Thomas 200, 224, 231, 233
Godesberg Declaration (1939) 64
Godot 4, 79–80
the good 93–4, 99, 101, 103–4, 106, 108–9, 111, 122–3, 127, 132, 137, 160–3, 200, 209–15, 217, 219–20, 222, 224–5, 228, 231
good Samaritan, parable of 5, 80, 93, 105, 107, 168
grace 6, 18–20, 27–8, 32, 35, 46, 53–4, 56–7, 68, 74, 93–4, 109, 118, 142–3, 172–3, 185, 193, 199–200, 219, 222–3, 225, 227–30, 232
grievance 200–204, 218, 230
Grotius, Hugo 27, 50

Habermas, Jürgen 93, 107–10
Hale, Emma 172
happiness 5, 130–46, 150, 159, 164, 166, 177, 209, 218, 225
harm 20, 122–3, 132, 195, 200, 203–6
heaven 33–4, 53–4, 91, 113, 121, 165–6, 169, 173–4, 176–8, 180–2, 184, 186–7, 190–2, 232
Helm, Paul 13
Hendrianto, Stefanus 5, 130–46
He Pasa Ekklesia: An Original History of the Religious Denominations at Present Existing in the United States (1884) Daniel Rupp 164, 170
Herbert, Edward 230
Hesselink, John 16
Hill, Marvin S 182
Hirsh, Emanuel 65
Hitler, Adolf 64–6
Hobbes, Thomas 18, 198, 203
Holborn, Hajo 75
Holderlein, Friedrich 209
holiness 118, 164–6, 175, 189, 195
Hollerich, MJ 45

Holy Bible 58, 59, 65, 67, 82, 103, 166–7, 173, 176, 185, 191, 206
Holy Spirit 39, 59, 174–5, 199, 221–2, 226–7
Höpfl, Harro 27
human depravity 18–19, 23, 55, 166
human flourishing 97, 102, 104, 142, 156, 160, 198, 229
hypocrisy 26, 82, 123, 181, 193
Hythloday, Raphael 90

image of God 10, 15, 17, 20, 23, 29, 107, 108, 110
Inazu, John 97
individualism 90, 186, 188, 198–9, 210
injustice 35, 59, 98, 204–11, 215, 232
Institutes (McNeill ed, Philadelphia, 1960), Calvin 9, 16
iudicialia 139

Jackson, Timothy 207
James (author of the Epistle) 65, 70–1, 167
James, St 2
Jefferson, Thomas 197
Jehovah 173–4
Jeremiah 194
Jerusalem Council 1–2
Jetsons cartoon 196
Jews 1, 2, 14, 22, 58, 65–8, 73, 75
Judaism 1–2, 81, 192
Judeo-Christian tradition 1, 192
Judgment 3, 16, 33–5, 40–2, 74, 98, 122, 132–3, 138, 184, 190, 192, 201, 204–12, 216, 218–21
jurisprudence 1, 4, 6, 32, 40, 42–3, 57–76, 80, 113, 124, 130, 186, 187

Kaufman, Peter 52–3
Kelsen, Hans 72–3
kingdom ethics 112, 122, 128
Koch, Eric 64
Köhler-Ryan, Renée 3–4, 44–56
koinonia 222
koinos bios 86
kristallnacht 68

Laborde, Cecile 108
Landesvater 62
Lang, August 24–5
latreia 4, 44, 46, 54–6
law: concept of 1, 13; content of 1, 10–11, 21; divine 4–5, 10, 14, 22, 25–7, 29–30, 65, 119, 126, 130–46;

function of 9–10, 18–20 (coercive/
  legislative 18–20, 25, 30; pedagogical
  18, 20, 25, 30; theological 18–20,
  25, 30); higher 27, 72, 182–3, 186–
  97; human 71, 120, 126, 130–46,
  179, 195; letter of 26, 189; moral
  12–16, 18–23, 26–7, 29, 121–3, 126,
  161; Moses *see* Moses, law of; natural
  13–22, 24–9, 73, 119–20, 126, 130,
  136, 138–9, 142, 149–63; Rome 61,
  189, 191; spirit of 10, 14, 17, 23–7,
  188–9; spiritual 17–18
law of love 3, 5, 9–30, 39, 42, 48, 56,
  93–111, 149–63
law of the Gospel 190
Lawrence, Frederick G 199, 209–10,
  213, 223, 227
lawyers 36, 72–4, 91, 168
Lee, Constance Youngwon 3, 9–30
Lee, Gregory W 46, 53
Lee, James K 53–4
legal positivism 4, 43, 69–75
Leigh, Edward 117
Les Miserables (1862) Victor Hugo 124
Levinas, Emmanuel 5, 8, 149–63
Lewis, CS 18, 63, 123–4
lex aeterna 136
lex divina 136, 138
lex humana 136
lex moralis 14
lex naturalis 14, 136
lex nova 138
lex talionis 113, 122, 128, 191
lex vetus 138
liberal virtues 102
Lincoln, Abraham 184
Little, David 15
living laws 11–12
Locke, John 187, 198, 203
Lonergan, Bernard 199, 212–15, 219,
  226, 230, 232
love, law of 3, 5, 9–30, 39, 42, 48, 56,
  93–111, 149–63
love of Christ 226; *see also* pure love of
  Christ
love of God 5, 25–6, 35, 44–6, 48, 52,
  56, 99, 118, 130–1, 133–6, 139–40,
  145, 162, 172
love your neighbour 5, 93, 99, 122
loving sword 112–29
loving violence 123
Lucifer 173
Luther, Martin 3, 7, 57–76, 232
Lutzer, Erwin 63, 66, 68

MacIntyre, Alasdair 4, 12, 79–80, 89,
  92, 204, 214, 231
magistrate, civil 9–12, 14, 26, 29,
  113, 126
Maine, Henry James Sumner 186, 188,
  192, 194
Marcellinus 47–8
marketplace of ideas 93
Markus, RA 44–5, 48–56, 84, 86
The Marriage of Heaven and Hell
  (1794), William Blake 165
Mathewes, Charles 40
McCabe, Herbert 87, 218
McNeill, John T 9, 11, 16, 21–2
Mein Kampf (1925), Adolf
  Hitler 66
Melanchthon, Philip 68
Memory and Reconciliation (1999) 3,
  33, 38–9
mens rea 189
mercy 5, 33–5, 40–3, 56, 71, 74–5,
  103, 109, 112–14, 118–19, 122,
  125, 127–9, 167, 172, 201
Metaxas, Eric 57, 64, 66, 68–9
Methuselah 176
Milbank, John 5, 45, 53–4, 93–4,
  100–104, 106, 109–11
Miller, Mark T 223
Minow, Martha 6, 31, 37, 198–204, 230
monasticism 4, 79–92
Montaigne, Michel de 213
Montesquieu, Charles Louis de
  Secondat 187
moral engagement 93–4, 96–8, 101,
  103–7, 109–11
morality 2, 10, 15–21, 26, 28–9, 31,
  79–80, 103, 126, 141, 228
More, St Thomas 4, 88–92
Mosaic law *see* Moses, law of
Moses, law of 5, 13–14, 16, 21, 58,
  121, 128, 186, 188–91
Murray, John 118

Nathaniel 191
National Socialism 64–74
natural law of love *see* law of love
necessary opposition 172–4
neighbour principle 1, 5, 18, 22–3,
  25, 74, 84, 93, 94, 99–100, 105,
  107, 112, 122, 130, 140, 143, 145,
  156–9, 168, 190, 216, 224, 232
Neoh, Joshua 1–6, 79–92
Noah 176–7
Noonan, John T Jr 231

Oaks, Dallin H 179, 182
obedience 6, 17, 24, 46, 60, 71, 75, 81–5, 87, 91–2, 99, 104, 164, 169, 176–7, 189, 192
Occam, William of 69
O'Donovan, Oliver 39, 41
offender 82, 127, 215–16, 218–20, 223, 229–30
Ogle, Veronica Roberts 47, 54, 56
one mind 85, 87, 176
On Secular Authority (1523), Martin Luther 59
ora et labora 86
ordinology 60
O'Regan, Cyril 221
Oriental rule 83
other, the 10, 40, 137, 149–63, 217–18, 220, 223–4, 230
other cheek 112, 191, 196
Otherwise than Being (1974, Alphonso Lingis trans, Pittsburgh, 1998) 149, 156–62
Outka, Gene 224
overlapping consensus 44, 51–2
Owen, John 117

Pabst, Adrian 103, 110
paternal ruler 62–4
Paul, St 1–4, 13, 15, 24, 29, 61, 70, 80–2, 84, 86, 92, 99–101, 118, 121, 123, 188, 193
Pearl of Great Price 167
peasant's revolt 59–60
Perelman, SJ 230
perpetual rule of love *see* rule of love
persecution 171–2, 177–8
Peter, St 1, 2, 20, 123, 191
philosophy 70, 73–4, 107, 131, 137, 144, 163, 200, 205, 208
Philpott, Daniel 36
Pieper, Josef 207, 216, 218–20, 229
Plato 14, 208
political theology 4–5, 12, 58–62, 74–5, 77
political theory 4, 17, 23, 44–5, 62, 199
politics of virtue 103–4, 106
Pollock, Frederick 186
Pope, Stephen 40
pounds, parable of 193
poverty 82–3, 87, 105, 158
prayer 66–7, 86, 88, 171, 176, 196, 223, 225, 230
pride cycles 172
Prima Pars, St Thomas Aquinas 134

primogeniture 187, 192
principles of civility 5, 93–111
prison-temple 179–82
privatio boni 212
proving contraries 6, 164–85
proximity 149–63, 167
public religion 94, 98–9
pure love of Christ 25, 175, 185, 193
pursuit of happiness 5, 130, 164

Radbruch, Gustav 73–4
rapporte 152
rational love 5, 130–46
Rawls, John 44–5, 49–52, 55, 107, 199, 203, 208
Rechtsphilosophie (Philosophy of Law) (1950), Gustav Radbruch 73–4
redamation 224
reductionist 199–200, 202, 221, 230, 232
reflection 35, 74, 104, 192–3, 196–7, 199
refugees 104, 192, 197
relative adequacy 205–6
ressentiment 199, 221
resurrection 192–3
retributive justice 112–13, 128
revelation 13, 25, 57, 99, 110, 168–72, 175–6, 178, 222
revenge 35, 112, 127, 191, 202–4, 212
Rhonheimer, Martin 208
Rice, Charles 73
rich man and Lazarus, parable of 193
Rigdon, Sidney 183
Rousseau, Jean-Jacques 18, 198
Royal Commission into Institutional Responses to Child Sexual Abuse (Australia) 124
rule of love 3, 9–10, 14, 20–7, 29
Rule of Macarius 83
Rule of Saint Augustine 82–3
Rule of Saint Benedict 4, 80, 83, 91–2
Rule of the Four Fathers 83
Rule of the Master 83
Rupp, Daniel 164–5, 167, 169–70, 178, 183–4
Rust, Bernard 65

sacraments 44, 55, 57, 229
saeculum 51, 56, 85
Saeculum: History and Society in the Theology of St. Augustine (1970), RA Markus 44–5, 48–50

sanctification 17, 20, 70, 108, 124, 178, 228
Sasse, Martin 68
Satan 123, 173–4, 177
Saunders, Benjamin B 112–29
Schleitheim Confession (1527) 113–14
Schmitt, Carl 4, 72
Schulz, Michael 107–10
scilicet moralia 139
Scruton, Roger 206
Second Rule of the Fathers 83
A Secular Age (2007), Charles Taylor 49–50
secularism 3, 4, 44–56, 59, 93, 105–6, 108, 199
Seitzer, Jeffrey 72
séjour 150
selfishness 44, 46, 54–6, 74, 100–101, 103, 186, 188, 196, 219
separation 6, 149, 153–5, 158, 160, 186, 195–7
se recuiellant 151
Sermon on the Mount 6, 113, 186, 189, 192, 194
Shaffer, Thomas 41, 43, 113, 124–5
sheep and goats, parable of 193
Sherwin, Michael 209, 216–18, 222–3, 227–9
Skinner, Quentin 59–60, 68
slavery 104, 122, 183, 187
Smith, Christian 212, 214
Smith, Gary Scott 74
Smith, Hyrum 179, 184
Smith, Joseph Jr 164–85
Smith, Randall 139
societas 47, 222
soft love 114, 122, 124–5, 127
sola scriptura 57
sower, parable of 193
Spencer, Nick 58–62
spiritual liberty 18–19
spiritual optics 149, 163
Stanton, Elizabeth Cady 203
status 6, 11, 18, 42, 64, 72, 81, 90, 95–6, 110, 121, 152–3, 167, 186–8, 192
strangers 158, 162, 179, 192, 194, 197, 225
Stuntz, William 42
suffering 6, 34, 61, 64, 149, 156, 159, 177, 180, 181
Summa Contra Gentiles, St Thomas Aquinas 139
Summa Thealogica/Thealogiae, St Thomas Aquinas 131, 136, 141–2

summum bonum 191
supernatural inclination 131, 143–5
superveniret 138

Talmud 67, 162, 192
Taylor, Charles 49–50
Temporal Authority (1523), Martin Luther 58–9
ten commandments 22, 120–1, 189
tension: in the act of judgment 33; between the City of God and the earthly city 47; in contraries 167; between generosity and the desire for security 155; at the heart of human existence 162; in human ethics 149; between law and love 40, 41, 92, 122, 127–9; in the nature of God 128; between present and future 43; between punishment and love 35
ten talents, parable of 192–3
ten virgins, parable of 192–3
Tertullian 223
Thayer, Donlu 6, 164–85
theocracy 3, 9, 27, 94, 111
theological secularism 199
theology 2–6, 17, 25, 27–8, 33, 38, 40–3, 45, 48, 57–62, 65–6, 68, 72, 74–5, 77, 82, 99, 109–11, 114, 117, 119, 128, 200, 215, 229
A Theory of Justice (1971), John Rawls 44, 45, 51
thesaurus ecclesia 88
Third Rule of the Fathers 83
Thompson, A Keith 1–6, 186–97
Thornhill, Christopher 72
Totality and Infinity (1961; Alphonso Lingis trans, Pittsburgh, 1969) Emmanuel Levinas 149–57, 162–3
tough love 114, 123–5
Tracy, David 203, 205
Treatise on Law, St Thomas Aquinas 136, 138, 145
Trinity 39, 99, 115
triune God 221–2
trust 62, 91, 99–101, 103, 175, 183, 195, 228–9
Truth and Reconciliation Commission, South Africa 33, 36
two cities 9, 46–9, 52–4
two kingdoms 58, 61, 74
two loves 46–9
tyranny 58–61, 63, 68

unforgiveable acts 202–5
Utopia (Clarence Miller trans, New Haven, 2014), Thomas More 4, 88–92

Valjean, Jean 124
Vining, Joseph 231
virtue 4, 18–19, 22, 45–6, 48, 99, 101–6, 109, 111, 138–9, 141, 143–5, 164, 175, 181, 194, 200, 208, 212, 216, 222, 225, 227–8, 230
visage 153
volksgeist 65
vulnerability 6, 149, 154, 156–7, 159–60

Waddell, Paul 209, 222, 224–5, 227, 229
Weil, Simone 207

welfare state 63–4
Wendland, Heinz-Dietrich 66
Wentworth, John 182
Westminster Confession of Faith (1646) 115
Wilberforce, William 104
Williams, Rowan 97, 105–6
Wilson, Bill 228–9
Witte, John Jr 62, 65, 99
Wolterstorff, Nicholas 42, 93, 96–8, 103, 113
Work of Monks (Mary Muldowney trans, Washington DC, 2014) 82

Zimmermann, Augusto 4, 57–76
Zion 170, 174–9

Printed in the United States
by Baker & Taylor Publisher Services